AIRCRAFT
OF
WORLD WAR II
A VISUAL ENCYCLOPEDIA

MICHAEL SHARPE · JERRY SCUTTS · DAN MARCH

PARKGATE
BOOKS

First published in 1999 by
PRC Publishing Ltd,
Kiln House
210 New Kings Road, London SW6 4NZ

This edition published in 2000 by
Parkgate Books Ltd
London House
Great Eastern Wharf, Parkgate Road
London, SW11 4NQ
Great Britain

British Library Cataloguing in Publication Data:
A catalogue record for this book is available from the British Library.

ISBN 1 902616 62 6

Printed and bound in China

CONTENTS

PREFACE

The period 1939-45 witnessed a revolution in the design and employment of military aircraft, while the concept of air power moved rapidly from the periphery to occupy a central position in strategic planning. As in 1914-18, it was conflict, and the need to create more and better machines of war, that forced the pace of change. The diversity of aircraft that emerged during the Second World War and the operations in which they were involved seem set to remain a source of fascination for those of us who share an interest in military aviation.

This comprehensive and highly-illustrated new book provides a detailed guide to the most important military aircraft in use with the air forces of the Axis and Allied powers during the Second World War. The aircraft are grouped according to country of origin and manufacturer. The more significant types command entries of greater length, but all have detailed specifications to accompany the text. In the introduction to the book, I hope to provide a glimpse into the background of the major air forces and then provide a brief look at the major events of the 1939-45 air war and the development of air operations.

Right: Preserved Hurricane leading a Spitfire.

8

INTRODUCTION

The First World War

The 1914-18 war acted as a powerful catalyst for developments in aircraft technology and laid the foundations for the future use of air power. Speed, firepower, ceiling and other performance measurements increased during the four years of war. In turn, the role of aircraft progressed from the original 1914 concept of aerial observation, to a wide tactical application and strategic design, as seen in the German Air Service's long-range bomber offensive against Britain. Tactics evolved from primitive, limited means of fighting, to the use of large formations organised for high-altitude, controlled combat. Germany led the way in other fields. In the March 1918 Kaiser Offensive on the Western Front its commanders pioneered the use of *Schlachtstaffeln* (specialised ground-attack air units) in support of advancing troops. Armed with light bombs, anti-personnel darts, machine-guns for strafing (from the German word *strafe*, meaning strike) and controlled by a rudimentary ground-air signalling system, these units proved highly effective. In the closing months of the war Britain refined these tactics, using aircraft to attack field artillery in the path of advancing tanks. In 1939 the German forces used similar tactics in its Blitzkrieg offensive on Poland, and again in the Low Countries, in France and during Operation Barbarossa.

During the interwar years defence cutbacks forced widespread reductions in European and US military air fleets and in the field of military aircraft design and development little progress was made. But while developments in military aviation stagnated in the decade after the war, civil aviation, which prior to the war had been in its infancy, took advantage of advances made in the war years and became the greatest catalyst for technological progress. Commercial pressures, rather than warfare, thus now stimulated aircraft production. There was a reawakening of the pioneer spirit of the prewar years through competition. The Schneider Trophy and the National Air Races in the USA attracted great interest among the public and stimulated manufacturers to research and develop ever more powerful engines, materials and airframes. Metal replaced wood for airscrews, undercarriage became retractable in response to the need for clean aerodynamic lines, and, most importantly, the biplane came to be replaced by the monoplane.

Military aviation was slow to the adopt these advances. In 1930, fighter aircraft were remarkably unchanged from the form in which they had emerged from the First World War. Performance was improved, but in essence they were the same. It will be noted that most of the aircraft in this book were designed in the mid-to late-1930s to directives that were based on speculative predictions of the role of aircraft in future warfare. In general, there was a very marked but ultimately damaging emphasis on the primacy of offence in aerial operations throughout the interwar years, one that prompted the British, French and US air forces to build small numbers of inadequate bombers whilst holding true to the belief that well-regimented formations of bombing aircraft with defensive armament held the key to the projection of air power. In 1939 none of the bombers in service were capable of the task which they were expected to fulfil. The ambitious predictions of the bomber theorists were in fact far in advance of the technology of the day. Germany, as we shall see, developed a tactical air force primarily for army support and equipped it with aircraft that were more than adequate in this role, but failed to envisage a situation where it would be expected to fight a long, strategic war.

Germany

Under the terms of the Versailles Treaty Germany lost the right to maintain her military air forces. Almost every major aircraft factory was forced to cease production, although some continued clandestine development work, and it is not until the rise of the Nazi party and the Third Reich that German military aviation again became a significant force. Air Minister Hermann Göring formally announced the existence of the Luftwaffe in March 1935, although plans for an independent German air force had been secretly under way since 1923. During the period 1933-39 Göring was content to delegate much responsibility for the Luftwaffe to his two subordinates: Inspector General of the Luftwaffe, Erhard Milch, and his Chief of Staff, General Wever, while he concentrated on furthering his political career. As deputy to Göring at the Ministry of Aviation from 1933, Milch was the prime architect of the fledgling Luftwaffe and took practical charge for its

Below: Focke-Wulf developed the Condor in the mid-1930s for commercial routes across the Atlantic. In wartime the aircraft was easily adapted to the long-range reconnaissance role.

organisation. He was greatly aided in his task by the pre-existence of a framework for a military air force, for in the years since the war the German Sporting Union had discreetly trained some 50,000 pilots from which Milch could draw. The best of the thousands of pilots who volunteered for service formed the cadre of the new air force. Milch also galvanised the civil aircraft industry, which built aircraft that were the forebears of the wartime German bomber fleets. By discreetly building transport and passenger-carrying aircraft that were, in fact, easily converted into military aircraft (wartime aircraft such as the Dornier Do 17, Heinkel He 111 and Focke-Wulfe FW 200 Condor were adapted from prewar civil designs) the

Below: The faithful Junkers Ju 52. In Spain it was used as a bomber, but proved its real value in the transport role.

Luftwaffe was able to disguise its offensive capabilities and intents.

In 1936, the Luftwaffe lost its first Chief of Staff, General Wever, in an air accident. Wever was one of the old school of bomber protagonists and in him the Luftwaffe lost its leading advocate of long-range strategic bombing. After this time development of heavy bombers was almost abandoned in favour of medium and dive-bombers and the Luftwaffe was geared toward a sophisticated army support role, reflecting Hitler's complete belief in offensive warfare. To support the medium bombers the Germans built a new generation of low-wing monoplane fighters, the best of them designed by Willy Messerschmitt at the Bayerische Flugzeugwerke. In 1935, Messerschmitt introduced his legendary Bf 109 to the world and also produced the Bf 110 for entry into service in 1939 in the vague *zerstörer* (bomber destroyer) role. Junkers designed and built the

Above: Willy Messerschmitt's Bf 109 was blooded in Spain by the Condor Legion.

fearsome Ju 87 dive-bomber, a perfect tool to support the army.

The Condor Legion in Spain
In the summer of 1936, Hitler sent a detachment of Luftwaffe pilots (the Condor Legion) to Spain in support of the fascist leader Franco, providing Luftwaffe pilots with ample opportunity to test their machinery and to refine tactics. The combat experience gained in Spain proved invaluable. Here were developed the Schwarm and Rotte fighter formations, based on mutually-supporting pairs, that were used throughout the Second World War to such effect, and also the close-support and dive-bombing tactics that formed the basis of Blitzkrieg. Such was the success of the few Junkers Ju 87 dive-bombers used operationally in Spain that the very concept of dive-bombing became central to Luftwaffe dogma. In 1939, it was the Stukageschwader that were held in the greatest esteem.

Only in the autumn of 1939, after war with Britain became a certainty, was interest in the heavy bomber renewed, as realisation of the need for a strategic bomber force suddenly became abruptly clear. This was but the first in series of mistakes that

Above: Reginald Mitchell's elegant Spitfire. K5054 was the first Spitfire prototype, although this is a actually a Mk II painted to represent it.

were to dog the Luftwaffe. Another was the decision taken by Göring to appoint his old comrade Ernst Udet to lead the Technical Office of the Luftwaffe. Udet, though a fine pilot and a good judge of fighter aircraft, was an astoundingly incompetent administrator under whose supervision the wartime German aircraft industry descended into chaos. Milch does not escape blame, for it was he who cancelled Germany's strategic bomber programme. Another fatal oversight was the fact that during the late 1930s the Luftwaffe planned almost to the last moment for a war starting in 1942 or 1943.

Ignoring these underlying deficiencies, by September 1939 the Luftwaffe was technically the most powerful air force in the world with a strength of some 3,750 aircraft. And in terms of its organisation, the quality of its pilots and its aircraft,

the Luftwaffe was certainly dominant, and more than capable of fulfilling the task for which it had been designed — that of supporting the army.

Britain

In the aftermath of the First World War domestic financial pressures in Britain forced a reduction in the size of the peacetime Royal Air Force (RAF) from 133 squadrons to 33, and only through pursuing a successful and cost-effective campaign of 'air policing' in Mesopotamia, the Middle East and, later on, the Northwest Frontier of India and in Somaliland, was the RAF able win lasting independence. This was done at the expense of the home defence, which by 1922 comprised only one squadron of ageing aircraft. With most of RAF strength on overseas detachment, its commander Lord

Trenchard struggled against financial limitations to build a strong framework for the service. His contribution was not only to keep the service alive in its early days but can also be seen in the institutions of training and support, the raising of its image in the public eye, the development of clear doctrines and modern theories of aerial warfare and in its structure.

Planning for War

During the early 1930s the RAF sought to establish the guidelines under which it would fight a future war. At this time the most prominent theories of the role of an independent air force were based either on the principles of air superiority, that is denying the enemy the use of the air as a prelude to an attack on their vital centres, or else the strategic theory of simply destroying their centres of production and communi-

Right: The Bristol Blenheim. Originally conceived as a high-speed transport for a newsaper magnate, it was Britain's standard light bomber in 1939.

cation. Emphasis on the primacy of offence in air operations was popularised by Trenchard in the First World War and maintained by the RAF right through the 1920s and 1930s, up until the last 18 months of peace. In practical terms, this policy meant that resources were funnelled into equipping the RAF with a substantial, but ultimately inadequate, strategic bomber fleet. Supporters of strategic bombing gave lofty voice to the theories of General Guilo Douhet, an Italian who believed that armies and navies were best employed as defensive forces while bomber fleets conquered the enemy. In Douhet's futuristic text *The War of 19-* he prophesied that in a future war aerial bombing would have such a profound effect on the civilian population that it would bring pressure or even an open revolt against the government. Douhet's theories conveniently ignored the natural advantage that defensive forces enjoy in warfare, yet they were eagerly digested by high-ranking airmen such General Billy Mitchell in the USA, Lord Trenchard in Britain, and others in France, in Germany and in Italy. Resources were concentrated on the development of bombing aircraft that could not possibly, given the available technology, ever hope to fulfil the demands of the theorists. The belief that Germany, which during the 1930s emerged as the greatest threat to Britain, would concentrate its rearmament on bomber aircraft, caused great consternation among the British public and press and influenced the Chiefs of Staff in their decision to build up the front-line bomber strength of the RAF, albeit with obsolete aircraft without the range to attack Germany from Britain. This led to the neglect of air defence forces that was only rectified after the Munich agreement.

Countdown to War

The realisation that Britain faced a new threat to her national security resulted in eight prewar rearmament schemes, the first of which was approved by the Cabinet in 1934. This planned to match the Luftwaffe in strength, and concentrated on expanding the bomber fleet. The plan was constantly revised over the following four years, until by 1938 emphasis was finally on fighter production. But by this stage Germany had taken a very substantial lead in developing modern aircraft, and there were some very worrying deficiencies in British defence planning. Firstly it was believed that Germany had only limited industrial capacity, and that this would not be bolstered in the event of war by the resources of Western Europe, and secondly the Chiefs of Staff had not considered the possibility that Britain would also br forced to fight in the Far East.

Although the lack of a cohesive and modern strategy handicapped the RAF in the late 1930s, a positive move in 1936 was the consolidation of the RAF into Bomber, Fighter, Coastal and Training Commands. The basic organisational unit remained the squadron, and these were divided into two flights of eight aircraft with two in reserve. Squadrons were organised into wings. Despite this pragmatic reorganisation, in September of 1939 the RAF was faced with the fact that it had no modern aircraft for the

Below: A Hawker Hurricane. This was the most prolific fighter in service with the Royal Air Force in 1939.

Above: The Tiger Moth, the standard RAF trainer of the late 1930s. Note the folded blind-flying hood on the rear cockpit.

Below: A Blenheim night-fighter, a role to which the aircraft was wholly unsuited.

Above: Spitfire Mk XI, which helped to bridge the gap created by the FW190.

Right and Below Right: Hurricanes being fuelled and serviced at a forward base in France.

ground-attack, reconnaissance, transport, or coastal defence roles. Control of naval aviation passed to the RAF in April 1918, and was neglected in the intervening years.

Rather too late, as Europe descended into conflict, the Air Ministry realised that it had focused for too long on the light bomber as its primary weapon. This rationale explains why aircraft of such dubious operational value as the Fairey Battle figured so strongly in the RAF inventory in 1939. Only after its mauling in France did the RAF acknowledge the poor combat capabilities of its front-line aircraft.

Italy

Italy was the first nation to use aircraft in combat (during the Italo-Turkish War of 1911–12), producing some of the finest heavy bombers of the First World War and, with Great

Britain, was the only other nation to establish an independent air force during that conflict. The privations forced on the Corpo Aeronautico Militare after the war were reversed with the accession to power of the Fascist Benito Mussolini, 'Il Duce', in 1922. Mussolini chose General Guilo Douhet, the exponent of strategic bombing whose theories influenced postwar military policy throughout Europe, to build an air force that could be instrumental in his grand plans to expand the Italian Empire. This new Italian air force, the Regia Aeronautica, was formed in March 1923. Re-equipping this force, and a corresponding expansion in the civil aviation market, brought something of a revival to the Italian aircraft industry after four years of stagnation. In the 1920s Italian aircraft won the Schneider Trophy no less than three times, and also gained records for long-distance flights. In the mid-1920s the Regia Aeronautica was engaged in operations to put down an insurrection in Libya, one of the African colonies that Italy had been granted at Versailles.

By 1933, Italy possessed what was regarded as the most powerful air force in the world. The strength of the Regia Aeronautica stood at some 1,200 first-line machines, and most of these were advanced types such as the manoeuvrable CR.20 fighter. Throughout the interwar years (and no doubt with the enthusiastic support of General Douhet) Italy demonstrated similar enthusiasm for strategic bombing and for developing large bomber aircraft, as it had in the First World War. Out of this enthusiasm grew the Caproni series of bombers that were the mainstay of Italian bomber units in the Second World War. Eager to expand his African possessions, Mussolini invaded Abyssinia in 1935. His bombers went into action against tribesmen armed with only the most basic of weapons, and achieved easy victory. In 1936, elements of the Regia Aeronautica were sent to Spain and in the absence of effective opposition

its aircraft performed admirably. Bolstered by these successes senior Italian airmen failed to modernise an air force that by the late 1930s was falling behind its more technologically advanced European neighbours and that entered the war with equipment that was markedly inferior in many respects to the Royal Air Force.

USA

America came late to the First World War, reversing a policy of isolationism that characterised its foreign policy for the early years of the 20th century. Airmen of the US Army Air Service that were attached to the American Expeditionary Force fought alongside British and French pilots from April 1917 and a number of them distinguished themselves in battle. American aviation industry made rapid advances to regain the ground it had lost in terms of technology, and in the years after the war emerged as the vanguard of progress.

Despite gaining autonomy in May 1918, the Air Service again came under the direct control of the Army in June 1920, which promptly reduced it in size to 27 squadrons, instead of the 87 that had been planned. The protestations of General William 'Billy' Mitchell (who had commanded the air units of the AEF in the war) were in vain, and his persistent attempts to convince the Army Chiefs of Staff to

create a strategic air force only led to court-martial and subsequent dismissal from his post. Mitchell, like Trenchard and Douhet, was an enthusiastic supporter of strategic bombing. The Air Service found itself in competition with the US Navy Bureau of Aeronautics, which was established the following year, for the scant resources allocated by the Department of Defense.

In 1926, the US Army Air Corps was organised and while calls from leading airmen for full independent status continued to be ignored, a slow process of expansion and re-equipment was begun. Stifling bureaucracy hampered the Corps until 1935, preventing the military from taking advantage of the advances in aviation technology that had been made in the ensuing period. Military aviation suffered from both a lack of investment and lack of interest among the men who controlled it and left the Corps weak by the time that America entered the war in 1941. However, it should be noted that in 1939 the USAAC possessed the only four-engine strategic bomber fleet in the world, equipped with the important Boeing B-17 Flying Fortress.

Below: B-17 *Miss Angela* **of the 8th Air Force.**

Japan

Japan began to emerge as a leading industrial power at the turn of the 20th century and in the aftermath of the First World War (from which her industries profited to a great extent) began to modernise her armed forces. Japan's army and naval air arms were formed prior to the First World War with French and British aircraft, but in 1916 an indigenous aero industry was founded by Nakajima and Kawanishi. International treaty agreements limited the expansion of these domestic industries until the early 1930s and until that time Japanese aviation relied on imports, licence designs and copies for its equipment. This led to the dangerous supposition in the West that Japan was only capable of making good copies and ignored the innovation shown by the Japanese engineers in adapting Western technology for their own needs. The Japanese Army Air Force (JAAF) began to gain combat experience in 1931 during the invasion of Manchuria. During the five-week military campaign the professional and ruthless Japanese Army,

supported by *chutais* (squadrons) of Nieuport 29 fighters and Salmson 2 reconnaissance aircraft, made huge territorial gains. There was no air opposition, and Japan's aircraft were engaged solely in bombing and tactical reconnaissance.

The naval air service played little part in the Manchurian campaign, but in the Shanghai invasion of January 1932 was able to prove its worth. Aircraft from the carriers *Hosho* and *Kaga* were fully involved in this action, supporting ground-attack sorties in which Chinese fighters were encountered for the first time. After a resounding Japanese victory, armistice terms were agreed on May 5. However, victory in Manchuria could not detract from the fact that Japanese expansion would always be hampered by a crippling lack of raw materials, save a little coal, and this prompted its economists and politicians to formulate plans for a Japanese-led economic empire known as the Greater East Asia Co-Prosperity Sphere, a kind of Asian brotherhood free from the oppression of the Western colonisers.

Above: A line-up of World War II veterans; Mitsubishi A6M Zero-Sen; Harvard trainer; Ryan PT-6; Harvard; P-38 Lightning.

The increasing stability of the Chinese economy and growing strength of its military, which Japan viewed as a threat to its plans for the Co-Prosperity Sphere, prompted a full-scale invasion of China in July 1937. In the resulting war Japan made devastating use of a formidable array of modern air weaponry and demonstrated that it possessed the best and most refined aircraft carrier forces in the world. The 72 chutais of the JAAF and 29 *buntais* (naval air squadrons) of the JNAF easily won superiority in the air, but their early successes were not matched by the land forces and as the Chinese air force (assisted by Captain Claire L. Chennault's Flying Tigers) regrouped and reorganised they began to suffer losses.

Japan realised that to sustain a war against China it needed raw materials, most importantly crude oil and

18

minerals. Some 90% of these materials were imported from the USA and the Dutch East Indies and restrictions placed on these imports after the invasion of China pushed Japan towards war. The strategists in Tokyo turned their eyes to the Dutch East Indies, rich in oil, and to Malaya, the British colony that produced 60% of the world's rubber. The plan to capture these islands was formulated under the guise of creating the Co-Prosperity Sphere. Burma, India, even Australia and New Zealand were a part of this Japanese ambition. In 1939, the Japanese army and navy began planning for war against the United States, the United Kingdom and the Dutch East Indies, in which air operations would play a very major part. The equipment of both the JAAF and JNAF was by this time generally superior to the badly maintained air forces that the US and UK held in the Pacific. Pilots and crews had been blooded over 10 years of warfare, with many averaging over 600 hours of combat time. As we shall see, an arrogant disregard for the qualities of the Japanese military among both British and American officers cost them dearly.

Soviet Union

Although Russia entered the First World War with numerically the strongest air force in the world it was poorly equipped and organised and made little contribution to the war effort. When the Bolsheviks became the new masters of Russia in October 1917 they inherited some 2,500 aircraft from the Imperial Army and Navy and an extensive, if primitive, aircraft industry. The renamed Workers and Peasants Red Military Air Fleet (RKKVVF) was subordinated to Trotsky's Revolutionary Military Council (*Revvoensovet*) and charged with supporting the ground forces during the civil war. The surviving Sikorski IM heavy bombers were used in attacks against the White Armies and proved so effective that the

Revvoensovet ordered an immediate replacement to be built, thus spurring the development of the first generation of Soviet heavy bombers.

The Civil War cost the RKKVVF dearly in terms of experienced pilots and commanders, and although the deficit in pilots was eventually made up by new flying schools, the air force lacked an effective officer cadre until 1930. One notable early achievement was the establishment in 1922 of the Zhukovski Air Force Engineering Academy. Among its early pupils were such luminaries of Soviet aviation as Sergei Il'yushin, Aleksandr Yakovlev and Artyom Mikoyan. And much tactical and technical experience was gained through links with the German aviation industry, notably the Junkers company, and no doubt helped by the presence of a secret German air training school at Lipetsk.

In 1923, the Red Air Fleet was reorganised. Each of the military districts into which the Soviet Union was divided (by 1938 there were some 14 of these) had one air brigade, under the command of a brigade commander who was himself subordinate to the Military District Commander. The air brigades consisted of squadrons (*eskadrilya*) made up of three flights of nine machines, these divided into three zvenya. The naval air units of the Black Sea and Baltic Fleets functioned in parallel with the district air commanders, with Fleet Commanders retaining overall control. In 1928, Stalin instigated the first of his Five-Year Plans to expand the collective strength of the Soviet air force units from less than one thousand aircraft to some 2,700 by 1933. Production of fighter and bomber aircraft was given priority and by 1937 the annual production of all combat aircraft types had reached 3,756. By then these included the very capable Polikarpov I-15 and I-16 fighters and the Tupolev SB-2 bomber; these aircraft were tested in combat during the Spanish Civil War, operating with

Right: Heinkel He 111 medium bomber en route to England.

considerable success in support of the Republican forces. Development of specialised anti-tank aircraft (*shturmovik*) was begun in the early 1930s, and although this was hampered by the lack of effective armament, the programme proved to be a far-sighted venture.

The influence of the doctrines of strategic bombing on Soviet policy began to emerge in the early 1930s, and was confirmed in 1936 with the creation of the Special Purpose Air Arm (AON), a strategic bomber fleet whose first leader, Vasili Khripin, subscribed to Douhet's treatise on air warfare. Under his command the bomber component of the Soviet Air Forces (Voenno-Vozduzhnoye Sily, or V-VS) was increased dramatically until by 1936 it represented some 60% of the total force. The AON was not planned, however, as an exclusively heavy bomber force. Its function lay equally in the support and supply of the Red Army in the new age of fast mechanised warfare foreseen by Soviet theoreticians such as Tukhachevski, who through his close association with high-ranking German officers was aware of the new doctrines of Blitzkrieg. This inspired the Soviets to develop airborne forces and to develop the V-VS as essentially an offensive force. Resources were poured into the development of heavy bombers that had become obsolescent by the outbreak of war.

In the mid-1930s, Stalin undertook a wholesale purge of the V-VS. This action robbed the V-VS of its most experienced leaders and theoreticians (Khripin and Lapchinski among them), and the aero industry of its finest engineers. Thus when the V-VS faced the Luftwaffe in the summer of 1941 it had innumerable aircraft, but a severe lack of tactical awareness among its leaders.

HISTORY OF THE AIR WAR

In the winter months of 1939-40, German land and air forces swarmed across Europe, achieving victories that stunned the world. Poland fell in 27 days, Denmark in 24 hours, Norway in 23 days, Holland in five, Belgium in 18, and then France in barely more than five weeks. In May 1940, Hitler's armies stood poised on the western coast of France ready to strike across the English Channel at Britain and deliver the *coup de grace*. The devastating effectiveness of German forces in those months was due in no small part to the strategy of Blitzkrieg. Blitzkrieg, the 'lightning war', was neither a new nor an untested theory, yet in 1940 few European military commanders had fully understood it, or knew how to counter it. The Germans had used fast-moving units to break through an enemy's defences, harass his rear guard forces, lines of communication, supply depots, and most importantly his headquarters, during the First World War, and later in Spain. The revolutionary German approach during the early months of the Second World War was to link this basic strategy with the most sophisticated aircraft and armour in the world.

Fall Weiss — the Invasion of Poland

At 04.45 (CET) on September 1, 1939 Blitzkrieg theory met its first test, as the air and ground forces of the Wehrmacht poured over the Czech border into Poland. A force of some 1,580 first-line aircraft were committed to the campaign. In the north Kesselring's Luftflotte I supported von Bock's army group. Löhr's Luftflotte IV operated in the south. Despite persistent bad weather and by making use of effective tactical photo-reconnaissance, the Luftwaffe was able to achieve its primary aim by destroying much of the Polish air force on the ground and in the air in the first hours of the war. Nine *Kampfgruppen* (bomber wings) of Dornier 17Z-1s, 17Z-2s and M-1s, and 15 Gruppen of Heinkel He 111H-1s carried out medium-range bombing on railheads and communications centres, disrupting mobilisation of Polish forces, while at the front a sustained aerial and ground bombardment by Ju 87 squadrons and heavy artillery

Left: A picture taken from the rear cockpit of a Junkers Ju 87 dive-bomber as it pulls up from an attack.

Above: Weary-looking Ju 87s over the Eastern Front.

in support of the armoured and motorised units (which comprised only one-sixth of the German forces) broke down the Polish resistance. The bombers were escorted by Messerschmitt Bf 109D-1s and E-1s and Bf 110C-1s, which proved far superior to anything that the well-trained, highly motivated but poorly equipped Polish fighter units could field.

Within 48 hours the Polish air force ceased to exist as an effective force. The Luftwaffe was thereafter able to turn its full attention to the secondary objective, supporting the armies. The fighting ended on September 27, marking the end of one of the most astounding military campaigns in military history. For the Luftwaffe, it confirmed the capabilities of the Ju 87 and Bf 110 long-range fighter. In the Polish campaign these aircraft performed admirably in the role for which they were built and against weak opposition. When used against a better-equipped enemy and without the benefit of air superiority their deficiencies were exposed.

Europe Prepares

When Britain declared war on Germany on September 3, 1939, the RAF could call on a strength of 114 squadrons. Fighter Command held

39, 25 of them equipped with Hurricanes and Spitfires and the remainder equipped with Gloster Gladiators, Gloster Gauntlets and even a few Hawker Hinds. Bomber Command was the largest of the RAF commands, in line with prewar doctrine, with 920 aircraft in 55 squadrons. Although on paper this looked an impressive force, 10 squadrons of Fairey Battles and two squadrons of Bristol Blenheims were committed to France with the Advanced Air Striking Force and another 17 were withdrawn to form Operational Training Units, leaving a strength of only 352 aircraft. Coastal Command had 10 squadrons, equipped with aircraft ranging from the Shorts Sunderland to the Supermarine Walrus.

Opposing them were 4,204 Luftwaffe aircraft, 90% of which were serviceable at any time. Despite the hasty rearmament of the late 1930s many people questioned whether the RAF had the material strength to challenge this force. The quality of training among its personnel was extremely variable, mainly because of inadequate and outmoded equipment. In marked contrast many of the German airmen had combat experience, and their tactics were based on experience rather than classroom theory.

France, which declared war in unison with the United Kingdom, had a small force of bombers supported by fighters that lacked the speed and firepower of the

Luftwaffe's Bf 109. Although new and more effective aircraft had been ordered both at home and from the US, they were slow to reach squadron service, hampered by a national aircraft industry just emerging from the disruption of recent nationalisation.

The Phoney War

After the crushing of Poland the British population nervously awaited the arrival of German bombers over their cities. The predicted attacks did not come and Britain was afforded a temporary respite, popularly referred to as the 'Phoney War', in which to fortify its air defences. Bomber Command operations during this time were restricted to daylight attacks on the havens of the German fleet and night-time leaflet dropping — the 'Nickel' raids. Few tangible successes were scored, save proving that the RAF could penetrate German airspace. On these missions the Fairey Battles, Vickers Wellingtons, Armstrong Whitworth Whitleys and Handley Page Hampdens of Bomber Command had no fighter escort and endured heavy losses against German fighter pilots flying aircraft with cannon armament and with a speed advantage of up to 100 mph. The heavy losses sustained during daylight raids peaked in December, and made it apparent that losses would rapidly become unsustainable. By comparison the night-time raids were less expensive in terms of men and aircraft, showing a possible way forward for the bombing offensive.

Pilots of Fighter Command squadrons at home and on deployment in France with the Advanced Air Striking Force (AASF) saw little action during this unnerving lull in the fighting. Few targets of worth appeared over the British positions save the odd German reconnaissance machine. The only really notable development was the creation of a dedicated photo reconnaissance unit within the RAF. As with so many other essential aspects of air

Above and Right: Vickers Wellington heavy bombers are prepared for a night raid on Germany. Although the 'Wimpy' was the best RAF bomber at the outbreak of war, it suffered heavy losses in the early daylight raids.

Below: Spitfire Mk I is turned around by armourers during the Battle of Britain.

operations photo reconnaissance had been badly neglected during the 1930s. The RAF was quick to appreciate the value of this intelligence and as the war progressed its reconnaissance and interpretation units played an increasingly important role in strategic and tactical planning.

Norway

Two factors lay behind Hitler's decision to invade Norway in April 1940. The first was Norway's important strategic position in the eyes of the German Navy. The second was the vital need to protect the supply of iron ore from Sweden to the Ruhr. The airborne and sea operation began in the early hours of April 9, 1940. An RAF Short Sunderland reconnaissance aircraft spotted the invasion fleet en route, but the Royal Navy failed to intercept the Kriegsmarine as it sped toward Trondheim, Bergen, Egersund, Arendal, Kristiansand and Oslo. The air aspect of the operation was under Generalleutnant Geisler whose 1,000 aircraft comprised approximately 500 transports and the remainder of them combat types. Geisler's main task was to neutralise the threat posed by the Royal Navy and as such the primary instrument

of air power was the long-range medium bomber — the Junkers Ju 88A-1s and Heinkel He 111H-1s. These were supported by 30 Bf 109Es (which had superseded the less powerful 'D' model) and 70 Bf 10 fighter escorts, and a small number of Ju 87R-1s with long-range tanks. Also available were 30 Heinkel He 115A-1 seaplanes.

Opposing them were the six Gloster Gladiators and Caproni Ca 110 Libeccio light bombers of the Norwegian Air Force, and elements of the Royal Air Force.

During the invasion RAF Bomber Command mounted daylight raids against the German invasion fleet, but not a single vessel was hit, let alone sunk. Within hours of the initial airborne and naval assault German paratroopers secured the important airfields at Aalborg Ost and West. The loss of the airfields meant that very limited support of the British and French expeditionary forces that came ashore at Namsos, Aandalsnes and Narvik in the following weeks was possible.

Attacks against occupied airfields confirmed that daylight operations were highly vulnerable; no fewer than nine of the 83 aircraft sent to attack two German cruisers on April 12 failed to return, and apart from

Above: The Sea Gladiator was immortalised in the defence of Norway and, later, during the battles for Malta.

occasional raids by Blenheims of No 2 Group, Bomber Command switched to night-time attacks after this date. The defenders of Norway were overcome by June 4 and an evacuation of men and equipment began. The RAF was dealt a further blow on June 8 when the eight Hurricanes and eight Gladiators that had been committed to the defence, and successfully evacuated back to the aircraft carrier HMS *Glorious*, were lost, together with almost the entire complement, when the vessel was sent to the bottom of the North Sea by the German fleet.

As in Poland, the Luftwaffe had proved to be the decisive factor in the success of the campaign. Airborne forces were used to great effect in capturing the vital airfields, in advance of a highly successful logistical operation that provided invaluable experience for the Transportgruppen. British attempts to establish points of resupply were hounded by the Luftwaffe bomber units enjoying conditions of air supremacy.

Fall Gelb — the Invasion of the Low Countries

Planning for *Fall Gelb*, the invasion of the Low Countries and France, began during the Polish campaign. Hitler's War Directive No 6, issued to his Chiefs of Staff on October 9, 1939, highlighted the key tasks of the Luftwaffe for the operation. These were protection of the land armies from aerial attack, support of their advance, preventing the Allied air forces from establishing themselves in Belgium, and prohibiting landings by British troops along the coast of Holland and Belgium. For the operation was assembled the largest Luftwaffe task force of the war. Von Bock's Army Group B in Belgium and Holland was to be supported by Luftflotte II, under the command of Albert Kesselring, while Von Runstedt's Army Group A, which was to attack through the Ardennes, was allocated Luftflotte III under Hugo Sperrle. Some 3,350 combat aircraft of a total Luftwaffe strength of 4,417 were available. In addition were 475 transports and gliders. Ju 87B-2 and Henschel Hs 123A-1 aircraft of VIII Fliegerkorps were tasked with providing close-support for the twin offensives.

In May 1940, two elements constituted the RAF force on the Continent. The Air Component of the British Expeditionary Force was made up of five squadrons of Westland Lysanders for tactical reconnaissance, four squadrons of Blenheims intended for strategic reconnaissance and four squadrons of Hurricanes for air defence. It was by any standards a meagre force and was later strengthened to 10 squadrons at the insistence of the French, much to the reluctance of Dowding. The Advanced Air Striking Force had 10 squadrons of Fairey Battles and Bristol Blenheims, which were to attack German columns, and four squadrons of Hurricanes for air defence. These squadrons could be allocated to any part of the front, and, to some extent, they could draw on the strength of home-based units.

The French Armée de l'Air, under Général Vuillemin, had a strength of 703 fighter aircraft, including 278 Morane-Saulnier MS 406s; these were bolstered by 100 Potez 631 long-range day and night fighters and a bomber force of approximately 175 Amiot 143, Farman 222 and Bloch 200 types and a few of the excellent Lioré et Olivier LeO 451 bombers. The Dutch air force was comprised almost solely of Fokker aircraft, save 11 Douglas DB-8A-3Ns. Fighter

Above: Junkers Ju 52e/3m, used to drop paratroopers onto Crete in the first airborne invasion in history.

strength amounted to approximately 28 single-engine Fokker D.XXIs and 23 twin-engine G.1As. Total strength was 132 aircraft. From these figures alone it is clear that, aside from its undoubted technical superiority, a considerable numerical advantage also favoured the Luftwaffe. It could also rely on the vital element of surprise.

On May 10, 1940, Blitzkrieg was unleashed on the West. In the darkness before dawn X Fliegerdivision carried out sea-mining sorties off the British and Dutch coasts. At 03.30 the air operations intensified with medium and low-altitude bomber attacks on airfields, strongpoints and communications centres in Belgium and Holland. Next came the airborne assault. Fifty-five German assault troops glided onto the roof of the imposing and supposedly impregnable Belgian fortress of Eben Emael, situated at a vital strategic point on the Albert Canal where it joins the River Maas. Belgium had maintained its neutrality after the invasion of Poland, but the concept

Above and Below: A Spanish-built version of the Bf 109, which dominated the skies over France until Spitfires were committed to the fight.

of neutrality did not suit Hitler. As airborne units seized key objectives along the canal, 12 Heinkel He 59 floatplanes landed on the River Maas, in the centre of the Dutch city of Rotterdam. German troops disgorged into inflatable boats and converged on the Willems Bridge.

At the same time, the 18th Army of General Georg von Kuchler, with the 9th Panzer Division at its head, stormed over the Dutch border and towards Rotterdam. To the south, Panzer Divisions 3 and 4 came over the River Maas via the captured bridges. The Dutch air force fought bravely, but lost over half of its serviceable aircraft on the first day. The Belgian air force lost 53 of its operational aircraft in the same time span.

During the initial air assault on France, nine of the RAF forward bases were attacked. The first RAF counter attacks were not ordered until 12.05. The Luftwaffe achieved air superiority against the unco-ordinated RAF and Armée de l'Air units with consummate ease.

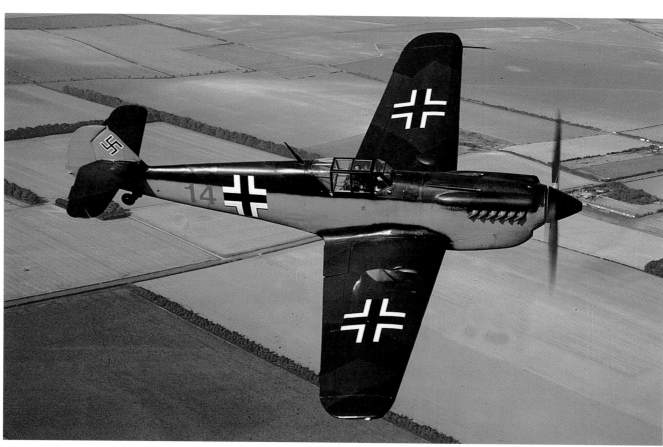

Above: Spanish-built (by CASA) version of the He 111, painted in the colours of the Luftwaffe.

Numerous attacks against the advancing German forces were launched by RAF Battle and Blenheim squadrons, and the Armée de l'Air Bloch and Amiot squadrons, over the course of the first 48 hours, but their losses were horrendous. On May 12, seven of the nine Blenheims of No 139 Squadron that set out to attack an enemy column near Maastricht failed to return. On that same day No 12 Squadron was tasked with attacking bridges over the Albert Canal near Maastricht. Every member of the squadron volunteered and six aircraft were dispatched. One returned after it had become unserviceable while the rest of the force pressed on with their desperate and heroic attack on bridges. One of the two bridges was destroyed but all five aircraft were brought down. For this action two airmen, Flg Off D. E Garland and Sgt T. Gray, were posthumously awarded the Victoria Cross.

The Allies had predicted the attack would come through Belgium, and the British Expeditionary Force and the French Seventh, First, and Ninth Armies duly began to move north to halt the German advance. Unbeknown to the Allied commanders, Army Group

A was threading its way through the narrow forest roads of the Ardennes region. This army group included the majority of German armoured divisions, including that of Heinz Guderian. The 5th and 7th Panzer Divisions, the latter commanded by Erwin Rommel, reached the River Meuse near Dinant in the Charleville-Sedan region on May 12. The next day the first assault across the river into France began, supported by II Fliegerkorps and Stukageschwader 77. Pontoon bridges were constructed under heavy French artillery fire, and after crossing the Panzers began their race across France.

Allied attacks on the bridgehead commenced on the morning of May 14. At 15.00, in a desperate attempt to halt the advance, every available aircraft of the AASF was committed to attacks on Sedan, Donchéry and Mouzon and 56% of the 68 aircraft were lost. Blenheim losses amounted to 75% of those engaged — totalling some 28 aircraft. The next day 40 of the 71 aircraft that took-off to attack German positions failed to return.

In an attempt to crush the final pockets of Dutch resistance in the city, Rotterdam was mercilessly bombed from the air on May 14 by

57 He 11IH-1s of Kampfgeschwader 54. The government fled to London and surrendered.

By May 15, a 50 mile (80 km) gap had been torn in the French defences. At Sedan, Guderian's XIX Panzerkorps sped forward with such momentum that he was ordered to slow down by senior commanders. In just two days the bomber strength of the AASF was nearly halved, and losses continued to mount in the days that followed. Despite the pleas of Hugh Dowding, the Fighter Command leader, Churchill sent reinforcements of fighter aircraft, but these could not halt the rout and on May 19 the surviving RAF aircraft were flown to England. Yet another disaster befell the RAF during the retreat. One hundred and twenty of the vitally important Hurricane fighters had to be destroyed to prevent their capture. This meant that out of a total of 261 Hurricanes deployed to France only 66 were returned.

On May 22 the leading elements of the 2nd Panzer Division reached Abbeville on the French coast. Evacuation through the port of Dunkirk was planned and both the Air Component and the AASF were gradually evacuated. Over the course of the next six days Spitfires of Fighter Command were committed to the battle in numbers for the first time, and achieved notable successes against the Bf 109s and Bf 110s against which they were pitted. During the withdrawal British ground forces were well-protected, and Luftwaffe air superiority was challenged for the first time. Much to their consternation, the Panzer groups found that they were no longer operating under conditions of air supremacy. One of the problems facing Luftwaffe units was one of range. Such had been the speed of the advance, its airfields were now far behind the front line.

Operation Dynamo

During the week of May 20-26, the British forces fell into headlong retreat. Some 500,000 tons of equipment and supplies were abandoned or sabotaged to prevent them from falling into German hands. Evacuation began on May 26, and by June 4 some 338,226 men had been brought to English ports in a rag-tag collection of yachts, fishing boats, and pleasure cruisers. Operation Dynamo was a hugely significant aspect of the Second World War. If one quarter of a million British and Allied troops had been captured it is unlikely that public support for the continuation of the conflict could have been maintained. Contrary to opinion at the time, the RAF were heavily engaged over the evacuation beaches during the evacuation. Dowding foresaw the need to conserve his fighter aircraft for the vital battle over Britain that was to follow, but nevertheless some 2,739 missions were flown, and air superiority over Dunkirk was achieved for much of the time. By the end of the withdrawal on June 4, RAF losses amounted to 959 aircraft — 229 of the AASF, 279 of the BEF Air Component, 219 of Fighter Command, 166 of Bomber Command and 66 of Coastal Command. Far more serious was the fact that between May 10 and June 4, no less than 432 Hurricanes and Spitfires were lost. These losses deeply undermined RAF strength and its capacity to defend Britain from air attack, and did little to bolster the confidence of its pilots. The Luftwaffe had suffered numerically worse losses, but few of its leaders expected Britain to fight on. Hitler himself believed Britain was defeated.

His generals were rather more conservatively minded but had good reason to feel optimistic of success if they had to take the fight on to British soil, provided that German troops could be transported safely across the Channel. They commanded 120 well-equipped divisions, whereas in Britain the army had barely 21, all of them seriously short of arms and equipment. The Royal Navy, which was numerically stronger to the Kriegsmarine, presented the main threat to the invasion fleet, but if air superiority could be achieved over the Channel this could be extinguished. The Luftwaffe were therefore ordered to proceed with all haste in defeating the RAF, in time for a planned invasion date in early autumn.

Having driven the British back across the sea, the German armies marched south, unopposed by the ineffective and poorly led French divisions. On June 16, Marshal Pétain sued for peace and signed the armistice with Hitler on June 22. The remainder of the Armée de l'Air was conscripted into the collabora-

Below: The redoubtable Hurricane made a vital and often highly underrated contribution to the defence of Britain defence in 1940.

tive Vichy air force, including those aircraft in France's North African colonies. French aircraft factories thereafter manufactured aircraft for both the Luftwaffe and the Vichy government.

In a six-week Blitzkrieg campaign, the Germans conquered all of western Europe. No assurances that Britain had accepted its supposedly inevitable defeat were forthcoming from the British Prime Minister, Winston Churchill, and so Hitler readily accepted Göring's assurances that he would blast the RAF from the sky in advance of an invasion planned for autumn. Hitler considered Operation Sealion a side issue to the invasion of Russia, and ordered that it be concluded as rapidly as possible.

BATTLE OF BRITAIN

Myths and legends abound in the many works published on this subject; what is certain is that it was the first and probably the greatest of all air battles. Indeed, it is the only major battle to have been fought solely in the air. Its outcome proved decisive on the outcome of the war.

Below: The wreckage of a Dornier Do 17 in a fenland dyke is examined by experts from the Air Ministry.

Command and Control

The key decisions in the battle rested with two very different men. Hermann Göring , the Luftwaffe commander, was a skilled politician, given to flamboyant gestures and posturing, but lacked a grasp of the realities of modern air war. Hugh Dowding, who led Fighter Command, was a quiet, rather serious man, often at odds with his ambitious superiors, but possessing a formidable strategic mind. He was a career RAF officer whose brusque manner had earned him many enemies among the Air Staff.

But although Dowding lacked the political skills of his adversary, he had been personally responsible for creating the RAF air defence network. At the forefront of this network were the 42 'Chain Home' early warning radar sites — tall, exposed steel towers concentrated along the eastern approaches. Supplementing the radar were the men and women of the Observer Corps. The successful defence of Britain in 1940 depended largely on the vital early warning that was provided by these elements, and an efficient system of command and control had been established prior to the war that linked Fighter Command airfields to the radar and observer sites.

For the duration of the Second World War Britain was divided into four parts each the responsibility of a designated group. No 13 Group covered the north of the country, No 10 Group looked after the south-west, No 12 Group was responsible for the Midlands and the Wash areas, and No 11 Group had the area between East Anglia and West Dorset, including London and the Home Counties. It was this group, commanded by Air Vice Marshal Keith Park, a tough and resourceful New Zealander, that bore the brunt of the fighting.

Each group was divided into sectors; No 11 Group, for example, was made up of seven different sectors, each controlling a number of separate airfields. Radar sites and observer sites were joined via two separate overland links to Air Marshal Dowding's Fighter Command headquarters at Bentley Priory in Middlesex, and to all the group and sector airfields. Acting on the basis of this information HQ Fighter Command could give an order to intercept to the relevant group fighter controller. These men were perhaps the key part of the whole system. It was their responsibility to allocate a raid to a particular sector according to the height and direction of the attacking force, and the readiness of the defending aircraft (the operational readiness of each squadron or flight was indicated on large board in the Operations Room at Bentley Priory). He could

then order a particular squadron or squadron flight to scramble and vector it to the interception point via radio.

Shoring up the Defences

Dowding also had operational control of Anti-Aircraft Command. By the start of the battle this important resource amounted to some 1,000 heavy AA guns and 600 lighter weapons, although this was only approximately half the total that was required. Augmenting the AA batteries were 1,400 barrage balloons, deployed around vital targets such as airframe and engine works to deter low-level and dive-bombing attacks. As mentioned previously, the strength of the RAF had been seriously depleted both in terms of men and machines during the Battle of France. The shortfall in aircraft was made good in the two months after Dunkirk largely through the energies of the dynamic newspaper proprietor Max Beaverbrook, who was appointed by Prime Minister Churchill to head a new Ministry of Aircraft Production. By the middle of August 700 aircraft were available, and production levels were increasing. Pilots were not so easily replaced. Despite the fact that the RAF had been strengthened by squadrons of volunteer Czech and Polish pilots, and by men from Canada, New Zealand, Australia, South Africa, India, the West Indies and America, by mid-August Dowding still lacked 154 pilots.

While Britain made good its defences, the Luftwaffe sought to recover its own strength. Aircraft losses of nearly 40% had been sustained in eight months of successive campaigning. Recovery was ominously swift — the most reliable source estimates the total combat strength of the Luftwaffe by mid-August at 1,481 twin-engine bombers, 327 dive bombers, 289 twin-engine fighters and 934 single-engine fighters. These were divided between Luftflotte III in northwest France, Luftflotte II in northern France and the Low Countries and Luftflotte V in Norway. The single-engined fighters were Bf 109E-1 models, which could outperform the Supermarine Spitfire II below 23,000ft and in a dive, and the Hawker Hurricane under any conditions.

It was not merely a numerical superiority that the German pilots enjoyed. The tactics employed by the RAF at this time were better suited to the air display than the rigours of aerial combat. Pre-training focused on disciplined flying in vee formations, a legacy of the belief in the prewar RAF that air combat would be a question of fighter against bomber. Instead of maintaining a vigilant look-out for enemy aircraft a pilot had to expend his energies on trying to keep station. Although many squadrons adopted their own tactics as experience taught, important differences of opinion divided the group commanders of Nos 11 and 12 Groups, Keith Park and Trafford Leigh-Mallory, which would have best been resolved before the war.

The Luftwaffe, drawing on its experiences in the Spanish Civil War, used a different system based on a mutually-supporting pair of aircraft called a Rotte. In this formation the wingman flew to the side and rear of his leader and was responsible for guarding the rear, leaving the lead man to direct all attention on the sky ahead. Pairs of Rotte were known as a Schwarm. These formations were far more flexible and manoeuvrable than the Fighter Command 'vic', and enabled all four pilots to keep a good lookout while staying in formation.

Although most British accounts consider July 10 as the starting point for the Battle of Britain, the Luftwaffe was active over the Channel from late June. From July 10 until August 8 the Luftwaffe intensified harassing attacks on ports on eastern, southern and north-western Britain, and against convoy shipping bringing coal from northern pits, in an attempt to draw Fighter Command into a decisive engagement over the Channel. Dowding refused to commit large forces to these battles. On July 19 Hitler again urged the British to surrender and threatened that failure to comply would result in her complete destruction. Göring ensured his Führer that the RAF was seriously weakened, and at the July 21 meeting of the German commanders-in-chief Hitler issued orders to Kesselring and Sperrle to plan the destruction of the RAF in order to prepare for an invasion. The main strike was planned for August 10, and codenamed *Adlertag* ('Eagle Day'). The aim of this operation, laid down by Hitler in Directive No 17 of August 1, was to 'destroy the Royal Air Force using all available force against primarily the flying units, their ground facilities and their support, but also the aviation industry, including that manufacturing anti-aircraft equipment'.

'Eagle Day'

Poor weather on August 10 forced a postponement, and only on August 12 did the attacks begin. Heavily escorted formations of bombers attacked radar stations and airfields near the English coast. Five radar facilities were damaged, but all but one of them, Ventnor, was back in operation within a few hours. Of the airfields Manston was put out of action and operations at Hawkinge and Lympne were seriously disrupted. The following day saw the start of the attack proper. Two major attacks were launched against airfields in the south and south-east, causing minor damage for the loss of 45 aircraft,

Above Right: A classic image showing a Heinkel He 111 over the docks in the East End of London.

Right: Luftwaffe service crews working on the Daimler Benz Db605 engine from a Bf 109.

Above: A crashed, but virually intact He 111. The aircraft has been fitted with special balloon cable-cutting equipment, which had a marked and negative effect on performance.

most of them Ju 87s. By comparison the RAF lost 13 aircraft, and three pilots. August 15 saw another day of heavy fighting, with attacks by all three Luftflotten on targets in the north, east and south. In the late morning a force of 110 Ju 87s and 50 Bf 109s attacked airfields in the south-east, badly damaging Lympne. Another three-pronged attack by 170 aircraft was plotted by radar in the afternoon, but the strength of the defenders deflected many of these raiders from their intended targets. Later in the afternoon a force of approximately 250 aircraft was intercepted along the southern coast, and the raid had only very limited effect. In the early evening a raid by 90 Dornier Do 17s escorted by 130 Bf 109s and a diversionary force of 60 Bf 109s crossed the Channel. Ten RAF squadrons intercepted, but some of the attacking aircraft were able to penetrate well inland and cause damage at West Malling and Croydon. In total, the number of

sorties flown that day by the Luftwaffe amounted to 1,750. Göring made a crucial decision that day to discontinue attacks on the radar sites, as these had so far produced few tangible results. In retrospect this proved a be one of his most basic mistakes. On August 16, a temporary let-up in the fighting gave the RAF time to count its losses and make good the damages as best it could. Between August 8 and 17, Fighter Command had lost some 154 aircraft, yet fighter production at this time was running at approximately 100 a week. More importantly, 154 pilots were lost in the same period. Only 63 pilots were available as replacements, and they were mostly inexperienced. The other commands were trawled for replacements but even with these men and the foreign and Commonwealth volunteers, aircrew losses remained the most serious problem that faced Dowding.

Battle of Attrition

This pattern of attack continued almost unabated until September 6. With the exception of a brief spell between August 19 and 23 when bad weather restricted daylight Luftwaffe operations, there was not a single day when less than 600 sorties were

flown against targets in Britain. During the lull, large formations of bombers attacked targets from South Wales and Liverpool to East Anglia at night. One of these formations mistakenly bombed London, prompting the Cabinet to order a retaliatory attack on Berlin on August 25/26. Although this caused little material damage, the attack was to have great significance. Daylight raids commenced on August 24, with renewed attacks on the RAF bases at Manston, Hornchurch and North Weald as well as Dover, Ramsgate, Portsmouth and other centres. All of the airfields ringing London were subjected to repeated attacks in the next two weeks, sometimes as many as three a day. It is sometimes assumed that the RAF had been brought to its knees by September 6, and that two further weeks of attacks would have been sufficient to seal its fate, but the reality is rather more complex. In fact the RAF could draw on large reserves of aircraft from No 13 Group and the rate of aircraft production in Britain was now double that which the Germans could manage. Even more crucially, the Luftwaffe was losing far more aircrew every day, either captured or killed, than the RAF. RAF pilots

were regularly rotated to relieve them of combat stress. Those pilots who were available to the Luftwaffe were almost constantly in the front line, and suffered as a result. Although intelligence reports were continually assuring them that the RAF was down to its last 150 aircraft, it was clear that the RAF still possessed a formidable force.

Storm over London

On September 7 Hitler ordered the Luftwaffe to concentrate its attacks on London. In the mistaken belief that the RAF could no longer offer effective opposition, he lunged hastily to deliver the *coup de grace*. Göring supported the change in tactics, but it was roundly derided by the weary fighter pilots. They recognised that forcing the fighter units to perform escort duties for the bomber formations would leave both vulnerable to attack. The Messerschmitt Bf 109E had a limited combat range and the fighters would

be forced to abandon their escort duties in order to ensure a safe return to France. The twin-engined Bf 110 fighter had a longer range, but was outclassed by both the Hurricane and Spitfire. This in turn would leave the lumbering bomber fleets to the mercy of the RAF on the return flight to France.

The first attacks concentrated on the docks, the industrial areas and the East End. The raids on London continued through the second week of September, although with nothing like the intensity of the first night. Bombs fell on many different parts of the city, including the Admiralty, the War Office and Buckingham Palace. On September 15 the Battle of Britain reached its zenith. During the late morning a huge German

formation gathered over France before setting course for London. Heavy fighting took place over the Home Counties as the bombers flew towards their target. Later in the afternoon three more waves of attackers came in, a total force of some 200 bombers escorted by 300 fighters. No fewer than 31 RAF squadrons rose to intercept the third wave, but many of the aircraft reached the London area and their bombs caused widespread damage and heavy casualties. Although claims were understandably exaggerated at the time, modern research has shown that the Luftwaffe lost 60 aircraft that day, compared to an RAF loss of 26. Far more significant than these statistics is the fact that the Luftwaffe was still opposed by nearly 300 RAF

Above and Right: Hurricane Mk II of the Battle of Britain Memorial Flight. Note the insignia of a Polish squadron on the left engine cowling.

aircraft after a month of attacks. While the RAF seemed to be growing stronger, many Luftwaffe pilots were showing signs of combat fatigue in the face of such concerted opposition. On September 18, Hitler postponed Operation Sealion indefinitely and restricted his bomber force to night time operations. High level daylight raids by fighter-bombers and fighters continued until October 31, and these posed many problems for the defenders. Not least among these was the inability of the radar network to measure the height of the incoming raids, which could amount to 1,000 sorties in one day, but as October drew to a close these raids became increasingly infrequent and attention switched firmly to night-time bombing — The 'Blitz'.

Blitz

After failing to win the war of attrition against the RAF, Hitler turned his attention to British cities. He believed that attacks against major population centres would destroy the will of the British people to continue fighting and as a result, through the autumn and winter of 1940-41, thousands of tons of bombs were indiscriminately dropped at night on the British mainland. Worst hit was

London, but countless other towns from Liverpool to Portsmouth experienced the terror of these attacks. The RAF could do little to prevent them prior to the arrival of effective airborne radar. Between September 7 and November 13, night fighters managed to shoot down only eight enemy aircraft — the total for all the defences combined amounted to less 1% of sorties dispatched.

A raid on Coventry on the night of November 14/15 killed 554 people and seriously injured another 865. These figures seem modest by comparison with later operations, but at the time they were considered extremely grave. Considerable effort was expended in devising effective passive means to counter the German radio navigation systems, Knickbein and X-Gerät, and in constructing dummy targets. More important than these passive measures were the improvements in the night-fighter force. This was equipped with Hurricanes, Spitfires and a few radar-equipped Blenheims, later supplemented by the Boulton-Paul Defiant with its dorsal turret and the heavily armed Bristol Beaufighter. But despite the arrival of new and better aircraft the campaign against the Luftwaffe

during the Blitz could hardly be considered a success. The relentless bombing was brought to a halt not by the actions of the night fighter squadrons, but the redeployment of much of the Luftwaffe to the east in preparation for Operation Barbarossa.

By June 1941 only about a quarter of Luftwaffe operational strength remained in occupied Western Europe and Germany, and the pressure on air defence in Britain was greatly reduced. In the event three key factors had worked to the RAF's advantage. Firstly, the system of early warning removed some of the vital element of surprise from the Luftwaffe. Secondly, the fact that the battle was fought over southern Britain meant that Luftwaffe pilots who baled out were out of the war, whereas RAF airmen could reasonably expect to be rejoin the battle, barring serious injury. Coupled with this the RAF also possessed an excellent repair network that meant that many seriously damaged aircraft

Below: Spitfire Mk XXI, Mk IX and Mk II (far), formate on a much rarer veteran, the Hurricane Mk II.

could be returned to service with all possible haste. Some 35% of the aircraft delivered to Fighter Command during the battle were salvaged machines. Lastly, the combat radius of the Luftwaffe's single most important fighter, the Messerschmitt Bf 109E, was limited to 125 miles. This meant that although the *Jagdgeschwader* (single-seat fighter units) could escort the bomber formations as far as London they had precious little fuel for combat. The Luftwaffe lost fewer fighter pilots during the battle than the RAF, but could not sustain the losses endured by its bomber units. It had tried to fight a strategic war and had failed, because it had never envisaged fighting such a war. A narrow British victory was thus won. Aside from the renewed vigour it gave to the British people, America was also persuaded that with a base in occupied Europe, the war against Germany could be continued.

Fighter Command Goes on the Attack

In the early spring of 1941 Fighter Command was ready to go on the attack. Rested, and re-equipped, its pilots began a series of raids on Luftwaffe airfields in northern France — the so-called 'Rhubarb' sweeps. Deployment of many of its units to the East in preparation for Barbarossa meant that Luftwaffe strength was depleted, but the introduction of the formidable Focke-Wulf 190 gave its fighter pilots a significant performance advantage over the Spitfire that was not redressed until the Mk IX model became available. The Rhubarb sweeps proved costly and indecisive, using aircraft that could have been better employed in Africa and the Far East. In the fighter battles over northern France between 1941 and 1943 the Luftwaffe Jagdgeschwader emerged victorious, until the effects of numerical inferiority and the pressure of fighting in Africa and the Soviet Union began to take their toll.

AIR WAR EAST

On July 31 1940, while still embroiled in the Battle of Britain, Hitler told his OKW chief of operations Alfred Jodl to begin planning the invasion of the Soviet Union. In time, Hitler's arrogant boast that he would crush the Red Army proved to be his costliest blunder. The operation was codenamed Barbarossa after an old Germanic hero, and it was planned to take no more than four months. Some British intelligence sources thought the Russians would capitulate in 10 days.

Plans were laid for an attack along a 2,000 mile (3,200 km) front by Army Groups North, Centre, and South with each group supported by air and by an armoured group. The Luftwaffe was tasked with its most testing commitment to date — the destruction of Stalin's mighty Red Air Force. Units were pulled wholesale from across occupied Europe until, by June 21, the Luftwaffe could field 2,770 combat aircraft in the east. Luftflotte I under Keller was to support Army Group North. Kesselring's Luftflotte II, barely rested from the Battle of Britain, was

attached to Army Group Centre, and Luftflotte IV under Löhr was given Army Group South. In hindsight it is clear that the Wehrmacht was woefully ill-equipped for the task. Any attack on Russia would be heavily reliant on motor vehicles, yet the Germans had too few, and of insufficient quality. The number of tank divisions was doubled, but only by stripping those that already existed of half their Panzers and pressing captured ones into service. The limited Russian rail network, running on a different gauge to the German, was a further hindrance. Also of considerable significance is

Below: Ilyushin Il-2 Shturmovik of the post-war Czech air force. This incredibly tough machine helped to drive back Hitler's Panzers on the Eastern Front.

Bottom: The excellent Lavochkin La-5 and La-7 fighters helped to redress the once huge imbalance in equipment between the Red Air Force and Luftwaffe.

the fact that the German aviation industry was still geared to peacetime rates, so for the Luftwaffe the impending campaign had to be of short duration. Against the Luftwaffe the Red Air Force could field some 7,700 aircraft stationed in western Russia, but this total does not include the naval units or the 3,500–4,000 aircraft held in the east. The quality of the aircraft varied enormously, but the Luftwaffe correctly adjudged the 2–300 MiG fighters as the greatest threat to its air superiority.

Zero hour was set for dawn on June 22, to gain maximum advantage from the favourable weather and the long daylight hours. At dawn on that day, from the Arctic Circle to the Black Sea, an army of 3.2 million men advanced into the Soviet Union. The Luftwaffe launched attacks on 66 airfields of the V-VS, catching the majority of its units on the ground. Over 1,000 Soviet aircraft were destroyed on the first day alone. The Panzer units raced forward as they had in France; Army Group Centre, including Guderian and Hoth's Panzer Groups drove towards Moscow capturing 300,000 of the Red Army and the city of Minsk. In the weeks after the German attack, Soviet industry began to evacuate wholesale from the west to areas behind the Ural Mountains. Between July and November 1941, over 1,500 industrial plants (1,360 of them armament manufacturers) moved east. The Red Air Force tried to stem the tide by mounting bombing raids in

regiment strength, but the closely formatted aircraft were cut from the sky in droves. Some Soviet fighter pilots resorted to using their Polikarpov I-16 in ramming attacks on the German bombers. On July 22, 200 Luftwaffe Ju 88s began the two-month bombing campaign against Moscow. Throughout the heat of the Russian summer the German armies fought dust, supply train problems and the never-ending waves of Red Army troops. The capture of Kiev on September 26 was only achieved after bitter fighting, which cost the Red Army nearly 500,000 men killed or captured. By the end of the month the Luftwaffe was able to announce that it had destroyed 4,500 Soviet aircraft.

Operation Taifun

On October 2, as the Russian winter began to close in, the race began to capture Moscow. Luftflotte II had been reinforced and had concentrated some 1,320 aircraft in the centre of the line between Smolensk and Konotop. The devastated V-VS could field little to oppose them. The campaign, codenamed *Taifun* (Typhoon) by the OKW, began successfully. Rostov fell in mid-November, as well as the strategically vital Perekop isthmus commanding the Crimea. But as the winter rains set in, mud turned the lightning war in Eastern Europe into a vast immovable traffic jam of German armour. Temperatures plummeted during November catching the Germans wholly unprepared, and on 27 November

the advance on Moscow ground to a halt only 19 miles north of the city. In the desperate defence of Moscow V-VS pilots flew some 51,300 sorties in all weathers, while the Germans lost an estimated 1,400 aircraft.

By the beginning of December, Army Group North, and Army Group Centre had been driving toward Moscow for five months and needed time for vital repairs. Hitler ordered a suspension in operations on December 8. Kesselring's Luftflotte II began to withdraw to the Mediterranean, weakening Luftwaffe strength in the east to around 1,700 at the end of December. The temporary lull in fighting allowed the Red Army to regroup its shattered forces on the western front. During that week the Soviets launched a massive counter-attack at the weak points in the German lines, and by January 1 the immediate threat to Moscow had been lifted. To support the ground forces the V-VS could offer only a token force of 350 aircraft. The bitter winter weather hampered Luftwaffe operations for weeks, and the inevitable problems with supply proved an added hindrance to the German forces. The counter-attack continued throughout January and February of 1942. Soviet attacks were made along the whole of the front from Crimea to Finland, pushing the Germans back an average distance of 150–200 miles. The situation degenerated into a stalemate during the spring thaws, as men and machines bogged down in seas of mud. Aircraft serviceability suffered in the bitter and primitive conditions.

During the period of Russian stalemate further elements of the Luftwaffe were redeployed to the Mediterranean and northern Europe. As losses mounted, the inability of the German aircraft industry and the pilot training system to keep pace became apparent. During these winter months the illustrious Il'yushin Il-2 Shturmovik began to make its mark. This aircraft more than any other turned the tide of the air war in the east. Other important types introduced at this stage were the Yakovlev Yak-1 and Lavochkin LaGG-3, both of them fighter aircraft that came near to upsetting the superiority of the Messerschmitt Bf 109F-2. On May 8, the Germans renewed their onslaught to eliminate the gains achieved by the Red Army during its winter offensive. Substantial advances were made in the Crimea, and by July 2, Sevastapol was captured. In support of the campaign to capture the city the VIII Fliegerkorps flew some 23,750 sorties, for the loss of 18 aircraft.

Fall Blau — The Push Towards Stalingrad

The brief respite that followed the spring offensive was shattered by the opening of the Fall Blau offensive on June 28. The attacks were aimed at Rostov and the symbolic target of Stalingrad, the gateway to the Caucasus and the Russian oilfields. Luftflotte IV, now under Generaloberst Wolfram, Freiherr von Richtofen and with a strength of 1,500 aircraft, was allocated to support the operation. On July 13, Hitler decided to split the attack and attack these targets in unison. By dividing Army Groups A and B he risked fatally weakening their attacking strength, and creating a vulnerable gap between the two forces. The drive on the Caucuses and Stalingrad began on July 13. Army Group A quickly captured Rostov, but the advance to Stalingrad was hampered by the diversion of forces to the south. Angered by the slow advance to Stalingrad, Hitler then withdrew vital forces form Army Group A to support the attack on the city. The Caucasus campaign, hampered by inadequate resources, then ground to

a virtual halt as all focus switched to the attempt to take Stalingrad. The autumn of 1942 the German Army fought in Stalingrad what its soldiers referred to as the *Rattenkrieg* or 'war of the rats'. The Luftwaffe, enjoying conditions of local air supremacy, bombed the city mercilessly but Chuikov and Shumilov, the two Soviet commanders charged with the defence, seemed to have almost limitless resources to throw at the German attackers. Von Paulus, commander of the German Sixth Army in Stalingrad received meagre reinforcements in the form of five assault pioneer battalions and an under strength Panzer division in the second week of October. They could make little impact on the battle. On November 19, a surprise Soviet counteroffensive drove south and cut off the Sixth Army. The encircled army were now trapped within the city they had set out to capture. Von Manstein was ordered by Hitler to reopen a channel to Stalingrad with Army Group Don but they failed to salvage the situation.

Air Supply at Stalingrad

By December 1942, supply had become the crucial factor in the battle for Stalingrad. Hitler's refusal to allow von Paulus to surrender his forces trapped inside the city meant that they were forced to rely on Göring's promise to supply 700 tons per day by air. This was rapidly reduced to 300 tons, but even this could not be maintained in the brutal Soviet winter. While they held

the vital Gumrak airfield to the west of the city, the German forces had been able to rely on a constant stream of Junkers 52 transport aircraft to ferry in food, fuel and ammunition. Even so the losses to the Transportgruppen of VIII Fliegerkorps were catastrophic. By mid-December the stream had been reduced to a trickle — about 50 tons a day. Hitler continued to refuse von Paulus permission to attempt a breakout, but when the snowbound Gumrak airfield fell to Soviet forces on January 22, 1943, the thin trickle of supplies that had been reaching the Sixth Army stopped completely. On February 2, von Paulus surrendered 91,000 men, the remnants of his once proud army, to the Red Army.

Retreat

The rapid Soviet counterattack at Stalingrad dealt a stunning blow to the Germans. The Luftwaffe alone lost nearly 3,000 aircraft in the battle for the city. This was partly due to the fact that the V-VS was rapidly narrowing its qualitative gap with the Luftwaffe. Under the leadership of Colonel General A. A. Novikov it had slowly recovered from almost complete destruction in the summer

Below: A Hawker Hurricane of the Red Air Force, which appears to have nosed over in the snow. Britain supplied a large number of Hurricanes to the Soviets.

Right: Bell P-39 Airacobra, pictured here carrying a long-range centreline fuel tank.

of 1941, and Soviet industry, by the end of 1942, was producing in excess of 2,000 aircraft per month. The Luftwaffe found itself with the problem of having to knock out large numbers of Soviet tanks, and thus developed variants of the Ju 87, Ju 88 and Henschel Hs 129 with large calibre anti-tank guns. These were organised into Panzerjäger units in early 1943, and specialist training was provided for pilots.

By the start of February 1943, with the Sixth Army hopelessly trapped in Stalingrad, the Soviet armies were threatening General Manstein's northern flank around Kharkov, a vital rail supply depot. Hitler ordered the city to be held and was furious when the SS Panzer division deployed to hold Kharkov abandoned it on February 15. Hitler immediately ordered von Manstein to recapture the city. Given the fact that his Army Group A had been forced to retreat hastily across the Black Sea to the Crimean Peninsula in the face of the Soviet offensive, it is remarkable that von Manstein could even contemplate fighting back. However, he had succeeded in luring the Soviet forces some 425 miles (700 km) west of Stalingrad in a short space of time, to Dnepropetrousk on the River Dneiper. The sheer scale of the Soviet forces, the speed of the advance, and poor organisation had thrown their logistics into chaos. Soviet tactics played little attention to the needs of supply, and atrocious winter weather and the German practice of converting wide gauge Russian railway lines to a narrower European gauge proved a considerable hindrance.

Right: Although US pilots were rather indifferent to the Airacobra, the Red Air Force welcomed it with open arms.

To take advantage of this situation Manstein launched a counterattack, supported by I and IV Fliegerkorps and Fliegerkorps Dontez. These flew an average of 1,000 sorties a day in support of the assaults. Von Manstein's forces had nearly a seven to one superiority in tanks and the Luftwaffe outnumbered the Red Air Force in the region by three to one. On February 20, the Fourth Panzer Army attacked South West Front. The Soviets, low on fuel and supplies, were rapidly driven back. Vatutin tried to rally his troops to halt the retreat and continue the drive southwest, but the Panzers kept rolling. By the end of the month, the Soviets had retreated back behind the River Denets, having lost over 600 tanks. Germans subsequently turned to the Voronezh Front, the line south of Kharkov, which had already been weakened by the need to redirect troops to the South West Front. Kharkov fell on March 15, the last time the city would be in German hands. The victory temporarily took the spotlight off the desperate state that Army Group South was in. Its 16 divisions could

muster only 140 serviceable tanks between them. And a huge salient still existed in the German line from Belgograd to Orel. From a Soviet perspective, Kharkov represented a major disaster. They lost over 72,000 troops and another 600 tanks. Yet they had no such problems with reinforcements, and could afford to lose legions of tanks and men seemingly with impunity. At Kursk this strength would prove decisive.

Zitadelle

In order to straighten the line a limited German offensive was planned to take Kursk by a pincer movement. During May and June the forces assembled: over 900,000 troops, with over 10,000 artillery pieces, and some 2,730 tanks. The Luftwaffe, meanwhile, prepared itself with what was destined to be the last great Blitzkrieg of the war. For Zitadelle von Manstein's Army Group South was given Luftflotte IV and VIII Fliegerkorps. In the northern sector of the Kursk bulge Army Group Centre was supported by Luftflotte VI and I Fliegerdivision. First-line strength was around 2,100

Above: MiG-3, clearly in the process of restoration!

aircraft from a total of 2,500 German aircraft in the east. However, by June 1943 a problem of fuel shortage was becoming apparent, largely due to partisan activity. The start of the offensive allowed the Soviet forces under Zhukov considerable time to prepare defensive works around the salient. Some 5,440 aircraft were available to the V-VS. Fighters included the latest Yakovlev Yak-9s and Lavochkin La-5FNs, and Bell P-39Q Airacobras supplied under the Lend-Lease scheme. Principal ground attack aircraft remained the Il'yushin Il-2 Shturmovik armed with a formidable barrage of weaponry that included 20 mm and 23 mm guns, rockets, 37 mm anti-tank cannon and hollow charge anti-tank bombs. The German attack was planned for July 5, with General Walther Model's Ninth Army driving south from Orel in a two-pronged attack. On the southern flank of the salient von Manstein's Fourth Panzer Army and Army Detachment Kempf would drive north-east to cut off the Soviet retreat. During the build up the Luftwaffe launched long-range penetrations against strategic targets (one of its rare attempts to disrupt Soviet industry), while the V-VS attacked Luftwaffe airfields. Many fierce air combats were fought, and on June 2, a bitter air battle was fought that cost the Luftwaffe 58 aircraft.

Prewarned by a Hungarian deserter of the exact time of the German attack, the V-VS launched a massed attack on airfields in VIII Fliegerkorps' sector. Every German fighter was scrambled and there ensued one of the biggest air battles of the war as some 400 aircraft fought above Kharkov. The German advance was chaotic and rapidly got bogged down in densely sown minefields. The attack stopped dead in its tracks only 12 miles (19 km) from its starting point. Many of the new Panther tanks broke down, and by July 12, Model had lost half of his tanks. The losses to the V-VS were substantial, amounting to 176 aircraft on the first day. The Luftwaffe fared worse, losing some 260.

In the south the numerical superiority of the Panzers proved an advantage, but heavily wooded countryside gave the Soviet anti-tank gunners superb cover and Kempf was unable to break through until July 8. Air battles were most intense in the period July 5-8, when sources state that a total of 566 V-VS aircraft were destroyed against 854 German. By July 10, a salient had been forced in the Soviet line almost to Prokhorouka. On July 11, German units crossed the River Psel, the last natural line of defence in front of Kursk. At this point the Soviet commander Nikolai Vatunin launched a counterattack with 850 T-34 and KV-1s. The 700 German tanks that opposed them were compressed into an area barely three miles square, and any advantage the Germans had previously possessed

with the range of their guns was negated. The Soviet tank crews fought with a tenacity and heroism that after eight hours of battle had seriously weakened the Panzer units.

On July 15, the forces under Marshal Rossokovsky drove north from their positions on the northern flank of the Kursk salient toward Orel. The other half of the Red Army's counter offensive was delayed by the need to reinforce and regroup, but on August 3 an attack split a 40 mile (64 km) gap in the German defensive line. On August 20, Hitler made a rare decision to retreat from Kharkov. By August 23, the hammer and sickle was flying over Kharkov again. The Panzers had been defeated at last. The Kursk campaign coincided with the Allied decimation of German air power over Sicily and southern Italy, and an escalation in attacks on the Reich by Bomber Command and the US 8th Air Force. Between June 1 and August 31, the Luftwaffe lost 2,183 aircraft on the Eastern Front and from this time the theatre no longer enjoyed top priority. The ground attack units were reorganised and re-equipped, but gradually fighter units were withdrawn for the defence of the Reich.

The abandonment of the German offensive was a decisive turning point in the war and marked the beginning of the Russian advance. Even while the tanks battled around Prokhorouka they launched a massive offensive against the Germans. Its basic simplicity was a characteristic of Russian strategy.

An attack at one point in the line would draw reserves and thus weaken another area of the front. It was a strategy that relied on numerical superiority — one factor that the Soviets certainly enjoyed. At the start of the summer offensive in the south the V-VS had some 8,000 aircraft against the 1,750 of the Luftwaffe. By mid-October, the Germans had been pushed back across a 440 mile (708 km) front. On November 3, Soviet forces assaulted Kiev, the hub city of the Ukraine, but encountered stiff resistance from the Fourth Panzer Army, who held it until the 12th. A remarkable German counterattack on November 15 retook Zhiomur and helped to stabilise the situation in the Ukraine. There followed a lull as freezing weather once more took its vice-like grip on the exhausted men who had already endured two such winters.

The air war in Russia had developed into a battle between fighters, close-support aircraft and medium bombers, whilst tactical reconnaissance played a vital role. Strategic bombing played little part in the war on the Eastern Front.

In January 1944 revitalised Soviet armies launched new offensives along all their fronts from Leningrad to the Crimea. In the north an assault by two army groups on the German 18th Army besieging Leningrad retook the city on January 26. The winter offensive in the Ukraine launched the 1st and 2nd Ukrainian Fronts on a south-western advance, capturing Zhitomir, Karosten, and Korovograd and encircling 100,000 German troops near Korsun. This south-western Ukrainian town formed the centre of the infamous Cherkassy Pocket. The six German divisions in the pocket fought desperately to break out while they were resupplied from the air by hastily adapted Heinkel He 111H-6 bombers and Ju 523/ms of Luftwaffe Transportgruppen that dropped a daily total of 100-185 tonnes. Von Manstein sacrificed an estimated 20,000 men and all his tank reserves in his failed attempt to relieve them.

With Korsun taken, the Soviets crossed the Bug and Dniester rivers, before advancing steadily toward Rumania. On April 8, a massive Soviet offensive was launched against the German armies trapped in the Crimea. Sevastapol, a vital bridging point between the Soviet forces and the Balkans, was retaken on May 12. By this time there were insufficient numbers of German fighters on the Eastern Front for the huge task of covering the various withdrawals. But despite its massive numerical disadvantage the Luftwaffe fighter units continued to fight hard. Hartmann, the highest scoring ace of all time with 352, scored his 100th kill on September 14, 1943. Many others — Rall, Barkhorn and Nowotny among them — reached and passed the 200 mark.

Soviet successes on the ground enraged Hitler, who lost no time in replacing the Southern Army Group commanders General von Kleist and Field Marshal von Manstein with Walter Model and General Schörner. Despite the opening of the second front after the Allied invasion of Normandy, Hitler refused to contemplate a strategy that talked of retreat. He could still command forces in the east totalling some three million men, 3,000 tanks (of varying degrees of battle worthiness) and 3,000 aircraft, and ordered these to be spread along a 1,400 mile (2,250 km) defensive front, reinforced by fortresses and with command of high ground. It looked to all around him like a strategy of desperation. The Russians could field 6.5 million men, supported by 8,000 tanks, and 13,000 aircraft.

Operation Bagration

Thus, when the Soviet command launched the summer offensive to clear Belorussia and destroy Army Group Centre on June 22, 1944, there could be little doubt about its outcome. In the north, the 21st and 23rd Armies on the Karelian and Leningrad fronts supported by 757 aircraft of the 13th VA and P-VO counterattacked Army Group North, forcing it back toward the Baltic states. The Finnish air force was active on this front, flying Bf 109G-2s and G-6s, but could do little to stem the advance. The major thrust of the offensive came in the centre. Around 6,000 V-VS aircraft were concentrated for the support of the ground forces. The quantitative effort not withstanding, the V-VS received three truly outstanding types in the summer, these being the Tupolev Tu-2, the Yakovlev Yak-3 and the Lavochkin La-7. The Red Army, supported by considerable numbers of Il-2 Shturmovik attack aircraft, punched north and south of Vitebsk to Minsk. Minsk was retaken on July 4, together with some 50,000 German troops. The Soviet advance continued apace toward the Polish border. In the north, the drive through the Baltic states took Vilnius (Lithuania) and Daugaupils on July 13. The bulk of Army Group North became trapped in a huge 'Baltic pocket' and despite a temporary check to Marshal Rokossovsky's advance east of Warsaw, the 1st Ukrainian Front forces under Konev captured Luov and reached the upper Vistala and Baranov Rivers by August 7.

The focus of the offensive now switched to the Balkan states, Hungary, Rumania, Yugoslavia, and Bulgaria. Hitler had massed the bulk of the Luftwaffe units here, fearful of the threat to the vital oilfields and refineries in the giant Ploesti complex. But the massive assault in the centre had denuded the strength of the Luftwaffe to a point where it could field only 200 aircraft in this sector. Rumania was invaded on August 20, and capitulated soon after, along with the bulk of the German 6th and 8th Armies, and the Ploesti fields were lost. On September 5, the Soviet Union declared war on Bulgaria, which had joined the Axis in March 1941 but had not joined Barbarossa. A rapid about face, on September 7, had Bulgaria declaring war on Germany. During the autumn and winter of 1944 the remaining fighter and ground-support forces of Luftflotte IV fought against overwhelming Soviet air superiority in the Hungarian sector. By the end of October, Soviet forces had entered eastern Prussia. With winter once more placing its vice-like grip on the landscape, operations were wound down. The final Soviet offensive was launched on January 12, across a 750 mile (1,206 km) stretch of the front from the Baltic to the Carpathians. The V-VS by now enjoyed a 15-1 numerical superiority over the Luftwaffe on the Eastern Front. Overwhelmed by the sheer weight of men and armour, the German defence crumbled. Zhukov, hero of Kursk, reached the Oder River with his 1st Byelorussian Front on January 31. Taking advantage of a shrinking perimeter the Luftwaffe fought back savagely. During the latter part of January 1945 some 650 fighters were transferred from the Western Front to the Oder-Silesia theatre, but these had little impact against now-battle hardened Soviet pilots. A last-ditch German offensive was launched against Marshal Tolbukhin's forces in the south, but this was rapidly overwhelmed. Crossing the Austrian

frontier on March 20, Marshal Malinovsky's 2nd Ukrainian Front drove into Vienna on April 13. The scene was now set for the final assault on Berlin. Three Soviet fronts under Zhukov, Konev, and Rokossovsky were more than a match for the old men, boys, and shattered German units left to defend Berlin. Many simply fled west to prevent capture by the Red Army. A twin-pronged attack by the Soviets had encircled the city by April 25. Just over one week later the surrender was announced, bringing to an end the fighting in what was the costliest and bloodiest theatre of war.

WAR IN THE PACIFIC

In August 1941 the US placed a total embargo on shipments of raw materials to Japan, an act that was perceived as outright hostility. Continuing Japanese aggression in China, a country many Americans held dear, and the close relationship between Japan and Nazi Germany, had increased the tension between the US and Japan from 1939, but the decision to curtail supplies of oil and other commodities vital to Japanese industry pushed the two countries into war. On the first day of December 1941, the decision was made to attack the US Pacific Fleet anchorage at Pearl Harbour, Hawaii,

a move that most Japanese commanders thought would bring the Americans to the negotiating table and force them to concede the US possessions at Wake Island, Hawaii, and the Philippines. The air attack on Pearl Harbour began at 7.55 am on Sunday December 7, a date chosen because it was estimated that a large part of the US Fleet would be in port. The first wave of aircraft consisted of 183 dive and torpedo bombers, with A6M2 Zeros providing top cover. These were flown off six carriers that had sailed undetected to within 250 miles (402 km) of the Hawaiian Islands. Although the approaching formation of Japanese aircraft was detected by radar operators at Opana, it was confused with a flight of USAAC B-17 bombers that was expected that same morning.

While part of the attacking force attacked and destroyed USAAC fighter aircraft parked wingtip-to-wingtip at Hickham Field airbase, torpedo bombers made low-level runs across the water toward the battleships anchored off Ford Island. By 8.25 am six of the battleships were sunk, sinking, or very badly

Below: A Harvard heavily modified to play the role of a Japanese 'Val' (Aichi D3A) for filming.

damaged. A second wave of 167 aircraft arrived at 8.40 am and continued to pound predesignated targets, specifically the airfields. By denying the Americans aircraft, the Japanese were preventing any possible counterattack against their carriers. In all they destroyed 188 aircraft and damaged 159 other, many of them Curtiss P-40 Tomahawks. Their own losses were minimal. However, crucially, the US Navy carriers *Enterprise* and *Saratoga* were at sea that day.

Two hours after the Pearl Harbour attack, Japanese aircraft were bombarding the Iba and Clark Field air bases in the Philippines. Douglas MacArthur, the chief military adviser on the islands, had full knowledge of the attack on the fleet, but he completely failed to make preparations. His aircraft were caught in the open, on the ground, and parked neatly in lines. Not surprisingly, they were destroyed in large numbers. The bombing attacks were followed by an amphibious assault on the islands. After a heroic defence Bataan eventually fell in April 1942.

Malaya

Singapore was selected as the main British base in the Far East in the early 1920s, and its defence depended upon coastal batteries and torpedo bombers. The aircraft chosen for this were Vickers Vildebeest biplanes, which were operated alongside No 205 Squadron with Shorts Singapore flying boats. In July of 1940 it was realised that the defence of the base would depend entirely on air power and that to defend all British interests in the area would require a force of some 566 aircraft. The modest force at Singapore was strengthened with

Left: Tora! Tora! Tora! The Harvard forms the basis for a Nalajima B6N Tenzan lookalike. How well done can be judged against the real thing (Inset Above), about to take off to bomb Pearl Harbor.

Blenheims, Hudsons and Catalinas but when the Japanese attack was launched RAF strength across the whole region amounted to only 326 aircraft. In Malaya these aircraft were operated from 22 airstrips, but all of these were poorly protected and only a handful were surfaced. The needs of communication and early warning were also poorly served. Only two hours after the attack on Pearl Harbour, forces commanded by Lieutenant-General Tomoyuki Yamashita battled their way ashore at Kota Bahru and Patani, on the northern astern coast of Malaya. The invasion fleet was spotted 300 miles (500 km) offshore by a Hudson of No 1 Squadron Royal Australian Air Force (RAAF) and was attacked with vigour during the landings. The only fighters available to the defenders were four squadrons of Brewster Buffaloes, an aircraft that had been rejected by the RAF as inadequate for the European theatre. Against the agile Mitsubishi A6M Zero it proved equally unsuited. More aircraft were lost in daylight raids on Japanese airfields.

Yamashita's forces proceeded to drive down the coastal plain on the west of the island at a stunning pace, with the Commonwealth forces in headlong flight before them. On December 10, the British suffered a devastating loss when the battleships *Prince of Wales* and *Repulse* were sunk by Japanese aircraft while sailing north to pressurise the invasion fleet. Confusion between Air Vice-Marshal Pulford, Commander-in-Chief of the RAF in the Far East, and the fleet commander meant that the fleet had not been provided with air cover and the British were dealt an appallingly costly lesson about the importance of air cover for modern naval forces.

By January 10, Kuala Lumpur was in Japanese hands and 17 days later Lieutenant-General Percival, commander of the Commonwealth forces, ordered a withdrawal to Singapore. Reinforcements for the final defence of Singapore including some Hurricane fighters began to arrive on Christmas Day and these were able to put up a more effective defence when unescorted Japanese aircraft bombed Singapore Island on January 20. On the following day the raiders returned with an escort of Zero fighters and five Hurricanes were lost. The light, manoeuvrable and comparatively heavily-armed A6M Zero-sen fighter was set to dominate air combat in the Pacific theatre until 1943. By the end of January virtually all the RAF and

Above: Mitsubishi G3Ms — codenamed 'Nell', the G3M was the backbone of the JNAF's medium bomber fleet in the early war years.

RAAF aircraft had been evacuated, with the intention of continuing the fight from Sumatra, across the Strait of Malacca. The assault on Singapore began on February 7, and on February 15, Percival surrendered the garrison of 80,000 men to Yamashita. Churchill called it 'one of the greatest disasters in British military history', and it had taken a mere 70 days.

The early months of the war brought Japan some stunning successes. By June 1942, the Philippines, Burma, Malaya, and Dutch East Indies were occupied by Japanese forces. In the first six months of its Pacific campaign, Japan had established a defensive island barrier around the Pacific Basin on which to base its aircraft and captured crucial raw materials. The initial Japanese campaign in the Pacific is regarded as a model in the use of offensive air power. But the supply lines to the homeland were long and highly vulnerable, and in the United States the Japanese had taken on a powerful enemy.

Above: Curtiss C-46 Commando, widely used to fly supplies over the 'Hump' into China.

Left: Another Curtiss product, the P-40 Warhawk, which did valuable service in the Burma campaign.

The Burma Campaign

Burma formed part of Britain's extensive colonial territories in South East Asia, and was thus a likely target for the expansionist policy of the Japanese. In December 1941, 35,000 men of the Japanese 15th Army crossed the border from China. Their primary objective was to halt the flow of arms along the Burma Road to the Kuomintang (the Chinese resistance forces). They were opposed by a slender, inadequately trained, and poorly equipped British force, supported by perhaps 30 aircraft of US Major General Chay Chennault's 'Flying Tigers' volunteer force and an RAF squadron with 16 Buffaloes on its strength. Air attacks on the capital, Rangoon, began on December 23. A squadron of Blenheims arrived on January 7, followed by 30 Hurricanes. These

aircraft acquitted themselves well, but in the following months the Japanese advanced steadily north, taking Pegu on March 4, before launching an assault on Rangoon. Despite the presence of the very capable General Harold Alexander, Rangoon was abandoned on March 6. The remaining RAF and American units pulled back to Lashio, a vital staging point on the Burma Road and were subjected to heavy bombardment at the base. By April 30, Lashio had been captured, although some RAF personnel were evacuated to India by Dakotas. Pursued by the highly-mobile Japanese forces, the British made a long retreat back to India, and at the end of May, Burma was in Japanese hands. The monsoon season then enveloped the region, affording the British a vital respite to build up their forces for the expected attack on India.

At this stage of the war Burma was a low priority in comparison to the European and Mediterranean theatres. Under Air Marshal Sir Richard Pierse, who arrived in March 1942 to take over command of the RAF, the service strength in India was rapidly built up in the summer to 26 squadrons. These aircraft were used in support of a limited counteroffensive on the Arakan coast in December, which had the primary aim of capturing the port of Aryab. The operation was an unmitigated disaster, and for the next two years the Allies satisfied themselves with the small scale successes of Orde Wingate's Chindit guerrillas. An interesting aspect of this opera-

tion, which lasted between February and May 1943, was that Wingate's forces depended entirely on air resupply by two squadrons of RAF Dakotas.

Part of the reason for the reluctance to launch a counteroffensive during this two-year period was that an American air link across the Himalayas had ensured vital supplies were still reaching the Chinese and the Allies were reluctant to commit forces to the area. South East Asia Command was formed under Lord Louis Mountbatten in November 1943, and by early the following year this had expanded to include 48 RAF and 17 USAAF squadrons, based at a huge complex of 275 new airfields that were protected by a vital radar network.

These aircraft proved a vital asset when on February 3, 1944, the Japanese 28th Army attacked the southern sector of the Indian frontier, with the object of capturing Kohima and Imphal. RAF Dakotas brought vital supplies to the defenders of these towns while Allied aircraft strafed the Japanese attackers. The strengthened 15th Corps under the British General

Slim met the attack and forced the 28th Army to begin withdrawing three weeks later. Further attacks in the central and northern areas of the frontier proved unsuccessful and costly for the Japanese, and when they began a general withdrawal on July 4, only 30,000 of the original attackers remained. Japanese defence hampered the Allied attempts to recapture Burma but with a force that amounted to some 90 RAF and USAAF squadrons, against which the Japanese could pit only 125 aircraft. Slim possessed an overwhelming advantage. Allied troops continued their advance south under overwhelming air support and by March of 1945 the British 14th Army had crossed the Chindwin river and was on the outskirts of Mandalay. Remorseless attacks on enemy supply dumps preceded the advance and when the capture of Wanting by Chinese forces in January 1945 permitted the reopening of the Burma Road, victory was more or less assured. On May 3, a combined airborne and amphibious offensive was launched to retake Rangoon. Effective Japanese resistance ended within a week.

The Doolittle Raid

One of the most important air actions in the Pacific theatre was the raid on Tokyo, Yokohama, Yokusuka, Kobe and Nagoya undertaken on April 1, 1942, by 16 twin-engine North American B-25 Mitchell bombers flown off the USS *Hornet*. Led by Lieutenant-General James Doolittle, the raid had little military impact, but the strategic implications were immense. Large proportions of Japanese aircraft were thereafter committed to national defence, while the attack greatly boosted American morale.

Above Left: C-46 Commando runs up its 2,000hp Double Wasp radials prior to take-off.

Left: The Douglas C-47 Skytrain, reckoned by General Eisenhower to be one of the four key weapons of the war (alongside the Jeep, the bazooka, and the atom bomb).

Battle of the Coral Sea

The first major carrier battle in the Pacific theatre was fought between May 7-8, 1942, in the Coral Sea. This was part of a wider Japanese offensive, code-named Operation Mo, that aimed to extend the limits of the defensive perimeter to Midway and the Aleutian Islands, and to provide them with bases for air attacks off the northern coast of Australia. In this action the Japanese fielded five aircraft carriers, supported by 120 land-based aircraft. American signals intelligence prewarned the US Navy of the Japanese actions, and allowed them to take defensive actions. May 7, saw the start of the battle, with both forces launching air attacks. Land-based B-17 bombers and Douglas SBD Dauntless dive-bombers attacked the Japanese carriers; *Shoho* was sent to the bottom and *Shokaku* was seriously disabled, while the *Lexington* was sunk by torpedoes launched by B5N2s and D3A1s. Although the US Navy lost the *Lexington* (carrier), the loss of two Japanese carriers prevented them from playing a role

Below: The Curtiss SB2C Helldiver carrier-borne dive-bomber.

in the later Battle of Midway. Japanese commander, Admiral Inoue was forced to abandon the invasion of Port Moresby on southern Papua, one of the objectives of Operation Mo. However, despite this setback Admiral Yamamoto, Commander-in-Chief of the Japanese Combined Fleet, thought he could destroy the US Pacific Fleet under Admiral Chester W. Nimitz in one decisive action on the high seas.

Battle of Midway

He chose Midway, some 1,000 miles west of Pearl Harbour, and assembled a formidable force that included four carriers and three battleships, one of them the giant *Yamato*. Embarked on these ships were some 227 battle-ready aircraft, piloted by veteran crews. Unbeknown to the Japanese, US Intelligence experts had again intercepted signals relating to the planned attack. When the Japanese fleet arrived off the north-west of Midway during the night of June 3, the Americans were fully prepared, with two task forces under Admirals Fletcher and Spruance. They had some 232 aircraft on call, including Douglas TBD-1s, SBD-3s and Grumman F4F-4 Wildcats, while shore-based units contributed another 119 assorted types. In the actions that followed, aircraft from

the *Yorktown* and *Enterprise* sank the *Akagi*, *Soryu*, *Hiryo* and *Kega*, for the loss of the *Yorktown*. As well as the catastrophic loss of four carriers, the Japanese Navy had also sacrificed 332 of her aircraft and 216 of her most experienced air crews. The Americans were easily able to replace their losses of aircraft (150) and crew and had learned valuable lessons in naval air warfare. American aircraft production by this stage of the war was five times greater than the Japanese could manage. At Midway air power had again proved the decisive factor. Flushed with the victory at Midway, MacArthur and Nimitz began planning for the first American offensive of the war. Code-named Operation Watchtower, it aimed to secure communications with Australia, take Guadalcanal in the Solomon Islands and New Guinea, and reduce the important Japanese base at Rabaul. From early 1942, Rabaul Japanese G4M1 bombers flew raids against Port Moresby in Papua and from the Celebes to attack Darwin in northern Australia and, in September 1943, Japanese strength in the area reached some 300 aircraft. Until the end of 1943, fighting in the Pacific concentrated in this area at the south-eastern edge of the Japanese defensive perimeter.

Guadalcanal

In May 1942, the Japanese had a limited military presence in Guadalcanal — less than 3,000 men. Importantly though, they were constructing an airbase, which could dominate the area if it became operational. On August 7, a poorly trained and under-equipped Marine Division landed unopposed at Tenaru and captured the airbase the following afternoon, under the cover of the air groups from USS *Saratoga*, *Wasp* and *Enterprise*. Under considerable duress, the Marines on Guadalcanal established a limited defensive perimeter with the few supplies of mines and wire they had. There were few tools for digging, but plant equipment left behind by the fleeing Japanese enabled Marine engineers to finish the airfield, renamed Henderson Field, and by August 20, the first American aircraft were landing. This was the first US counter-offensive of the war.

In the autumn of 1942, Japanese supply convoys, nicknamed the 'Tokyo Express', continued to bring thousands of reinforcements to points east and west of Henderson Field. They were thrown into a series of unceasing attacks on the Marine defenders, who demonstrated extreme courage and resilience in holding them off. After the with-drawal of the carrier forces, the defence of the island fell to the F4F-4s of VMF-223. In the seas surrounding the islands, the United States and Japanese navies fought seven major naval battles to secure control of the approaches. Slowly the American air presence at Henderson Field grew, and by the end of October included Lockheed P-38F Lightnings and Curtiss P-40 Tomahawks. Mounting losses in the air, on land and at sea forced a Japanese withdrawal on December 31, 1942, and by February 9, 1943 the island was secured. For the Americans and their allies the successful seizure and defence of Guadalcanal brought immense advantages. Australia and New Zealand were safe, and Allied Forces now stood on the outer cordon of the Japanese Empire. On New Guinea, Australian troops made contact with Japanese troops advancing across the Owen Stanley Mountains toward Port Moresby on August 16, 1942. A month of savage combat along the narrow Kokoda Trail, the only viable route through the mountains, forced the Japanese into defensive positions at Buna, Gona and Sananda. They were captured in January 1943, but only after some of the most bitter and costly fighting of the war. Fierce fighting for control of

Above: Grumman TBF Avenger torpedo bomber.

the Huan Peninsula, the south-eastern tip of Papua, continued through the spring.

While it still held the balance of carrier air power, the battle for Guadalcanal cost the Japanese 350 aircraft, which carried the cream of its best air crews. The strength of the Japanese Naval Air Force stood at 1,721 aircraft in November 1942, of which 465 were carrier based, while the first line strength of the Japanese Army Air Force stood at 1,642. 1943 saw the real development of the American challenge to Japanese domination. Having failed to secure a decisive victory, defeat for the Japanese against the industrial might of the US was inevitable. In 1943, the US would produce 92,196 aircraft in comparison to the Japanese effort of 16,693. In March 1943, a Japanese relief convoy to the beleaguered Japanese forces in New Guinea was hammered by B-17 Flying Fortresses, North American B-25s and Douglas A-20s of the USAAF, and Bristol Beaufighters and Beauforts of the RAAF, in the Battle of Bismarck Sea. In April, Admiral

Right: Grumman F6F Wildcat, the US Navy's standard fighter in December 1941.

Yamamoto flew to the Rabaul to mastermind an all-out air assault aimed at destroying Allied air power in the Solomons known as Operation I-Go. Fierce air battles culminated in a massed attack on Port Moresby by 200 Japanese aircraft, but I-Go had little impact. Of far greater importance was the loss of Admiral Yamamoto, when his transport was intercepted and destroyed by P-38s while en route to Ballale. In Yamamoto the Japanese lost their most capable strategist.

These actions effectively isolated the Japanese forces on New Guinea, underlined Allied air superiority in the Bismarck Sea and led the Allied Joint Chiefs of Staff to revise their strategic aims. They planned a two-pronged attack, code-named Operation Cartwheel. Admiral William 'Bull' Halsey's 3rd Fleet began a drive in July through the Solomon Islands, with the objective of capturing Rabaul. Landings on the New Georgia island group were co-ordinated with assaults on New Guinea by forces under MacArthur. At the latter's disposal were 772 aircraft of the US 5th Air Force and 1,441 RAAF machines. To oppose MacArthur's invasion, increasing numbers of Japanese army aircraft went to Rabaul, but despite the introduction of impressive new aircraft such as the Nakajima Ki-43-IIKai, the Kawasaki Ki-61 Hien 'Tony' and the twin-engine Kawasaki Ki-45 Toryu 'Nick' operations were severely hampered by poor logistical back up. The rapid advance of MacArthur's troops along the Huan Peninsula was achieved by a series of leapfrogging amphibious assaults, under the cover of massive air support and culminating in the capture of the strategically vital port of Finschhafen on October 2. By

December 20, Allied supremacy on the Huan Peninsula was assured.

The air fighting over the Solomons and Rabaul was the most contested of the Pacific War, as the JNAF fed in the bulk of its carrier air groups to try and halt the US advance. Halsey's forces battled through the Central Solomons during the summer. The airfields on New Georgia fell to American forces on August 22, after the Japanese had withdrawn to Bougainville, the most westerly of the Solomon Islands. Prior to the amphibious assault on Bougainville scheduled for November 1, units of the RNZAF, 5th and 13th Air Forces pounded the Japanese airfields at Kara, Kieta, Ballale, Buka, Bomis and Kahili. Japanese strength on the islands was estimated at 40,000, but by the end of the year effective opposition had ended. Isolated Japanese soldiers continued to harry Allied Forces well into 1945, but construction of a US bomber base on the island was largely unopposed, allowing the Americans to attack Rabaul. From the Bougainville airfields American F4U-1 Corsairs of the US Marine Corps and Navy quickly established air superiority over the remaining Japanese fighter forces at Rabaul. With over 90,000 Japanese troops stationed on New Britain, based primarily around Rabaul, Halsey and MacArthur decided to bypass the island. Air attacks continued until February 20, 1944, after which the remaining Japanese aircraft were withdrawn to

Truk. In the battles for the Solomons and Rabaul, the Japanese lost 2,935 navy aircraft along with the remaining nucleus of experienced pilots and crews. MacArthur recaptured the Admiralty Islands with a daring operation that began in February 1944, completing the encirclement of Rabaul. By the start of the summer, JAAF opposition in New Guinea had been neutralised by units of the RAAF and 5th Air Force.

Central Pacific

In the Central Pacific an ambitious assault was launched by Admiral Nimitz in the summer of 1943. With the return of Halsey's Fleet to his command after the successes in the Solomons, and with the aircraft of the 7th Air Force at his disposal, he now possessed considerable forces with which to strike deep within the Japanese perimeter. For the campaign in the Baker and Gilbert Islands, US 5th Fleet commander Vice-Admiral Spruance commanded 11 carriers in all with 703 aircraft. These operations saw the introduction of the 27,000 ton 'Essex' class carriers and the Grumman F6F-3 Hellcat, which although less manoeuvrable than the latest A6M5 fighter had a 20 mph (32 kmh) speed advantage and could absorb far more damage. On November 20, 1943 Makin and Tarawa were easily taken.

Despite concerted attacks by Japanese Mitsubishi G4M2 and Nakajima B6N2 torpedo-bombers on the invasion fleet the capture of the Marshall Islands followed swiftly

Left: The Vought F4U Corsair outclassed any of the contemporary Japanese fighters that were pitted against it.

after. So effective had been the actions of the US fast carrier groups that no Japanese aircraft were left in fighting condition by the time of the various landings on the Marshalls. Truk, a major Japanese headquarters and base for the formidable battleship *Musashi* was bypassed, leaving it to 'wither on the vine'. On February 17, the 155 aircraft that constituted Japanese air strength on Truk, along with 180 aircraft under repair, were smashed by Task Group 58.1 and TG 58.3. By the end of the following day 252 Japanese aircraft had been destroyed, forcing the Japanese to tighten the defensive line to the Marianas, eastern Carolines and the Palaus. JNAF strength was thereafter focused on the Marianas.

The Philippine Sea — Last of the Great Carrier Air Battles

Under the threat of converging US drives, the Japanese fleet under Vice-Admiral Ozawa sailed to challenge Nimitz's forces, and suffered a heavy defeat at the Battle of the Philippine Sea. The battle, which lasted June 19-20, 1944, was the last of the large-scale carrier force battles of the Pacific War. In the action three Japanese carriers were lost along with countless aircrew. The battle brought an end to any real counter threat and clearly demonstrated the superiority of the American forces. They could now focus on the Marianas Islands, which from February 1944, had been the target of aircraft from Task Groups 58.2 and

58.3. Reinforcements amounting to some 120 aircraft were sent from the mainland to the 22nd and 26th Air Flotillas at Guam, Sinian and Taipan, but these had been almost wiped out by the time of the amphibious assault on Guam on July 21. With naval forces dominant, the amphibious assault on Guam was a success. Fierce Japanese resistance on the island and neighbouring Saipan and Tinian had ended by mid-August, for the loss of over 40,000 Japanese troops. A large American airbase was rapidly constructed on the island that allowed attacks industrial targets on the Japanese mainland by giant US B-29 Superfortresses. Aircraft production dropped dramatically after this date, as the frightened and exhausted Japanese work force began to disperse, and the shortage of raw materials became increasingly acute. Although Japanese aircraft production increased in 1944 to a record total of 28,180 aircraft, the focus remained firmly on offensive aircraft, not the high-altitude fighters and radar-equipped night fighters that were urgently needed to defend the industrial centres.

The Philippines

With the battles for the Southern and Central Pacific islands won, Allied attentions could now focus on the Philippines, and Japan itself. As it was deemed impossible to assault Formosa until the New Year, General MacArthur's advocacy of an attack on Luzon in the Philippines was favoured, commencing with a major assault against Leyte. The battle for

Left: Spitfires with tropical kit are flown off the deck of a carrier.

Leyte Gulf remains the largest naval engagement in history and confirmed the aircraft carrier as the primary weapon of naval power in the Pacific theatre. The Japanese were fully aware that the establishment of US air bases on Leyte, 300 miles (483 km) to the south east of Luzon, would bring to an end the Japanese presence in the Philippines, leaving their defensive perimeter in tatters. A last-ditch operation codenamed Sho-Go had been planned for just such an eventuality. As part of this larger operation the Japanese planned to draw Halsey's 3rd Fleet into a decisive naval action and save the Philippines. The plan called for the deployment of every remaining Japanese Navy warship in two strike forces, with a third decoy force of Japan's four remaining carriers.

The battle ended on October 26, with a decisive defeat for the Japanese Navy, who lost four carriers, three battleships and 10 cruisers, finally expending in one battle what remained of her mobile fleet and naval air force. The surviving Japanese ships could no longer provide any effective opposition to the US Pacific Fleet, nor guard the sea approaches to Japan. However, Kamikaze attacks were making operations increasingly hazardous in the theatre. The campaign to take Luzon began on December 15, and despite the appointment of General Tomoyuki Yamashita, 'The Tiger of Malaya,' MacArthur's forces had forced the Japanese into isolated pockets of resistance by the end of the year. With overwhelming forces at their disposal, fighting an enemy

Above: The B-29 will be remembered for its role in dropping the atomic bomb but it would see much more action than this in the Pacific Theatre.

Below: Boeing B-29 Superfortress *Enola Gay*, used to drop the first atomic weapon, dubbed 'Fat Man' by ground crews, on Hiroshima in August 1945.

crippled by supply problems and trained manpower, the final nine months of the war seemed a foregone conclusion.

But the closer to Japan and victory the Allies came, the more resolute the defenders became. The strategic bombing offensive against the Japanese mainland was not proving decisive, despite the superiority of the aircraft over Japanese air defences. With the Philippines secure, the Americans had cause to ponder their next move. Despite the Allied successes in the theatre, Japan remained in control of Burma, the Dutch East Indies, and a huge area of Manchuria, Korea, and China, though little of the resources of those countries were reaching Japan, thanks to US submariners, but the Japanese appeared resolute. It seemed that an assault on the mainland of Japan would be appallingly costly.

Iwo Jima and Okinawa

Iwo Jima, known as Japan's 'unsinkable aircraft carrier', and Okinawa were final linch pins in the US Pacific campaign. Amphibious assaults began on February 19, and April 1, respectively aimed at providing the Americans with a strategic airbase for a concerted Allied attack on the Japanese home territories. The 23,000 strong force of Japanese defenders held out for over five weeks against a massive US invasion force of over 250,000. Mount Suribachi was finally taken on February 23. By the end of March the three air bases on Iwo Jima were ready to receive vast fleets of US B-29 bombers. Many of the men who had endured the hell of Iwo Jima were part of the task force that set sail in late March to assault Okinawa, last Japanese bastion in the Pacific. The amphibious assault would prove to be the largest and most ambitious of the Pacific campaign. Preliminary air operations began with attacks on the Japanese air bases on Kyushu, and the industrial centre of Honshu. A massive naval bombardment commenced on March 23 coinciding with air bombardment of Japanese positions on the island. At sea, the last remnants of the Japanese fleet engaged the US Navy in a futile sea battle that resulted in the loss of the giant *Yamato*. A 700-plane Kamikaze raid launched in a final act of desperation on

April 6, sunk and damaged 13 US destroyers. On May 3, the Japanese defenders of Okinawa launched a massive counterattack. In the sea off Okinawa, Kamikaze attacks continued against the American fleet with renewed ferocity. In all, 21 American vessels were sunk and another 43 put out of action. On June 22, the headquarters of the Japanese commander Ushijima was finally overrun.

With the suicidal resistance of the Japanese defenders overcome, the final phase of the Strategic Air Offensive began in earnest. Through February and March, B-29 bombers rained incendiaries and high explosives on Japanese industrial targets. On March 9-10, a raid on Tokyo by 334 US aircraft dropped some 1,667 tons of incendiaries on the Japanese capital, creating a devastating fire storm. These actions and a protracted naval blockade failed to bring about a Japanese surrender, and the American commanders began preparations for an invasion of the Japanese mainland. President Truman finally made the decision to use atomic weapons after the Western leaders had arrived at the conclusion that an invasion of the mainland would cost the Allies huge numbers of casualties. A joint ultimatum to the Japanese went unheeded.

Hiroshima and Nagasaki

On August 6, 1945, USAAF B-29 Superfortress *Enola Gay* from Tinian

Above: The sole suviving B-29 Superfortress, *Fifi*, which makes regular appearances during the show season.

in the Marianas dropped an atomic bomb, the most powerful and destructive weapon the world had yet seen, on the Japanese city of Hiroshima. Nearly 80,000 people died as an immediate effect of the explosion, and 75% of the buildings in the city were destroyed. Three days after the Hiroshima explosion, another device was exploded in the sky above the Japanese industrial centre of Nagasaki. Forty thousand people died and nearly half the city was destroyed. Japan capitulated the following day.

NORTH AFRICA AND THE MEDITERRANEAN

When Mussolini committed his country to war in May 1940, he envisaged sharing in the spoils of Britain's defeat and adding her African and Mediterranean possessions to his plan for a great Italian empire. British interest in the region focused on the Suez Canal, the narrow link through Egypt to the resources of the Far East, but despite extensive operations in the Middle

East during the 1930s, in June 1940 RAF strength in the region amounted to only about 300 aircraft. The operational commander of RAF Middle East, Air Chief Marshal Sir Arthur Longmore, realised that this was a pitifully small force with which to defend an area that included Egypt, the Sudan, Kenya, Palestine and Gibraltar. He also knew that with the crisis at home he could expect precious few reinforcements. Longmore's force comprised 14 bomber squadrons, nine of them equipped with Bristol Blenheims, four maritime squadrons, two of which operated Sunderlands and five fighter squadrons, none of them equipped with anything better than Gloster Gladiator biplanes. Making up the rest of the force were an extraordinary mixture of Fairey Battles, Vickers Wellesleys, Vickers Vincents, Hawker Audaxes, Hawker Harts and other of types of even older vintage. To exacerbate the problem the aircraft were dispersed widely across the command. Opposing them, the Italian air force had some 282 aircraft stationed in Libya, from where the first attack against the Egyptian garrison was expected. A further 150 were stationed in Italian East Africa, but the main force of 1,200 was held in

southern Italy, within easing flying distance of Egypt and the British bases in Malta. Longmore knew that lengthy preparations would be necessary before the Italians could mount an attack on Egypt and that when they did strike he would have few replacement aircraft. A limited number of crated aircraft were available for delivery, but to run the gauntlet of the powerful Italian fleet and air force in the central Mediterranean was clearly too hazardous and the route around southern Africa was prohibitively slow. Alternatively, aircraft could be flown out via Gibraltar and Malta, but this method had its own hazards. In the event crated aircraft were sent by sea to the Gold Coast and after assembly were flown across the barren deserts of northern Africa to Egypt. This operation began on August 24, 1940, and continued to supply British forces in North Africa for the duration of the war.

Operations in the Mediterranean began on June 11, 1940, with a massed attack on the Grand Harbour at Malta by 10 Savoia-Marchetti SM 79 bombers. The strategic value of the island of Malta was clear to the Italians. As a vital staging post for the British Mediterranean Fleet and a haven for convoys resupplying the

Eighth Army it became the subject of almost continual attack from the summer of 1940. At the time that Italy entered the war the air defence fleet amounted to five antiquated Swordfish biplanes used for reconnaissance work and three Gladiators. During the first major air assault on Malta that coincided with the Italian invasion of Greece, these three Galdiators — nicknamed 'Faith', 'Hope' and 'Charity' — made a useful contribution to the defence. The arrival of No 830 Squadron, FAA, at Malta on June 24, with Swordfish Mk I torpedo bombers provided for a limited offensive capability. Through the summer No 830 carried out a series of daring offensive operations against Italian ports. In September attacks by the Regia Aeronautica on Malta escalated, with CANT Z.1007 medium bombers deployed alongside German-supplied Ju 87-B-2 dive-bombers.

Below: Martin's B-26 Marauder gained a reputuation for being tricky to fly, but in the right hands it was a useful weapon and achieved the lowest attrition rate of any other US aircraft in the European theatre.

Operation Judgement — The Attack on Taranto

Offensive carrier operations of the Royal Navy during the period June 1940 to March 1941 were outstandingly successful, and were noted with interest by the Japanese Navy. Attacks on Italian ports at Benghazi, Rhodes and Leros took place in July and August. With the Mediterranean Fleet strengthened by the arrival in August of HMS *Illustrious*, the Fleet Air Arm was ready to undertake one of its most important actions of the war. On the night of November 11-12, 1940, 21 Swordfish of Nos 813, 815 and 819 Squadrons were flown off HMS *Illustrious* for a low-level torpedo attack on the Italian Fleet moored in Taranto harbour. Three battleships were hit and disabled, for the loss of two Swordfish, effectively crippling the Italian Fleet. This action, the world's first carrier based air attack, redressed the balance of naval power in the Mediterranean in favour of the British.

The Western Desert

By September 1940, 165,000 Commonwealth troops were opposed by 500,000 of the enemy in the Western Desert, a vast barren area at the northwest tip of the African continent. There were further substantial Italian forces in Eritrea and Abyssinia, comprising some 200,000 men. General Sir Archibald Wavell, Commander-in-Chief of Allied Forces in the Middle East, recognised that if the Italians attacked on all fronts there was little he could do to prevent their advance to Cairo. Wavell's opponent, however, the timid Marshal Graziani, was not a man for bold strokes. In September the Italian Tenth Army advanced tentatively into Egypt from Cyrenaica (Libya). Sollum on the north coast fell followed by Sidi Barrani, where they constructed a series of fortified encampments.

On October 28, 1940, with his forces in North Africa delaying their attack on Egypt, Mussolini invaded Greece through neighbouring Albania. Although Longmore was reluctant to weaken his slender forces he found himself required to dispatch a force to aid the Greeks. This comprised No 30 Squadron, equipped with a mixture of Blenheim bombers and fighters. Ground attack operations carried out by these aircraft proved a useful asset to the Greek Army, who inflicted some notable defeats on the Italian Army up until the following spring. Some offensive activity was launched from Malta, through whose airfields Wellingtons were by now being routed as reinforcements to Egypt. Luftwaffe presence in the Mediterranean was strengthened by the deployment of X-Fliegerkorps from the Channel coast to Sicily from January 1941. Its presence severely curtailed the Royal Navy's freedom of operation in the supply of Malta and the British troops in Greece. Junkers 87R-2s and Junkers 88A-1s carried out innumerable attacks on Maltese airfields and British supply convoys resupplying the island, with top cover provided by Macchi MC.200s and Fiat CR 42 Falcos, but failed in their attempts to sink the

Left: A Consolidated B-24 Liberator, pictured over a snowy Alpine landscape.

Above: Vickers K-gun equipped Hurricane, designed specifically for anti-tank work in North Africa.

Illustrious. By the end of February 1941, the Luftwaffe had achieved almost complete air superiority over Britain's island aircraft carrier, and much of X Fliegerkorps was redeployed support the Afrika Korps in North Africa.

By April 6, the Italian Army had still failed to deliver victory in Greece. Fearful that the RAF would use the airfields in the country to launch air strikes against his precious oilfields in Rumania, Hitler ordered a full-scale German invasion with a force of 27 divisions supported by 1,200 aircraft redirected from the Barbarossa build-up. despite the arrival of four more RAF squadrons from Egypt — two of Blenheim light bombers, one of Hurricanes and another a mixture of Hurricanes and Lysander reconnaissance aircraft — together with reinforcements from Malta the odds were overwhelming. After nine days of fighting only 46 RAF aircraft remained serviceable and on April 20, the rest of the British force was evacuated. RAF flying boats proved invaluable during this operation, but it was clear to all that the whole Greek campaign had been a costly folly.

Operation 'Bestrafung' — Yugoslavia Brought to Heel

Hitler's plans to secure the southern flank of the Axis powers as a prelude to Barbarossa were dealt a blow by the need to provide assistance to Italian forces for their campaigns in Greece, North Africa and in the Mediterranean. They also depended on the signature of Yugoslavia on the Tripartite agreement that would bring the Balkan region under Axis influence. Failure to comply resulted in attacks on April 6, 1941, on the capital Belgrade by Dornier Do 17Z-2s, Junkers 88A-4s and Junkers 87B-2s from forward bases in Hungary. Luftwaffe fighter units were opposed by the Yugoslav Air Force flying imported Hawker

Left: Ground crew unload the film drum from a PR Spitfire, somewhere in North Africa.

Hurricanes and Messerschmitt Bf 109E-1s, but the considerable numerical advantage enjoyed by the German land and air forces brought victory in just 12 days.

NORTH AFRICA

In the Western Desert, British forces counterattacked on December 9 1940, driving the Italian Army back across northern Cyrenaica. The RAF force in Egypt had been reinforced by two squadrons of Wellingtons and one of Hurricanes, while another Hurricane and three Blenheim squadrons had been transferred from the Canal Zone. The Italian ports of Tobruk, Benghazi, Bardia and Derna were all bombed from Egypt, while Wellingtons from Malta attacked Tripoli and intercepted merchant ships crossing the Mediterranean to supply the Italian forces. Few Italian aircraft were encountered over the battle field, enabling RAF aircraft to roam with impunity and making it possible for the Hurricanes to switch from air defence to the ground attack role. On January 22, 1941 the Italian fort at Tobruk fell. It was the first significant British victory of the war.

Top: Hurricane and Spitfire in flight. The first aircraft has desert paint scheme. The aircraft below wears the late colour scheme and markings of South East Asia command.

Above: RAF and RN armourers working on a Spitfire in a blast pen on one of Malta's hard-pressed airfields.

Above: 'Black Six', the sole surviving Bf 109G, which was written-off in an accident in 1998.

Rommel's First Offensive

British celebrations were short lived. Hitler was fully aware of the strategic significance of the North African oil reserves and the Suez Canal. On February 14, 1941, the first of the units that came to be known as the Afrika Korps began arriving in Tripoli. To command this desert army Hitler appointed General Erwin Rommel, one of his foremost tacticians. Rommel had at his disposal some 150 aircraft; about 50 of them were Bf 109Es that had been transferred with their experienced aircrew from the Channel coast. Their arrival quickly enabled the Luftwaffe to destroy the air superiority that the RAF had gained. In spite of the slenderness of his resources Rommel went on the offensive on March 21, attacking the long and vulnerable British line which stretched from the Nile to Beda Fomm. To support this offensive were 40 Ju 87s and the Bf 110C-4s and D-3s of III/ZG 26. The Greek campaign had considerably weakened RAF strength and although strenuous efforts were made by Hurricanes of the RAAF against the Stukas and their Bf 110 escorts, and by RAF Blenheims on enemy airfields and troop concentrations, El Agheila, Agedabia and Benghazi fell in rapid succession. Within two weeks the British were driven back as far as Egypt, leaving only Tobruk to hold out against the German armies.

The Allies were determined to prevent the vital port of Tobruk from falling into German hands. On April 10, the first German attacks were launched against 15,000 Australian infantry under Major-General Leslie Morshead, who could take advantage of the extensive works prepared by the Italians. Two squadrons of Hurricanes, Nos 6 and 73, were left to operate within the perimeter of the defence while Nos 3, 45 and 55 Squadrons were pulled back to Egypt. Rommel decided to set up a cordon around the town, and laid siege to the town for two months while his forces regrouped. Tobruk was a vital link in the Allied supply lines and to lose it completely would spell disaster in North Africa. Two British counter offensives to retake Cyrenaica in May (Operation Brevity) and June (Battleaxe) failed, costing the RAF more of its resources; with the losses over Greece and Crete, RAF Middle East Command had reached a low ebb.

Supply problems were daunting for all the forces operating in North Africa. Supply lines stretched across thousands of miles of desert and grew longer with each advance. In the baking heat and dust the Luftwaffe began to suffer serious reliability problems compounded by the fact that by the summer of 1941 its supply lines were stretched to breaking point across North Africa. In the Mediterranean Axis supply convoys were sought out by RAF PR units based at Malta and attacked by anti-shipping aircraft. In November 1941, 14 of the 21 ships sent from Italy were sunk. The RAF suffered similar depredations, and on top of these the RAF in the Middle East at this time was in dire need of effective organisation. One of the most pressing problems was that of technical support. Conditions in the desert were particularly hard on machinery, and the only source of spares was the long and fragile supply route to Britain. Reorganisation of the engineering infrastructure during the summer enabled the RAF to increase its front line strength from 200 to almost 600 aircraft in November 1941. Another key change was successful organisation of air/ground operations by the establishment of Air Support Control Units. These were mobile, jointly manned units located at the headquarters of each Army Corps, with links to the HQ Western Desert Air Force and the HQs of the RAF Wings. American support in the form of Curtiss Tomahawk IIBs and Martin Marylands began to arrive in the autumn, together with increasing numbers of Hurricane IICs with 20mm cannon armament. But both the Tomahawk and Hurricane were markedly inferior to the Bf 109F-2s and F-4/Trops that were sent to reinforce the Luftwaffe. The Italians also received improved aircraft, including the Macchi MC.202 Folgores of the 1 Gruppo for Operation Crusader.

Operation Crusader

On the night of November 18-19, 1941, reinforced British and Commonwealth troops under Claude Auchinlek launched Operation Crusader, a large scale armoured offensive toward Tobruk. For 35 days prior to the attack RAF and RAAF squadrons had sought to gain air superiority over the Luftwaffe and Regia Aeronautica with attacks on airfields in the Derna-Benghazi sector. The results were inconclusive, serving to confirm the superiority of the Bf 109Fs over both the Hurricane and Tomahawk. In the opening week of Crusader, the 49 squadrons available to Air Marshal Sir Arthur Tedder, the successor to Longmore, gradually gained air superiority over the bat-

tlefield. The Axis forces were driven back as far as El Agheila, the siege of Tobruk was lifted on December 8 and Benghazi was recaptured on the 23rd. Rommel had been pushed back to the Tripolitanian borders, from where he had advanced in early spring. Desperate shortages of aviation fuel, resulting from the actions of the tiny RAF anti-shipping force at Malta, meant that Luftwaffe units were restricted to an average of 100 sorties during the campaign. The attack petered out in the spring of 1942, by which time it had cost the Allies some 300 aircraft and exposed the worrying limitations of British tanks. The mounting demands of the Pacific campaign had robbed Tedder of many aircraft, and heralded the prospect of a cutback in reinforcements. Urgent supply problems were now the lot of the Allies.

In contrast, retreat had halved Rommel's supply lines, and, although the Axis losses amounted to some 232 German aircraft, plus at least 100 Italian machines, the Bf 109F had again proved superior to Allied fighters in the air. To compound

Allied problems, in November 1941, the importance of the Mediterranean theatre in Axis strategy was finally recognised by the OKW, prompting Hitler to redeploy II Fliegerkorps from the Russian front to Sicily, with the express task of nullifying Malta. This was followed by the whole of Kesselring's Luftflotte II. An escalation in air attacks on Malta became evident in December and in that same month two convoys carrying vital stocks of aviation fuel and other supplies reached Tripoli. With the RAF under siege in Malta supplies poured in.

The first Spitfire Mk VBs — the first in the Mediterranean theatre — were flown off HMS *Eagle* to Malta on March 7, 1942. They could not

Below: In an attempt to squeeze more performance from the Bf 109 airframe Messerchmitt fited increasingly powerful engines. The 'G' series was built in larger numbers than any other.

have arrived at a better time. During the months of March and April II Fliegerkorps threw everything it had at the island. April was particularly savage and by the 23rd of the month the RAF had only six serviceable Spitfires available, 30 of the reinforcements having been shot down. On May 10, a crucial decision was taken to resupply the island, despite the losses, but with such concerted air action many of the ships failed to get through. In July, the air offensive against Malta reopened, but with 200 aircraft now available to them the defenders were able to put up a stout resistance. Some 567 Axis aircraft were ranged against the RAF force; by August 14, 44 of these together with their crews had been lost. Against that the RAF had lost 39 aircraft, but 26 pilots survived to fight again. Finally, in mid-August, the remnants of a convoy limped into the island's Grand Harbour. With it came the ship *Ohio* carrying vital aviation fuel and relief for the island.

Rommel's Last Triumph

On May 26, 1942, Rommel launched a final counteroffensive from his positions. At his disposal was a considerable air armada comprising Luftflotte II, II Fliegerkorps and X Fliegerkorps, with 657, 97 and 129 aircraft respectively. The RAF had some 536 fighters, 246 medium bombers and 105 Wellington bombers. The best aircraft were still tied to Britain. Despite the considerable efforts of Air Vice-Marshal Coningham's Desert Air Force, which engaged the enemy both on the ground and in the air, the Germans made rapid advances all along the Gazala-Bir Hakeim line. Bristol Beaufighters were extremely active, ranging far behind the lines to attack enemy supply lines. The speed of the retreat forced RAF squadrons to operate from wherever the existence of suitable airstrips made it possible. The Luftwaffe also found it difficult to keep pace. A conciliatory note for the Allies was that attacks on Malta eased off as German

aircraft based in Sicily and southern Italy were redeployed in support of this attack and to the Russian Front. Between February and April a lull in ground operations allowed both sides much needed time to rest and re-equip, although air superiority was still keenly contested. In May the offensive was renewed. After an intense aerial bombardment by Luftflotte II and dwindling ammunition supplies had sapped the capabilities of the hardy defenders of Tobruk, the last symbol of British strength in North Africa, the Afrika Korps captured the town on June 21, 1942. Nearly 30,000 troops were taken prisoner, together with vital stores.

El Alamein

The capture of Tobruk encouraged the OKW to drop plans for the invasion of Malta, and to proceed with all haste to Libya and Egypt. This allowed the small air force on the island to recover its strength, and attacks on the Axis shipping were renewed with fresh intensity. Fuel shortages again became the Achilles heel of the Fliegerfëhrer Afrika, which had expended much of its strength on the air fighting over Tobruk. The Allies had retreated in good order to make their last stand at El Alamein, barely 55 miles (88 km) west of Alexandria and the Suez Canal, entrenched along a position flanked to the south by the impassable Quattarra depression. This forced Rommel to make a frontal attack with extremely limited forces, and by June 16 they had been repulsed with heavy losses. The Allied Chief-in-Command Claude Auchinleck counterattacked on June 21, but made little impression on the Afrika Korps attackers.

Realising the desperation of the position in North Africa, Churchill visited the beleaguered British troops in Egypt on August 5, appointing Bernard Montgomery as Chief-in-Command in Auchinleck's place. Montgomery and Tedder established a good working relationship that

greatly facilitated the effective tactical use of aircraft for the rest of the campaign. The crisis led to the deployment of aircraft from Australia and India and American entry into the war brought the Eighth Army and Desert Air Force enormous material support, in terms of both tanks and aircraft. By September 2, the German attacks at El Alamein had been called off. Rommel's supply lines across the Mediterranean were under heavy attack by the Royal Navy and RAF, starving him of the one commodity he desperately needed — fuel. Although his forces had occupied airfields from which to strike against the vital RAF bases in the Canal Zone, the Luftwaffe had no fuel for its aircraft. Almost all supplies had to be brought in by air from Greece, and even the ceaseless efforts of Junkers Ju 52/3m crews could not make good the shortfall. Furthermore, Axis attacks on well-dug positions around Alamein were proving too costly both in terms of fuel and equipment. By August 20, the Fliegerfëhrer Afrika had only 160 aircraft available, and although the Jagdgflieger were achieving notable successes against Allied fighters in their new Bf 109G-2s, qualitative superiority, as was proved time and again in the 1939-45 air war, could not offset numerical inferiority.

The Second Battle of Alamein

Through the autumn Allied forces, bolstered by American Army Air Force units from India and by a steady flow of reinforcements for the

Above Right: North American B-25 Mitchell of the RAF and Bell P-39 Airacobra of the Red Air Force. Under the Lend-Lease Act both Britain and Russia received US-built machines.

Right: Focke-Wulf FW200 Condor crews parade in front of their machines.

Eighth Army, prepared to go on the offensive. Ninety-six squadrons were available to the Tedder, 60 of them RAF and Fleet Air Arm units. For three weeks prior to the attack these units pounded German airfields by day and night. The Second Battle of Alamein began at 9.40 pm on October 23. A huge 882-gun artillery barrage pounded the German lines, prior to the advance of infantry. The Allied air operations had left only 690 aircraft available to the Luftwaffe in North Africa, although nearly 2,300 were spread across the rest of the Mediterranean. The massive air superiority enjoyed by the Allies was a key feature of the battle. While medium bombers made constant attacks on enemy positions, fighter-bombers attacked armour without fear of attack by enemy fighters. The fighting was locked in stalemate until November 3, when Rommel, whose forces were critically short of petrol and ammunition, ordered a withdrawal. A furious Hitler signalled Rommel to halt the withdrawal on November 5, but the logistical position the 'Desert Fox' faced left him with few other options.

Operation Torch

The final blow for the Afrika Korps was struck at 5.15 am on November 8, 1942, when 100,000 men of the Central, Western and Eastern task forces began to land on the beaches of Morocco, Algeria and Tunisia under Operation Torch. Hitler was forced to send reinforcements to Rommel, now sandwiched between two armies far greater in strength than his own. Fliegerféhrer Afrika was resupplied by stripping units at the Eastern Front and in Norway, which could not afford them, strengthening German air forces in North Africa to some 1,220 aircraft by December 12. Reinforcements of Focke-Wulf 190A-4s were sent from France to Tunisia to stem the advance of Montgomery from the West and to try and secure supply lines over the Mediterranean.

Despite difficult conditions, and severely handicapped both by poor logistic and maintenance facilities and by lack of suitable airfields, squadrons of RAF Spitfires struggled to support the Allied forces as they fought their way through Tunisia. Winter rains, and determined resistance from the Luftwaffe bogged down the western advance in December. In the Mediterranean heavily armed Bristol Beauforts and Vickers Wellingtons destroyed almost every Italian vessel that attempted to cross.

Defeat in Africa

During the winter of 1942/43, the Desert Fox led his Afrika Korps in a skilful retreat to Tunis, their vital port of supply. The Allied First Army under Lt Gen Sir Kenneth Anderson pushed the Germans to within 30 miles (50 km) of Tunis by January 1943, but as winter rains reduced the volume of air operations and hampered further movement on the ground, his troops dug in to wait for the arrival of the US II Corps. In January Tedder was appointed overall commander of all Allied air units in the region, simplifying chains of command that prior to his appointment had been somewhat disjointed. From the west the advance of the II Corps was slowed by stiff German resistance. The relative inexperience of US pilots, despite the arrival in theatre of very capable aircraft such as the Lockheed P-38F 10 Lightning, Bell P-39D Airacobra, Martin B-26 Marauder and Douglas Dakota, only compounded the problem. The Eighth Army continued its march up the coast of Libya throughout January and February, forcing Rommel into a narrower and narrower pocket around Tunis. In March, Luftwaffe Transportgruppen in Sicily and Greece began a brave but futile operation to resupply the Afrika Korps, with a fleet of Ju 52/3ms, Junkers Ju 90s, Junkers Ju 290s, Gotha 242s and Messerschmitt Me 323D-1 Gigants. The lumbering

aircraft were shot down in droves; no less than 20 of the giant Me 323s were lost. On April 22, the combined forces of Anderson and Montgomery attacked German lines. Rommel had flown to Germany on March 9, to beg Hitler to evacuate, but his pleas fell on deaf ears. The Führer replaced the Desert Fox with General von Amim, yet the new commander was in a hopeless position. Tunis fell on May 7, and by May 14, all the Axis forces in North Africa were in captivity. By this time much of Fliegerkorps Afrika had successfully evacuated to Sicily, in preparation for the invasion of Italy that was now inevitable. Defeat of the Luftwaffe in North Africa came not at the hands of the Allies, but through a desperate shortage of fuel, spares, experienced pilots and a chaotic and directionless German aircraft industry that could no longer keep pace with the demand of fighting on three fronts.

THE ITALIAN CAMPAIGN

Plans for Operation Husky, the invasion of Sicily, were made during the spring of 1943. For six weeks prior to the planned invasion day, airfields, ports and industrial targets on Sicily, Sardinia and in southern Italy were the subject of continual Allied air attacks by the Strategic Air Force. On July 10, some 180,000 men of the US Seventh Army and British Eighth Army landed on the shores of Sicily, off the south-western coast of Italy. Complete air cover was assured by the deployment of 4,000 Allied aircraft. The RAF contingent in this huge aerial armada was represented by 121 squadrons For their part the Axis forces could muster only 550. The Allied air forces were given four main tasks: firstly, to gain air superiority, second, to give air cover to the convoys at sea; third, to operate over the beach-heads so as to provide cover for Allied ships offshore, and to attack enemy defences on shore; and fourth, to support the subsequent advance of the armies through Sicily. The Eighth Army, under Montgomery, met with little

Right: Ground crew of the
Regia Aeronautica tend to Fiat
C.R.42s in the desert.

opposition at their landing point just south of Syracuse. Resistance at the Gulf of Gila, disembarkation point for the US forces, was stiffer but easily overcome. Syracuse fell on July 12, but Montgomery's direct drive to Messina on Sicily's northeastern coast faltered in the face of determined German defences around Catania. The US forces, under General Patton, were hampered by the hilly Sicilian terrain, and he chose instead to make a looping attack around the northern coast, taking Palermo on July 22. Units of the US 3rd Division reached Messina on August 22, shortly after the German evacuation across the straits. Although they had lost 12,000 men, the Allied death toll was nearly 20,000. The five-week campaign cost fewer than 400 aircraft, for the destruction or capture of 1,850 enemy machines.

The Invasion of Italy

At the end of July, Mussolini was placed under house arrest. Intelligence reports indicated to the Allied leaders that the Italians would soon desert the Axis. Negotiations centred on this possibility delayed plans for the invasion of Italy, and after they had rescued Mussolini and reinstated him as a puppet leader the Germans poured men and equipment into the Italian peninsula. On September 3, the Eighth Army finally crossed the Straits of Messina under massive air cover and made unopposed landings at Taranto. In marked contrast, the amphibious assault on Salerno by the US 5th Army very nearly proved disastrous. The German defenders were easily able to predict the landing sites and the 16 divisions under General Mark Clark had to fight long and hard to establish a beachhead. The British plan was to drive through Calabria

and link up with Clark, trapping the Germans in the process. The skill and ferocity of the German defenders forced the Allies to rethink, and enabled Field Marshal Kesselring's forces to escape the pincer movement. Superiority and command of the skies again proved the greatest asset as the Allies slowly advanced north. To aid the advance the 'cab rank' system was pioneered, whereby standing patrols of ground attack aircraft could be called down by radio to strike at targets by ground forces with the shortest possible time delay. Naples fell on October 1, and the air bases at Foggia were in Allied hands by October 5. These were the two prime Allied objectives, as the latter brought Hitler's Romanian oilfields within striking range of nine squadrons of No 205 Group, which commenced operations in April 1944. The Allies continued their drive north on either side of the

Apennine Mountains and with winter rapidly approaching, Kesselring formed a defensive line (the 'Gustav' line) stretching across the peninsula from the Liri Valley to the approaches to Rome. Hopes of an early victory dashed, the Allied commanders decided to focus on the capture of Rome. The elaborate and imposing Gustav line stood directly in their path, persuading the Allies to embark on an amphibious assault behind the line at Anzio. Operation Shingle, as the assault was codenamed, was nothing short of a disaster. Although an attack on the Gustav line at Cassino diverted some of Kesselring's forces, General Clark failed to consolidate the beachhead after an almost unopposed landing

**Below: A Savoia-Marchetti
S.M.79 Sparviero in desert
camouflage.**

on January 22. A rapid German counterattack nearly drove the US Sixth Corps back into the sea. For the next four months, the American forces were subjected to intense bombardment and attack and fought a bitter defensive battle against the German 14th Army.

Along the Gustav line, a renewed offensive began on May 11, code-named Operation Diadem. Twelve Allied divisions were opposed by six German divisions. On the west coast, the corridor through Cassino allowed General Clark to advance on Rome. Clark ignored General Alexander's order to cut the German retreat, allowing them to escape again. On June 5, Rome fell to the Allies, and the Germans once again stabilised a defensive line across the peninsula as their troops were diverted to Normandy in droves. The line was drawn from La Spezia to Pesaro, and as the winter of 1944 drew in, there was a lull in operations. The fighting in northern France had shifted the focus of Allied and German strategy. In the spring of 1945, the US Fifth Army and British Eighth Army, 17 divisions in all, launched a final attack along the Senio River. Massive aerial bombardment of the German forward

divisions and their reinforcements had weakened their defences, and they crumbled in the face of the advance. Throughout the following week, Allied aircraft systematically destroyed bridges across the Po River, so denying the Germans any possibility of retreat. The surrender of General Heinreich von Vietinghoff's Army Group C on May 2, 1945, brought to an end the bitterly contested and costly Italian campaign.

THE ALLIED FIGHTBACK

Writing after the war, Churchill revealed that of all the aspects of the war only the losses sustained by the north Atlantic convoys had caused him concern. The task of protecting these convoys became the single highest priority for Royal Air Force Coastal Command and may be seen as its most important contribution to the war. The ineffectiveness of Bomber Command operations in the early stages of the war, albeit in the face of many obstacles, was a similar cause for concern, and was offset only by the tenacity and bravery of the air crews. Revitalised with more effective equipment and organisation and the establishment of US bomber bases in Britain from

August 1942, the Allies were ready to mount a concerted strategic campaign against Germany which by 1944 was delivering devastating blows against Germany's ability to wage war.

Coastal Command

Few flying boats of any ability, or land-based aircraft with suitable range for the demands of maritime operations, were available to the RAF at the outbreak of war. The most capable aircraft on the inventory of Coastal Command was the Avro Anson. Soon after war broke out British merchant shipping crossing the North Atlantic from

Right: Avro Lancaster heavy bomber of the Battle of Britain Memorial Flight.

Below Right: B-25 Mitchell *Yellow Rose* — American bomber crews popularised the practice of nose-art.

Below: Boeing B-17 Flying Fortress. The bright tail surfaces indicate that this aircraft is a bombing leader.

Above: Short Sunderland maritime reconaissance flying boat on display outside the RAF Museum at Hendon.

Canada came under devastating attack from U-boats operating in the Atlantic Gap, the long stretch of their voyage where no air cover was available. Allied losses during the first six months of the war were appallingly high. The Royal Navy was fully occupied in the Mediterranean and could spare few destroyers for escort duties, and few of these were equipped with radar to detect submarines running on the surface. These were dark days for Coastal Command. They had sunk only two U-boats and the toll on merchant shipping convoys began to escalate to unsustainable levels during the summer of 1941.

Gradually the Ansons were phased out of service by the Lockheed Hudson, a military version of the Lockheed 188A airliner with heavier armament and twice the range. Coastal Command squadrons also began to take delivery of Beaufort torpedo bombers, to supplement the increasing numbers of Sunderlands, Whitleys and Wellingtons on Coastal Command strength. The only notable victories that were scored in the early phase of the war were the attacks on the German battleship *Gneisenau* and cruiser *Létzow* by torpedo-carrying

Beauforts which badly damaged the former vessel and put out of commission the other. The Beaufort also proved highly effective in the anti-shipping role particularly against Axis convoys in the Mediterranean. Command strength was further boosted by the arrival, later in 1941, of American long-range Consolidated PBY Catalina and Liberator aircraft, and stood at 633 aircraft by the end of 1941. In February of the next year, however, the Command endured a very public setback when a substantial German fleet that included the German battlecruisers *Scharnhorst* and *Gneisenau* left Brest and after slipping through the English Channel escaped to home waters. During the course of the year increasing commitments in the Mediterranean and Far East theatres resulted in the redeployment of all the Beaufort squadrons to these theatres and depleted the strength of the home force, which for a time had to rely on unsuitable Handley-Page Hampdens for anti-shipping work.

The equipment that revolutionised the war at sea was undoubtedly radar. When the first Air to Surface Vessel (ASV) sets were made available to Coastal Command in 1941 results began to improve. The anti-submarine bombs that had proved so ineffective against U-boats in the early stages of the war were also gradually replaced by a new and powerful depth charge. A significant innovation in the battle against

submarines was pioneered from June of 1942. U-boats recharging their batteries on the surface under the cloak of darkness were difficult to spot, even with radar. By equipping maritime patrol aircraft with a powerful spotlight that could illuminate the target after radar acquisition the hunters became the hunted. In the following 12 months Coastal Command sank 71 U-boats, a rate that the German boat yards were unable to sustain, particularly as the Strategic Bombing Offensive began to have some effect. The RAF were aided in the war against the U-boats by British Intelligence, whose interceptions of German Enigma radio traffic became increasingly accurate and allowed U-boat movements to be plotted.

Rocket-firing Beaufighters began to make their mark on Axis coastal shipping in the latter part of 1943, in both the northern European and Mediterranean theatres. As mentioned in the preceding chapter, Coastal Command units operating in the Mediterranean theatre were instrumental in denying Rommel the vital supply route to southern Italy. By the autumn of 1943 it was clear that the German shipyards could no longer keep pace with the rate of losses to the Allies. The first Strike Wing, consisting of one anti-flak squadron and a torpedo-carrying squadron, had been formed the previous November and the effectiveness of this unit prompted the formation of another five by

Right: Consolidated PBY-6 Catalina of the Danish Air Force. This model was one of the last military Catalina variants.

June 1944. Although German radar countermeasures were constantly improving, advances in Allied radar science allowed Coastal Command to maintain its lead in the anti-submarine war, which was further helped by Portugal's decision to allow the Azores to be used as a base for Coastal Command operations from October. This was a major factor in the battle, as it allowed for additional coverage of the shipping lanes. Between July 1943 and D-Day, Coastal Command sank 114 U-boats. Although the German navy was able to increase U-boat production, the loss of experienced crews was far outstripping the rate at which they could be trained. The volume of men and material brought to Britain from the US during preparations for the Second Front demonstrates the dramatic reversal in fortunes in the Battle of the Atlantic.

Bomber Command

Bomber Command entered the war as the strongest of the three RAF home commands, with an operational strength amounting to 325 aircraft in five groups (Nos 1, 2, 3, 4 and 5). The total strength was closer to 952, but 17 squadrons were withdrawn to form Operational Training Units and a further 10 sent to France. The aircraft were a mixture of Vickers Wellingtons, Armstrong Whitworth Whitleys, Fairey Battles, Bristol Blenheims and Handley Page

Hampdens. By comparison with the modern bomber aircraft that the Luftwaffe could field, these aircraft appeared obsolescent and incapable of mounting an effective strategic bombing campaign. This was underlined in early operations, yet a crucial difference lay in the fact that whereas the Luftwaffe was essentially a tactical air force subordinated to the army, equipped with medium

bombers of limited capacity, Bomber Command had been designed from the outset as an independent strategic force that could operate across the whole extent of the Empire. In 1940 the first of the 'heavy' bombers designed specifically for this role were just entering production, whereas in Germany no such aircraft was even near to the production stage.

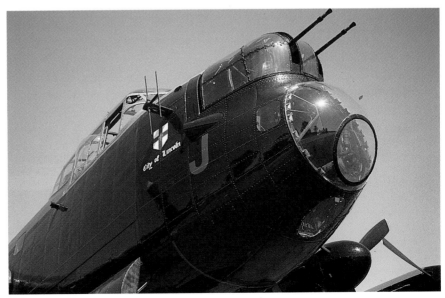

Above Right: More nose-art, this time adorning a Liberator.

Right: *City of Lincoln* is the sole airworthy RAF Lancaster bomber in existence.

The Battle of Heligoland Bight

From the outbreak of war on September 3, 1943, both the Luftwaffe and the RAF were restricted to attacks on purely military targets at sea. Bomber Command sent its Wellingtons, Blenheims, Hampdens and Whitleys to make attacks on the German fleet in the North Sea and the coastline from Emden to Kiel. On December 18, off Heligoland Bight, no less than 50% of the attacking force of 24 Wellingtons were lost, 10 to the guns of II/JG 77 and another two in ditchings. This action was instrumental in the RAF decision to withdraw bomber squadrons from daylight operations, and made a nonsense of the belief that a bomber force flying in close formation could beat off a fighter attack. As we have seen the Battles of the Advanced Allied Striking Force and the Blenheims of No 2 Group suffered terrible losses during the Battle for France.

In May 10, 1940, amidst an air of crisis, Churchill authorised unlimited bombing to the east of the Rhine. This decision marked the start of the strategic bombing campaign against Germany. Attacks began on the night of May 15-16, 1940, and continued until the final surrender in May 1945. During the Battle of Britain bomber operations were focused on selected German industrial targets and on the ports and airfields preparing for the invasion of mainland Britain. Here Bomber Command was able to make a significant contribution, sinking many of the invasion barges in their harbours during repeated attacks, and despite the inadequacy of the aircraft in service German industrial targets in the Ruhr, Munster and Cologne were attacked, albeit without significant success, primarily because of poor navigational aids and weather intelligence. At this time aircraft still carried out their own navigation — although there were no specialist navigators in the crews — and unless the aircraft could be flown with great precision and the target was not covered by the thick cloud that often blanketed the Ruhr, then accuracy was often very poor.

In October, the threat of German invasion began to fade and Bomber Command was able to concentrate on the strategic bombing campaign vigorously championed by many

Above: Incendiary bombs await loading onto a Lancaster.

senior officers. Nevertheless, RAF commanders remained overly optimistic about the damage these raids were causing to German industry, despite the clear evidence provided by the pilots and interpreters of the RAF Photo Reconnaissance Unit. In one notable report from the Photographic Interpretation Section on bomber raids against two synthetic oil plants at Gelsenkirchen, it was shown that in almost 300 sorties no major damage had been caused. Yet despite this, and further evidence provided by the PRU, the commander of Bomber Command, Air Marshal Sir Richard Pierse, held firm in the belief that targeting these oil facilities should remain the focus of the RAF bomber squadrons through the winter of 1940 and early spring of 1941. Allied Losses to flak and fighters escalated, however, during the early months of 1941 as opposition in the skies over German grew stiffer.

Above: The de Havilland Mosquito.

Right: Hawker Typhoon at a forward base in France during summer 1944.

Flak and Nightfighters

In the spring of 1940, as the bombing campaign against German industrial targets began in earnest, Göring ordered the formation of special nightfighter units (Nachtgeschwader). German airborne radar was somewhat less advanced than its British equivalent at this time, and these units were reliant on skilled operators using the GEMA FuMG 80 Freya ground-based radar. The first airborne interception using this equipment was made by a Dornier 17Z-10 on October 2, 1940. The main weapon of the flak arm was the fearsome 88mm Flak 36 (later used to devastating effect against Allied armour), sighted using information from the Kommandogerät 36 predictor. The gun-laying FuMG 39L and 40L radar sets were superseded in May 1940, by Telefunken's FuMG62 (Würzburg) equipment, which were installed on the coastline of northern Europe.

Right: Short Sunderland in its element, hunting for U-boats over the North Atlantic.

The Submarine Threat

Because of the increasing threat presented by U-boats operating from Lorient, St-Nazaire and Bordeaux, in March 1941 Churchill instigated a directive ordering Bomber Command to concentrate on reducing this threat by bombing the French bases and the shipyards in Kiel, Bremen and Hamburg. This saw the start of a shift towards area targeting that was to develop over the next four months. During this period a total of 12,721 sorties were flown against these and other targets, for a loss of 321 aircraft, yet no readily appreciable impact was made on submarine operations. After the fall of France the Germans had lost no time in constructing massively strong

• AIRCRAFT OF WWII •
A VISUAL ENCYCLOPEDIA

concrete U-boats pens at the Atlantic ports and these proved highly resistant to RAF bombing.

By July the threat to the Atlantic sea routes had receded somewhat, and Bomber Command was free to return to the strategic bombing campaign once again. Significantly, attention was turned in yet another directive of July 9, to the dislocation of the German transportation systems and to 'destroying the morale of the population as a whole and of the industrial workers in particular.' But in the following months, both navigation and bombing accuracy within the Command were again shown to be hopelessly inadequate. An analysis of 100 raids carried out between June and July 1941, showed that only one in four crews who had even reached the target had bombed within five miles of it. The position did not improve during the autumn and after a disastrous raid on November 7-8, when out of 169

aircraft dispatched against Berlin, only 28.8% reached the target and 9.4% of these attacking aircraft were lost, Pierse was summoned to the Prime Minister's retreat at Chequers to answer some searching questions. The result was that operations against Berlin were suspended, and Bomber Command retired to lick its wounds and re-equip with new navigation and bombing aids in preparation for the new strategic bombing offensive planned for 1942.

Strategic Bombing Offensive

In the winter of 1941 the Air Staff drew up a new plan for attacking 43 of the main industrial centres in Germany, with a fleet which was to be bolstered by a sizeable US strategic bomber force based in the United Kingdom. In February an important change in RAF policy was established. The concept of bombing specific industrial targets was abandoned in favour of area bombing,

and henceforth the primary objective would be breaking the morale of the civilian population. Much emphasis was attached in the Directive to the new 'Gee' navigational aid, which relied on pulsed transmissions from ground stations in Britain which were interpreted in the air through a cathode ray tube to guide aircraft to their targets. Although the first equipment was crude and not especially accurate, it was the first of four important systems that were used during the course of the war.

In February 1942, Pierse was replaced in command by the man whose name is synonymous with Bomber Command, Air Chief Marshal Sir Arthur Harris. Harris has attracted considerable controversy for his unflinching belief in area bombing, but his dynamic personality and dogged determination made him a hero among his men. Morale in the command had been sapped by constant criticism, and Harris played an important part in reviving flag-

Below: Consolidated B-24 Liberator, adorned with the names of its sponsors.

Above: A Griffon-engined Spitfire, with the five-blade constant speed Rotol propeller.

ging confidence. During the spring, massed raids were undertaken against German cities that caused widespread destruction and deaths among the civilian population, culminating in the first '1,000 bomber raid' against Cologne at the end of May.

In August, Sir Charles Portal, the Chief of the Air Staff and alongside Harris the chief advocate of strategic bombing within the RAF, ordered that a special Pathfinder unit should be raised to further boost bombing accuracy. This was to be made up of the best crews and would be charged with finding and marking the target with flares as a guide to the main fleet. Bombing accuracy, even with 'Gee' equipment, was far below the level required and it was clear that another method was required. Although strongly resisted by Harris, the unit was created under Gp Cpt Donald Bennett and began assembling at its newly assigned bases on the same day that B-17s of the US Eighth Air Force carried out their first attacks. The Pathfinder Force (PFF) was established from Nos 7, 35, 83, 109 and 156 Squadrons, flying a mixture of Halifaxes, Stirlings, and Wellingtons. This force eventually became No 8 Group. The first operation was not a success. The target, Flensburg on the Baltic coast, was not hit at all but during the autumn results began to improve with the introduction of specially designed incendiary marking devices. In the later part of the year an improved navigational aid, code-named Oboe, began to equip PFF Mosquitoes. These light, fast and high flying aircraft were the ideal tool for the Oboe equipment, which had a strictly limited range and could control only a single aircraft to the target at any one time. Oboe was used exclusively by PFF Mosquitoes until the end of the war.

The Eighth Air Force

The United States entered the war with the only four-engined strategic bombing fleet in the world, of which the primary component was the Boeing B-17 Flying Fortress. American strategists held that 'area bombing' practised by Bomber Command achieved little at great expense. They pointed to the night-time raids on Britain in the winter of 1940-41. These had failed to break down civilian morale to a point where the will to fight was lost. Why then, they reasoned, should such a strategy work on the German population? Instead the Americans favoured pinpoint attacks on German military, economic and industrial resources. The conflict of opinions were not resolved and for the remaining duration of the war, the Allies pursued two separate policies. While the British carpet bombed at night, American aircraft precision bombed by day. The Lend-Lease Act of March 1941 had geared the American aviation industry to high output, thus allowing the USAAF to triple its bomber fleet in the year after Pearl Harbour. To bases in eastern England US President Roosevelt sent the 8th Air Force, under the command by General Carl Spaatz. The Eighth's first operation, an attack on targets at Rouen-Sotteville in northern France, took place on August 17, 1942. This type of attack, a short range penetration, set the pattern for Eighth Air Force operations until October 1942, as priorities in North Africa and the Pacific took pride of place. During the winter of 1942-43 an offensive against the U-boats pens at Lorient, St Nazaire and La Rochelle was mounted. These missions received escort from Supermarine Spitfire Mk VBs equipped with long-range tanks, during the first 40 miles of penetration over the coast, but losses steadily rose until by December they had reached 8.8%. This situation was to endure until May 1943. In January of that year, American aircraft made their first daylight attacks on German soil, in the face of concerted attacks by defending fighters and without escort.

H2S

In January 1943, a device came into service that was to prove a considerable asset to Bomber Command. This was the H2S equipment, a primitive ground-mapping radar that could with skilled operation be used to distinguish targets on the ground. Importantly, it enabled aircraft to bomb through cloud, could be carried by all aircraft as it was self-contained and did not rely on ground stations, and could not be jammed by the enemy. The Luftwaffe responded to this new threat with their own innovations. The night fighter force were equipped with efficient airborne radar by mid-1942 and took an increasingly heavy toll on Bomber Command.

The scale of the Ruhr attacks by Bomber Command were stepped up in February, with a revitalised Bomber Command strengthened to 50 squadrons and 18 of them equipped with the vitally important Avro Lancaster four-engine bomber. High capacity 8,000 lb and 4,000 lb 'cookie' blast bombs were by now in use, together with the accurate Mk XIV bombsight. A directive to RAF Bomber Command dated February 4, 1943, released Harris from the strictures of having to bomb the U-boat pens and freed his forces for an all-out attack on the German industrial heartland of the Ruhr. Over nearly four months, from March 5 to June 28, the major cities

of Essen, Duisberg and Désseldorf were subjected to 26 major raids in which 34,705 tons of HE and incendiaries were released, for the loss of 628 aircraft. On the night of June 28-29 the famous Dambusters raid on the Mohne, Sorpe and Eder Dams caused massive flooding in the Ruhr basin, but production was not very much affected by the loss of hydroelectric power.

During this time the major part of VIII Bomber Command (USAAF) was engaged in daylight raids against the U-boat bases in the Bay of Biscay and their construction yards in Kiel and Bremen, this being later dubbed the Battle of Kiel. The US airmen met with intense opposition from the Luftwaffe; on June 22, no less than 120 FW 190s and Bf 102s rose to meet the 235 aircraft sent to bomb Nordeutsche Chemische Werke GmbH at Hüls near Hannover, shooting down 16 and damaging 66 other. In response to the upsurge in Allied bombing German defences were strengthened, and although the Luftwaffe's priorities remained the Mediterranean and the Soviet Union, increasing numbers of aircraft were now being withdrawn from the Eastern Front to defend the Reich. Among the newcomers to LwBefhmitte on June 22, was I/JG 'Udet'. Nightfighter

strength was increased to 493, many of them new Bf 110G-4s and Dornier Do 217N-1s with FuG 202 Lichtenstein airborne radar. In the summer of 1943, strengthened defences, a mounting casualty rate on the daylight raids and the poor results achieved thus far by the US bomber groups, gave Allied commanders cause for thought. A directive of June 10, 1943, ordered that they now concentrate on destroying the German fighter arm, while the urgent need for long-range fighter escort was addressed. On July 24, massed attacks by up to 303 B-17s began in earnest on targets in the Ruhr and continued for a week. For the first time the bombers enjoyed the protection of P-47 Thunderbolt fighters equipped with long-range tanks on the initial part of the outbound journey, and these proved very successful against the Bf 110 Zerstörer fighters sent against them.

Below: Douglas Dakota of RAF Transport Command. The vertical bars on the empennage and wings were applied to all aircraft prior to D-Day to help visual indentification in the crowded skies over Normandy.

Operation 'Gomorrah' — the Hamburg Raids

At the end of July 1943 Hamburg was subjected to the most devastating aerial attacks of the war thus far. By night massed formations of Bomber Command aircraft utilising Window (lightweight strips of reflective material that were ejected from aircraft to obscure the German radar screens) and guided by Pathfinder Force aircraft equipped with H2S radar attacked Germany's second city. During the day the US Eighth Air Force dispatched more. A huge fire storm created by a raid on July 27-28, killed some 41,800 people, injured 38,000 more, and prompted a mass exodus of 1,200,000 others from the city. The attacks continued unabated for a week, during which some 8,621 tonnes of bombs rained down on the city. The scope of these combined attacks was widened to include other German cities through the summer, supplemented by raids on northern Italy by Bomber Command aircraft in early August. The damage rendered during these raids was undoubtedly a factor in the decision of the Italian people to agree an armistice with the Allies on September 8.

The climax of Gomorrah came at a disastrous time for the Luftwaffe, which had lost hundreds of aircraft in the attempt to stem the Allied invasion of Italy. 'Window' temporarily threw its defences into disarray, but further strengthening of both the day and night fighter forces with units withdrawn from other fronts and the introduction of the new Wilde Sau tactics that allowed single-engine fighter pilots relying on visual interception to range freely in flak free zones, led to a dramatic rise in its successes against night raiders. On September, 18 a massed attack by 596 Bomber Command aircraft hammered the German missile-producing facility at Peenemunde on the Baltic coast, causing substantial damage and generating crucial delays in the V2 project. However, the efficiency of the German defences, particularly the night-fighter units, cost some 40 aircraft. In October the USAAF suffered such losses during a series of raids on targets deep into Germany, most notably against the ball-bearing factories at Schweinfurt on October 14, that it was forced to abandon deep-penetration unescorted daylight raids. Bomber Command, by contrast, launched a massive offensive against Berlin that

Above: Republic P-47 Thunderbolt.

aimed ultimately at bombing Germany out of the war. This was its most bitter campaign of the war.

The assault on Berlin commenced on the night of November 18-19, when 444 bombers were sent against the city; another force of 325 heavy bombers attacked Mannheim. In the period that followed lasting until the end of March Berlin suffered 16 major raids. During the winter both the Vickers Wellington and Short Stirling bombers were withdrawn to less demanding roles in the face of mounting losses to the German defenders. The Luftwaffe night-fighter crews were aided by some important electronic innovations. One of these was a device codenamed 'Naxos' that allowed the fighters to home in on British H2S radar transmissions. Harris ordered a partial H2S silence for October, and a tail warning device was introduced on British aircraft. Unbeknown to the British, however, this equipment acted like a beacon to guide the enemy into the attack. But despite the heavy losses of the autumn and the forced withdrawal of nearly one

third of his fleet by January 1944, Harris remained convinced that strategic bombing held the key to victory and pressed on with the attacks on Berlin through the winter. The losses sustained during these attacks were quite insupportable; from November 1943 to March 1944, a total of 587 aircraft were lost, almost all of them Lancasters. The Battle of Berlin failed to deliver the final victory Harris had promised and was considered by many as a resounding defeat.

Arrival of the Mustang

A key turn in events came with the arrival in service of the North-American P-51B-1NA Mustang. Never has an aircraft been more keenly received than this. Equipped with two 75US-gal tanks, plus a rear fuselage tank, the aircraft could range deep into Germany, providing cover for the bombers of the 8th Air Force for the duration of a mission. It was vastly superior to anything that the Germans could field, and more than any other aircraft (with the possible exception of the Spitfire) it helped turn the tide of the war firmly to the advantage of the Allies. Mustangs began operations over Germany in early 1944. By this time the Luftwaffe was running desperately short of experienced pilots and aircraft. On December 31, 1943, it could field only 343 single-engine fighter aircraft for the defence of the Reich, to which could be added 196 twin-engine heavy fighters. Against them were pitted some 1,500 B-17s and Consolidated B-24 Liberators of the US 8th and 15th Air Forces, backed by over 1,200 fighters. But Hitler still failed to accord his defence forces the resources they

Left: Examples of the North American P-51 Mustang, the finest offensive fighter of the war.

needed. Bomber aircraft continued to be built at the expense of fighters and these were wasted in a hopeless bombing offensive launched on January 20, 1944 against London. Crisis deepened during the all-out day and night bomber offensive that has become known as 'Big Week'. This aimed at obliterating centres of German aircraft production and was launched in late February. At the end of a week of intensive bombing the Luftwaffe had lost 293 fighters destroyed and 90 damaged. The Allied losses had been equally heavy, but replacements were more easily at hand. But the events in March proved that the Luftwaffe, or at least its Nachtgeschwader, was still a formidable foe.

The epic Battle of Berlin drew to a close on March 24, 1944. Losses had been high but sustainable, whilst the nightfighter force had grown ever more skilful. No sign of an impending collapse in the German nation's will to resist had been signalled. Earlier in the month Harris had ordered his Command to commence operations against German transportation centres in preparation for the Second Front. Harris was fully aware that he would be required to sacrifice more aircraft to this cause, as would the US Eighth Air Force, but on the night of 30-31 dispatched 795 heavy bombers to Nuremberg. In the clear moonlit sky over the target 95 of the bombers were shot down, and a further 71 were badly damaged. It was the biggest night battle of the war, and victory went to the Luftwaffe. Once again it proved that for a successful bomber offensive opposition in the air had to be defeated.

D-DAY AND THE FALL OF FRANCE

Plans for the cross-Channel invasion of France had been drawn up by the British Joint Planning staff as early as September 1941, but serious discussion of the viability of an invasion began in earnest after American entry into the war. The invasion

force, comprising nearly three million men, was to be supported by massive strategic and tactical air support. The Allied Expeditionary Air Force was formed in November 1943 to co-ordinate this support under Air Marshal Leigh-Mallory. To the AEAF were subordinated air forces of the 2nd Tactical Air Force, formed in late 1943 (including No 2 Group which had left Bomber Command on June 1st), the US 9th Air Force and the whole of Fighter Command. The man chosen to be deputy leader of this vast aerial task force was desert veteran Air Chief Marshal Sir Arthur Tedder.

Air superiority was a vital part of the Allied plan, and Eisenhower decided to delay the invasion by one month to further reduce the operational strength of the Luftwaffe. Control of the AEAF, including Bomber Command, passed to General Eisenhower in mid-April 1944 in order to simplify the chain of command. Although both Bomber Command and the 8th Air Force continued to attack German cities in the late spring most effort was concentrated into attacks on transportation centres in France so as to hinder enemy movement after the Normandy invasions. To maintain the secrecy surrounding the operation simultaneous raids were carried out throughout northern France, particularly in the Pas de Calais region. From the end of May the heavily fortified defensive positions forming the Atlantic Wall were targeted, and once again, so as to conceal the intended invasion area, the sites attacked stretched right down the coast. During the build up to the invasion aircraft of 2TAF and the 9th Air Force struck at rail targets, V-1 missile sites and Luftwaffe bases while the fighters flew on protection missions. The resources of the Luftwaffe were increasingly overstretched and fighter combats over France were becoming rarer. Its aircraft were now being conserved for operations against the daylight bombing raids of the 8th Air Force.

By June 1944, the strength of the Allied air formations committed to Overlord amounted to 3,467 heavy US and British bombers, 1,645 light, medium and torpedo-bombers, 5,409 fighters, and 2,316 transports and troop carriers. On May 31, the Luftwaffe had a strength of 6,141 first-line aircraft dissipated through Europe and on the Eastern Front. In France and the Low Countries were some 827 of these aircraft. It was a seemingly paltry force with which to oppose the Allied onslaught. Furthermore, the Allied air offensive against German synthetic oil production centres was creating a desperate shortage of fuel.

In the hours prior to the invasion on June 6 Bomber Command flew 1,200 sorties against enemy targets and in the hours after the troops had begun pouring onto the beaches its crews flew over 1,000 sorties, dropping over 5,000 tons of bombs on enemy communications, airfields and ports. In the Straits of Dover a unit of No 617 Squadron dropped 'Window' to confuse the enemy radar sites.

Forces of the British 6th Airborne Division and the US 82nd and 101st Airborne were the first in, conveyed across the Channel by an armada of RAF Transport Command Armstrong Whitworth Albemarles, Douglas Dakotas and US Douglas C-47s, some of them dropping by parachute with the heavier equipment in gliders. These units drew two attacking Panzer divisions into the battle and were supported by close-support aircraft of the Tactical Air Force. British and Canadian troops stormed ashore from landing craft onto Gold, Juna, and Sword beaches, supported by a massive naval bombardment and heavy bombing attacks. The landings on the British beaches met with only light resistance, and contact with airborne forces of the 6th Airborne Division was rapidly made. Further west, the American landings on Omaha beach by V Corps were hampered by heavy surf, steep cliffs and stubborn German resistance. Hitler was slow to react, however, and delayed moving the 19th Army south from Calais. By the evening of June 6, all 150,000 men of the invasion fleet were ashore and beachheads had been established.

Close Air Support

After the bridgehead at Normandy was secured Allied tactical aircraft were deployed to operating strips built by airfield construction units. By June 27, there were 38 Allied fighter and fighter-bomber squadrons operating from 13 improvised airfields. While the fighter squadrons maintained air superiority over the battlefields, the fighter bomber squadrons were used in the close-air support role, a vital feature of the campaign through northwest Europe. The importance of tactical close air support was realised by Air Marshal Tedder during the campaign in North Africa. Co-operation between Tedder's Desert Air Force and Montgomery's Eighth Army worked effectively in this theatre because the air commander retained full control of his subordinate units, and could respond to various threats as he saw fit. The role of dedicated Tactical Air Force close-air support squadrons, equipped predominantly with aircraft such as the Hawker Typhoon and P-47 Thunderbolt, was to provide ground forces with a form of aerial artillery to suppress German defences. Field-based ground-to-air radio links meant attacks could be called in on targets at short notice. During the battle for France aircraft armed with armour piercing rockets and cannon were used to cripple German supply columns and columns of armour.

Below: A Republic P-47 Thunderbolt.

Breakout from Normandy

Air attacks continued to harry the German divisions in the week after the landings, and although storms in the Channel threatened to disrupt unloading at the beaches, the Allied advance from the beachheads continued apace. US forces captured the port of Cherbourg on June 26, and by July 1, the Allies had equalled the German forces in strength on the Continent. With nearly one million men and 177,000 vehicles opposing him, Hitler still continued to refuse to allow divisions in the Pas de Calais region to move south. Eisenhower seized this opportunity to breakout from the beachhead and between July 7 and July 15, six massive carpet-bombing raids were carried out in front of the Allied positions at Normandy. These attacks wreaked considerable destruction on the German troops, but also caused casualties among the Allied forces. Bradley's 1st Army divisions achieved a vital breakout to Avranches on July 31 and secured the Cotentin Peninsula.

On August 15, with the Allied breakout in full flood, an attack was launched between Cannes and

Right: Close-up of the Lancaster cockpit.

Toulon, throwing German defences into further confusion. In Normandy, 16 German divisions of Army Group B were trapped in a pocket around Falaise between the advancing Allied armies and were virtually annihilated by rocket-firing Typhoons of 2TAF in one of the most brutal displays of air power witnessed in the war. At the same time a bombing offensive was launched against ports along the Channel coast, where the isolated German garrisons were holding out. The ports were heavily damaged, and civilian casualties were high. Bomber Command alone flew nearly 6,000 sorties against them, losing only 14 aircraft in the process. Paris was liberated by August 25, with the

Above: *City of Lincoln* on final approach.

Germans now in headlong flight. The losses to Luftflotte III, charged with the defence of the Western ramparts, were staggering. Between June 1 and August 31, it lost some 2,195 combat aircraft. However, the rapid advance had left Allied supply lines overstretched, and the armies were still reliant on the temporary harbour at Normandy. The result was a significant loss of momentum, giving the Germans time to consolidate their defences. By early September, the Germans had retired to their defended lines in the Netherlands, and along

Above: The Gloster Meteor, Britain's first operational jet fighter.

the fortified Siegfried Line. Eisenhower continued to pursue his relentless advance, provoking further arguments between his field commanders, Montgomery and Patton, who were both anxious to see a concentration of forces behind their respective spearheads.

Eisenhower gave his support to Montgomery's disastrous airborne assault at Arnhem, Operation Market Garden, which was designed to capture three important Dutch river positions and hasten the Allied advance. The attack was launched on September 17 and rapidly ran into considerable opposition from two SS Panzer divisions. In the air the fighter opposition was considerable, and both the Allied transport aircraft and their fighter support received a mauling at the hands of the Luftwaffe. On September 25, the surviving ground forces were pulled out. Only 2,000 of the 9,000 British airborne troops survived. This costly defeat showed that although the Germans were on the back foot, they were far from beaten.

But reinforcements were continuing to pour into France, and as autumn began to descend on western Europe, the Nazi position was becoming increasingly untenable. Hitler's armies were fighting in northern and southern France, in northern Italy, and on the vast Eastern Front. In the German heartland, the mighty bomber fleets were reducing production lines to a shambles. The bomber crews, however, faced mounting opposition in the skies over the Reich, which by now including the revolutionary Messerschmitt Me 262 jet and Me 163B-1 rocket-fighter. Command of the heavy bomber groups was therefore returned to their respective commanders-in-chief. The freezing winter of 1944–45 would prove that the Germans were not yet prepared to accept the defeat that was now inevitable.

Below: Heinkel He162 Salamander—the *Volksjäger*.

Left: Meteors at dispersal.

Below: The Me262 *Schwalbe* lifts-off. This was the time when the aircraft was at its most vulnerable.

Bottom: A line-up of Me262s. Although it represented a huge technological achievement, introduction of the Me262 was fatally delayed by political meddling.

Battle of the Bulge

In late November, 25 divisions, virtually all the German reserve, were assembled for an attack through the heavily wooded semi-mountainous Ardennes region that lay at the centre of the Allied line. Hitler aimed to punch through this line, split the British and American forces and stabilise the Western front. Even at this stage, and without knowledge of the Allied commitment to the total defeat of Germany, he believed the British and Americans would sue for peace. The scene was thus set for the last major German offensive in the West. On December 16, the German units, which included 11 Panzer divisions, attacked through the Ardennes achieving complete surprise. They rapidly overran the six US divisions guarding a 60 mile (97 km) front and began the race to Antwerp, creating a huge 'bulge' in the Allied line. Eisenhower was slow to react, and with heavy snowstorms grounding the Allied air forces the German forces made rapid advances. Soon they were plagued by the problem that had hampered their operations for months — shortage of fuel. A rapid reinforcement of 200,000 Allied troops was rushed into the battle and on December 23, the weather cleared and tactical air units were able to fly 600 missions. Attacks on German armour forced the attackers on to the back heel. By the end of the year the Germans were retreating through the forest and, by the end of January 1945, all German gains from the Ardennes offensive were in Allied control.

The Final Battles

Bomber Command resumed the air offensive on August 15, 1944, and was released from the control of Supreme Headquarters in mid-September. In August, a total of 65,855 tons of bombs were dropped by 1,200 aircraft, with much improved accuracy afforded by improved radar and navigation aids. Much of the edge was taken off the Luftwaffe night-fighter arm as early warning radar stations fell in the wake of Allied advance. The Air Staff were divided over the choice of target systems that should be attacked, but in the event a directive of September 25, 1944, prioritised the German petroleum industry.

Victory for the Eighth

In the early winter of 1944 came firm evidence that round-the-clock bombing of the German aircraft industry by the 8th Air Force and Bomber Command had failed. During 1944, a herculean effort by the embattled German aircraft industry produced a record number of fighter aircraft. Production peaked

in September at 3,375. With the introduction of types such as the Bf 109G-10 and K-4 and the FW 190D-9, some parity with the P-51D and Hawker Tempest was achieved, and these fought out the battle for air superiority over the Reich through the winter of 1944-45. But mere numbers could not assuage the handicap of inexperienced pilots and fuel shortages, and during November the German fighter arm was savaged by the 8th Air Force with losses totalling 672 aircraft destroyed.

In mid-October, massive attacks were launched against Cologne and Duisberg and with Allied air superiority virtually unchallenged losses were very low. Bomber Command had by this time reached a strength of 94 squadrons. On New Year's Day 1945 the RAF received an expensive warning against complacency when the airfields of 2TAF were attacked by a fleet of 800 German aircraft. Some 144 Allied aircraft were destroyed on the ground, but the aircrew losses suffered by the Luftwaffe effectively ruled out further air operations. The closing months of the war saw a continuation of numerous and widely scattered attacks across Germany and the remaining occupied territories. Two operations in particular were notable. The first was the sinking of the battleship *Tirpitz* in Tromso fjord by Nos 9 and 617 Squadrons on November 12, 1944. The vessel was struck by at least two 12,000 lb 'Tallboy' bombs before rolling over. Second was the controversial attack on Dresden on the night of February 13-14, 1945. This city had escaped heavy bombing thus far in the war, and was suggested by the Air Staff as a target to Harris in a letter of January 25, 1945. The raid was carried out by a force of 773 Lancasters in two waves, dropping more than 1,800 tons of bombs. A massive fire storm similar to that seen at Hamburg engulfed the old city, killing as many as 50,000 people and destroying many of its historic buildings.

Fall of Berlin

Hitler continued to refuse von Runstedt to order a withdrawal behind the Rhine in the spring as the bulk of the Allied forces returned to the offensive. Montgomery planned a set-piece assault across the Rhine, codenamed Operation Plunder, for March 24. Importantly, effective air preparation and support was organised and through the night prior to the assault, heavy bombing attacks were concentrated on bridges, railway centres, airfields and barracks. Early the next morning aircraft and gliders of Nos 38 and 46 Groups, RAF Transport Command, assaulted across the river. Soon after a unit of the US 1st Army had brilliantly snatched the Remagen bridge over the Rhine, Patton sneaked a unit of the 3rd Army across the river at Oppenheim. Effective German resistance ended after the Allies crossed the Rhine and advances were rapid. The Luftwaffe was by now reduced to cursory attacks, primarily because of a chronic shortage of fuel, enabling Allied aircraft to operate with impunity over Berlin. The last major bombing operation of the war was concentrated against the naval base at Kiel on May 2-3. The success of the Strategic Bombing Offensive is often judged in the simple terms of its prewar aims, and the fact German industry was not brought to its knees remains undisputed. Production in some sectors of industry actually increased. But by diverting valuable forces away from the front into defence during this period, the Allied bomber crews not only gave indirect and vital support to the Red Army at a crucial stage in the conflict but more importantly helped prepare for the second front.

The Reichstag was stormed by Russian troops on April 30, the same day that Adolf Hitler committed suicide. On May 2, with the position now hopeless, General Weidling, the Commandant of Berlin, called on his troops to lay down their arms.

FRANCE

AMIOT 143

Most numerous among France's chronically anti-quated bombers at the start of the Second World War, the Amiot 143 was designed to meet a 1928 specification for a Multiplace de Combat aircraft. It first flew as the Amiot 140 in April 1931. With a slab-sided, stepped fuselage and high wing, it had a fixed landing gear with the mainwheels enclosed in large spats, heavily braced to the fuselage sides. The wing was deep enough for a crew member to reach the rear of each engine in flight. As though to reflect its ungainly, flying boxcar appearance, the Amiot 140 managed a modest top speed of under 200 mph. Neither was it well armed, its defensive guns being of updated World War 1 vintage Lewis type with drum ammunition feed.

During further development towards a production machine, the 140 became the 143 which entered service in August 1935. When war came in 1939 the Amiots initially carried out leaflet raids, soon switching to more lethal payloads. Despite looking like a Messerschmitt pilot's dream, the Amiots proved remarkably resilient during the German invasion and in a total of 197 night bombing operations, they dropped 338,626 lb of bombs, losing only

four aircraft in the process. Daylight raids were an entirely different matter, two Groupes being practically wiped out during desperate operations in the Sedan area. Vichy

French forces continued to use the surviving Amiots, mainly as transports, after the armistice and they continued to serve in that role in Tunisia until 1944.

Specification: Amiot 143
Type: Twin-engined medium bomber
Manufacturer: Avions Amiot
Number built: 138
Entry into service: August 1935
Length: 59 ft 11 in (18.25 m)
Height: 18 ft 7.75 in (5.65 m)
Wingspan: 80 ft 6 in (24.53 m)
Weight empty: 13, 448 lb (6,100 kg)
Range: 746 miles (1,200 km)
Max speed: 193 mph (310 km/h)
Service ceiling: 25,930 ft (9,000 m)
Armaments: 4 x 7.5-mm MAC 1934 machine guns and up to 1,764 lb (800 kg) of bombs internally and on wing racks

Above: A line up of Amiot 143 bombers.

Left: The Amiot 143 saw little World War II service but performed the missions it did more capably than its appearance would suggest.

BLOCH MB 151/152

Few aircraft can have started out as badly as the odd-looking prototype Bloch 150 fighter, which would probably have been cancelled had it not been for the threat of war. On July 17, 1936 the squat aircraft, fitted with a 930 hp Gnome-Rhone 14 Kfs radial engine, failed to take off for its maiden flight. Drastic redesign was obviously necessary and the project was shelved in August 1936 but revived in 1937 when the single-seater was given a greater wingspan and more engine power which enabled test flying and development to proceed. The first flight took place on 29 September.

With France having a requirement for a substantial number of fighters — which could not be met entirely by the favored MS 406 — it was decided to produce the MB 150 and order the Hawk 75A from the USA. One reason was that the MS 406 was hampered by the low production rate of Hispano Suiza engines whereas the Gnome-Rhone 14N powerplant for the MB 150 was available in quantity. Alternative

Below: A Vichy French Bloch MB 151.

Specification: Bloch MB 152
Type: Single-seat interceptor fighter
Manufacturer: SNCASO
Number built: 628 (140 MB 151/488 MB 152)
Entry into service: 1939
Length: 29 ft 10 in (9.1 m)
Height: 13 ft (3.95 m)
Wingspan: 34 ft 6.75 in (10.5 m)
Range: 373 miles (600 km)
Max speed: 323 mph (520 km/h)
Service ceiling: 32,800 ft (10,000 m)
Armaments: 2 x 20-mm Hispano 404 cannon and 2 x 7.7-mm MAC 1934 machine guns or 4 x MAC machine guns in wings

powerplants were also investigated while the newly-state-owned SNCASCO factories struggled to build the complex MB 150, completing 25 examples before the MB 151 was introduced, followed by the more powerful MB 152. Only 85 had been delivered by the start of World War 2 and these lacked essential equipment such as gunsights and even propellers. These problems were quickly rectified however and examples were delivered to xx [ed: info missing?] Groupes de Chasse by the time of the German invasion in May 1940. Rugged and well armed for its day with two 20-mm cannon and two machine guns, the MB 152 saw

limited combat with the Luftwaffe although over 100 were destroyed on the ground during the initial assault. A difficult aircraft to fly, the MB 152 was the subject of further production contracts, but the fall of France put paid to them.

Development continued with the MB 155 powered by a 1,180 hp Gnome-Rhone engine and peaked at the projected and potentially very capable MB 157, which was never put into production. After the armistice, Vichy French forces flew the MB 155 and Germany and Greece used Bloch fighters as trainers; 20 were also passed to Rumania for similar use.

BREGUET 690

One of the best designs to meet the very demanding international trend for a twin-engined multi-place fighter able to hold its own against single-seaters. This was an ideal that was rarely achieved but the Breguet 690 series came very close. When it first flew on 23 March 1938, the prototype showed a potentially better performance than France's primary single-seat fighter, the MS 406.

With its distinctly curved 'tadpole' fuselage and closely-cowled engines, the twin-finned Br 691/3 performed well. The aircraft was very manoeuvrable and for ground attacks it had a useful close grouping of a single 20-mm cannon and two machine guns in the nose. This battery of guns could be swivelled downwards 15 degrees for ground strafing and a fuselage bay held up to eight 110 lb bombs

Put into production as a light attack type, the Br 691 (first flight March 22, 1939) had Hispano-Suiza radial engines and the subsequent Br 693 (October 25, 1939) two Gnome-Rhones, both sub-types having a similar performance. Only 224 examples were delivered to the Armée de l'Air but a percentage of

these fought well before the parent units were decimated by the German onslaught. Front-line units found the Breguet very simple to maintain, a huge asset in the type of unco-ordinated combat operations the French units found themselves faced with in 1940.

In addition to the main French-engined models, 50 Br 695s were re-engined with Pratt & Whitney Twin Wasp Junior engines by the time of the capitulation. Although the American engines had some

adverse effect on handling qualities, such problems could surely have been eradicated in time — but there was no time left. Many of the seized Breguets were passed on to Italy, the Regia Aeronautica using them mainly as operational trainers.

Specification: Breguet 691-695
Type: Twin-engined light attack bomber
Manufacturer: Soc Louis Breguet
Number built: 304
Entry into service: Spring 1940
Length: 33 ft 7 in (10.22 m)
Height: 10 ft 3.75 in (3.4 m)
Wingspan: 50 ft 4.75 in (15.3 m)
Weight empty: 6,834 lb (3,100 kg)
Range: 840 miles (1,350 km)
Max speed: 300 mph (483 km/h)
Service ceiling: 27,885 ft (8,500 m)
Armaments: 1 x 20-mm Hispano cannon and 2 x 7.5-mm machine guns in nose and 1 x MAC 1934 for rear defense; up to eight 110 lb (50 kg) bombs

Below: Prototype Breguet 690.

DEWOITINE D 520

S o many high-quality products of the French aircraft industry were stifled before they had a chance to prove themselves in combat and the D 520 well summed up the 'too little, too late' situation that prevailed by 1940. When the Germans showed how a well organised and led air force could achieve incredible results very quickly indeed, France paid heavily for a chaotic prewar industrial situation that simply did not deliver enough aircraft in time.

Designed as a private venture by the Dewoitine company and presented to the Air Ministry in January 1937, the D 520 was awarded a prototype contract in April 1938. The first example, the D 520-01, flew for the first time on October 2, 1938 at Toulouse-Francazals. Powered by an 895 hp Hispano-Suiza 12Y-21 engine driving a two-blade airscrew, the new fighter was found to have speed limitations imposed by poor radiator design. This was revised and a three-blade airscrew was fitted as were increased area vertical tail surfaces. Trials using three prototypes were completed in March 1939, a contract for 200 aircraft following soon afterwards. Delays occurred with the result that the first true pro-

duction D 520 was not completed until December 1939. More revisional work needed to be carried out resulting in the first combat ready aircraft not being delivered until April 1940. Only GC I/3 was fully equipped by May 10. Four more units became operational in time to combat the Luftwaffe and although there were more D 520s in air force hands, there was no time to convert more first line Groupes. In combat the D 520 was credited with 108 confirmed victories and 39 probables

for the loss of around 100 of the French fighters to all causes.

Development of the D 520 did not stop with the armistice and 10 units of the Armistice Air Force in North Africa flew the type at the time of Operation Torch. Some units went into action against the Allied air forces supporting the invasion, while others sided with the invaders. The D 520 saw little further combat until December 1, 1944 when the Armée de l'Air was reorganised and re-equipped with mainly Allied air-

Specification: Dewoitine D 520
Specification: Dewoitine D 520
Type: Single-seat interceptor fighter
Manufacturer: SNCA du Midi
Number built: 905
Entry into service: May 1940
Length: 28 ft 8.5 in (8.75 m)
Height: 11 ft 3 in (3.4 m)
Wingspan: 33 ft 5.75 in (10.2 m)
Weight empty: 4,630 lb (2,100 kg)
Range: 777 miles (1,240 km)
Max speed: 329 mph (530 km/h)
Service ceiling: 36,090 ft (11,000 m)
Armaments: 1 x 20-mm Hispano-Suiza 404 cannon firing through propeller hub plus 4 x 7.5-mm MAC 1934 machine guns in wings

Right: The D 520 continued in production after the fall of France and would see action in the hands of the Free French when recaptured in late 1944.

Overleaf: The fine lines of the D 520, undoubtedly France's best fighter when war began, are shown well in these photographs.

Above: Armée de l'Air D 520s circa 1940.

Right: A long nose hampered D 520 pilots' ground view.

Below right: Unique French camouflage pattern on a D 520, widely reckoned as France's best wartime fighter.

craft. The French fighter did fly further sorties with French pilots at the controls but the largest second line use was by the Luftwaffe, which equipped three training Gruppen, and the Regia Aeronautica, which deployed the D 520 in a similar role. Others were passed to Bulgaria and Rumania.

LEO 451

The best bomber produced in France in time to see combat during the 1940 invasion, the Lioré et Olivier 451 was one of a family of modern twin-engined aircraft designed to meet a 1934 specification. This called for a four-seat medium bomber with a 2,645 lb bomb load and cannon armament. The prototype LeO 451 made its maiden flight on January 16, 1937 as the LeO 45-01.

In July, trials with the prototype which had in the meantime had some tail modifications, included a recorded top speed of 388 mph in a shallow dive. Despite this, the 1,078 hp Hispano Suiza 14AA engines were shown to be quite unreliable, but without an alternative power-plant, 20 machines were ordered in January 1938. More modifications were made to the prototype and in August 1938 it was decided to switch to Gnome-Rhone 14N 20/21 radials of 1,030 hp, the aircraft being redesignated the LeO 451. The first production LeO 451 flew at Villacoublay on March 24, 1939.

Production was increased and by the outbreak of war the 31e Escadre had five LeO 451s on strength, these conducting some of the first operational reconnaissance missions over Germany. Having first dropped bombs in anger on May 11, there

Specification: Lioré et Olivier 451
Type: Twin-engined medium bomber
Manufacturer: Soc Lioré et Olivier (SNCASE)
Number built: 452
Entry into service: August 1939
Length: 56 ft 4 in (17.17 m)
Height: 14 ft 9.25 in (4.50 m)
Wingspan: 73 ft 10.75 in (22.52 in)
Weight empty: 17,225 lb (7,813 kg)
Range: 1,430 miles (2,300 km)
Max speed: 307 mph (495 km/h)
Service ceiling: 29,530 ft (9,000 m)
Armaments: 1 x 20-mm Hispano-Suiza 404 cannon in dorsal position pus 1 x MAC 1934 machine gun firing forward; up to 4,410 lb of bombs (2,000 kg) in internal bay

were eight first line Groupes by early June 1940. Thrown in to stem the Wehrmacht advance, these units generally acquitted themselves well, although casualties were high on some missions. The LeO 451's 20-mm cannon defence, although not as effective as had been anticipated, could hold off attacking fighters, one gunner shooting down two Bf 110s on a June 6, sortie. Bombing operations were also generally successful but these were curtailed when the armistice was signed on 23 June 1940. Therafter, the LeO 451 served in Vichy units and development aircraft, often under designations

derived from different engines, were completed while France enjoyed an uneasy peace. Action flared again after the Allies invaded North Africa in November 1942, there subsequently being numerous transport flights for the USAAF as well as bombing missions under Allied command — while spares for the aircraft lasted. The Italians and Germans operated many Leo 451s, the Luftwaffe drafting two into its clandestine unit KG 200.

Below: A LeO 451 prototype.

MORANE-SAULNIER MS 406

Most numerous of the French fighters at the outbreak of war, the MS 406 was a rugged and reliable aircraft without being outstanding in any one area. In response to an Air Ministry specification of 1934 for a single-seat fighter Morane-Saulnier submitted its MS 405 design. The company proceeded with a prototype even though a winner was not immediately chosen from a number of submissions and the prototype first flew on August 8, 1935 at Villacoublay.

A dumpy, low-wing monoplane designed to have a 20-mm cannon mounted between the cylinder banks of its Hispano-Suiza Vee inline engine, the MS 405-01 was followed by a second prototype. In the meantime a small production order for the fighter, as the implied winner of the 1934 competition, was confirmed. By the autumn of 1937 both these machines had been lost in accidents but the first order for 15 aircraft was completed, the design

Specification: Morane Saulnier MS 406
Type: Single-seat interceptor fighter
Manufacturer: Aeroplanes Morane Saulnier
Number built: 1,098
Entry into service: 1.098
Length: 26 ft 9.25 in (8.16 m)
Height: 9 ft 3.75 in (2.83 m)
Wingspan: 34 ft 9.75 in (10.60 m)
Weight empty: 4,189 lb (1,900 kg)
Range: 497 miles (800 km)
Max speed: 302 mph (485 km/h)
Service ceiling: 30,840 ft (9,400 m)
Armaments: 1 x 20-mm Hispano-Suiza HS-9 or 404 cannon firing through propeller hub plus 2 x 7.5 mm MAC 1934 machine guns in wings.

number having previously been changed to MS 406.

With some basic modifications the MS 406 was set for volume production but various delays, particularly in deliveries of engines, meant that service debut did not take place until the late autumn of 1938. Apart from some criticism of the

vulnerability of hydraulic and electrical systems to enemy fire, the MS 406 was welcomed by the Armée de l'Air. Production picked up significantly before the German invasion.

Combat-worthy MS 406s had an 860 hp Hispano-Suiza inline engine, the centerline 20-mm cannon and

Above: An MS 406 with its telescopic gunsight well shown.

Below left: An MS 406 saved to become a museum exhibit.

Below: More MS 406s were available than any other French fighter when the Germans struck on May 10.

two 7.5-mm machine guns in the wings. Maximum speed at 6,560 ft was 281 mph and although the aircraft had a useful ceiling of 32,800 ft, pilots complained that the guns had a tendency to freeze up at such altitudes.

When the French air force was mobilised for war in 1939 there were 13 Groupes de Chasse combat ready with the MS 406 and these carried out numerous operational flights during the Phoney War. Up to the

German invasion, French pilots scored 32 confirmed victories for the loss of 13 MS 406s shot down and 33 written off.

Although the number of combat units flying the Morane was increased before the German onslaught there was an urgent need to replace it with a fighter better able to combat the Bf 109. Losses were heavy in the first days of the fighting and re-equipment did go ahead to the extent that by the armistice there

Above: The angle of the MS 406's landing gear is well shown in this view.

were only four MS 406 Groupes left in France.

In common with many French aircraft, the MS 406 found as much if not more deployment with post-armistice Vichy and foreign air forces which had ordered it or taken out licence-build agreements. Although some export orders could not be fulfilled, the MS 406 saw service in Finland where its 20-mm cannon was a useful ground strafing weapon. The Finns found the Morane to be an excellent fighter and in late 1943 a Soviet development of the Hispano engine was fitted to provide a much needed power boost to 1,100 hp. By the Russo-Finnish armistice the MS 406 had scored 121 victories. Tha last country to use the MS 406 was Switzerland which license built its own version with some modifications and kept it in service until 1959.

Below: Many MS 406s were abandoned when the Armistice was signed.

POTEZ 630/631

Yet another effort to produce an effective strategic fighter with dual role capability in twin-engine configuration, the Potez 63 was the winner of a 1934 competition for a multi-seat fighter for the Armée de l'Air. An impressively streamlined, low wing design with end plate fins, the Potez 63 was powered by two 725 hp Hispano-Suiza 14AB radials. The prototype flew for the first time on April 25, 1936.

Early production concentrated on meeting export orders from such countries as Greece, Rumania and Switzerland and 10 prototypes were ordered for evaluation prior to French service. These were config-ured to fufill various roles: two- or three-seat day/night fighter; conver-sion trainer; light bomber; army co-operation and reconnaissance aircraft and attack bomber.

In the event the Potez 631 and 633 were ordered for the French air forces and 208 were delivered, enough to equip five air force fight-er squadrons, two of the Aeronaval squadrons and numerous smaller units. These machines gave a good account of themselves during the German invasion, scoring 29 aerial victories during the course of the battle. The variant most used by France was, however, the Potez 63-11. Given a deeper front fuselage,

Specification: Potez 63-11
Type: Twin-engined fighter bomber
Manufacturer: Avions Henri Potez
Number built: 1,300 (approx)
Entry into service: November 1939
Length: 36 ft 4 in (11.07 m)
Height: 11 ft 9.75 in (3.6 m)
Wingspan: 52 ft 6 in (16 m)
Weight empty: 6,912 lb (3,205 kg)
Range: Over 800 miles
Max speed: 264 mph (425 km/h)
Service ceiling: 26,250 ft (8,000 m)
Armaments: 7 x 7.5-mm MAC 1934 machine guns in fixed forward fuselage (including four in wing fairings) plus 3 x MAC 1934s in fixed aft-firing positions and 2 x MAC 1934s on flexible mount for rear defense; up to four 110 lb (50 kg) bombs on wing racks

Left: A Potez 630 bomber in French markings used in 1940.

Above: Well armed for its day, the Potez bomber series gave good if brief service.

Below: Extensive nose glazing hallmarked the Potez bombers.

nose glazing and shortened, raised cockpit canopy, it was virtually a new design, though not as aesthetically appealing as its forerunners. Many Potez 631 components were utilised and it was a sound enough combat aircraft which inherited the pleasant flight characteristics of its predecessor. Intended primarily as a reconnaissance aircraft, the 63-11 first flew in prototype form on December 31, 1938. Examples were operated by pro-Allied units in North Africa as well as Vichy French forces, the Luftwaffe, Greece and Rumania.

Right from the start the aircraft had been designed to take different powerplants and armament configurations and the French 63-11s usually had Gnome-Rhone 14 radials. Armament options included a relatively heavy (maximum) forward firing battery of four machine guns faired into the wing underside plus three in the fuselage. In addition, rear defence could comprise up to five machine guns in dorsal and ventral positions. A light bomb load was accommodated on inboard wing racks.

GERMANY

ARADO AR 196

A diminutive floatplane that became an important if modest contributor to Germany's neglected maritime airpower, the Arado Ar 196 was originally designed as a spotter for the Kriegsmarine's capital ships. It mainly replaced the biplane He 60 in this role, concurrently being deployed on patrol and reconnaissance duties from coastal land bases.

The Ar 196V-1 first flew in May 1938; there were five prototypes, all powered by the 880 hp BMW 132C radial engine with a two-blade propeller, these testing various float configurations prior to entering service. A single main float was tried but a twin, strongly braced arrangement was chosen for the first production model, the Ar 196A-1. Armament trials were also conducted, shortly before series production commenced in late 1938. The Arado 196A-1 had a 960 BMW 132K engine. The aircraft, stressed for catapulting and armed with two machine guns, could carry a small bomb load on underwing racks. Embarked on capital ships by the second half of 1939, both the Ar 196A-1 and the succeeding Ar 196A-3 had more powerful armament in the shape of two 20-mm MG FF cannon in the wings. These weapons supplemented the single fuselage machine gun and the twin guns provided for the observer who occupied the rear cockpit.

Increasing the armament was intended to broaden the type's role into that of coastal patrol and provide some attack capability, although unlike some of its foreign counterparts, the Ar 196 was not designed to have a dual configuration as a landplane. And while the deployment of floatplanes operating from

coastal waters had some limitations, the Arado units could be quite effective combat aircraft within their radius of action. For example, considerable audacity was required to persuade an enemy submarine to surrender to such an aircraft but that happened to HMS *Seal* on 5 May 1940. Caught on the surface and unable to dive due to mine damage, the *Seal* had little choice but to surrender to the floatplane crew after

it had attacked with guns and bombs.

Also operated widely in the Mediterranean and Adriatic as well as European coastal waters, the Ar 196 proving highly versatile, covering friendly shipping and driving off intruders with equal success. A dozen units, rarely larger than Staffel size, operated the Ar 196 which remained on Luftwaffe strength throughout the war.

Specification: Ar 196A-3
Type: Single-engined reconnaissance floatplane
Manufacturer: Arado Flugzeugwerke GmbH
Number built: 593
Entry into service: August 1939
Length: 36 ft 1 in (11 m)
Height: 4 ft 7.25 in (4.45m)
Wingspan: 40 ft 8.25 in (12.4 m)
Weight empty: 6,593 lb (2,990 kg)
Range: 665 miles (1,070km)
Max speed: 193 mph (310 km/h)
Service ceiling: 22,960 ft (7,000m)
Armaments: 2 x 20-mm MG FF wing cannon; 1 x 7.9-mm MG 17 machine gun in forward fuselage and 2 x MG 17 machine guns for rear defence; up to 220 lb (100 kg) of bombs on wing racks

Above: Many Ar 196s were used by Luftwaffe coastal patrol units.

Right: An Ar 196 is readied on its shipboard catapult.

Below left: An Ar 196 is hoisted aboard a ship under way.

Below: Building up the engine revs, an Ar 196 crew braces for the launch.

ARADO AR 234

As the world's first practical jet bomber, the Arado 234 did not see combat in numbers comparable to German jet fighters and was deployed mainly in the reconnaissance role in which it excelled. But by 1945 the ability to obtain photo coverage of targets all but immune from Allied interception was somewhat academic — there was little chance that those same targets would be bombed, even by Ar 234s. None of that lessened an outstanding achievement by Arado.

Arado began studies into a jet bomber in 1940 in response to an official requirement for a high speed reconnaissance aircraft powered by the turbojets then being developed. Late delivery of these new and temperamental engines delayed the first flight of the Ar 234 V1 until June 15,

Specification: Ar 234B
Type: Twin-engined jet medium bomber
Manufacturer: Arado
Number built: 222
Entry into service: 1944
Length: 41 ft 5.5 in (12.64 m)
Height: 14 ft 1.5 in (4.29 m)
Wingspan: 63 ft 3.5 in (14.44 m)
Weight empty: 11,464 lb (6,500 kg)
Range: 765 miles (1,215 km)
Max speed: 530 mph (852 km/h)
Service ceiling: 36,091 ft (11,000 m)
Armaments: Bomb load up to 3,000 lb (1,500 kg) on external racks

1943, Junkers Jumo 004B-0 power-plants having been installed in the meantime. Prototype testing continued and on April 8, 1944 the Ar 234 V6 flew, fitted with BMW 003A-1 turbojets.

Arado had also decided to fit a conventional landing gear instead of the skid arrangement originally proposed, the first aircraft so equipped flying for the first time on March 10, 1944. This, the V9, was the prototype

for the production model, the Ar 234B. Having decided after considerable testing to clear the engine for service use, the BMW power-plant was chosen and the first Ar 234B-0 flew in June 1944.

Issued to evaluation units, the Arado bomber quickly demonstrated its enormous potential and three Luftwaffe reconnaissance Staffeln commenced high altitude flights over Britain. A fourth Staffel received the Ar 234 in Italy. The first bomber Geschwader, KG 76, went operational during the 'Blitz' of the Battle of the Bulge in the winter of 1944 and there was subsequently much action around the Remargen bridge over the Rhine as the Luftwaffe tried to destroy the last Allied hurdle on the road to victory.

To boost its range the Arado 234 really needed four engines and development of the basic twin layout led to the Ar 234C. The prototype flew in September 1944 and examples of various sub-variants were flight tested before the German surrender. None entered service.

It was left to the victorious Allies, primarily the Russians, to complete some of the projects that had advanced beyond the drawing board stage. Arado's design expertise disappeared into the vastness of Russia, some German influence, particularly regarding engines, being reflected in later Soviet jet bomber design.

Left: Extensive nose glazing hallmarked the world's first jet bomber.

Below: An Ar 234 under evaluation in the US.

DORNIER DO 17/215

Nicknamed the 'Flying Pencil' when it was unveiled as a high speed mailplane for Lufthansa in 1934, the Dornier Do 17 was militarised and first flew in bomber configuration as the Do 17 E-1, able to carry a 1,102 lb (500 kg) bomb load internally. Developed from a common prototype shared with the early F series, the Do 17E-1 was intended primarily for reconnaissance duties. In 1937 15 Do 17F-1s were transferred to 1A./88 of the Condor Legion to see action in Spain and both the E and F series subsequently flew combat sorties in support of Franco's Nationalists.

A shortage of DB 600A inline engines led to the Do 17M and its Do 17P reconnaissance derivative being powered by the 865 hp BMW 132N radial. With three machine guns for defence the Do 17M-1 remained under-defended although Spain had highlighted this deficiency. A fourth gun was added to the small number of Do 17Us built, these aircraft entering combat use by the Luftwaffe in November 1939.

The Do 17Z was the most important of the early Dornier bombers and was built in the largest numbers, starting with the production of the Do 17Z-1. Still underpowered and consequently capable of carrying a bomb load no greater than the E and F, the early Do 17Zs were nevertheless pleasant to fly. The Do 17Z-3, -4 and -5 all had 1,000 hp Bramo 323P engines with a similar bomb load.

An important consideration for Germany following RAF night bombing raids was the need for night fighters, few of which were available. An interim solution lay in the Do 17Z-10. Fitted with a new 'solid' nose containing two 20-mm cannon and four machine guns the aircraft was alos equipped with the Spanner-Anlage infra-red sighting device. Only nine aircraft were completed but they indicated a useful secondary role for Dornier bombers. The Do 17Zs and earlir variants took part in the attack on Poland and operated over the Western Front but by the Battle of Britain the early Dorniers were fast disappearing, to be replaced by more modern bombers. By the time of the invasion of Russia only part of KG 2 and KG 3 were still using the Do 17 in

the bombing role, these being withdrawn by late 1942.

To be effective the Do 17 had always needed greater bomb capaci-

---

Specification: Do 17Z
Type: Twin-engined medium bomber
Manufacturer: Dornier GmbH
Number built: 528
Entry into service: 1939
Length: 52 ft 9.75 in (16.1m)
Height: 14 ft 11.24 in (4.55 m)
Wingspan: 59 ft (18 m)
Weight empty: 11,488 lb (5,210 kg)
Range: 721 miles (1,160 km)
Max speed: 214 mph (345 km/h)
Service ceiling: 26,904 ft (8,200 m)
Armaments: up to 6 x 7.9-mm machine guns in nose, windscreen, side windows, dorsal and ventral positions; bomb load of up to 2,205 lb (1,000 kg)

Above: One of many prototype
Do 17s.

Right: Luftwaffe personnel
examine the damage to a
Do 17.

Below right: Hand-bomb
hauling often saved time on
Do 17 airfields.

Below left: A Do 17 in Spanish
Civil War style markings.

Below: A Jumo-engined
Do 215.

ty, which meant at least a deeper
fuselage. This was partially addressed
in the interim Do 215 but the
answer lay in a comprehensive
redesign and this emerged as the
Do 217.

DORNIER DO 217

Evolving from the Do 215 to which it bore a superficial resemblence and from a naval requirement for a floatplane, the Do 217 became the last Dornier aircraft to see front line service in any numbers. An excellent aircraft, easy to fly and better defended than other German medium bomber, many Do 217s were expended in raids on England long past the time when 'pinprick' night raids had an effect on the outcome of the war. Many raids were ordered purely as vengeance for the Allied bombing of Germany, although the German defences were as powerless to stop the raids as the Luftwaffe was to destroy British cities with a few small aircraft.

First flying as the Do 217 V1 in August 1938 this and subsequent protypes had Daimler Benz or Junkers Jumo engines but the production Do 217E-1 of 1940 standardised on the 1,550 hp BMW 801 radial. Able to carry a 4,410 lb (2,000 kg) bomb load the Do 217E had good handling characteristics and was well defended by five machine guns and a 20-mm cannon.

Initially being deployed on long-range reconnaissance, the Do 217E, designed for a more offensive role, was first issued to II/KG 40 in the spring of 1941. KG 2, which became the main operating Geschwader, received its first aircraft that August. The Do 217E-3 with increased armour protection and eight guns was built before the Do 217E-2, both sub-types being similar; both had a dorsal turret, which was lacking on the Do 217E-1. Most Do 217s were built with a dive bombing capability although the tail dive brakes were often removed by combat units.

Adapted into other roles by issue of numerous Rustsatze (field conversion kits), the Do 217E became the first bomber in the world to release radio-controlled glider bombs against enemy ships. Adapted to launch the Hs 293A missile, the Do 217E-5 could carry two of them under the outer wing panels.

Night fighter conversions of the Do 217 continued to occupy Dornier, the Do 217J-1 appearing in 1942, and the succeeding J-2 being based on the E-2/3 bombers. Both were able to carry SN-2 airborne intercept radar which increased their ability to destroy enemy bombers, but the main drawback of the converted bombers was their high weight and a lack of manoeuvrabilty.

A new nose identified the last series of Do 217 bombers, beginning with the Do 217K which entered service with KG 2 in the autumn of

1942. Otherwise similar to the E models, the Do 217K had a completely new and larger nose which was extensively glazed without a

---

Specification: Do 217E
Type: Twin-engined medium bomber
Manufacturer: Dornier GmbH
Number built: 1,730
Entry into service: Winter 1940
Length: 59 ft 8.5 in (18.2m)
Height: 16 ft 6 in (5.03m)
Wingspan: 62 ft 4 in (19m)
Weight empty: 19,522 lb (8.950kg)
Range: 1,740 miles (2,800km)
Max speed: 320 mph (516 km/h)
Service ceiling: 29,529 ft (9,000m)
Armaments: 1 x 15-mm MG 151/15 cannon in nose plus 2 x MG 131 in dorsal turret and ventral position and 3 x MG 15 7.92-mm guns in additional nose and cockpitside windows; 8,818lb (4,000 kg) of bombs in internal bay and on wing racks.

cockpit 'step' as before. Powered by 1,700 hp BMW 801D engines the Do 217K could carry up to eight guns for defence and in K-2 and K-3 form, two Fritz X rocket-propelled missiles or two Hs 293As.

The Do 217M-1 was similar in configuration to the Do 217K apart from an engine switch to 1,750 hp DB 603A liquid cooled engines. Two sub-variants, the Do 217M-1 and the M-11 saw operational service. Dornier supplied the M series bomber equivalent as the Do 217N night fighter with four cannon and four machine guns in the nose, the stepped cockpit of the Do 217J being retained on all night fighter models.

Top right: The SN-2 AI radar was fitted to the Do 217J-2 night fighter.

Above right: A new nose distinguished the Do 217K.

Right: Bombs waiting to be loaded into a Do 217E.

Below left: A Do 217E prepares for a night sortie.

Below: An early Do 217N night fighter.

FIESLER FI 103

Known to those who had to withstand its impact as the 'Doodlebug', the first of Hitler's 'V for vengeance' weapons was a small pilotless airplane with an explosive warheasd. Developed by the Luftwaffe as the FZG 76, it was intended to deliver a 1,870 lb warhead from a fixed launching ramp powered by a fuel/air mix pulse jet. Originally developed as early as 1928, the pulse jet received more official backing in the late 1930s. Argus built the propulsion unit and by 1941 the first experimental models had flown, mounted on conventional bombers.

It was Hitler's intention to devastate the Operation Overlord invasion force in Normandy with V1s but Allied intelligence had advance warning of this and mass bombing of the first launching sites in France curtailed the offensive for a vital few weeks. No V1s were launched until June 13, but by the 29th, 2,000 had been aimed at London. Airborne attacks were also initiated by He 111s.

Bombing and the capture of the launching sites by Allied troops, plus countermeasures by massed AA guns and high speed fighters, rendered the V1 largely ineffective as 'war winning' weapon for the Germans. It did however cause widespread loss of life and damage to property in England, 2,419 falling on London.

In 1945, the SS took over the V1 program and numerous flying bombs were launched against the Dutch city of Antwerp.

Although it was a simple weapon to produce and some 50 times cheaper than the V2 rocket, the V1 suffered many 'dud' launchings and roughly four times the number had

Specification: FZG-76

Type: Unguided pilotless aircraft with explosive warhead

Manufacturer: Fieseler GmbH

Number built: c.35,000

Entry into service: First used mid-June 1944

Length: 25 ft 4.5 in (7.72m)

Wingspan: 17 ft 8.25 in (5.4m)

Weight: 4,750 lb (2,154 kg)

Range: 1,740 miles (2,800km)

Max speed: 360 mph (579 km/h)

Service ceiling: 2,500 ft (762m)

Armaments: 1,870 lb (848 kg)

to be fired compared to the actual hits. British and US fighters, including the RAF's jet Meteor, did their share in shooting down airborne V1s.

A 'last ditch' effort by the Nazis was to install a rudimetary cockpit on the V1 the intention being that unlike the kamikaze ideal of the Japanese, the German pilot would ostensibly bail out after aiming his bomb. Few believed this would be feasible as the V1's design all but prevented a safe exit. No actual sorties were launched.

Top: Many V1s still exist in museums.

Above: A preserved V1 complete with a section of launching ramp.

Left: Even the Germans contemplated suicide missions with piloted versions of the V1 flying bomb.

FIESLER FI 156

An aircraft that was so slow it was said to be able to fly backwards, the Fieseler Fi 156 Storch (Stork) was developed as an army co-operation aircraft for battlefield casevac and general liaison duties. It first flew in the spring of 1936 and deliveries to the Luftwaffe began early the following year.

A combination of wing flaps and slots enabled the Storch to virtually hover in a 25 mph headwind. It could land in 61 feet and take off in 213 feet, its maximum speed being 109 mph.Basically a three-seater aircraft it had a loaded weighed just short of 3,000 lbs.

The main service variant was the Fi 156C powered by an Argus As 10P engine. It operated wherever the Luftwaffe was engaged and was allocated to numerous staff officers as their personal transport. Reconnaissance duty and rescue flights saw Storch pilots making many hazardous trips behind enemy lines to bring back data and aircrew, the most famous Storch operation probably being that by commando Otto Skorzeny to recue Italian dictator Benito Mussolini. As German fortunes waned, a captured Storch was a prized possession by Allied units which often flew generals on front line visits in much the same way as their former owners.

Production extended to the similar Fi 156D, a production run of 2,549 examples ending with the Fi 156E. So useful was the Storch that French and Czech examples were built after the war.

Below: A preserved Fi 156 is ideal for mountain flying.

Specification: Fi 156C-3
Type: General communica tions and reconnaissance
Manufacturer: Fieseler GmbH
Number built: 2,549 (wartime production)
Entry into service: First flew 1936
Length: 32 ft 5.75 in (10.8m)
Height: 9 ft 10 in (3m)
Wingspan: 46 ft 9 in (14.25m)
Weight: 2,910 lb (1,320 kg)
Range: 236 miles (380 km)
Max speed: 109 mph (175 km/h)
Service ceiling: 15,090 ft (4,600 m)
Armaments: One 7.9mm rear-firing MG 15

Above: Its long landing gear legs made the Storch an ideal 'rough field' aircraft.

Right: Extensively used by the Germans the Storch was a favourite Allied 'runabout'.

Below: Air ambulance markings show another useful role for the Fi 156.

FOCKE-WULF FW 190

One of the best fighter designs of the wartime years the Focke-Wulf 190 was far more than Germany's 'second string' after the Bf 109. In most respects the 190 eclipsed its Messerschmitt counterpart and went on to become a versatile and effective ground attack aircraft, a role which reflected the Luftwaffe's changing fortunes. A switch from offensive to defensive operations saw FW 190s fed into some fronts in numbers far too small to make any difference because output was never to rival that of the Bf 109.

First flown on December 1, 1939, the FW 190V-1 was powered by a forerunner of the 1,660 hp BMW 801 radial engine. Having overcome some initial teething troubles with this powerplant, the service debut of the FW 190A took place in August 1941. Some problems remained to be solved but pilots on both sides of the Channel came to appreciate just how fine a job designer Kurt Tank had done on the 'Butcher bird'. The RAF was soon seeking an antidote to the fighter that proved alarmingly superior to the Spitfire V. The Spitfire IX, however, proved to be the equal of the 190 on most counts.

Having enjoyed something of a honeymoon as an interceptor fighter in many combats with the RAF, where its pilots could choose where and when to fight on their terms, the Focke-Wulf 190 was progessively developed to broaden its role. The original FW 190A series was revised as the A-4 which had a longer fuselage.

The FW 190 was soon thrown into the relentless attrition of attacking USAAF bombers and successful though it was, the bombers were very tough targets. When US fighters were able to escort the B-17s and

Specification: FW 190A-4
Type: Single-seat fighter
Manufacturer: Focke-Wulf Flugzeugbau GmbH
Number built: 20,051
Entry into service: 1941
Length: 29 ft (8.84 m)
Height: 13 ft (3.96 m)
Wingspan: 34 ft 5.5 in (10.49 m)
Weight empty: 7,055 lb (3,200 kg)
Range: 560 miles (900 km)
Max speed: 408 mph (653 km/h)
Service ceiling: 37,400 ft (11.410 m)
Armaments: 2 x 13-mm MG 151 machine guns in upper engine cowling plus 2 x 20-mm MG 151/20 in wing roots and 2 x MG 151/20 in outer wings; up to 1,100 lb (500 kg) of bombs on centerline racks

Specification: FW 190D-9
Type: Single-seat fighter
Manufacturer: Focke-Wulf Flugzeugbau GmbH
Number built: 1,805
Entry into service: Autumn 1944
Length: 33 ft 5.25 in (10.2 m)
Height: 11 ft 0.25 in (3.35 m)
Wingspan: 34 ft 5.5 in (10.49 m)
Weight empty: 7,720 lb (3,500 kg)
Range: 560 miles (900 km)
Max speed: 440 mph (704 km/h)
Service ceiling: 32,810 ft (10,000 m)
Armaments: 2 x 13-mm MG 151 machine guns in upper cowling plus 2 x 20-mm MG 151/20 cannon in wing roots and 2 x 20-mm MG 151/20 or 30-mm MK 108 cannon in outer wings; up to 1,100 lb (500 kg) of bombs on centerline rack.

B-24s, the FW 190 pilots had their work cut out and their numbers were gradually whittled down. Special heavily armoured attack models including the FW 190F and G (which were specialised versions of the FW 190A) failed to beat the

Above: The superb FW 190A fighter was extensively used as a fighter bomber.

Below left: FW 190A fighter bombers were used briefly in North Africa.

Below: An FW 190 preserved in the UK.

mounting odds, stacked increasingly heavily against the Luftwaffe.

Thrown into the melee of the Eastern Front from 1942 the FW 190 units were initially highly successful. Aces such as Hannes Trautloft and Walter Nowotny scoring kills at a rate that has never been equalled. Rugged and better able, due to its wide-track landing gear, to operate from rough forward fields than its Bf 109 counterpart, the Focke-Wulf 190 was well suited to conditions in Russia. It also became an effective ground support fighter bomber. In this role it largely replaced other types such as the Ju 87 from the autumn of 1943. Combat in the east slowly drained the Luftwaffe fighter force of its best pilots and aircraft, there rarely being enough FW 190s to fulfill all the tasks it was able to handle so well across a thousand-mile front. As the Red Air Force burgeoned so the Luftwaffe fighter force was forced to

Above: A rare FW 190 two-seater survived to become a UK museum exhibit.

Left: Both cockpits open on the FW 190 trainer.

Below left: The centre gear doors seen on early production FW 190s were soon eliminated.

Right: On of many 190As captured by the Allies and evaluated in the US.

Overleaf: An FW 190A flying in the US soon after the war.

act as a fire brigade, sending fighter units all over the front to stem enemy threats. Some FW 190 units on the Eastern Front managed to hold on right through the Soviet offensives but overall the losses were cripplingly high.

In the meantime Kurt Tank had taken steps to keep his potent fighter ahead of Allied development and in the FW 190D, the 'long nose', he achieved parity with the best the enemy had to offer. Powered by a Junkers Jumo 213A liquid-cooled engine in an annular cowling, the 'Dora 9' first entered service with JG 54 in the fall of 1944. Water-methanol injection boosted engine power to 2,240 hp for short periods, the aircraft being armed with two MG 151/20 cannon in the wings and two MG 131 machine guns above the engine cowling.

Few pilots proved able to get the best out of the Dora as Allied opposition was so heavy by the time it entered service. Development continued and Tank's work was honoured by having his later designs bear his name. Most variants, from the FW 190A to the FW 190D-9, remained in service until the German surrender, the pilot shortage and fuel restrictions proving to the last remnants of the Luftwaffe that its best fighters had come far too late.

Top left: The superlative FW 190D after thorough refurbishment for the USAF Museum.

Below left: An FW 190 fighter bomber is given the 'all clear' for another mission.

Bottom left: White paint helped hide the FW 190s of JG 51 from enemy fighters in Russia.

Right: Extensive hinged panels aided servicing of the FW 190s.

Below: Line up of newly completed FW 190As in Germany.

Bottom: A late-war FW 190 runs up before another sortie against Allied ground positions.

FOCKE WULF FW 200 CONDOR

As the only long-range German maritime bomber with a conventional four-engined layout, the FW 200 Condor was an expedient conversion of a prewar airliner that proved remarkably capable. Pressed into service on reconnaissance duties in support of the U-boat fleet, the Condor became the valuable airborne eyes to submarine crews, by shadowing Allied convoys and guiding them into ideal torpedo positions. By carrying out their own attacks on shipping, Condor crews of KG 40, the primary operating unit, sent many thousands of tons of vital supplies to the bottom of the sea and soon became a significant threat to Britain. As a makeshift counter fighters were mounted on merchant ships for 'one way' intercept launches, and escort carriers were introduced. Both combined to blunt the Condor's effectiveness but the loss of trained crews and a relatively modest production rate contributed equally to ending the threat.

Adapted to military configuration to meet a stillborn Japanese order, the FW 200V-10 prototype flew for the first time on 27 July 1937.

Production of FW 200A-0s and the following C series provided Fliegerfuhrer Atlantik with a useful fleet of maritime reconnaissance aircraft able to operate more than 1,000 miles from bases in France.

Most armed versions up to the FW 200C-8 were outwardly similar apart from armament variations

Using conventional bombs for most early sorties the FW 200 was subsequently adapted as a carrier aircraft for a pair of Hs 293 missiles. It did not fare particularly well in this later role because inherent weakness stemming from its airliner origins imposed unexceptable strains on the

Specification: FW 200C-3
Type: Four engined reconnaissance bomber
Manufacturer: Focke-Wulf Flugzeugbau GmbH
Number built: 276
Entry into service: 1940
Length: 76 ft 11.5 in (23.46 m)
Height: 20 ft 8 in (6.3 m)
Wingspan: 107 ft 9.5 in (30.85 m)
Weight empty: 28,550 lb (12,951 kg)
Range: 2,206 miles (3,550 km)
Max speed: 224 mph (360 km/h)
Service ceiling: 19,030 ft (5,800 m)
Armaments: 1 x 15-mm MG 151/15 cannon in dorsal turret; 1 x 20-mm MG 151/20 cannon in forward gondola position; 3 x 7.9-mm MG 15 machine guns in ventral gondola and in beam positions and 1 x 13-mm MG 131 in aft dorsal position; maximum bomb load 4,626 lb (2,100 kg) in ventral gondola; two Hs 293 missiles under outer engine nacelles.

Dornier Do 217 and He 177.

Its size made the FW 200 a useful military transport, following conversion of a number of aircraft to VIP configuration with luxury interiors to carry Hitler, Himmler and other high ranking officials. At Stalingrad several Condors were used to bolster the Luftwaffe transport force vainly trying to extricate the surrounded German Sixth Army. Transport duties were undertaken by the FW 200 throughout the war and the training of maritime crews was also an important secondary role for which the aircraft was better suited. Allied air opposition made the relatively slow Condor a tempting target and anti-shipping operations gradually reduced in scope as the U-boat fleet suffered similar war attrition.

Above: ASV radar assisted Condor crews to plot Allied convoys.

Right: An FW 200 low over the sea. Despite its civil airliner origins the Condor became an effective anti-shipping raider.

Below: Crews sweat to load a bomb into the Condor's dorsal gondola bay.

Above left: Early Lufthansa Condor airliners had a striking silver and black colour scheme.

Bottom left: A number of Condors were used as Hitler's personal transport.

FW 200's airfame, particularly during the necessary low flying over the sea to launch the missiles. Numerous accidents, directly traceable to its origins, wrote off many Condors even on normal operations and in the main, missile attacks were left to the

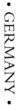

HEINKEL HE 111

The most numerous German bomber type at the beginning of the Second World War, the He 111 was easy to fly and well liked by its crews. Starting life in the guise of an airliner for Deutsche Luft Hansa, the He 111 was intended for the bombing role from an early date. The He 111V 1 flew for the first time on February 24, 1936, with production of the He 111B-0 starting that August. Powered by two DB 600C engines of 880 hp, the aircraft could carry a useful bomb load of up to 2,200 lb. To offset the small size of the internal bay the bombs were stowed vertically.

Bloodied, along with many of its contemporaries, under Nationalist colours in the Spanish Civil War, the He 111 was rapidly eclipsed in terms of defensive firepower and bomb load so that even by the start of operations in Western Europe it was outclassed. Following the He 111B and P series was the definitive He 111H series, which first appeared early in 1939. Although defensive armament had been increased to include cannon in some instances, the large formations of Heinkels sent over England in 1940 often received a severe mauling at the hands of more modern RAF fighters. But the He 111 was the aircraft the Germans had in substantial numbers and they had little choice but to deploy it extensively as a day and night bomber during the Blitz on England.

As long as it had a chance to survive against the air defences the He 111 was deployed and this kept its parent units active until well into the fighting on the Eastern front. It was there that the German policy of ignoring the long-range bomber was seen as a serious oversight when early large scale bombing raids on Moscow quickly dwindled to the

Specification: He 111H-3
Type: Twin-engined medium bomber
Manufacturer: Ernst Heinkel AG
Number built: 5,678
Entry into service: 1937
Length: 57 ft 5 in (17.5m)
Height: 14 ft 5.25 in (4.4m)
Wingspan: 74 ft 1.75 in (22.6 m)
Weight empty: 17,000 lb (7,720 kg)
Range: 932 miles (1,500km)
Max speed: 261 mph (420 km/h)
Service ceiling: 12,620 ft (7,500 m)
Armaments: 6 x 7.9-mm machine guns in nose, side hatches, ventral gondola and dorsal positions; up to 4,419 lb (2,000kg) of bombs in internal bay plus up to 3,968 lb (1,800 kg) on 2 x fuselage hard points

Above: He 111s carried out the majority of the Luftwaffe's medium bomber sorties.

Right: Famous photograph of an He 111 over London's River Thames in 1940.

Below left: Extensive nose glazing afforded Heinkel 111 crews an excellent view forward and downward.

Below: Pressed into service in the anti-shipping role, the radar-equipped He 111 was quite successful.

point that they were mounted by He 111 formations that rarely reached double figures. With attrition having taken a steady toll, medium bombers often flew sorties carrying supplies rather than high explosive.

With its Kampfgruppen flying aircraft that were increasingly vulnerable to fighter attack, the Luftwaffe's striking power waned and the Heinkel 111 and its ilk had little or no place in the strategic picture after late 1943, when the conventional bomber force was all but disbanded. When no suitable replacement appeared the bomber programme shrank in favour of fighters.

Above: Widely used though it was, the He 111 suffered from weak defensive armament. The dorsal position can be clearly seen here.

Right: The navigator/gunner of an He 111 watches the camera ship close in.

Below right: He 111s were also widely used as trainers with numerical identification.

Opposite page, above: To 'keep 'em flying' Spanish-built CASA C 2111s had Rolls-Royce Merlin engines.

Opposite page, below: The Merlin's radiators significantly altered the He 111's orginal configuration.

Overleaf: Fine in-flight view of a warbird 'He 111', all of which are ex-Spanish C 2111s.

The He 111 was successfully deployed in the demanding torpedo bombing role, units such as KG 26 achieving a measure of success against Allied shipping. Another duty that the He 111 undertook was that of mother ship to V-1 flying bombs. Designed to offset the steady toll taken of ground launched V-1s by Allied flak and fighters, units such as KG 3 operated off the coast of Britain. Approaching 'low and slow' at night or in overcast conditions they sometimes proved hard for defending night fighter crews to see and shoot down and a number of successful air launchings were carried out. The final He 111H-20 introduced a dorsal turret with a single machine gun. In 1942 two airframes linked by an additional wing section with an extra engine resulted in the He 111Z Zwilling glider tug.

Top: Most CASA C 2111s that are flyable carry Luftwaffe markings.

Above: 'Bought up' for the film *Battle of Britain* ex-Spanish 'He 111s' survive to thrill air show crowds.

Left: Modern avionics replace WWII-vintage instruments in many of today's flyable 'Heinkels'.

Opposite page, above: Luftwaffe crews fly their He 111s on an early war training sortie.

Opposite page, below: Temporary black paint was daubed on He 111s to help hide them from Allied night fighters.

Top: A Luftwaffe armourer selecting SC 500 lb bombs for his He 111 Staffel.

Center: Cumbersome balloon cable cutters were fitted to some He 111s but their heaviness rendered them largely ineffective.

Above: An economical glider tug was produced by joining two Heinkel bombers and adding a fifth engine to produce the He 111Z Zwilling.

Above right: Viewed from below the CASA C 2111 reveals its Spanish rather than German origins.

Right: Only from above is the illusion of an original German He 111 more or less created.

HEINKEL HE 177

An innovative design that suffered more than its fair share of technical problems, the He 177 found its moment of success far away from the adverse headlines that had followed its operations in Europe. Airmen far outside Luftwaffe circles were made aware of the results of a compromised design when He 177s caught fire, crashed and fell victim to Allied fighters in ever growing numbers.

Heavy bombing had never sat well with the Luftwaffe hierachy which had planned for a short war. Large bombers were materials and manpower resource sponges and after the death of General Wever, their main advocate, in 1937, little more was done.

Specification: He 177A-5
Type: Four-engined heavy bomber
Manufacturer: Heinkel AG
Number built: 1.146
Entry into service: 1942
Length: 66 ft 11.25 in (19.4 m)
Height: 20ft 11.75 in (6.4 m)
Wingspan: 103 ft 1.75 in (31.44 m)
Weight empty: 37,038 lb (16,900 kg)
Range: 3,417 miles (5,500 km)
Max speed: 303 mph (488 km/h)
Service ceiling: 26,248 ft (8,000 m)
Armaments: Combinations of 20-mm MG 151 cannon and 5 x 7.92-mm MG 81 and 131 machine guns in nose, dorsal, ventral gondola and tail positions; up to 13,200 lb (6,000 kg) of bombs internally; 2 x Hs 293A or FX 1400 stand-off missiles under wings

Above: Unique in being a four engined bomber that appeared as a twin, the He 177 had a checkered career in Luftwaffe service.

Left: Black finished for night operations this He 177 was probably operated by the famous anti-shipping unit KG 40.

But with a constant if unrealistic obsession with offensive air operations, the Luftwaffe found itself in dire need of new bombers by 1942. The He 177 was, accordingly, one of the important 'next generation' of replacements for the elderly He 111s and Do 17s which in many respects were obsolescent even before the war began. Germany's shortage of raw materials led to a decision to economise with the He 177 and mount two engines in one nacelle rather than four separate nacelles, as was usual in such a design. The result was a complex ignition train that was prone to in-flight fires, oil leaks and other malfunctions — so much so that service entry was critically delayed. Even when the He 177 was available for combat operations, a vague operational plan for the deployment of heavy bombers, in further disarray through ever

stronger Allied defences, tended to render it ineffectual. The hard-pressed anti-shipping unit KG 40 also dutifully did its best to make the He 177 a suitable replacement for its faithful but delicate FW 200 Condors. Flying long-range patrols out into the Bay of Biscay some of KG 40's He 177s were adapted for surface attack with guided missiles. Unable to deploy these in any number, the He 177 continued to disappoint, suffering as it did from numerous technical faults which regularly reduced aircraft availability.

It was not until 1944, when it was far too late, that KG 1 was able to put 80 plus He 177s into the air over Russia to carpet bomb hitherto invulnerable, out-of-range, targets and the aircraft finally proved itself in its intended role. Few engine fires were experienced on those sorties and some success was achieved. But

Above: With a wingspan inches less than that of a B-17, the He 177 was a large aircraft by WWII standards.

despite this being one of the few instances of a German heavy bomber campaign bearing even a tiny comparison with those of the Allies, KG 1's efforts were all but stillborn. It was left to the Allies, notably France, to complete, once hostilities had ceased, the derivative He 277 as a conventional heavy bomber with four engines in single nacelles — which might well have been a better design option in the first place.

HEINKEL HE 219

Potentially the best German night fighter of World War II, the He 219 introduced some novel features, including ejector seats for the crew. Most night fighters were adapatations of existing designs, Germany being one of the nations that aimed at specialisation, but the 'single use' aircraft had understandable limitation. Developed by Ernst Heinkel as a private venture, the He 219 was not originally intended for the night role but by 1941 with RAF bombing increasing, more official interest was shown in the project. The result was a first flight by the He 219 V1 on November 15, 1942.

Allied bombing adversely affected the future program however and Heinkel could not initiate mass production until after the V2 had made its combat debut on 11/12 June 1943. That night Maj Werner Streib shot down five Lancasters.

A handful of pre-production He 219A-0s were operationally evaluated by the Nachtjagd and some success was achieved, certainly enough to justify building a first major version, the He 219A-5.

Heinkel meanwhile had diversified into development versions rather than concentrate on a few service models and this, coupled with an official aversion to new aircraft as yet unproven, cut the number of He 219s to reach front line units. The upshot was that the He 219, further built in A-6 and A-7 versions, was never available to the Luftwaffe in high numbers. When it did see action however the He 219 was often effective, air and ground crew alike appreciating its tricycle landing gear, radar and heavy armament.

As with most German aircraft, various armament combination could be fitted to the He 219, the engines of which remained two Daimler-Benz DB 603s with some power variation, depending on variant. Production was, with hindsight, prematurely cancelled in May 1944 although Heinkel, on his own initiative, continued to build the aircraft in small numbers, a far from effective solution to devastating Allied bombing.

Specification: He 219
Type: Night fighter
Manufacturer: Heinkel AG
Number built: 268
Entry into service: 1943
Length: 50 ft 11.75 in
  (15.54 m)
Height: 13ft 5.50 in (4.1 m)
Wingspan: 60 ft 8.5 in
  (18.50 m)
Weight empty: 24,691 lb
  (11,200 kg)
Range: 1,240 miles
  (2,000 km)
Max speed: 416 mph
  (670 km/h)
Service ceiling: 41,665 ft
  (12,700 m)
Armaments: Two x 30-mm
  MK 108 cannon in wing
  roots, 2 x 30-mm MK 103
  and 2 x 20mm MG
  151/20 in ventral gun tray,
  2 x upward-firing 30mm
  MK 108 cannon in rear

Above: With its wings painted black and white for quick recognition by friendly flak gunners, a radar-equipped He 219 makes a night sortie.

Left: Potentially one of the best German night-fighters of the war the He 219 run headlong into the need for single-seat day interceptors and was curtailed before it could be developed fully.

JUNKERS JU 52

The ubiquitous 'Iron Annie', the Ju 52, was a literal lifeline to the Luftwaffe wherever it fought. In its own right as a paratroop transport the type bore German forces to capture the Eben Emael forts to open the assault in the west in 1940; it carried the ill-fated Fallschirmer to Crete and failed valiantly to bring the bulk of the Sixth Army out of Stalingard. Slaughtered by enemy fighters virtually anywhere they found it, the Ju 52 soldiered on, continuing until the last days of the war to ferry precious supplies of all kinds, personnel and equipment to combat formations.

Flying as a single-engined aircraft for the first time on 13 October 1930, the Ju 52 used a 'traditional' Junkers corrugated skin for airframe strength. A tri-motor configuration, which was very much in vogue for European airliners during the 1930s, was later adopted.

Bloodied over Spain where its outstanding transport capability was first realised by the Condor Legion, Ju 52s were pressed into front line service over Poland where they doubled as bombers during the assault on Warsaw. The ability to operate from rough landing fields stood the Ju 52 in good stead in the Second World War when it was often obliged to use landing areas — to call them airfields would be stretching credibility!

In North Africa Ju 52 transports were often the only means the combat units had to remain in action, for without them, supplies would have dwindled away. The more the Allies strangled seaborne lifelines the more reliance was placed on air transportation. And when the time came for the Germans to withdraw from their many battlefields, it was invariably Ju 52s that carried the bulk of them to safety, if only temporarily.

Throughout the war the Ju 52 outwardly changed little although the landing gear wheel spats of the 1930s were abandoned before the war began. The Ju 52/3m was the primary production model, the prototype having flown in April 1932.

In a move to give the Ju 52 a slightly better means of defending

Specification: Ju 52/3m
Type: Three-engined transport
Manufacturer: Junkers AG
Number built: 2,804
Entry into service: 1934
Length: 62 ft (18.9 m)
Height: 14 ft 9 in (4.5 m)
Wingspan: 95 ft 11.5 in (29.25 m)
Weight empty: 14,354 lb (6,510 kg)
Range: 795 miles (1,280 km)
Max speed: 168 mph (270 km/h)
Service ceiling: 18,046 ft (5,500 m)
Armaments: 1 x 7.9-mm machine gun in dorsal turret

Below: Another German aircraft that survived WWII in some numbers this Ju 52 taxies out at a modern air show.

Above: Paratroopers spill out of a Ju 52 during training. The old Junkers transport became the 'German C-47' in WWII.

Right: Dropping a 'stick' of men with their 'chutes already deploying a Ju 52 flight crew holds their aircraft steady.

Below: Prewar training formation of Ju 52s with markings that were revised for wartime operations.

itself a dorsal cupola was fitted in the cockpit roof and mounting a single MG 15 machine gun, on the last sub type, the Ju 52/3mg14e. First delivered in the fall of 1943, contracts for this version were completed in 1944.

Although it proved almost as irreplaceable to the Germans as the C-47 did to the Allies, the Ju 52 had clearly flown far beyond its normal phase out time even at the mid point of the war and it was updated in the Ju 352, a larger, but still tri-motored transport that flew some sorties before the German surrender.

Above right: An anti-magnetic mine ring slowed the Ju 52 down even more but it was used in action.

Right: The Ju 52 was built for pre-war Lufthansa operations, as seen here.

Bottom left: Mortal enemies a half century ago a Ju 52 formates with a Spitfire in peaceful air show skies.

Above: Little changed from WWII configuration, a Ju 52 displays typical Luftwaffe transport unit markings.

Below: Although it was slow and poorly armed the Ju 52 was the 'workhorse of the Luftwaffe'.

Left: The tough Fallschirmjäger (parachute troops) were carried into battle by Ju 52s on most of their successful early war operations.

Below: A Ju 52 painted in the airline colors of pre-Hitler's Germany.

Bottom: Ju 52s such as these were lifelines to forward air combat units in the Mediterranean theater.

Above: When Hitler came to power in 1933 Ju 52s and other airliners adopted a swastika on the tail.

Below: Black paint provided a suitable anti-glare effect for the Ju 52 crew.

Overleaf: With only slight cowling modifications, this modern day Ju 52 looks very authentic.

Top: A Luftwaffe Ju 52 on test prior to delivery to a service unit.

Above: Tail bands in white were characteristic of German aircraft — including the Ju 52 — operating in the Middle east.

Left: Typical German camouflage applied to a warbird Ju 52.

Right: Steeply banking a Ju 52 shows the trimotor layout, popular on pre-war airliners.

Below: Not for nothing was the Ju 52 known as 'Iron Annie' due to the corrugated aluminium skinning.

Bottom: A Ju 52 'out to grass' after Spanish air force service.

JUNKERS JU 87

Virtually any film footage of the European air war features Ju 87s in their stomach-churning 45-degree dives, the crank-winged Stuka acting as the Wehrmacht's aerial artillery. Stuka is an abbreviation of *Sturzkampfflugzeug* meaning dive-bomber (thus the abbreviation for dive-bomber wing — *Geschwader* — is StuG). Helping materially to smash Poland and the countries of Western and Southern Europe before laying waste to the Soviet Union and blasting Allied ships on the high seas, the Ju 87 gained an awesome early war reputation. This began in Spain when the Condor Legion's war rehearsal

Specification: Ju 87D
Type: Two-seat dive bomber
Manufacturer: Junkers AG
Number built: 4,890
Entry into service: 1939
Length: 37 ft 8.75 in (11.5 m)
Height: 12 ft 9.5 in (3.9 m)
Wingspan: 49 ft 2.5 in (15 m)
Weight empty: 8,687 lb (3,940 kg)
Range: 620 miles (1,000 km)
Max speed: 248 mph (400 km/h)
Service ceiling: 24,000 ft (7,320 m)
Armaments: 2 x wing-mounted MG 17 machine guns plus 2 x 7.92-mm MG 81 machine guns in rear cockpit; 1 x 3,968 lb (1,800 kg) bomb on centreline rack

Above: Wheel spats were often removed from front line Ju 87s to stop mud fouling the under-carriage.

Right: If Germany had finshed her aircraft carrier, *Graf Zeppelin,* Ju 87s with wing folding would have been the strike element. Wing folding was tested, as shown here.

Below right: Pioneers of dive-bombing, Germany brought the concept to a fine art with the Ju 87.

Left: A Staffel of Ju 87Ds running up.

included the 'daisy chain', a line of Stukas dropping down in turn to pulverise their targets. It was highly impressive and served the German propaganda machine very well indeed.

Given the Stuka's record, it came as some surprise to RAF fighter pilots to realise how easily the Ju 87 could be shot down if caught before

Above: The purposeful snout of a Ju 87G armed with tank buster cannon.

Right: Low-flying Ju 87Gs were the scourge of Soviet armour on the Eastern Front.

Below right: Cumbersome though they were, the 37-mm anti-tank guns were fearsomely effective against enemy armour.

Overleaf:
Top left: Few Ju 87s survived the war but this example is preserved in Britain.

Top right: Winter camouflaged Ju 87Ds en route home from an Eastern Front sortie.

Main picture: The sheer size of the Ju 87 is impressive for a single-engined type.

Right: A typical echeloned Stuka formation.

Below right: Ju 87Bs returning with empty bomb racks from a sortie on the Eastern front.

or after it had pulled out of a dive — over Dunkirk and the English Channel Stuka crews realised that modern enemy fighters could destroy them with impunity. But if after 1940 the Ju 87's reputation took a dent the Schaltgeschwadern (ground attack) units were by no means a spent force. New battlefields lay ahead in the east.

Dr Hugo Junkers' concern at Dessau built and flew the twin finned Ju 87V1 in spring 1935, powered by a 640 hp Rolls-Royce Kestral V engine. The distinctive inverted gull wing, trousered undercarriage and greenhouse canopy over the two crew seats would remain with minor changes, but a single fin and rudder replaced the original tail design on the Ju 87V-2.

The Ju 87A of 1937 was followed into Luftwaffe service by the much improved Ju 87B of 1938. Four models of the Ju 87B were built, five B-1s being sent to Spain for operational testing. These, following several Ju 87A-1s into Condor Legion service, were found to be even more effective under actual combat conditions — then came Poland where the Stukas were deployed to devastating effect. By 10 May 1940 the longer range Ju 87R had entered service, this and the 'Berta' being available for the Battle of Britain. Following some ambitious raids on airfields and radar stations, the Ju 87 units suffered such high losses from RAF fighters that they were withdrawn by 18 August.

Better results followed in the Middle East, the Balkans and Russia, the Ju 87D-1 and D-3 being the last sub types with the original wingspan. The Ju 87D-5 ground attack variant introduced a wing of 49 ft 3.5 in span which was used on the last major production model, the Ju 87G of 1942.

On the Eastern Front Ju 87D bombers and Gs armed with two 37-mm Flak 18 anti-tank cannon pulverised Soviet armour whenever their crews could penetrate Soviet flak and fighters. Aces such as Hans Rudel brought anti-tank warfare to a deadly art, flying an aircraft that by all the odds should not have survived. As big as an SB2C Helldiver, the Ju 87 represented a large target.

It was ironic that of, all the aircraft Germany had brought into service during the war, the Ju 87 should still be active in 1945. Along with fighters, Ju 87s were often encountered by the Allies in the last months of the war when ground attack targets remained in abundance on both fronts. The swansong of the Ju 87 was more spectacular than might have been anticipated, it being quite common for Ju 87s to put down on surrender airfields in company with the latest FW 190s and Bf 109s.

JUNKERS JU 88

If the Ju 87 reinstated the dive-bomber as an effective weapon of war, the Ju 88 showed that Germany's obsolescent prewar medium bomber force could be highly effective if new blood were brought in in time. Joining the Do 17 and He 111 in the front line Kampfgruppen, the Ju 88 surpassed them on nearly all counts. So versatile was it to prove that new roles were created specifically for this Junkers-designed aircraft to fill.

Flying for the first time on 21 December 1936 as the Ju 88 V1 and as the Ju 88A-1 on 7 September 1939, the aircraft's pre-war development included equipping it to make diving attacks. In this instance the German perchant to give all bombers such capability, paid off; the Ju 88 featured a reliable automated pull out device that enabled it to be highly effective against difficult targets such as ships under way. Over the Mediterranean and the Black Sea particularly, the Ju 88 became one of the most effective anti-shipping aircraft of all time.

An early requirement for an effective intruder and night fighter led to the Ju 88C-0 of 1939. Equipped with a solid nose containing cannon and machine guns Ju 88C intruders of NJG2 waged almost a private war against English bomber bases for the first years of the war.

As Germany's war fortunes waned, ever more effort was put into defense against bombers and the excellent Ju 88G was a partial answer to giving the night fighter arm more muscle. Try as they might, however, there were too few Ju 88 night fighters to stem the massive RAF night raids.

More adapatable than almost any other aircraft on either side, the Ju 88 also undertook torpedo bombing, long range reconnaissance and ground attack missions with equal alacrity. A big challange was to find an effective antedote to Soviet armor when Germany was forced onto the defensive. Ju 88s were among other types adapted to take large caliber anti-tank guns mounted in belly fairings. Cumbersome and detrimental to the aircraft's speed, these weapons

Above right: Ground crews ready a Ju 88 for another wartime sortie. The Ju 88 was easily the best German bomber of WWII.

Centre right: Refuelling a Ju 88A on a front line airfield.

Below right: With SN-2 airborne interception radar in a 'solid' nose the Ju 88G was a formidable night fighter.

Below: The distinctive nose of the Ju 88A with its twin 'beetle eye' rear gun positions aft of the cockpit.

Specification: Ju 88A-4
Type: Twin-engined medium bomber and night fighter
Manufacturer: Junkers AG
Number built: 16,911
Entry to service: 1939
Length: 47 ft 2.25 in (14.4 m)
Height: 15 ft 11 in (4.85 m)
Wingspan: 65 ft 10.5 in (20.13 m)
Weight empty: 17,637 lb (8,000 kg)
Range: 1,112 miles (1,790 km)
Max speed: 269 mph (433 km/h)
Service ceiling: 26,900 ft (8,200 m)
Armaments: (typical) 2 x 7.92-mm MG 81 machine guns firing forward plus 2 x MG 81 in rear of cockpit, plus 2 x MG 81 at rear of gondola; maximum bomb load 6,614 lb (3,000kg) in internal bay and external racks.

Specification: Ju 886-6
Type: Twin-engined night fighter
Manufacturer: Junkers AG
Number built: 3,915
Length: 54 ft 1.5 in (16.49 m)
Height: 15 ft 11 in (4.85 m)
Wingspan: 65 ft 10.5 in (20.13 m)
Weight empty: 20,062 lb (9,100 kg)
Range: 1,430 miles (2,300 km)
Max speed: 402 mph (643 km/h)
Service ceiling: 28,870 ft (8,800 m)
Armaments: 4 x MG 151/20 cannon in ventral pack plus 1 x 13-mm MG 131 machine gun for rear defence; 2 x MG 151/20 cannon in ventral installation (some aircraft only).

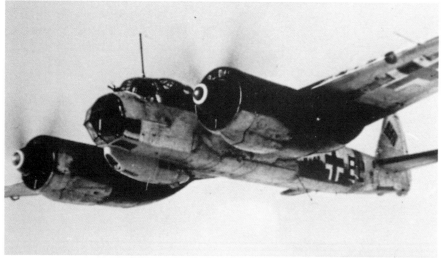

could not be made very effective even when carried by the Ju 88.

The majority of Ju 88s had a bulky forward fuselage dictated by grouping the entire crew in the

Below: The Ju 88 was also adapated a successful ground attack aircraft as these BMW-engined machines show.

extreme nose. A streamlining exercise resulted in the sleek Ju 88S which was the fastest of the series. Finally the proud Ju 88 suffered the ignominy of being turned into a flying bomb under the Mistel program. With a Bf 109 or FW 190 controlling it from a trapeze mounted on the fuslage, most variants of the Ju 88 were potentially adaptable to remote control for the delivery of high

Above: Unfortunately for the Germans a Ju 88 crew landed their fully equipped G model with its secret radar in England, thus giving the RAF a vital edge in the night battle over the Reich. This is that aircraft on test in the UK.

Left: A Ju 88A-4 banks over for a bombing run on a Russian target.

Above right: Carrying asymmetrical bomb loads was a feature of Ju 88 operations, types such as the A-4 having few handling problems.

Below right: In a desperate attempt to stem the 1945 Russian advance, the Luftwaffe tried the Ju 88/Bf 109/FW 190 Mistel combination, where the bomber became a pilotless flying bomb.

Top: This Ju 88D was flown to the United States for wartime tests.

Above: Ju 88s were given many exotic camouflage schemes at war's end.

Left: Ju 88G under test after its false landing in Britain.

explosive onto a selected target. Due to their vulnerability, few Mistels were actually expended in action before the end.

As with the Bf 110, the Ju 88 soldiered on in the night fighter role although a handful of units did retain it as a conventional bomber and undertook duties such as pathfinding and night ground attack until the surrender.

JUNKERS JU 188

A bomber that had its origins in the enormous number of projected variations outlined during the early development work on the Ju 88, the Ju 188 was resurrected in the Luftwaffe's disastrous 'Bomber B' programme. The only tangible survivor of this far-reaching 'second generation' bomber requirement, the Ju 188 was an efficient but not an outstandingly radical design. The Bomber B programme was too late and ran headlong into an escalating need for the Reich to have fighters, fighters and more fighters for home defence. Conventional bombers were hardly needed after early 1944, certainly not new ones that absorbed raw materials and manpower.

Specification: Ju 188E
Type: Twin-engined bomber
Manufacturer: Junkers AG
Number built: 1,076
Entry into service: 1942
Length: 49 ft 1 in (14.96 m)
Height: 16 ft 1 in (4.9 m)
Wingspan: 72 ft 2 in (22 m)
Weight empty: 21,825 lb (9,900 kg)
Range: 1,550 miles (2,480 km)
Max speed: 315 mph (494 km/h)
Service ceiling: 31,170 ft (9,500 m)
Armaments: 2 x 20-mm MG 151 cannon in nose and dorsal turret plus 3 x machine guns in lower dorsal and ventral positions; up to 6,614 lb (3,000 kg) of bombs internally and on wing racks.

Above left: An early Ju 188 on pre-delivery test flight.

Left: Equipped with radar the Ju 188 was a potent anti-shipping aircraft although targets were increasingly better defended.

Top: The Ju 188 undertook a late-war nocturnal bombing and flare-dropping role.

Above: The revised crew position of the Ju 188 compared to the Ju 88 can be seen in this view.

Right: With BMW engines the Ju 188 was rated as one of the best of German bombers.

MESSERSCHMITT BF 109

154

So important was the Bf 109 to Germany's military ambitions that it is nearly impossible to envisage any of the early successes being achieved had it not been available in substantial numbers. En route to the Channel coast of France, the Messerschmitt pilots overcame at least 10 different enemy single-seat fighter types, some equally good in direct technical comparison. But in most cases the 'other side' lacked the confidence, organisation and airmanship that imbued the German pilots and added not insubstantially to their victories.

Following the first flight of the Bf 109V1 on 28 May 1935, the aircraft chosen as the Luftwaffe's principal single-seat fighter entered production at a modest rate, and the Bf 109B, C and D models were produced in small numbers before the Jagdwaffe went to war in Europe, these being tested in combat in Spain where the Condor Legion helped Franco to ultimate victory. Near the end of the Spanish Civil War the Legion received examples of the Bf 109E which were handed to the grateful Spaniards when the Germans went home in triumph. The first line Jagdgeschwader at home in Germany were gradually re-equipped with the new Bf 109E, the Polish campaign requiring relatively few single-seat fighters.

Unfortunately for the Allies, the Bf 109E-1 predominated before the May 10, 1940 invasion of France and the Low Countries. Thrown into chaos and ill-served by its defence organisation, the French Air Force and RAF could not stop the advance. At Dunkirk the air umbrella over the rescue ships included Spitfires — where the Bf 109 began to meet its match.

Although it was well able to counter RAF fighters during the Battle of Britain, radar warning and the sound tactics followed by the British prevented the Bf 109 pilots from exploiting any advantage they believed they had.

With Operation Sealion postponed Göring ordered Bf 109 fighter bombers to help continue the fight aaginst England, while the Luftwaffe was gearing up to help the Italians in North Africa. First operating over the desert in 1941, the Jagdwaffe was gradually drawn into the protracted battle for control of the Mediterranean. The small German fighter force there did very well considering that it was usually outnumbered. In Western Europe

Specification: Bf 109E-4
Type: Single-seat fighter
Manufacturer:
  Messerschmitt AG
Number built: 31,8980
  (all models)
Entry into service: 1939
Length: 28 ft 4 in (8.64 m)
Height: 7 ft 5.5 in (2.28 m)
Wingspan: 32 ft 4.5 in
  (9.87 m)
Weight empty: 4,189 lb
  (1,900 kg)
Range: 365 miles (700km)
Max speed: [ed: text missing] mph (km/h)
Service ceiling: 34,450 ft
  (10,500 m)
Armaments: (Bf 109E)
  2 x MG 17 machine guns
  in upper engine cowling
  plus 1 x 20-mm MG FF
  cannon firing through
  airscrew hub and 2 x MG
  FF cannon in wings; up to
  551 lb (250 kg) of bombs
  on fuselage rack. (Bf
  109G) 1 x 20-mm MG FF
  cannon firing through
  airscrew hub and 2 x MG
  17 machine guns in upper
  engine cowling; up to
  551 lb (250 kg) of bombs
  on fuselage rack.

Below: One of the few flyable Bf 109s, this is a Bf 109G.

Specification: Bf 109K-4
Type: Single-seat fighter
Manufacturer:
   Messerschmitt AG
Entry into service:
   October 1944
Length: 29 ft 4 in (8.64 m)
Height: 8 ft 6 in (2.59 m)
Wingspan: 32 ft 6.5 in
   (9.92 m)
Weight empty: 6,000 lb
(2,721 kg)
Range: 365 miles (700 km)
Max speed: 452 mph
   (729 km/h)
Service ceiling: 41,000 ft
   (12,500 m)
Armaments: 1 x 20-mm
   cannon on fuselage centre
   line plus 2 x Mk in fuse
   lage; 2 x 20-mm cannon
   in gondolas under wing;
   up to bombs

**Above right: Bf 109E on
pre-delivery test flight.**

**Right: Front line exercises
honed Bf 109E units for their
decisive role in Europe in 1940.**

**Below: Duxford-based Bf 109F
and Bf 109G formate during a
brief outing together.**

the Bf 109F was also very capable of challenging British incursions over the Continent, which picked up from 1942 onwards. The Bf 109F, considered a real fighter pilot's aircraft, usually carried only one cannon and two machine guns, a modest armament that was exploited well by the best pilots.

The inevitable modifications to keep pace with changing requirements led to the Bf 109G, which was built in great numbers and flown wherever the Luftwaffe was committed. As in the F model, the light fixed armament of the 'Gustav' was often supplemented by a 'gunboat' configuration — two gondola-mounted

20-mm cannon. These gave that vital extra punch for the destruction of heavy bombers, for example, but pilots noted the drag the extra guns imposed. A 'clean' Bf 109F was an excellent fighter but no use to any pilot whose marksmanship was not of the highest order.

Bomber interception preoccupied the German fighter force for the last two years of the war and it became increasingly necesary for fighter pilots to press ever closer into the fire of massed guns.

Despite the rain of Allied bombs from the very aircraft that the

Above: Painted in Luftwaffe colours, the Spanish supplied most of today's warbird inventory of 'Bf 109s'.

Left: Famed for their appearance in the film *Battle of Britain* Buchons have since become well known.

Right: From head-on the intake of the Merlin-engined Buchon helps distinguish it from the wartime Daimler-Benz powerplant.

Below: Most of the Buchons fly in the US and UK where a 'near-Bf 109' is better than none at all!

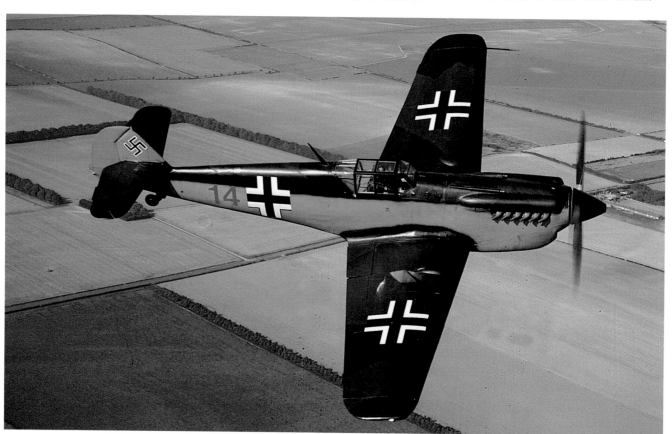

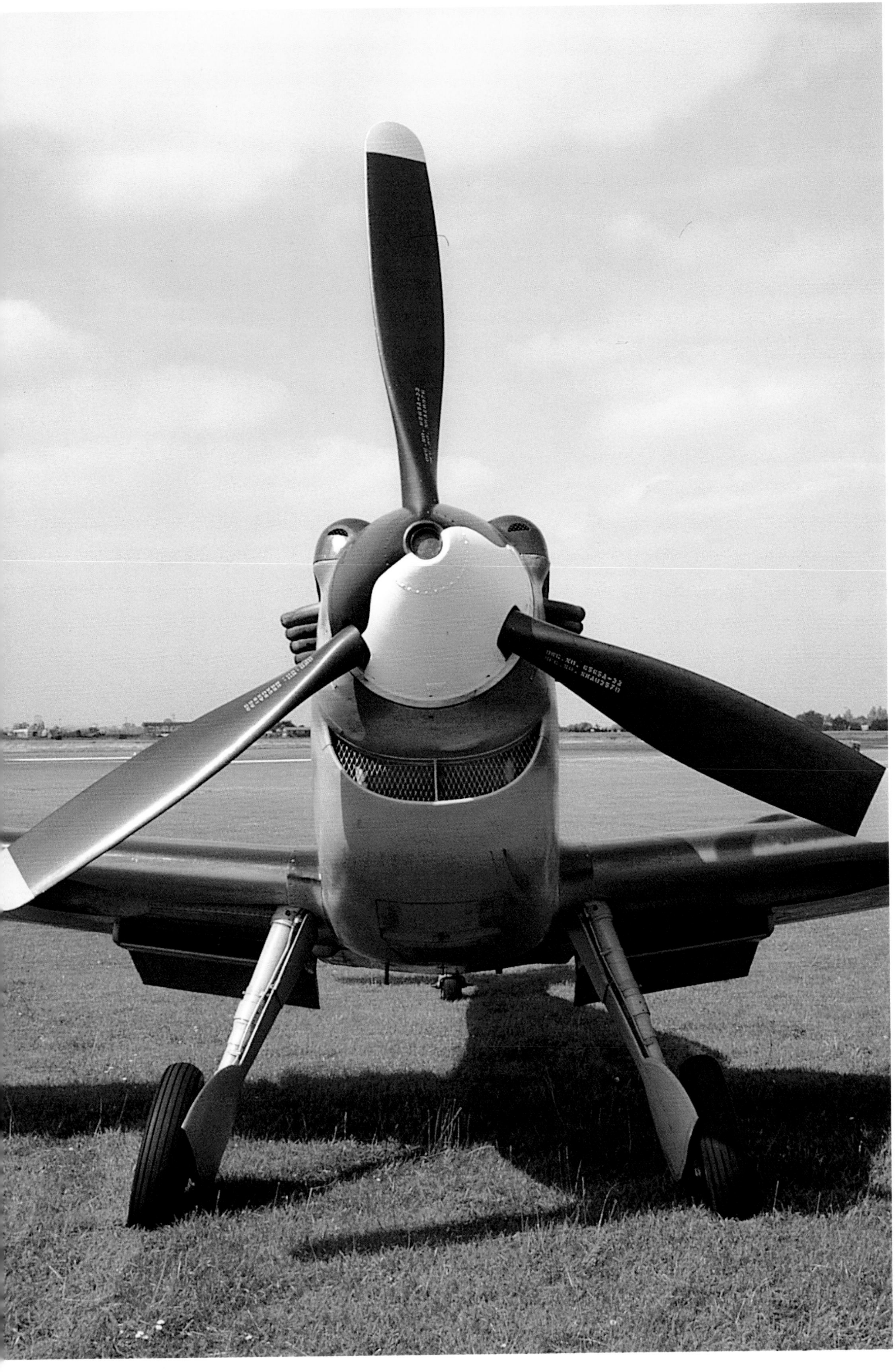

Messerschmitts were trying to destroy, the company factories continued to increase output and develop the Bf 109G series to include the G-6, which was the most produced model at over 12,000 examples, the G-8 for tactical reconnaissance and the G-10 and G-14 fighters which closely paralleled the K series. In the meantime the Bf 109G-12 became a long overdue two-seater to ease conversion training.

A potent fighter lacking enough skilled pilots to fly it to its limits in combat, the Bf 109K-4 was delivered to front line units in mid-1944. Although nothing could be done to

improve the pilot shortage, which was even then being felt, individuals such as Erich Hartmann, who scored 352 kills, were not alone in flying the 109 throughout his war service and surviving.

Willy Messerschmitt had turned away from any major stress problems by deleting wing-mounted cannon from the Bf 109F onwards but it was planned to reintroduce such armament in the Bf 109K-6. This was tested but none reached wartime units, the Bf 109K-4 proving to be the last of a line which had in nearly a decade, stretched to well over 30,000 examples.

Top: Years of restoration work created the first flyable Bf 109 in Britain for decades. An authentic desert camouflage scheme was applied to the F model painted as 'Black 6'.

Above: Bf 109Gs of a training formation checking out new pilots during the mid-war years.

Right: Many Luftwaffe Bf 109 aces are represented by the colour schemes adopted by private owners for their Buchon 109s.

Previous pages
Main picture: The Bf 109F flying in Engand during the early 1990s.

Top left: Coming in to land the Bf 109F shows its classic lines.

Top right: The 109F power-house.

Above right: Dispersed under camouflage netting on a French airfield, Bf 109Es await another Battle of Britain sortie.

Right: A late-war Bf 109G with dulled-downed national insignia.

Below: False guns and cylinder bank fairings identify a warbird Buchon 109.

Above: This Bf 109G was refurbished in the UK for a German customer who was a night fighter pilot.

Below: 'Black 2' was subsequently painted with tail kill markings, but the German authorities will not allow the swastika to be displayed.

Right: Pilots of the famous JG 27 get a briefing soon after arriving in North Africa.

Far right, above: Bf 109G 'Black 2' on finals showing the taller wooden tailplane of late model Gs and Ks.

Far right, below: The RAF Museum in London has this Bf 109E on display.

Below: A Bf 109E fighter bomber flown by the adjutant of JG 54 Grünherz over Russia.

Bottom: The fighter bomber Staffel of JG 26 flew Bf 109Es similar to its fighter counterparts in the same unit.

MESSERSCHMITT BF 110

Much trumpeted as Hermann Göring's 'ironsides', the Gruppen equipped with the Bf 110 long-range heavy fighter seemed an inspired idea at a time when air arms the world over were obliged to diversify into many different combat aircraft types to fill an expanding number of roles. The Me 110 exemplified the Zerstörer (destroyer) concept of combining the best attack features of single- and twin-engined fighters in one airframe. Basically this meant heavy armament, substantial range and good performance. Attributes such as manoeuvrability and airframe strength were also desirable and when the Bf 110V1 emerged for its first flight on May 12, 1936, it appeared to have all these qualities in good measure.

Powered by two 1,100 hp DB 601A liquid-cooled engines, the Bf 110C series was the most numer-

Below: Also displayed at Hendon is the world's only Bf 110G night fighter.

Specification: Bf 110G-4
Type: Twin-engined fighter bomber
Manufacturer: Messerschmitt AG
Number built: 6,257
Entry into service: Spring 1943
Length: 39 ft 8.5 in (12.1 m)
Height: 11 ft 6 in (3.5 m)
Wingspan: 53 ft 4.75 in (16.53 m)
Weight empty: 9,920 lb (4,500 kg)
Range: 528 miles (850 km)
Max speed: 349 mph (562 km/h)
Service ceiling: 32,800 ft (10,000 m)
Armaments: 2 x 20-mm MG FF cannon and 4 x 7.92-mm MG 17 machine guns in fuselage nose plus 1 x 7.9-mm MG 17 for rear defense; (Bf 110G-4) 2 x 7.9-mm MG 17s for rear defense; 2 x 20-mm MG FF cannon in oblique rear cockpit *Schräge Musik* mounting plus combinations of cannon and machine guns in nose and fuselage pack, depending on mission requirements.

ous of the early models, this entering Luftwaffe service in February 1939.

Three Gruppen were equipped with Bf 110C-1s by the outbreak of war and these were bloodied over Poland where for the first and arguably only time it operated in its intended role, the Bf 110 seemed to

have proven the Zerstörer concept. It was used over Poland in some numbers and was in fact the leading fighter type. The Messerschmitt twin became an integral part of the Luftwaffe order of battle for the assault on Scandinavia and western Europe. Enemy opposition en route

Above: Bf 110s were widely used during the early part of the war but their use in daylight was curtailed by Allied fighters.

Right: Bf 110Cs carrying the *Wespen* (Wasp) nose marking of Zerstörergeschwader 1 over Russia.

Below: Bf 110 night fighter.

to the French coast did not highlight any particular drawbacks in the Bf 110, but cross-Channel sorties against England in 1940 were an entirely different prospect. While dogfighting Spitfires and Hurricanes, crews flying the Bf 110C and D variants found themselves out-manoeuvred if not outgunned, for they still had heavy cannon armament which could be devastating when it could be brought to bear. Tactically the Bf 110 crews found that their broadly defined role could not be exploited in such an action and they often ended up having to be escorted by

Below: A formation of Bf 110Cs.

Bf 109s. That was definitely not what the Bf 110 was for!

A more useful role was that of fighter bomber and during the battle some important lessons were learned. Losses were often high but in the ground attack role Bf 110s fitted with fuselage and wing bomb racks continued to be used throughout the war. It remained a versatile type and was adaped to carry a comprehensive list of Rustsatz field conversion kits which included heavy calibre guns, underwing rocket tubes and external fuselage fuel tanks to extend range.

Despite a disappointing showing on the Channel coast, the Bf 110 still equipped Zerstörer units and it was also drafted into the Nachtjagd where it was to prove outstanding. In an area where aircraft were often lone hunters of night bombers the Bf 110 began steadily piling up kills.

For some time the Bf 110D and D models operated at night with few equipment changes.

In 1943 the night fighter arm began to equip its Bf 110s with SN-2 airborne radar and when installed in the improved Bf 110G powered by two 1,475 hp DB 605B engines this aid significantly increased the crews' chances of detecting and bringing down enemy bombers. Despite an initial reluctance to fly Bf 110s with the drag-inducing 'Stag's antlers' nose aerials, numerous night fighter aces including Heinz-Wolfgang Schnaufer with an eventual total of 121 victories, soon saw the advantages radar gave them.

In 1942-43 Bf 110 Zerstörer crews were pressed into service against American daylight raids and before escort fighters became a deadly adversary they were well able

to shoot down heavy bombers with cannon and rockets. American fighters found them easy targets, however, and the main use of the Bf 110 remained at night for the rest of the war. One of its most effective weapons was *Schräge Musik*, a pair of upwards-firing cannon used to fire on the belly of bombers where they were most vulnerable.

Left: Bf 110Gs with twin rocket mortar tubes under each outer wing.

Below: Two early Bf 110C night fighters in pre-radar days.

Bottom: A dapple camouflaged Bf 110C on a daylight sortie over the Eastern Front.

Above: A Bf 110 flying off Dover during the early stages of the Battle of Britain.

Left: Bf 110 crews prepare to take off for a mission late in the war. Such operations became increasingly hazardous as Allied fighter strength built up.

Inset, above: Long range tanks helped to boost the endurance of the Bf 110 operating in its original Zerstörer role.

Inset, below: A yellow Eastern Front fuselage band on Bf 110s of SKG 1; note the unit retained the striking Wasp emblem of ZG 1.

MESSERSCHMITT ME 210/410

One of the less successful products of the Third Reich's aero industry, the Me 210/410 series was not alone in supplementing rather than ousting the type it was designed to replace. By the outbreak of war in 1939 the Me 210 V1, the prototype of an eventual successor to the Me 110 Zerstörer, had been completed. Following a basically similar layout to the Bf 110 but with a single fin, the Me 210 flew for the first time on September 2, 1939.

Powered by two 1,395 hp DB 601F engines, the Me 210A weighed around 12,000 lb in empty condition compared with 15,530 lb for a fully loaded Bf 110 and its performance suffered accordingly, this being revealed during early flight trials. Production was consequently restricted to 352 aircraft against an initial order for 1,000. The Me 210 was used primarily to equip recon-naissance units in the Middle East but otherwise the deployment of the type in Europe was very limited. This did not prevent Allied intelli-gence widely circulating details of the Me 210 before its operational debut after its operational debut in the summer of 1940 and later in the war pilots constantly reported encounters with Me 210s when they were, in fact, Me 410s.

Specification: Me 410B
Type: Twin-engined fighter bomber
Manufacturer: Messerschmitt AG
Number built: (Me 210) 356; (Me 410) 113
Entry into service: January 1943
Length: 40 ft 10 in (12.45 m)
Height: 14 ft 0.25 in (4.3 m)
Wingspan: 53 ft 7.75 in (16.4 m)
Weight empty: 13,500 lb (6,150 kg)
Range: 1,447 miles (2,330 km)
Max speed: 385 mph (620 km/h)
Service ceiling: 32,800 ft (10,000 m)
Armaments: 2 x 20-mm MG 151/20 cannon and 2 x 7.92-mm MG 17 machine guns in nose plus 2 x 13-mm MG 131 machine guns in remotely controlled fuselage bar bettes; up to 2,204 lb (1,000 kg) in internal bay plus wing ordnanace

Above left: As a Bf 110 replace-ment the Me 210 was highly disappointing.

Left: A 210 rebuild to create the Me 410 was successful but its role had all but disappeared by the time it entered service.

Top right: An early production Me 410 ready for flight testing

Above right: An Me 410 that went to the US for testing after capture.

Right: An Me 410 survives today as museum exhibit in the UK.

To rectify the Me 210's faults, Messerschmitt embarked on a major modification programme that resulted in a virtually new aircraft. This time the formulae of new 1,750 hp DB 603A engines, revised crew accommodation, the introduction of rearward-firing armament, and other changes, worked well enough. The Me 410 *Hornisse* (Hornet) was hardly faster than its forerunner but it had vastly improved handling qualities and was more manoeuvrable. However, the role of the Zerstörer, never very well defined, was even more difficult to justify in 1943 with the Luftwaffe being increasingly hard-pressed on every war front. The demand was for single-engined bomber interceptors not twins which could do little to effectively combat enemy fighters as their performance would always be compromised by weight and size considerations.

Nevertheless, the Me 410 was pressed into service as a bomber interceptor, and it also became a useful long-range intruder and reconnaissance aircraft in addition to a limited deployment in the night fighter role carrying SN-2 radar. In all these roles the aircraft performed well enough but Allied advances in the twin-engined fighter field had all but overtaken it by the time it was available in large numbers. The original German Zerstörer concept for twin-engined fighters was perpetuated by the Me 410 and a number of units deployed it in this way, using a variety of ground attack weapons.

MESSERSCHMITT ME 163

Remembered as the world's first practical rocket-powered fighter, the Me 163 achieved little in actual combat but represented a seemingly significant step forward in terms of aeronautical propulsion.

When American bomber crews were attacked by a Me 163 for the first time, few of those present had any idea what it was. No wonder — nothing could touch an Me 163 climbing at full power.

A war emergency expedient following development of numerous tailless aircraft tests by Dr Alexander Lippisch, the Me 163 was tiny. To save weight a landing gear was not fitted, the aircraft instead taking off from a wheeled dolly which dropped away as airspeed was gained, the landing being cushioned by a retractable skid built into the lower fuselage.

Initial flight trials were conducted by towing the Me 163 aloft and by numerous gliding sorties. These proved the soundness of the 'tailless' design and there followed test flights with the Walter R–II–203 rocket motor installed. This powerplant used a mixture of T-Stoff (hydrogen peroxide and water) and C-Stoff (hydrazine hydrate, methyl alcohol and water) to produce enormous thrust. Early flight tests easily exceeded the world speed record in a shallow dive, after which the Me 163 was timed for a 'straight and level' run which took place on October 2, 1942. The flight returned a speed of 622.8 mph (1,004.4 km/h). Military officials could hardly ignore such a performance and Me 163B prototypes were ordered on December 1, 1941.

For such a small airframe the Me 163Ba-1 carried the heavy armament of two MG 151 20-mm

Specification: Me 163B	
Type: Single-seat rocket-powered interceptor	
Manufacturer: Messerschmitt AG	
Number built: 470	
Entry into service: May 1944	
Length: 18 ft 8 in (5.69 m)	
Height: 9 ft (2.76 m)	
Wingspan: 30 ft 7 in (9.32 m)	
Weight empty: 4,191 lb (1,905 kg)	
Range: 50 miles (80 km)	
Max speed: 516 mph (830 km/h)	
Service ceiling: 39,690 ft (12,100 m)	
Armaments: 2 x MK 108 30-mm cannon or (Me 163Ba-1) 2 x MG 151 20-mm cannon in wing roots	

cannon built into each wing roots. This was increased by the installation of two 30-mm MK 108 cannon in the Me 163B-1a but the most innovative armament for the rocket fighter was a dorsal mortar system triggered by the shadow of an enemy bomber as the Me 163 slid under it.

The main problems with the Me 163, apart from a demanding pilot training programme, included engine reliability and fuel volatility

that made it highly dangeous to handle. Lack of endurance was also a major drawback for a combat aircraft; although its lethal rocket fuel gave it a climbing speed of 33,470 ft per minute (10,200 m/min) it carried only enough to last for an eight-minute powered 'burn'. With

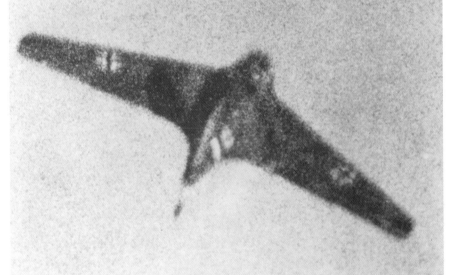

Above: One of the UK's Me 163s painted in an authentic Luftwaffe camouflage scheme.

Left: Fascination with the rocket fighter concept made the Allies to ship many Me 163s home for evaluation and several exist today.

Above right: Me 163s were vulnerable when their 'short burn' fuel load was exhausted and some were shot down by Allied fighters.

Right: Early test flights with the Me 163 were very dangerous as its fuel was so volatile.

his fuel expended, the Me 163 pilot had to glide back to base for a potentially dangerous landing, for the fumes accumulated in its fuselage tanks could detonate with the slightest jolt — indeed Me 163s were known to explode for no apparent reason.

First contact by the Me 163 with Allied bombers was on August 16, 1944 when I Gruppe JG 400 based at Brandis made an unsuccessful interception of B-17s. Other operating units were formed but the Komets delivered to operational units achieved only nine confirmed kills, two of which were 'probables', during their entire operational career.

Below: Its rocket motor on the point of ignition, an Me 163 taxies out, probably at Brandis, in 1944.

Top left: Another preserved Me 163 in typical markings of the only operational unit, JG 400.

Above left: Though an interesting idea, the Me 163 failed to score many kills in air combat.

Above: Engineers gingerly top up the Me 163's tanks with its highly explosive fuel.

Right: A special tractor was developed to tow the Me 163 to the take-off point.

Below right: An early Me 163 takes off. In seconds the little airplane would go into a phenominal climb.

Left: A wartime Me 163B with a US evaluation number on the tail. Part of the remarkable innovative effort of German wartime scientists, the Me 163 largely failed to achieve its potential.

Top left: A partially refurbished Me 163 pictured at Biggin Hill during the 1960s.

Above: Top Pilot and engineer prepare an Me 163 for flight.

Below: The Germans filmed the entire starting sequence for the Me 163, this being a still from the refuelling sequence.

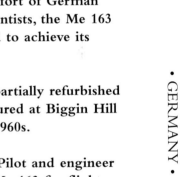

MESSERSCHMITT ME 262

The most advanced jet fighter in the world at the time of its combat debut, the Me 262 brought to the fore numerous problems, quite apart from its undoubted potential. First entering combat in 1944 its record was uneven for by then the Germans could no longer afford the luxury of a lengthy pilot conversion program which was very necessary in order to get the best from the aircraft. Even if pilots did manage to fly the aircraft reasonably well, the very speed of the Me 262 mitigated against it. An aircraft technically 10 years ahead of other wartime fighters, the Me 262 was not equipped with enough advanced air-to-air missiles or sights that could have made it far more effective. Nor were pilots trained to correctly use the weapons they had at the high closure speeds they were using to intercept piston-engined bombers.

That said, the Allies were unaware that the Germans had their own troubles with the Me 262 — all they saw was an enormous threat from an aircraft that even the P-51 could not catch in level flight.

Specification: Me 262A-1
Type: Single-seat twin turbojet interceptor fighter
Manufacturer: Messerschmitt AG
Number built: 1,430
Entry into service: September 1944
Length: 34 ft 9.5 in (10.6 m)
Height: 12 ft 7 in (3.8 m)
Wingspan: 40 ft 11.5 in (12.5 m)
Weight empty: 8,820 lb (4,000 kg)
Range: 650 miles (1,050 km)
Max speed: 540 mph (870 km/h)
Service ceiling: 37,565 ft (11,500 m)
Armaments: 4 x 30-mm MK 108 cannon in fuselage nose; up to 1,100 lb (500 kg) on forward fuselage racks.

The Me 262V1 flew for the first time on April 18, 1941 and its fine aerodynamics promised an excellent performance despite the fact that it had to use a piston engine as no turbojets engines were then available. Its selected powerplant, the Jumo 004, of 1,980 lb (900kg) static thrust was barely developed to a state of full reliability but Messerschmitt had little alternative choice but to use it if the Me 262 was to enter Luftwaffe service without delay. The Me 262's first flight under turbojet power was made on July 18, 1942.

There was a lengthy gestation period however and apart from Hitler's demand that a proportion of production aircraft be adapted to carry bombs, the disruption caused by Allied bombing, the continuing loss of fighter pilots and the use of untrained slave labour in the assembly plants all mitigated against the Me 262 being available any earlier than September 1944. When it was

Specification: Me 262 B-1a
Type: Two-seat twin-turbo
  jet interceptor fighter
Manufacturer:
  Messerschmitt AG
Number built: 67
Entry into service:
  September 1944
Length: 38 ft 9 in (11.8 m)
Height: 12 ft 7 in (3.8 m)
Wingspan: 40 ft 11.5 in
  (12.5 m)
Weight empty: 9,700 lb
  (4,400 kg)
Range: 650 miles
  (1,050 km)
Max speed: 497 mph
  (800 km/h)
Service ceiling: 37,565 ft
  (11,500 m)
Armaments: 4 x 30-mm
  MK 108 cannon in
  forward fuselage nose

on hand its units such as Kommando Nowotny, JG 7, KG (J) 54 and Adolf Galland's JV 44 did their best with slim resources to use the aircraft effectively.

Ever inventive, the Germans tested ejector seats in the Me 262 and planned a host of derivative models including those with dual rocket/turbojet power, increased wing sweep and a towed fuel supply.

In the end the Germans were unable to field the Me 262 in the numbers required to force any kind of cutback in the bomber offensive that had already all but destroyed the country's means to wage war.

Just before the end the Me 262 became a night interceptor and began to enjoy some success against the main antagonist of the conventional night fighter force, the Mosquito. As a jet night fighter the Me 262 claimed another 'first' and but for low numbers and enough trained crews it could undoubtedly have been most effective in this arena.

Me 262B-1a

It was clear that duplicating the performance, handling and flight controls of such a revolutionary aircraft as the Me 262 really demanded a two-seat conversion trainer right from the start. Numerous factors delayed such a development of the basic design which was why would-be jet pilots drafted into Me 262 Staffeln often had to make do with unrepresentative training aircraft such as the Si 204 if they had not previously had any twin-engined experience. Fortunately many pilots had come from the bomber arm, so this kind of basic experience was not lacking. Nor was navigation the problem it might have been.

Messerschmitt began studies into a two seat Me 262 as early as August 1943 as part of a far-reaching series of projected versions of the basic airframe. The prototype, known as the Me 262S5, actually flew for the first time on 28 April 1944.

With a new canopy over the two seats and standard armament, the first Me 262B was completed in September 1944. After four aircraft had been delivered to operational units, Allied bombing caused a halt, production resuming in January 1945. Lufthansa and Blohm und Voss facilities were combined to build most of the total of 67 aircraft.

By the time the first two-seater was ready for service in its intended conversion training role, Germany's military position was dire. With numerous aircraft projects dropped in deference to fighters, it was expedient to count the two-seat Me 262 as an combat aircraft rather than a trainer. The night fighter arm could,

Below left: A pristine Me 262A preserved as a museum exhibit.

Below: From head-on the sleek shark-like fuselage of the Me 262 shows just how advanced it was at war's end.

it was estimated, make particularly good use of a jet interceptor with the added advantage of carrying a radar operator/navigator. Consequently, a small number of trainers, probably no more than 20, were converted into Me 262B-1a/U1 interim night fighters, the suffix indicating the installation of SN-2 radar and advanced radio equipment. Kommando Welter was formed early in 1945 to defend Berlin at night with about ten aircraft. By the time

Above right: Lift off for an early production Me 262.

Right: Even with its wheels down, the Me 262 was the most streamlined fighter of WWII.

Below: Luftwaffe ace Adolf Galland likened the Me 262's flight 'as though an angel was pushing'.

Above: Preserved Me 262 in South Africa. All Allied nations were fascinated by the potential of jets and many were 'liberated' when Germany fell.

Left: Well marked Me 262 superbly refurbished by the Smithsonian Institution.

Below left: Operational line up of Me 262A fighters in 1945.

Overleaf
Inset, Left and Right: Crudely re-marked with German insignia, this Me 262B two-seater was captured intact and shipped to the US. The 'FE' the stands for 'foreign evaluation'.

Main picture: Fanciful colour scheme on another Me 262B in the US after the war.

Above: The small frontal area of the Me 262A and heavy armament gave it huge potential.

Right: Taking the camouflage nets off an Me 262A at an operational base in Germany.

Below right: Taxying an Me 262A had to be done with care to prevent engine 'flame out'.

this experimental unit had been redesignated 10./ NJG 11 in April, it had proved that few Allied aircraft were available to intercept the Me 262 at night, and even the superlative Mosquito had finally meet its equal. Only one example of the intended night fighter, the Me 262 B-2a, was flown before the war ended.

GREAT
BRITAIN

AIRSPEED OXFORD

In the mid-1930s the RAF's massive modernisation programme included new types for Bomber Command such as the Whitley, Hampden, Wellington and Blenheim. In order to train crews to operate modern bombers, a new advanced training aircraft was required, and to fulfill this role the Air Ministry selected the Airspeed Oxford. First flying in June 1937, the all-wooden Oxford was based on the AS 6 Envoy civilian transport and only minor changes to the assembly line were required before construction of production aircraft could begin.

Powered by Armstrong Siddeley Cheetah engines the Oxford Mk I entered service in 1938 and by the outbreak of war was serving with the Central Flying School and various Flying Training Schools. The aircraft proved very versatile being used not only for training pilots, air gunners (using the Armstrong Whitworth gun turret) and bomb-aimers with the Mk I but also navigators, camera operators and radio operators using the Oxford Mk II. The other major production variant was the Mk V which was similar to the Mk II except for the installation of Pratt & Whitney R-985 Wasp engines.

In addition to RAF units the Oxford was also delivered in vast numbers for the Commonwealth Air Training Scheme which trained many thousands of Allied wartime aircrew. Other examples were used in the anti-aircraft co-operation and radar calibration roles, as air ambulances and for communications. A total of 8,586 Oxfords were eventually produced playing a vital part in the massive training campaign which ensured that sufficient aircrew were available for frontline squadrons.

Specification: Oxford Mk V
Manufacturers: Airspeed, de Havilland, Percival, Standard Motors
Number built: 8,586 all types (inc 5384 Mk I, 3004 Mk II)
Entry into service: November 1937
Powerplant: Two 450 hp Pratt & Whitney R-985-AN6 Wasp Junior
Length: 34 ft 6 in (10.52 m)
Height: 11 ft 1 in (3.38 m)
Wingspan: 53 ft 4 in (16.26 m)
Weight empty: 5,670 lb (2,572 kg)
Service ceiling: 21,000 ft (6,400 m)
Max speed: 202 mph (325 km/h) at 4,100 ft (1,250 m)
Range fully loaded: 700 miles (1,127 km)
Armament (Mk I): 1 x 0.303-in (7.7-mm) machine gun in dorsal turret; up to 12 x 25 lb practice bombs

Previous page: The de
Havilland Mosquito.

Left: Affectionately known as
the 'Oxbox', the Oxford was a
docile twin well suited to the
training task.

Above: An early production
Oxford Mk I.

Right: Turrets were added to
the Oxford for
gunnery training.

Below right: RAF Oxfords on
an airfield in the UK.

ARMSTRONG WHITWORTH WHITLEY

Built in greater numbers than any other Armstrong Whitworth aircraft, the AW 38 Whitley was designed to meet a 1934 Air Ministry specification for a heavy bomber as part of the British Government's rearmament programme. By the time the first prototype Whitley flew in March 1936 a production order for 80 aircraft had already been placed, the first of which was delivered to the RAF early in 1937. The Armstrong Siddeley Tiger-powered Whitley Mk I was the first aircraft with a stressed-skin fuselage to go into production for the RAF, and was soon joined in squadron service by the Mk II (featuring supercharged Tiger engines) and the Mk III (with improved armament and an enlarged bomb bay).

In 1939 production switched to the Rolls-Royce Merlin-powered Mk IV and Mk V, endowing the aircraft with increased performance, range and bomb-carrying capacity. By the time the UK committed itself to the Second World War Whitleys of different marks equipped four front line RAF squadrons; Nos 10, 51, 58 and 78. On the first night of the war the Whitley was committed to

Specification: Whitley Mk III
Manufacturer: Armstrong Whitworth
Number built: 1,814 inc 80 Mks I and II, 80 Mk III, 40 Mk IV, 1,466 Mk V and 146 Mk VII
Entry into service: March 1937
Powerplant: Two 845 hp Armstrong Siddeley Tiger VIII
Length: 69 ft 3 in (21.11 m)
Height: 15 ft 0 in (4.57 m)
Wingspan: 84 ft 0 in (25.60 m)
Weight empty: 15,475 lb (7019 kg)
Range fully loaded: 1,315 miles (2,116 km)
Max speed: 209 mph (336 km/h) at 14,250 ft (4,343 m)
Service ceiling: 23,000 ft (7,010 m)
Armament: 1 x 0.303-in (7.7-mm) machine gun each in nose and tail turrets, 2 x 0.303-in (7.7-mm) machine guns in ventral turret plus up to 5,500 lb (2,495 kg) of bombs

Specification: Whitley Mk V
Powerplant: Two 1,145 hp Rolls-Royce Merlin X
Length: 70 ft 6 in (21.49 m)
Height: 15 ft 0 in (4.57 m)
Wingspan: 84 ft 0 in (25.60 m)
Weight empty: 19,350 lb (8,795 kg)
Range fully loaded: 1,500 miles (2,414 km)
Maximum speed: 230 mph (370 km/h) at 16,400 ft (4,999 m)
Service ceiling: 26,000 ft (7,925 m)
Armament: 1/2 x 0.303-in (7.7-mm) machine gun each in nose, 4 x 0.303-in (7.7-mm) machine guns in tail turret plus up to 7,000 lb (3,175 kg) of bombs

Left: A Whitley Mk I on a pre-delivery test flight.

Above right: Whitleys could carry the largest bombs the RAF had early in the war.

Right: It could of course take multiple small bombs as well.

operations with 10 Mk IIIs from Nos 51 and 58 Squadrons flying a propaganda leaflet dropping raid over Bremen, Hamburg and the Ruhr. A number of other leaflet raids (codename 'Nickle') followed during the autumn, ranging as far as Berlin and Poland.

As more squadrons began to receive the definitive Mk V, Bomber Command's Whitleys began more aggressive operations, starting with a bombing raid on seaplanes departing Borkum air station on the Friesian Islands on the night of December 12/13 1939. More raids against targets in German coastal waters continued in the early part of 1940 before on the night of March 19-20 Whitleys from Nos 10, 51, 77 and 102 Squadrons, joined by Hampdens, dropped the first bombs on German soil in a raid against the Hornum seaplane station. Whitley raids intensified during the spring and early summer attacking railway stations and supply routes into

the Netherlands. On June 10, 36 Whitleys made the first bombing raid against Italy although only 13 reached their targets due to bad weather and engine problems. In August 1940 Whitley Mk Vs from Nos 51 and 78 Squadrons took part in the first bombing raid of the war against Berlin and continued night raids against targets in Germany and occupied Europe over the next 12 months.

Throughout 1941, the more capable Wellington gradually replaced the Whitley in front line squadrons, and the last operational raid by Bomber Command Whitleys was carried out on the night of April 29, 1942 against Ostend harbour. However, some Whitleys assigned to operational training units were called up to participate in the '1,000 Bomber' raid on Cologne on the night of May 30, 1942.

Although designed as a heavy night bomber, the Whitley also admirably fulfilled a number of other

vital roles during the conflict. In September 1939 No 58 Squadron was temporarily transferred to Coastal Command for anti-submarine patrols. The aircraft's good endurance made it ideal for the task and No 502 and 612 Squadrons subsequently re-equipped with the Whitley for patrols over the Atlantic. Their success led to the development of the specialised Whitley Mk VII fitted with ASV Mk II anti-surface radar. The capabilities of the Mk VII were demonstrated on 30 November 1941 when an aircraft from No 502 used the radar to attack and sink U-boat U-206 in the Bay of Biscay. The type remained in Coastal Command service until mid-1943.

From 1941 British forces turned to more offensive operations and the Whitley was employed in the deployment of airborne forces. Able to carry 10 fully laden paratroops in each aircraft, the Whitley was used extensively for parachute training with No 1 Parachute Training School before entering operational service. The first deployment occurred on February 7, 1941 when eight Whitleys from No 78 Squadron dropped 37 SAS troops behind enemy lines in southern Italy during Operation Colossus. More drops were carried out in France the following year including Nos 138 and 161 (Special Duties) Squadrons deploying agents in occupied territory. Whitleys were also earmarked for the glider-towing role. Much of the development work in using gliders operationally was completed by Whitleys of Nos 295 and 296 Squadrons, however by the time gliders were used operationally the Whitley tugs had been replaced by the Halifax.

Although largely obsolescent by 1939, the Whitley played an important part in the early war years as the only fully trained night bombing force. The aircraft developed many of the bombing techniques and procedures that were used with such telling effect by four-engined bombers later in the war.

AVRO ANSON

Developed from the Type 652 civilian passenger and mail transport aircraft for use by Imperial Airways, the Avro Anson was submitted to the Air Ministry in 1934 in answer to a specification for a twin-engined coastal reconnaissance aircraft. Winning the contract in preference to the de Havilland DH 89, the Anson was placed immediately into production and, when introduced to RAF service with No 48 Squadron in March 1936 became one of that service's first all-metal monoplane types and the first with a retractable undercarriage.

Fitted with Armstrong Siddeley Cheetah engines, forward fuselage and dorsal turret mounted machine guns and capable of carrying two 100-lb and eight 20-lb bombs, the Anson equipped a total of 21 Coastal Command squadrons by the outbreak of the Second World War. Used extensively for reconnaissance and anti-shipping duties in the first two years of the war, Coastal Command Ansons played a vital role in monitoring German warships in the English Channel and achieved some success against lighter vessels such as E-boats. Although lacking sufficient defensive firepower the Ansons were not helpless against attacking fighters. On June 1, 1940 an Anson from No 500 Squadron, attacked by three Messerschmitt Bf 109s, managed to

Specification: Anson Mk I
Manufacturers: Avro, Federal Aircraft (Canada)
Number built: 6,704 (Mk I), 1,832 (Mk II), 223 (Mk III and Mk IV), 1,070 (Mk V), 103 (Mk X), plus postwar production
Entry into service: March 1936
Powerplant: Two 335 hp Armstrong Siddeley Cheetah IX
Length: 42 ft 3 in (12.88 m)
Height: 13 ft 1 in (3.99 m)
Wingspan: 56 ft 6 in (17.22 m)
Weight empty: 5,375 lb (2,438 kg)
Range fully loaded: 660 miles (1,062 km)
Max speed: 188 mph (303 km/h) at 7,000 ft (2,135 m)
Service ceiling: 19,000 ft (5,790 m)
Armament: 1 x 0.303-in (7.7-mm) forward-firing machine gun and 1 x 0.303-in (7.7-mm) machine gun in dorsal turret

down two using the nose and dorsal machine guns.

In 1942 the Anson was retired from front line service, but had by then begun a new career with the RAF and the Commonwealth Air Training Plan as a navigation trainer serving in vast numbers. Further variants, fitted with various power-plants, replaced the older Mk I versions during the war and the air-craft remained one of the most important British training aircraft up to 1945 and beyond.

Below left: 'Annie' was a trainer familiar to RAF cadets for decades.

Above right: This Anson has mid-war RAF trainer markings.

Right: Pre-war 'silver' Ansons.

Below: Very slow and docile the Anson was also pressed into combat on occasions.

AVRO LANCASTER

Without doubt the most important RAF bomber of the Second World War, the Avro Lancaster owed its existence almost entirely to the failure of its predecessor, the twin-engined Avro Manchester. Designed to meet an Air Ministry specification for a twin-engined medium bomber, the Manchester was plagued by severe problems with its Rolls-Royce Vulture engines that were never resolved, and production was quickly abandoned.

Meanwhile Handley Page had designed a four-engined heavy bomber using four Rolls-Royce Merlin engines, and initially the RAF wanted Avro to abandon Manchester development in favour of setting up a Halifax production line of its own. However, Avro had adapted a standard Manchester airframe with the same Merlin engines and the aircraft, known then as the Manchester Mk III, was delivered in January 1941 to the A&AEE at Boscombe Down for acceptance trials. The aircraft's exceptional load-carrying capacity, allied to Avro's insistence that it would be simpler and cheaper to adapt existing production lines rather than establish Halifax production, secured the future of the Lancaster which went on to become the most numerous Bomber Command aircraft.

First delivered to No 44 Squadron at the end of 1941, the Lancaster Mk I started its operational career with a mine-laying sortie over the Heligoland Bight on March 3, 1942. In April No 97 Sqn joined No 44 Sqn on a 12-aircraft raid which would change Bomber Command policy for the rest of the war. Flying unescorted during daylight against the heavily defended MAN diesel factory at Augsburg, seven of the aircraft were shot down, and even though the raid inflicted considerable damage the losses were deemed unsustainable, prompting all future raids to be conducted at night. Squadron Leaders Nettleton and Sherwood became the first Lancaster aircrew to receive the Victoria Cross for their part in the raid.

As more squadrons equipped with the Lancaster from mid-1942 the frequency of raids intensified and several new bombing techniques were inaugurated. On the night of August 18 the first pathfinder operation was made when Lancasters from No 83 Squadron marked target areas around Flensberg. The success of the raid prompted the formation of the dedicated Pathfinder Force (PFF) which, equipped with pyrotechnic bombs and flares, would be involved in marking targets for Bomber Command's main force for the remainder of the war. From 1944 the PFF received a small number of Lancaster Mk VIs fitted with radio countermeasures equipment which helped confuse intercepting Luftwaffe night-fighters.

From the spring of 1943 the Lancasters of Bomber Command began massed raids against the industrial factories and installations centred on the Ruhr. With Arthur 'Bomber' Harris formulating policy, the targets were soon to include major cities such as Berlin and Hamburg. Almost every night operational Lancaster squadrons relentlessly attacked targets deep within Germany not only destroying German industrial capacity but also having a dramatic effect on civilian morale. By the summer of 1943, as operations were reaching their most intensive phase, 132 tons of bombs were being dropped for every Lancaster lost. The capability and importance of the Lancaster is illustrated by the fact that the corresponding figures for the RAF's other heavy bombers were 56 tons for the Halifax and 41 tons for the Stirling.

The capability to carry a larger bombload than any other wartime

---

Specification: Lancaster Mk I

Manufacturers: Avro, Metropolitan-Vickers, Vickers Armstrong, Austin Motors, Armstrong Whitworth, Victory Aircraft (Canada)

Number built: 7,378 (3,479 Mk I, 300 Mk II, 3,021 Mk III, 18 Mk VI, 130 Mk VII and 430 Mk X)

Entry into service: December 1941

Powerplant: Four 1,280 hp Rolls-Royce Merlin XX

Length: 69 ft 4 in (21.04 m)

Height: 20 ft 0 in (6.10 m)

Wingspan: 102 ft 0 in (31.09 m)

Weight empty: 36,900 lb (16,738 kg)

Range: 2,530 miles (4,072 km) with 7,000-lb (3,175-kg) bombload

Max speed: 287 mph (462 km/h) at 11,500 ft (3,505 m)

Service ceiling: 22,000 ft (6,706 m)

Armament: 8 x 0.303-in (7.7-mm) machine guns in nose dorsal and tail turrets plus one 22,000-lb (9,979-kg) bomb or up to 18,000 lb (8,182 kg) of smaller bombs

Above: Lancaster Mk Is on a daylight training flight.

Left: Early Lancaster Is had no dorsal turret fairings.

Below left: A Lancaster on a late-war daylight raid when these were less hazardous.

Above: With good defensive armament except for below the Lancaster carried the heaviest wartime bombs such as the 'Grand Slam' and 'Tallboy'.

Right: This frequently depicted Lancaster Mk I served with No 50 Squadron.

Insets Top right, Below left and Bottom right: Popular at air shows, this rare preserved Lancaster is maintained by the RAF as part of its 'Battle of Britain Memorial Flight'. Squadron markings are changed regularly.

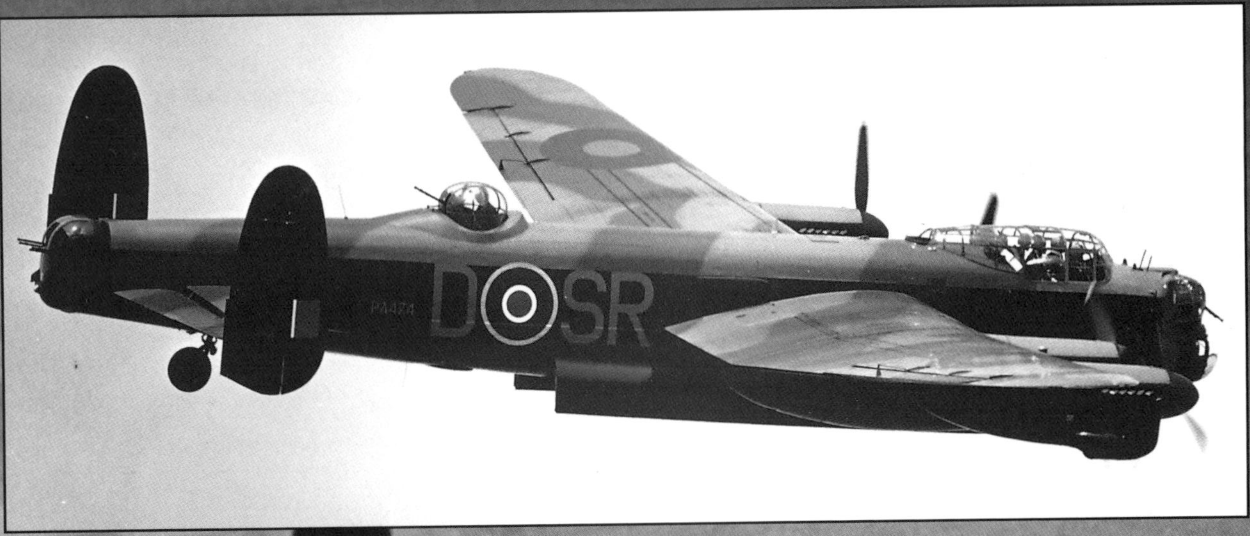
PA474
D SR

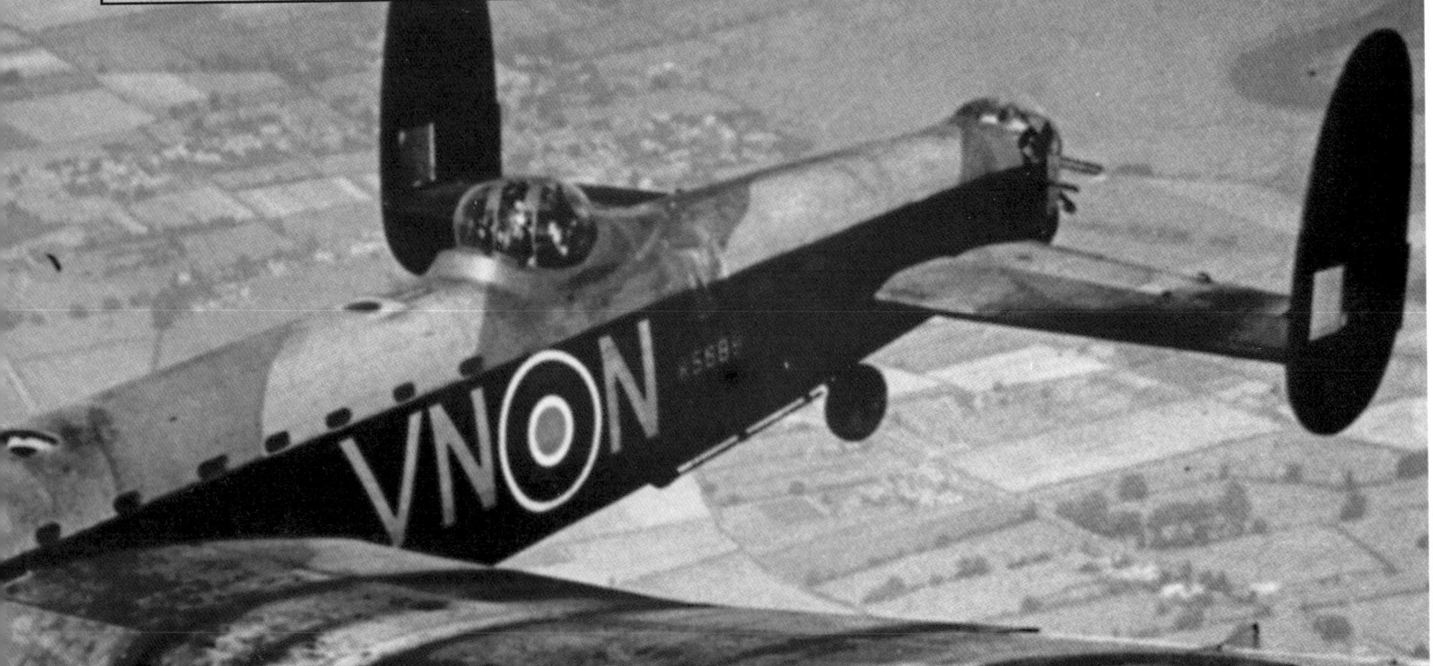
VN N

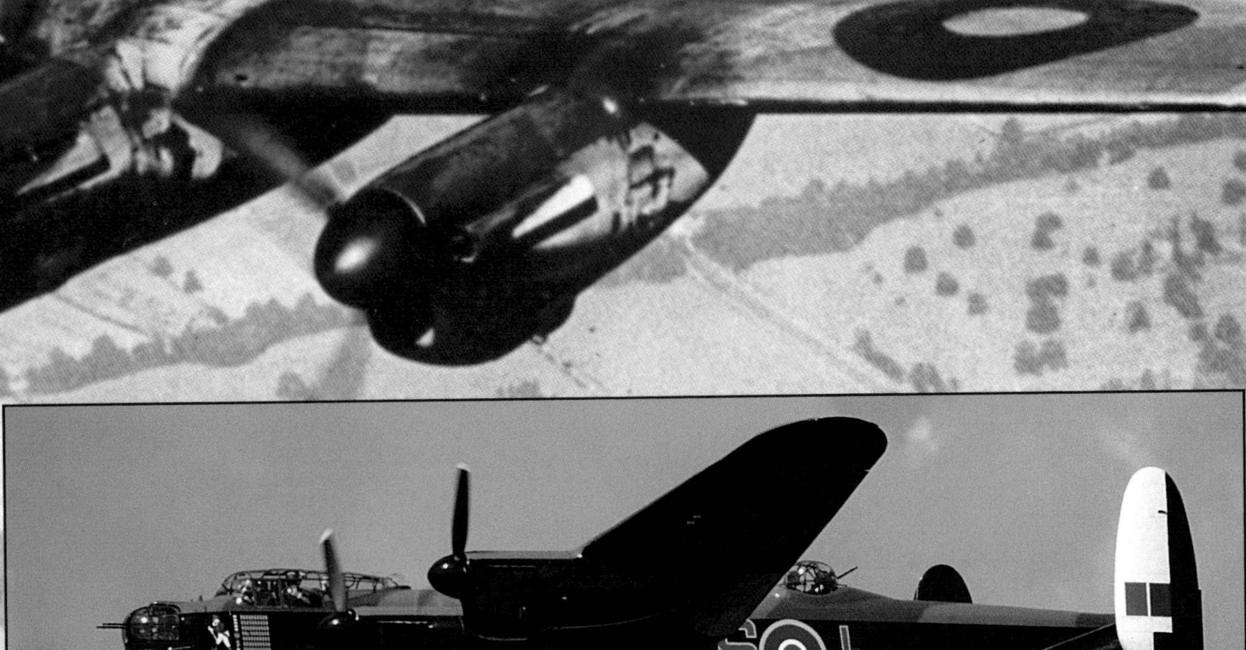
WS J
PA474

bomber allowed the Lancaster to deliver a number of unique weapons. The most famous of these weapons was undoubtedly the cylindrical 'bouncing bomb' invented by Dr Barnes Wallis. On the night of May 16, 1943 17 specially-modified Lancaster Mk IIIs from No 617 Sqn, led by Wing Commander Guy Gibson, conducted Operation Chastise - the famous 'Dambusters' raid. Using a specially developed low flying release technique, the bombs breached the Möhne and Eder dams cutting power supplies to the industry on the Ruhr and providing a huge propaganda coup for the Allies. Other important weapons included the 12,000-lb 'Tallboy' bomb, which was used to sink the German battleship *Tirpitz*; anchored in a Norwegian fjord as well as inflicting severe damage on numerous industrial targets, and the massive 22,000-lb 'Grand Slam' which was instrumental in destroying the Bielefeld viaduct.

After the D-Day invasion, Lancasters were pre-eminent in the attacks on tactical targets and lines of communication in a resumption of daylight raids. The accuracy of the continuing night raids against German cities was improved by the introduction of the H2S target location device to the bombers. Attacks on German targets continued until VE-Day with one of the last raids being conducted against Hitler's Berchtesgaden retreat on 25 April 1945. After Germany's capitulation a number of Lancasters were 'tropicalised' for use in the Far East as B.Mk 1(FE)s and B.Mk VII(FE)s, however the war was to end before they were introduced.

Lancasters were also used for a number of other tasks during the war such as training and, in the spring of 1945, the dropping of humanitarian supplies to the starving Dutch population during Operation Manna. However, it is as the main instrument of the RAF's devastating night raids on German industrial centres and cities that the Lancaster will be best remembered. The fact that the 7,300 Lancasters, built both in the UK and Canada, dropped 69% of the total delivered by the RAF (a total of 608,612 tons) gives credence to Sir 'Bomber' Harris' claim that 'the Lancaster was the greatest single factor in winning the Second World War'.

Right: To keep its preserved Lancaster flyable, the RAF carefully restricts the hours it flies each year.

Below right: One reason why the Lancaster was so effective was its massive bomb bay.

Below: The RAF 'Battle of Britain Memorial Flight'.

BOULTON PAUL DEFIANT

The design origins of the Boulton Paul Defiant can be traced back to the use of a power-operated turret on 59 Hawker Demons manufactured for the Hawker company by Boulton Paul. The aircraft was deemed a success and many experts within the Air Ministry were of the opinion that a turret arrangement would be suitable for a new high-performance fighter. Able to provide both defensive and offensive capability over a large field of fire this arrangement would free the pilot, allowing him to concentrate on flying the aircraft.

In 1935 Boulton Paul submitted its initial Defiant designs in response to an Air Ministry specification for a two-seat fighter with a power-operated turret. The first prototype, powered by the ubiquitous Rolls-Royce Merlin engine, made its maiden flight in August 1937 and a troubled development period followed. Performance and agility was severely diminished by the weight of the turret and, however cleverly the turret was faired into the fuselage, its sheer bulk created sufficient drag to degrade performance still further.

Specification: Defiant Mk I
Manufacturer: Boulton Paul
Number built: 1,075 (725 Mk I, 210 Mk II and 140 TT1)
Entry into service: December 1939
Powerplant: One 1,030 hp Rolls-Royce Merlin III
Length: 35 ft 4 in (10.77 m)
Height: 12 ft 2 in (3.71 m)
Wingspan: 39 ft 4 in (11.99 m)
Weight empty: 6,078 lb (2,759 kg)
Range: 465 miles (748 km)
Max speed: 304 mph (489 km/h) at 17,000 ft (5,181 m)
Service ceiling: 30,350 ft (9,250 m)
Armament: 4 x 0.303-in (7.7-mm) machine guns in dorsal turret

There were also numerous teething troubles including engine and turret malfunctions. Despite this, many in the Air Ministry were still convinced that the concept was the way forward in air combat and, following the outbreak of the Second World War, the first production Defiant Mk Is were delivered to No 264 Squadron in December 1939.

The type was first deployed operationally during the evacuation of Dunkirk on May 12, 1940 and

initially it seemed that the doubters of turret fighters would be proved wrong. Often mistaking the Defiants for Hurricanes No 264 Squadron aircrew gained complete tactical surprise over attacking Luftwaffe pilots. Many aircraft, attacking from the rear, were downed by the powerful four-gun turret which also proved devastating against enemy bomber formations. In the first 20 days of operations 65 enemy aircraft were downed including 38 in one day, but losses were increasing at an alarming

**Top, Above and Below left:
Defiant day fighters were not a
success but it performed better
as a night–fighter.**

**Below: Defiant Is on patrol in
1940.**

daylight operations and a new role
for the aircraft was found.

As the Battle of Britain progressed the Luftwaffe switched
increasingly to night raids. To
counter the threat it was decided to
install the new and largely untried
AI.Mk IV interception radar in the
Defiant. Aircraft modified to carry
the radar were fitted with flame-
dampening exhausts and were
redesignated Defiant NF.Mk IA.
These aircraft, along with new-build
Defiant NF.Mk IIs fitted with the
more powerful Merlin XX engine,
were to prove an invaluable addition
to the UK's night defences during
the most intensive period of night
bombing between October 1940
and March 1941. During this period
the Defiants scored more 'kills'
per interception than any of its
contemporary night–fighters. By
the end of this period 13 frontline
squadrons were operating the type;
however, the introduction of the
superior Beaufighter led to the
withdrawal of the aircraft from
frontline duties.

Many of the surviving aircraft
went on to be converted into target-
towing aircraft which, in addition to
140 new production TT.Mk IIIs,
served in this role throughout the
remainder of the war. Another 50
examples were converted for the
air/sea rescue role serving with five
operational squadrons.

rate. Luftwaffe pilots soon discovered
that attacking Defiants from the
front or below left the aircraft virtually defenceless and to experienced
pilots were more or less 'sitting
ducks'. Within two months unac-
ceptably high loss rates prompted the
withdrawal of the Defiant from

BRISTOL BEAUFIGHTER

Possessing excellent performance, heavy firepower and unmatched versatility, the Beaufighter was one of the most widely used and important combat aircraft operated by the Allies during the Second World War.

By 1936 the British Air Ministry and the designers at the Bristol Company were aware that war with Germany was becoming a distinct possibility. As part of the mass re-equipment programme for the RAF the need for new long-range heavily armed fighters was regarded as a priority. The Westland Whirlwind and Boulton Paul P.92 were selected for this role, but by the end of 1938 major technological problems with these projects were resulting in delays that left a serious shortfall in frontline RAF assets. Bristol recognised the problem and, shortly after the first flight of the Beaufort, began to develop a fighter derivative fitted with the more powerful Bristol Hercules engine.

Married to the wings, rear fuselage, tail unit and landing gear of the existing Beaufort was a redesigned front fuselage section shortened to allow the larger diameter propellers fitted to the Hercules engines to rotate in front of the aircraft's nose. The Air Ministry was immediately enthusiastic about the design and, thanks to its commonality with the Beaufort, the prototype made its first flight on July 17, 1939 within six months of the first design drawings.

Production contracts were signed and, thanks to many of the component production jigs already in use with the Beaufort, production was quickly established. Named Beaufighter Mk I (from Beaufort Fighter) the first aircraft were delivered to frontline squadrons in September 1940, one of the shortest gestation periods of any combat aircraft used in the Second World War. In the following months the Luftwaffe bombers turned increasingly to night operations and the Beaufighter was earmarked to receive the newly developed AI.Mk IV interception radar. Beaufighter Mk Is from Nos 25, 29, 219, 600 and 604 Squadrons with the new radar were delivered during late 1940 and on November 19 Flt Lt John 'Cats Eyes' Cunningham claimed the first 'kill' using the radar against a Junkers Ju 88. The five squadrons continued in operations against the night Blitz until attacks began to peter out in May 1941. During the last major raid on London on May 10, 14 enemy aircraft were downed by the Beaufighters - the most number claimed on any one night. Fitted with six machine guns and four cannon the Beaufighter was the most heavily armed fighter employed by the RAF during the war, an attribute which was later put to devastating effect against ground targets

As an insurance policy against a shortage of Hercules engines, which were in heavy demand for heavy bomber types, Bristol developed the Beaufighter Mk II with Rolls-Royce Merlin engines. The fastest of all variants, over 400 were built as Mk IIF night-fighters serving in this role with UK-based squadrons from April 1941. Instability problems

Specification: Beaufighter Mk IF (late production)

Manufacturers: Bristol, Fairey, Rootes Securities plus the Department of Aircraft Production, Australia

Number built: 5,918 inc 364 in Australia (553 Mk IF, 397 Mk IC, 597 Mk IIF, 693 Mk VIC, 879 Mk VIF, 2,205 Mk X, 163 Mk XIC and 364 TF Mk 21)

Entry into service: September 1940

Powerplant: Two 1,400 hp Bristol Hercules III, X or XI

Length: 41 ft 4 in (12.60 m)

Height: 15 ft 10 in (4.82 m)

Wingspan: 57 ft 10 in (17.63 m)

Empty equipped weight: 14,069 lb (6,381 kg)

Normal range: 1,500 miles (2,414 km)

Max speed: 323 mph (520 km/h) at 15,000 ft (4,572 m)

Service ceiling: 28,900 ft (8,809 m)

Armament: 4 x 20-mm cannon in forward fuselage plus 6 x 0.303-in (7.7-mm) machine guns mounted in wings

Specification: Beaufighter Mk X

Powerplant: Two 1,770 hp Bristol Hercules XVII

Length: 41 ft 8 in (12.60 m)

Height: 15 ft 10 in (4.82 m)

Wingspan: 57 ft 10 in (17.70 m)

Empty equipped weight: 16,930 lb (7,686 kg)

Range: 1,470 miles (2,366 km) with 1,700-lb torpedo

Max speed: 303 mph (488 km/h) at 1,300 ft (395 m)

Service ceiling: 15,000 ft (4,572 m)

Armament: 4 x 20-mm cannon in forward fuselage, 6 x 0.303-in (7.7-mm) machine guns mounted in wings, 1 x 0.303-in (7.7-mm) machine gun in dorsal position plus one 1,650 lb (748 kg) or 2,127 lb (965 kg) torpedo and either 500-lb of bombs or 8 x 90-lb (41-kg) rocket projectiles.

which manifested themselves during low-speed flight on both Mk Is and Mk IIs were remedied during the production run by fitting a 12 degree dihedral tailplane which was adopted on these and all subsequent variants.

By mid-1941 the Beaufighter had been adopted by RAF Coastal Command in the form of the Mk IC long-range strike fighter. With the RAF desperately requiring an aircraft able to mount long-range strike missions in the Mediterranean theatre, the machine guns were replaced by additional fuel tanks to increase range and this new variant entered service with No 252 Squadron on Malta in May 1941. Joined in the region by No 272 Squadron the Mk ICs enjoyed considerable success against German and Italian shipping during the summer months. In November 1941 No 272 Squadron mounted airfield attacks during Operation Crusader in North Africa destroying 44 aircraft in four days.

Below left: Rocket-firing Beaufighters were the heavyweight punch of the coastal strike squadrons.

Below: A Mk I Beaufighter in early camouflage.

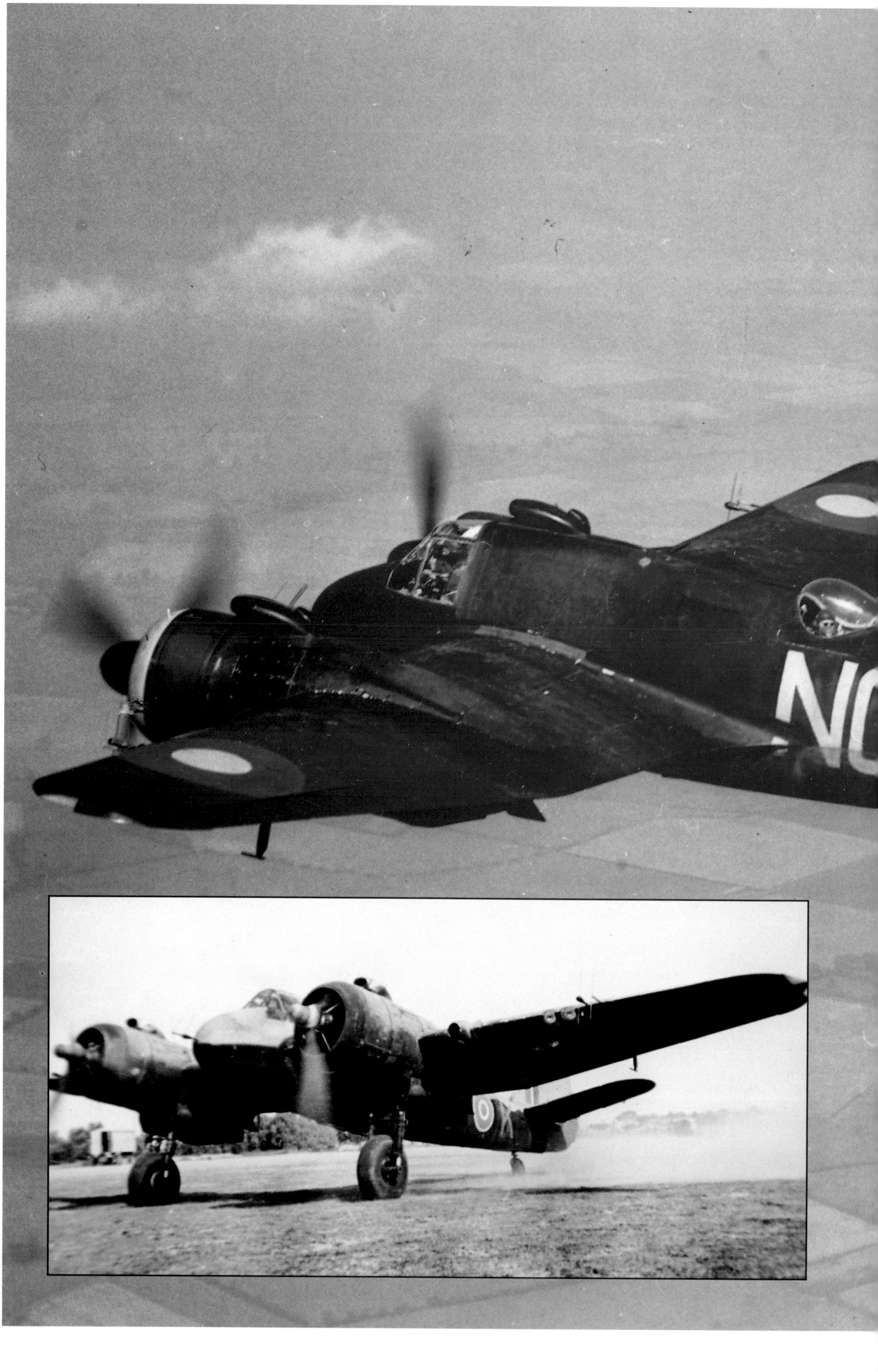

Above: By D-Day Beaufighter strike squadrons had made the seas highly unsafe for enemy shipping.

Left: Night finish was used for No 604's Beaufighter Mk Is.

Below left: AI radar made the Beaufighter an effective night hunter.

The next production version was the Mk VI, produced like the Mk II in VIC (coastal) and VIF (fighter versions). For night fighting the Mk VIF was mainly equipped with the new AI.MK VIII radar housed in a 'thimble' nose. The ever-decreasing raids on the UK in 1942 freed many of the home-based squadrons to fly night raids over northern France attacking trains, convoys, railway installations and other such targets. The Mk VIFs were also used to escort Main Bomber Force raids, luring away Luftwaffe night fighters.

This variant was also deployed in the Far East theatre to great effect, attacking Japanese lines of communication in Burma. From the end of 1942 Nos 27, 176 and 177 Squadrons mounted daily low-level raids using the aircraft's devastating firepower to claim, amongst other targets, 66 locomotives, 123 ships and

96 road vehicles destroyed in the first nine months of operations. Such was the aircraft's effect on Japanese morale that they nicknamed the aircraft 'Whispering Death'. The introduction of rocket projectiles further increased the effect of the low-level attacks and Mk VIs continued to serve in the theatre until the end of the war. From September 1942 the RAF squadrons were joined in the theatre by RAAF Beaufighters which were used to equally devastating effect especially during the 'island hopping' stages of the final two years.

Replacing the Mk ICs in the Mediterranean, Mk VIs played a vital role in the victory in North Africa, ranging over vast areas to attack targets of opportunity. Beaufighters were also used to 'soften up' enemy defences before the invasions of Italy

and Sicily in 1943 and to support allied ground operations until the Italian surrender.

Coastal Command Mk VICs were active in the North Sea and the Bay of Biscay from 1942 and, using rocket projectiles and cannon, sank or crippled thousands of tons of enemy shipping and submarines over the following three years. The success in the anti-shipping role led to the development of the final major production version, the Beaufighter TF.Mk X torpedo-carrying anti-ship aircraft. Developed from the Mk VI(ITF) interim torpedo fighter, the aircraft could carry one 2,000-lb torpedo beneath the fuselage or, alternatively, eight rocket projectiles. A modified version of the AI.Mk VIII radar in a thimble nose proved to have excellent air-to-surface capabilities and the

Above: A 'Torbeau' on a flight test from the Bristol factory.

Above right: Combining with rocket-firing Beaus, the strike units sank many enemy ships.

Right: Its Hercules engines gave the Beaufighter a mighty swing on take off.

'Torbeau', as it was unofficially known, became the standard Coastal Command variant for the last two years of the war, equipping a number of Beaufighter Strike Wings. Notable successes included the sinking of the 51,000-ton Rex after have been struck 55 times below the water-line by rockets fired from attacking Beaufighter TF.Mk Xs.

BRISTOL BEAUFORT

In 1935 the Air Ministry issued two separate specifications for a torpedo bomber and a general reconnaissance bomber. Bristol immediately set to work on adapting its existing Blenheim design to meet the requirements of the former. After detailed design work including modifying the fuselage to hold a torpedo and the installation of more powerful engines, Bristol realised that its new design could fulfill both roles and adapted its proposal as necessary to be presented to the Air Ministry as the Type 152. Bristol received the go-ahead to proceed with the design with an 'off the drawing board' order for 78 examples received in August 1936.

With the Bristol Perseus engine unable to deliver sufficient power it was decided to switch to the Bristol Taurus engine although this engine was not yet cleared for production. Problems with overheating engines delayed the first flight until October 1938, and this event only revealed further problems with the main undercarriage fairings causing extreme yawing of the aircraft during asymmetric retraction or extension of the undercarriage. The problem was cured by incorporating 'clamshell' undercarriage doors on

Specification: Beaufort Mk I
Manufacturers: Bristol, Department of Aircraft Production (Australia)
Number built: 1,930 (966 Mk I, 164 Mk II by Bristol; 700 Mk V-IX by DAP)
Entry into service: November 1939
Powerplant: Two 1,065 hp Bristol Taurus II or 1,085 hp Bristol Taurus VI
Length: 44 ft 3 in (13.49 m)
Height: 14 ft 3 in (4.34 m)
Wingspan: 57 ft 10 in (17.63 m)
Weight empty: 13,107 lb (5,945 kg)
Normal range: 1,600 miles (2,574 km)
Max speed: 260 mph (418 km/h) at 6,000 ft (1,830 m)
Service ceiling: 16,500 ft (5,030 m)
Armament: 5-8 x 0.303-in (7.7-mm) machine guns in forward-firing, nose turret, dorsal turret and beam positions plus up to 1,500 lb (680 kg) of bombs or 1 x 1,605-lb (728-kg) torpedo

Specification: Beaufort Mk II
Powerplant: Two 1,200 hp Pratt & Whitney Twin-Wasp S3G4G
Length: 44 ft 3 in (13.49 m)
Wingspan: 57 ft 10 in (17.63 m)
Height: 14 ft 3 in (4.34 m)
Weight empty: 14,070 lb (6,395 kg)
Max speed: 278 mph (448 km/h) at 6,000 ft (1,830 m)
Normal range: 1,450 miles (2,333 km)
Service ceiling: 21,000 ft (6400 m)
Armament: 5-8 x 0.303-in (7.7-mm) machine guns in forward-firing, nose turret, dorsal turret and beam positions plus up to 1,500 lb (680 kg) of bombs or 1 x 1,605-lb (728-kg) torpedo

production aircraft and, in November 1939, No 22 Squadron became the first operational unit to receive the Beaufort Mk I. However, the cooling problems had not been fully resolved and, with torpedo trials yet to be carried out, it wasn't until April 1940 that the first operational mission was flown. The initial missions mainly involved convoy patrols and mine-laying missions in the North Sea and later in the month No 42 Squadron became the second unit to receive the type.

In May 1940, persisting problems with the Taurus engines caused the aircraft to be grounded for three months. The only action carried out during this period being the attack on the German cruiser *Scharnhorst* by nine No 42 Squadron Beauforts. Although a number of bombs hit their target the cruiser escaped and three aircraft were lost in the attack. Late 1940 and early 1941 saw the two squadrons mainly occupied in attacking enemy shipping in the English Channel and the North Sea. In September 1940 No 22 Squadron made the RAF's first anti-shipping torpedo attack of the war and in April 1941 Flying Officer Campbell completed a gallant lone raid against the German battleship *Gneisenau* in Brest harbour. The torpedo struck home putting the ship out of action for nine months and earning Campbell a posthumous VC.

In August 1941 two more units (Nos 86 and 217 Squadrons) brought the number of UK operational squadrons to four and these units continued anti-shipping operations until the spring of 1942 when the type was withdrawn from frontline UK-based units. In the meantime Nos 39 and 47 had re-equipped with the improved Beaufort Mk II for operations in the Mediterranean. During the first half of 1943 the two squadrons achieved considerable

Above: The moment of torpedo release as a Beaufort makes a training run.

Left: Britain's first modern torpedo bomber, the Beaufort kept helped keep the sea lanes clear.

Right: 'Tin fish' ready for loading into Beauforts of No 22 Squadron.

Above: Bristol aircraft including the Beaufort, featured rearward-firing guns.

Right: Wartime colour view of a No 217 Squadron Beaufort.

Below right: Good though it was, the Beaufort was out-classed by the Beaufighter as an anti-shipping aircraft.

success torpedoing many Axis supply ships heading for North Africa as well as assisting the Allied Torch landings.

In the Far East theatre No 217 conducted offensive patrols against Japanese shipping, but it was Royal Australian Air Force Beauforts that were to make a vital impact in this campaign. Powered by Pratt & Whitney Twin Wasp engines, Beaufort Mks V–VIII served with 10 Australian squadrons and were instrumental in crippling the Japanese invasion fleet at Normanby Island in September 1942. From this time until VJ-Day the RAAF Beauforts destroyed vast amounts of Japanese shipping and harbour installations including the annihilation of a large Japanese convoy during the Battle of the Bismarck Sea in March 1943. It was undoubtedly in the Pacific theatre, in the hands of RAAF aircrew, that the Beaufort made its most telling contribution to the war.

BRISTOL BLENHEIM

The fact that the Bristol Blenheim equipped more RAF bomber squadrons than any other type at the outbreak of war was almost entirely due to the desire of Lord Rothermere in 1934, then proprietor of the *Daily Mail* newspaper, to obtain a fast and spacious private aircraft that would prove Britain was at the forefront of aviation design. The Bristol company had already begun preliminary designs for such an aircraft in 1933, and when the prototype Type 142 named 'Britain First' first flew in April 1935 it was a revelation. Trials conducted at Martlesham Heath in June revealed that the Type 142 was over 30 mph faster than the latest RAF fighter, causing much embarrassment.

The Bristol company and the Air Ministry had, by this time, already anticipated the military applications such an aircraft could fulfill, and in August 1935 Bristol received an order for 150 Type 142M bombers based on the design of 'Britain First'. Powered by two Bristol Mercury engines the first operational Blenheim Mk Is, as the type had then been named, were delivered to No 114 Squadron in spring 1937.

Specification: Blenheim Mk I
Manufacturers: Bristol, Avro, Rootes Securities
Number built: 6,355 for the RAF (1,427 Mk I, 3,983 Mk IV and 945 Mk V)
Entry into service: March 1937
Powerplant: Two 840 hp Bristol Mercury VIII
Length: 39 ft 9 in (12.12 m)
Height: 12 ft 10 in (3.91 m)
Wingspan: 56 ft 4 in (17.17 m)
Weight empty: 8,100 lb (3,682 kg)
Range: 1,125 miles (1,810 km) at 165 mph (265 km/h)
Max speed: 285 mph (459 km/h) at 15,000 ft (4,575 m)
Service ceiling: 25,500 ft (7,772 m)
Armament: 1 x 0.303-in (7.7-mm) forward firing machine gun, one 0.303-in (7.7-mm) machine gun in dorsal turret plus up to 1,000 lb (454 kg) of bombs

Specification: Blenheim Mk IV)
Powerplant: Two 920 hp Bristol Mercury XV
Length: 42 ft 9 in (13.03 m)
Height: 12 ft 10 in (3.91 m)
Wingspan: 56 ft 4 in (17.17 m)
Weight empty: 9,790 lb (4,445 kg)
Maximum range: 1,460 miles (2,350 km)
Max speed: 266 mph (428 km/h) at 11,800 ft (3,595 m)
Service ceiling: 27,260 ft (8,310 m)
Armament: 5 x 0.303-in (7.7-mm), one forward-firing, two in dorsal turret and two rear-firing remotely controlled below nose plus up to 1,320 lb (599 kg) of bombs

Above: An early Beaufort IV light bomber.

Right: Bravely flying daylight sorties in Europe, Blenheim units suffered heavy losses.

Below left: As a makeshift night fighter the Blenheim I filled a gap.

Below: Confidently taxying out for the press, Blenheim IV crews were glad to get more modern aircraft.

Fitted with one forward-firing machine gun, a single gun Bristol B.1 Mk I dorsal turret and capable of carrying a 1,000 lb bombload, the Blenheim was hailed as one of the finest bombers in the world. To alleviate the cramped conditions Bristol developed the design with an extended nose and, to extend range, extra fuel tanks in the wings. With a 'stepped' windscreen and a scalloped forward hooding to improve the pilot's view ahead the new variant was originally named Bolingbroke (later applied to Canadian-built versions) but became known as the Blenheim Mk IV. Introduced in 1939 the Blenheim Mk IV steadily superseded Bomber Command's original force of Mk I bombers.

Within two hours of the declaration of war a Blenheim Mk IV from No 139 Squadron flew the first operational sortie of the war reconnoitring the German fleet at Kiel. The following day 10 Blenheims from Nos 107 and 110 Squadrons (along with 14 Wellingtons) made the first raid on a German target attacking warships at Wilhelmshaven. The attack was a disaster with five of the Blenheims being shot down. Like other RAF Bomber Command types the Blenheim suffered readily at the hands of Luftwaffe fighters during daylight attacks in the winter of 1939-40, but persisted sporadic raids and reconnaissance sorties continued until the Battle of France began in May 1940.

The six Blenheim Mk IV squadrons assigned to the British Expeditionary Force and the Advanced Air Striking Force were immediately pushed into intensive operations suffering crippling losses, due in part to their poor defensive armament. On 17 May No 82 Squadron lost 11 out of 12 aircraft and many other units suffered similar casualties. By the end of the battle, UK- and French-based squadrons had lost a total of 175 Blenheims. The Blenheim Mk IV Squadrons played an active role in the Battle of Britain making low-level attacks

against German installations and being heavily involved in reconnaissance. The defeat of the Luftwaffe in the autumn of 1940 led to a scaling-down of Blenheim operations with most being high-level small formation raids against occupied territory. The advent of the Boston and Mosquito ensured that by the end of 1941 the Blenheim had been withdrawn from front line Bomber Command units.

Many of the Blenheim Mk Is which had been replaced from 1938 by the Mk IV were earmarked for conversion to long-range fighters with a battery of four forward-firing machine guns in a pack beneath the bomb bay. Deemed unsuitable for daylight operations in 1940, the aircraft found a new role towards the end of that year as night-fighters.

One of the few aircraft able to carry the new AI.Mk III interception radar, the Blenheim Mk IF was one of the more successful types in intercepting German bomber during the night Blitz of the winter of 1940-41. The first 'kill' using radar was made on July 23, 1940 when a Mk IF from the Fighter Interception Unit downed a Dornier Do 17 and many others followed as the technique was perfected. The introduction of the Beaufighter in late-1940 freed the Blenheims for night intruder missions attacking German bombers as they left their bases. The Mk IF continued in this role until April 1941.

RAF Coastal Command also employed the Blenheim Mk IV in the anti-shipping and maritime patrol roles. From 1940, 11 Coastal

Above: A dedicated rebuild brought UK air show crowds a Blenheim after many thought it extinct.

Right: Blenheims lined up for a squadron inspection.

Above Left: Blenheim Mk IVs on a pre-war exercise.

Below left: Slow and ill-armed, Blenheim IVs were massacred over France when the Germans attacked in 1940.

Below: Coming into land, a preserved Blenheim reflects all the dedication of the restorers.

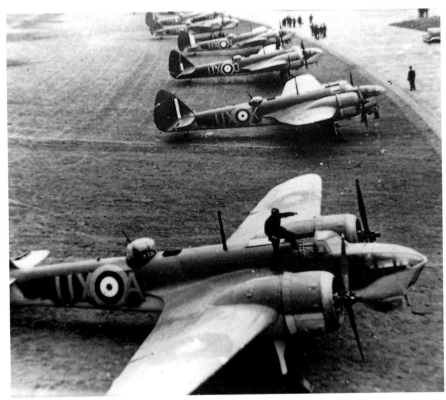

Command squadrons were equipped with the Mk IVF (fitted with the belly gun pack) and were used with moderate results against German shipping. These aircraft would have been the main attack aircraft used to destroy the invasion barges if Hitler's plans had ever been implemented, but the attack never materialised and by the end of 1941 most of the Coastal Command Blenheims had been relegated to secondary duties.

Blenheims were destined to have a much longer service career in the Mediterranean and Far East theatres. On June 11, 1940 a mixed force of Blenheim Mk Is and Mk IVs from Nos 45, 55 and 113 Squadrons based in Egypt made the first attack against an Italian target, bombing the airfield at El Adem, Libya. These units along with five other squadrons continued bombing and reconnaissance missions throughout 1940. In 1941 the invasion of Greece saw Nos 84, 211, 113 and 11 Squadrons involved in continuous raids against advancing Italian and then German forces suffering heavy casualties in the process. The Blenheim Mk IV squadrons were heavily involved in the Western Desert in 1941-42 before the last squadron withdrew the type in December of that year. In November four squadrons of the new Blenheim Mk V supported the Allied Torch landings although they too suffered heavy casualties at the hands of Messerschmitt Bf 109s. Nos 13 and 614 Squadrons retained the Mk V for the invasion of Sicily in 1943 before the type was finally withdrawn from this theatre in early 1944.

In the Far East Blenheim Mk Is were in action from the start although many were destroyed on the ground in bombing raids as the Japanese advanced. By the start of 1942 only 19 of 62 Blenheim Mk Is remained serviceable. In the spring of 1942 two squadrons of Blenheims were involved in a valiant, but unsuccessful, attempt to defend Sumatra from the Japanese but by June had withdrawn to India. The Blenheim Mk V began to re-equip the Far East units from October 1942, but the aircraft's unsuitability for tropical conditions ensured that their impact was marginal and by the end of 1943 all had been reallocated to second-line duties.

Above: A warbird Blenheim pictured on an early flight.

Right and Below left: Blenheims changed little during their RAF service.

Above left: A Blenheim of 13 OTU demonstrates its Lewis gun armament.

Below: In a black night intruder scheme, this warbird Blenheim has No 68 Squadron codes.

DE HAVILLAND MOSQUITO

De Havilland's 'wooden wonder' was one of the outstanding British aircraft of the Second World War. From the time of its introduction in September 1941, until early 1944, it was the fastest type in the RAF and remained the fastest aircraft in Bomber Command until the introduction of the Canberra jet bomber in 1951!

Like the Supermarine Spitfire and the Rolls-Royce Merlin engine that powered both the Spitfire and the new de Havilland design, the Mosquito was a private venture. Of all-wooden construction, it was intended that it carry no defensive armament, relying instead on its speed alone. Official interest was scant at first, but the outbreak of war brought permission to develop a light bomber based on the de Havilland design, able to carry a 1,000-lb bomb load over 1,500 miles. Work began at the end of 1939 and on March 1, 1940 50 aircraft

were ordered to Specification B.1/40. A prototype was completed in great secrecy and flown for the first time on November 25.

In the event, the first three Mosquitos were completed to fill three different roles and it was a photo-reconnaissance variant that entered service first. Ten of the first 50 aircraft were built as Mk I long-range, reconnaissance machines, the first successful mission by one of these aircraft taking place on 20 September 1941. By the end of 1943, three squadrons were equipped with the type, flying regular sorties well into occupied Europe.

The first Mosquito bombers, Mk IVs, carried four 500-lb bombs, twice the weight specified, and replaced Blenheims in No 2 (Light Bomber) Group. No 105 Squadron received its first examples in November 1941 and flew its first sortie on May 31, 1942 - a daylight raid on Cologne. Further raids

followed and on May 31, 1943 Berlin was targeted for the first time.

Meanwhile, the second Mosquito prototype to take to the air was a night-fighter, flown in May 1941. Conforming to RAF Specification F.21/40, the aircraft was fitted with the secret AI.Mk IV radar and was followed by 398 Mosquito Mk IIs, the first of which entered service with No 157 Squadron, Fighter Command in January 1942. Operations began in April and by the end of the year Mosquito NF.Mk II (Intruder) aircraft were based in Malta. As well as air-to-air operations, these aircraft were also engaged in train-busting using their four 20-mm cannon and four 0.303-in machine guns. While further night-fighter variants entered service, each with improved engines and radar, it was the Mk VI fighter-bomber, that was to be the most widely-used of the fighter derivatives. These entered service as day and night intruders, undertaking daring raids across the

Specification: Mosquito F.Mk II

Manufacturers: de Havilland, De Havilland Canada, de Havilland Australia, Airspeed, Percival and Standard

Number built: 7,785 (inc Canadian and Australian production; 467 Mk II, 343 Mk III, 273 Mk IV, 2,218 Mk VI, 270 Mk XIII, 432 Mk XIV, 1,200 Mk XVI, 220 Mk XIX, 145 Mk XX, 400 B25, 338 FB26, 526 NF30, 266 NF36)

Entry into service: July 1941

Powerplant: Two 1,460 hp Rolls-Royce Merlin 21/23

Length: 40 ft 6 in (12.34 m)

Height: 12 ft 6 in (3.81 m)

Wingspan: 54 ft 2 in (16.51 m)

Weight empty: 14,300 lb (6,492 kg)

Normal range: 1,705 miles (2,743 km)

Max speed: 370 mph (595 km/h) at 14,000 ft (4,267 m)

Service ceiling: 36,000 ft (1,0973 m)

Armament: 4 x 20-mm cannon in front fuselage plus 4 x 0.303-in (7.7-mm) machine guns mounted in nose

Specification: Mosquito B.Mk XVI

Powerplant: Two 1,710 hp Rolls-Royce Merlin 76/77

Length: 44 ft 6 in (13.56 m)

Height: 12 ft 6 in (3.81 m)

Wingspan: 54 ft 2 in (16.51 m)

Weight empty: 14,600 lb (6,628 kg)

Range: 1,485 miles (2,380 km) with maximum load

Max speed: 415 mph (668 km/h) at 28,000 ft (8,534 m)

Service ceiling: 37,000 ft (11,278 m)

Armament: 1 x 4000-lb or 4 x 500-lb bombs in bomb bay plus 2 x 500-lb bombs under wings

English Channel (latterly with 2nd TAF) equipped with underwing bombs and relying on their speed to evade Luftwaffe fighters. Others were equipped with eight rocket projectiles and issued to Coastal Command for anti-shipping sorties.

Of the radar-equipped aircraft, Mks XIX and XXX, the latter with Merlin 70 series engines with two-stage supercharging, were perhaps the most important and equipped not only Fighter Command units, but also squadrons within No 100 (Bomber Support) Group, Bomber Command, operating in the bomber streams over Germany to protect them from attack by Luftwaffe night fighters.

Following the success of the B.Mk IV, Mosquito bomber development progressed to the Mk IX, with Merlin 70 series engines and a ceiling over 36,000 ft. These aircraft

Below left: A preserved Mosquito typifying the RAF strike squadrons of mid-1944.

Below: Mosquito FB.Mk VI fighter-bombers were highly effective in their dual role.

carried extra bombs on underwing racks and a number carried 'Oboe' blind bombing radar and served as pathfinders within Bomber Command. All Mk IXs and the few Mk IVs still in use were eventually modified to carry a 4,000-lb bomb, hitherto the preserve of the heavy bombers, the weapon being carried by Mosquitos for the first time in February 1944. The next bomber variant was the B.Mk XVI, which introduced cabin pressurisation, allowing operations up to 40,000 ft, and it was this version that was to be the main equipment of the Light Night Striking Force, undertaking nuisance raids, independent of the Main Force 'heavies'. Mk XVIs were among those aircraft on Bomber Command's last raid of the war, on May 2 1945.

Before the war's end, one more Mosquito bomber variant flew, though the B.Mk 35 was too late for wartime service. With a top speed of 422 mph, the Mk 35 could carry 2,000 lb of bombs for 2,050 miles.

Photographic reconnaissance Mosquito development followed the

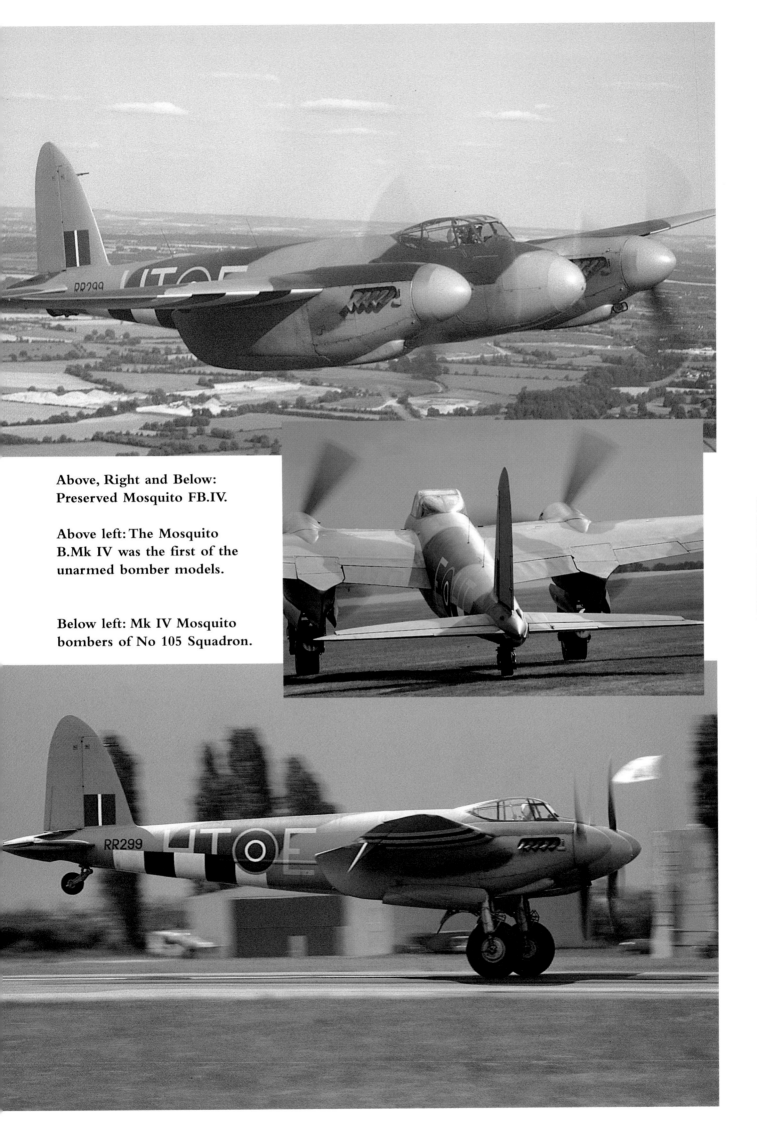

Above, Right and Below:
Preserved Mosquito FB.IV.

Above left: The Mosquito B.Mk IV was the first of the unarmed bomber models.

Below left: Mk IV Mosquito bombers of No 105 Squadron.

Above: Wartime view of a Mosquito Mk IV on test.

Right: Photo-recon was another role in which the Mosquito excelled.

Below right: A deep-bellied Mosquito with extra tanks taxying out during an air show.

pattern set by the bomber variants. PR.Mk Is were followed by 27 Mk IV bombers converted for PR use, one of which was fitted with Merlin 60 engines as the first of the Mk VIIIs. These were followed by a new high-altitude version based on the B.Mk IX bomber, the PR.Mk IX becoming the principal type within PR Mosquito squadrons during 1943/44. From the end of 1943, operations by the PR 'Mossies' began in the Far East.

The most widely-used of the camera-equipped aircraft was the Mk XVI, again a bomber derivative and one that served until the end of the war from bases in the UK, with the 2nd TAF in Europe and in the Far East. The final reconnaissance aircraft were very-long-range Mk 34s, based on the Mk XVI but fitted with underwing drop tanks and large tanks in the redundant bomb bay which boosted range to 3,500 miles. In service from late 1944, the Mk 34 was primarily intended for South East Asia Command and the expected campaign against Japan.

DE HAVILLAND TIGER MOTH

One of the most famous training aircraft in the world, the de Havilland DH 82A Tiger Moth was produced in large numbers both before and during the Second World War, to meet the escalating demands of elementary flying training for both British and Commonwealth air forces.

Developed from de Havillands highly successful DH 60 Moth the Tiger Moth, in DH 82A form, featured slightly swept wings with increased dihedral on the lower unit and a de Havilland Gipsy Major inline piston engine. To meet the RAF specification a blind flying hood was incorporated which could be positioned over the rear cockpit for instrument flying training and it was fully aerobatic.

Already in service with many of the Elementary and Reserve Flying Schools by 1939, the outbreak of war saw further substantial orders, many

of which were built at the Cowley works of Morris Motors, and many civilian aircraft impressed into RAF service as station hacks and trainers. In September 1939 Tiger Moths were dispatched to France as part of the British Expeditionary Force for

communications duties becoming No 81 Squadron. Operating under the most trying conditions during the Battle of France, the aircraft remained until the evacuation of the British Forces at Dunkirk. Other aircraft were allocated to Coastal

---

Specification: De Havilland DH 82A Tiger Moth
Manufacturers: De Havilland (Great Britain, Australia and New Zealand), Morris Motors
Number built: 8,280 (plus 420 Queen Bees)
Entry into service: 1932
Powerplant: One 130 hp DH Gipsy Major I
Length: 23 ft 11 in (7.29 m)
Height: 8 ft 9 in (2.68 m)
Wingspan: 29 ft 4 in (8.94 m)
Weight empty: 1,115 lb (506 kg)
Range: 302 miles (486 km)
Max speed: 104 mph (167 km/h) at 1,000 ft (305 m)
Service ceiling: 13,600 ft (4,145 m)
Armament: Could be adapted to carry 8 x 20 lb (9.07 kg) bombs on underwing racks

Command for reconnaissance of the English Channel in late 1939 and 1940. As the threat of invasion grew in the summer of 1940 Tiger Moths were adapted to carry small weapons racks for 20 lb bombs. In the event of invasion over 500 Tiger Moths would have been called on to attack the landing craft but the need never arose.

In the Far East modified Tiger Moths capable of carrying a single stretcher case saw service in the air ambulance role with No 224 Squadron. It was in the elementary training role, however, that the DH 82A made its most vital contribution serving with around 70 Flying Training Schools in Britain, Canada, Australia, India and South Africa.

Most famous of the de Havilland Moth line, the Tiger was built in large numbers and gave many RAF cadets their first taste of flying — and today wartime colours adorn many current Tiger Moths. Although a trainer Tiger Moths saw some combat duty in 1940.

FAIREY ALBACORE

Ordered off the drawing board in May 1937 as a replacement for the Swordfish torpedo bomber, the Fairey Albacore was to be outlived in operational service by the aircraft it was intended to supersede. Fitted with an enclosed cockpit to protect the three-man crew from the elements and the new and unproven Bristol Taurus engine, it was intended that the Albacore would be ready for operational service by the end of 1938.

When the first production aircraft was delivered to the A&AEE it soon became apparent that all was not well with the aircraft. The aircraft's controls were heavy and did not respond

Specification: Albacore Mk I
Manufacturers: Fairey
Number built: 802
Entry into service: March 1940
Powerplant: One 1,130 hp Bristol Taurus XII
Length: 39 ft 10 in (12.14 m)
Height: 14 ft 2 in (4.32 m)
Wingspan: 50 ft 0 in (15.24 m)
Weight empty: 7,250 lb (3,289 kg)
Range fully loaded: 930 miles (1,497 km)
Max speed: 161 mph (259 km/h) at 4,500 ft (1,370 m)
Service ceiling: 20,700 ft (6,310 m)
Armament: 1 x 0.303-in (7.7-mm) forward-firing machine gun and two 0.303-in (7.7-mm) machine guns in rear cockpit plus one 1,610-lb (730-kg) torpedo or up to 2,000 lb (907 kg) of bombs

well to the pilot's inputs, cockpit ventilation was poor with the front cockpit overheating in the sun and the rear position subject to icy draughts. The Taurus engine was also found to be unreliable.

Production was delayed pending solutions to the powerplant problems, and the first operational unit,

Above left: The 'Applecore' to its Navy crews, the Albacore was like a more comfortable Swordfish.

Left: A poor engine curtailed the Albacore's career but is saw some combat.

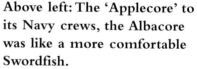

Above right: Albacores in the Middle East, a theater where they were most widely used.

Right: Designed for carrier operations, the Albacore did not replace the Swordfish, as intended.

No 826 Squadron, did not equip with the Albacore until March 1940. On May 31, 1940, it made its combat début when No 826 Squadron attacked a number of E-boats off the Belgian coast and by the autumn of 1940 had been joined by three more squadrons on mine-laying and anti-shipping duties. In the winter of 1940/41 Nos 826 and 829 Squadrons joined HMS *Formidable* for convoy escort duty to South Africa attacking the Italian battleship *Vittorio Veneto* during the Battle of Cape Matapan. Albacore deployment reached its peak in mid-1942 with 15 squadrons operating the type on convoys to Northern Russia, in the Mediterranean, the Indian Ocean and the North Atlantic, both from carriers and from land bases. From the spring of 1943 the type was rapidly replaced by the Fairey Barracuda and the last frontline FAA squadron withdrew the aircraft the following November.

FAIREY BARRACUDA

With the age of biplane warplanes drawing to a close the Air Ministry issued a specification in 1938 for a new monoplane torpedo/dive-bomber to replace the Swordfish and Albacore. The Fairey Barracuda was selected as the winning design and flown in prototype form in December 1940, powered by a 24-cylinder Rolls-Royce X engine.

Fitted with large flaps which could adopt a negative angle for diving attacks the Barracuda had vastly improved speed and climb performance compared to its predecessors. Testing of the prototype Barracuda Mk Is fitted with the Merlin 30 engine and service equipment revealed that the aircraft was underpowered. Production was quickly changed to the Mk II with the more powerful Merlin 32 engine, that largely cured the problem.

The aircraft entered operational service in Mk II form with No 827 Squadron in January 1943 and first saw action during the Salerno landings. Steadily replacing the Albacore and Swordfish, a total of 10 squadrons were equipped for anti-

shipping operations in the North Sea and English Channel by the beginning of 1944. Starting in April 1944 carrier-based Barracudas flew their most famous missions against the German battleship *Tirpitz* moored in a Norwegian fjord. In the first raid the ship was heavily damaged and over the following four months further raids prevented the ship from reaching operational status. In 1945

the Barracuda Mk III with ASV radar was gradually introduced, increasing the aircrafts capabilities.

From April 1944 Nos 810 and 847 Squadrons began operations in the Pacific theatre aboard HMS *Illustrious*. Dive-bombing attacks were made on Japanese land and maritime targets and continued to support the Allies advance until the end of the war.

Specification: Barracuda Mk II
Manufacturers: Fairey, Blackburn, Boulton Paul, Westland
Number built: 2,602 (23 Mk I, 1,637 Mk II, 912 Mk III, 30 Mk V)
Entry into service: January 1943
Powerplant: One 1,640 hp Rolls-Royce Merlin 32
Length: 39 ft 9 in (12.12 m)
Height: 15 ft 1 in (4.60 m)
Wingspan: 49 ft 2 in (14.99 m)
Weight empty: 9,350 lb (4,241 kg)
Range fully loaded: 1,150 miles (1,851 km) without weapon load
Max speed: 228 mph (367 km/h) at 1,750 ft (535 m)
Service ceiling: 16,600 ft (5,060 m)
Armament: 2 x 0.303-in (7.7-mm) forward-firing machine guns plus 1 x 1,620-lb (735-kg) torpedo or an equivalent weight of bombs, depth charges or mines

Above: Armed with a torpedo and little else, Barracuda crews bravely attacked the *Tirpitz* with some success.

Right: A carrier 'batsman' guides a Barracuda pilot down.

Below left and Below: As ugly as sin and only tolerated by its crews, fortunately the 'Barra' was not often exposed to enemy fighters.

FAIREY BATTLE

The Fairey Battle was hailed on its arrival into RAF service as the finest single-engined light bomber in the world. Capable of carrying a 1,000-lb bombload over 1,000 miles at speeds in excess of 240 mph the Battle certainly represented a big increase in capability over its predecessor, the Hawker Hart. However, within three years of its entry into service the Battle would be devastated during the Battle of France and from that point onwards would be destined for the less glamorous training or target-towing roles.

At the outbreak of war more than 1,000 Battles had been delivered to the RAF and a number of units were immediately deployed to France as part of the Advanced Air Striking Force. During the next eight months of the Phoney War it became clear that the Battle would be unable to defend itself against the Luftwaffes fighters suffering many casualties whilst engaged on daylight reconnaissance missions.

This problem manifested itself with disastrous consequences from May 1940 when, during the desperate defence of France, the Battle squadrons were literally ripped to pieces. With great bravery the Battle crews persisted, typified by the actions of five No 12 squadron aircraft which attacked two vital bridges over the Albert Canal at Maastricht on May 10. One bridge was seriously damaged for the loss of all five aircraft and crew. When 35 of 63 Battles failed to return from sorties on May 14 the RAF resigned itself to withdrawing the type from front line service. A high proportion of them were allocated to Commonwealth Flying Training Schools in Canada and Australia.

Specification: Battle Mk I
Manufacturers: Fairey, Austin Motors, Avions Fairey
Number built: 2,201
Entry into service: May 1937
Powerplant: One 1,030 hp Rolls-Royce Merlin I
Length: 42 ft 4 in (12.90 m)
Height: 15 ft 6 in (4.72 m)
Wingspan: 54 ft 0 in (16.46 m)
Weight empty: 6,647 lb (3,015 kg)
Range fully loaded: 1,000 miles (1,609 km)
Max speed: 257 mph (414 km/h) at 20,000 ft (6,100 m)
Service ceiling: 25,000 ft (7,620 m)
Armament: 1 x 0.303-in (7.7-mm) forward-firing machine gun in starboard wing and 1x 0.303-in (7.7-mm) machine gun in rear cockpit plus up to 1,000 lb (454 kg) of bombs

Above: Nobody knew when it first flew how bad the Battle would be, as it replaced biplanes — and obviously looked good!

Left: Another unfortunate RAF crew about the board a Battle for a sortie over France.

Far left: A poor idea that got worse in combat the Battle was cumbersome and slow, a disaster in combat.

Below: A use was found for the Battle far away from the war, as a trainer in Canada.

FAIREY FIREFLY

By 1940 the fighter assets of the Fleet Air Arm were deemed by the Admiralty to be inadequate. The current front line fighter, the Fairey Fulmar, was slow, relatively unmanoeuvrable and underpowered and a specification for a new reconnaissance fighter was issued in 1940. Performance would be of paramount importance for the new aircraft, however, the Navy insisted on retaining a two-man crew.

In response to the specification Fairey designed the monoplane Firefly powered by a Rolls-Royce Griffon engine. The aircraft was ordered into production from the drawing board in June 1940, and the first of four prototypes made its maiden flight on December 22, 1941. One of the most important features of the aircraft were the Youngman flaps which could be fully retracted for high-speed flight but extended outwards and backwards to provide excellent lift at slower speeds. The flaps could also be deployed in a 'turning fight' decreasing the turning circle and enabling the aircraft to out-manoeuvre many contemporary single-seat fighters.

The first operational unit to fly

Specification: Firefly Mk I
Manufacturers: Fairey, General Aircraft
Number built: 978 Mk Is (after 1945 645 FR4/AS6)
Entry into service: October 1943
Powerplant: Rolls-Royce Griffon
Length: 37 ft 7 in (11.46 m)
Height: 13 ft 7 in (4.14 m)
Wingspan: 44 ft 6 in (13.56 m)
Weight empty: 9,750 lb (4,423 kg)
Normal range: 1,300 miles (2,092 km)
Max speed: 316 mph (509 km/h) at 14,000 ft (4,265 m)
Service ceiling: 28,000 ft (8,535 m)
Armament: 4 x 20-mm cannon in wings plus up to 2,000 lb (907 kg) of bombs or 8 x 60-lb (27-kg) rocket projectiles

the Firefly FR.Mk I was No 1770 Squadron at Yeovilton in October 1943. No 1771 Squadron followed at the same base in February 1944, and the last of the trio of units to operate this variant type during the war was No 1772 Squadron, which was equipped in May 1944. The first combat action was conducted by No 1770 Sqn Fireflies, embarked on HMS *Indefatigable*, supporting the bombing raids on the *Tirpitz*. The aircraft strafed defensive gun positions before Fleet Air Arm

Baracudas attacked the battleship, returning for further raids later in the summer

No 1771 aboard HMS *Implacable* joined No 1770 Sqn in September 1944 and both squadrons were actively engaged in providing cover for mine-laying operations and attacking enemy shipping off the Norwegian coast with one troopship destroyed and four damaged.

At the end of 1944 the three Firefly squadrons were allocated to the British Pacific Fleet for service in

the Far East. The first to arrive was No 1770 Sqn, which was involved in attacks on oil refineries in Sumatra using rocket projectiles. During these strikes the first air-to-air 'kill' by a Firefly was made on January 4, 1945 when Lt D. Levitt downed a Ki-43 Hayabusa and six more Japanese aircraft were claimed by the unit before the end of the month. In the spring the unit attacked targets in the South China Sea and Taiwan before withdrawing to Australia in June. At this time No 1771 Sqn began operations in the theatre with strikes on the Caroline Islands and finally in July becoming the first FAA aircraft to attack mainland Japan. No 1772 Squadron aboard HMS *Indefatigable*

joined the strikes on Japan in July and these two units continued in the ground-attack role until VJ-Day.

The dedicated night-fighter Firefly NF.Mk II was plagued by instability problems caused by the installation of airborne intercept radar in the wings. With this variant unable to achieved operational status No. 746 squadron received Firefly NF.Mk Is and developed operational naval night-fighting procedures. In October 1943 the unit dispatched aircraft and crews to RAF Coltishall to intercept V-1 flying bomb-carrying Heinkel He 111s, but none were ever shot down. No 1790 Squadron became the first operational naval night-fighter squadron to be

Above and Below: Combat in Korea proved the Firefly's good combat capability.

Below left: Although its missed the limelight in WWII, the Firefly served the Fleet Air Arm well.

embarked on a carrier when it sailed for the Pacific in February 1945 equipped with Firefly NF.Mk Is, but arrived too late to see any action.

The Firefly had proven to be an exceptionally accurate and stable ground-attack aircraft and later variants were to demonstrate this ability during the Korean War.

FAIREY FULMAR

In 1934 the Fairey company designed an aerodynamically clean two-seat monoplane day bomber known as the P.4/34. Stressed to cope with dive-bombing the aircraft first flew in January 1937 and showed excellent performance for its intended role. Meanwhile the Admiralty had concluded that the standard of navigation aids was not sufficient to permit single-seat fighter operations and desperately required a new monoplane fighter. To meet the demand development of the day bomber version was abandoned and modifications were incorporated for the fighter role. A modified P.4/34 was used as a prototype and the aircraft was ordered into production in May 1938.

Named Fulmar Mk I the aircraft was introduced into service by No 808 Squadron in June 1940 and in the latter half of the year Nos 806 and 807 Squadrons also became operational with the type. In October 1940 No 808 Squadron aboard HMS *Ark Royal* began operations in the Mediterranean flying convoy patrol and fighter escort

sorties. In 1941 the squadron was joined by Nos 806 and 807 and these three units were heavily involved in actions against the Italian air force in the defence of the Malta Convoys in May November of that year. Nos 807 and 808 Squadrons shot down 15 enemy fighters in July-August and the aircraft held its own in dogfights until faced by superior German aircraft during the Greek campaign. The lack of rear-firing armament was undoubtedly the aircrafts weak point and once enemy

aircraft realised that they could safely attack from this quarter, the Fulmars days as a front line fighter were numbered. Deliveries to front line units continued in 1942 and early 1943 with over 15 squadrons equipped with the type by April 1943 flying valuable convoy escort and, in the Indian Ocean, long-range reconnaissance operations. However, the advent of the Firefly in the latter half of 1943 relegated the Fulmar to secondary units with the final example being withdrawn in March 1945.

Specification: Fulmar Mk I
Manufacturers: Fairey
Number built: 602
Entry into service: June 1940
Powerplant: One 1,080 hp Rolls-Royce Merlin VIII
Length: 40 ft 3 in (12.27 m)
Height: 14 ft 0 in (4.27 m)
Wingspan: 46 ft 5 in (14.15 m)
Weight empty: 6,915 lb (3,137 kg)
Maximum Range fully loaded: 800 miles (1,287 km)
Max speed: 280 mph (451 km/h)
Service ceiling: 26,000 ft (7,925 m)
Armament: 8 x 0.303-in (7.7-mm) forward-firing machine guns

Top: Unblessed with fighter performance, the Fulmar was only a 'stop gap' type.

Above: The sheer size of the Fulmar went against it in service.

Right: The Fleet Air Arm museum at Yeovilton, Somerset has a preserved Fulmar Mk II.

Left: Another unfortunate result of the single-engined light bomber concept, the Fulmar became a Royal Navy fighter.

FAIREY SWORDFISH

Obsolete at the outbreak of the Second World War the Fairey Swordfish was to go on to become one of the Fleet Air Arm's most successful warplanes of the conflict. Outliving its successor, the Fairey Albacore, it destroyed a greater tonnage of enemy shipping than any other Allied torpedo bomber.

Initially designated TSR.II, the Swordfish first flew in April 1934 and could be fitted with either wheeled or float undercarriage. The fabric-covered metal tube fuselage held a standard crew of three and the aircraft was capable of lifting a standard 1,610-lb torpedo from the deck of all Royal Navy aircraft carriers with a full load; its folding wings allowing easy storage on the crowded flight decks. Entering service with No 823 Squadron in February 1936 the aircraft was immediately recognised as an ideal for the reconnaissance and anti-shipping role and further orders were rapidly instigated.

At the outbreak of the Second World World War over 500 Swordfish Mk Is were in Fleet Air Arm service in both wheeled form (serving from aircraft carriers and land stations) and as floatplanes (from seaplane bases and with Catapult Flights on Royal Navy battleships and cruisers). During the Phoney War between September 1939 and May 1940 the Swordfish squadrons saw only limited action, using the time to perfect their torpedo and bombing skills. The German invasion of the Low Countries on May 10, 1940 immediately brought the Swordfish into offensive action. On May 11 Swordfish from the carrier *Furious* made the first torpedo attack of the war and this was followed two days later by the first U-boat 'kill'

Specification: Swordfish Mk II (landplane)
Manufacturers: Fairey, Blackburn
Number built: 2,391
Entry into service: July 1936
Powerplant: One 690 hp Bristol Pegasus IIIM3 or XXX
Length: 35 ft 8 in (10.87 m)
Height: 12 ft 4 in (3.76 m)
Wingspan: 45 ft 6 in (13.87 m)
Weight empty: 4,700 lb (2,132 kg)
Maximum range: 1,030 miles (1,658 km)
Max speed: 138 mph (222 km/h)
Service ceiling: 10,700 ft (3,260 m)
Armament: 2 x 0.303-in (7.7-mm) machine guns (1 x forward-firing, 1 x aft cockpit) plus 1x 1,610-lb (730 kg) torpedo or up to 1,500 lb (680 kg) of bombs mines or rockets or 8 x 60-lb (27-kg) rocket projectiles

when a catapulted floatplane Swordfish from HMS *Warspite* sank the submarine U-64 using bombs.

These early successes led to further orders, and the lack of capacity at Fairey factories resulted in all subsequent examples being licence-built by Blackburn. The RAF had also adopted the Swordfish for Coastal Command mine-laying operations and bombing attacks on German-held ports. To provide extra range two additional fuel tanks were mounted in the rear cockpit and sorties were normally flown with only two crew members.

Undoubtedly the Swordfish's greatest achievement of the war occurred on November 11, 1940 when 21 Swordfish from Nos 813, 815, 819 and 824 Squadrons embarked on HMS *Illustrious* attacked the Italian fleet in Taranto harbour. Launching at night and at low-level, the attack achieved almost complete tactical surprise. At 23.00 the first wave of 12 aircraft, carrying

Above: Dramatic peel-off for rocket-carrying Swordfish supporting the D-Day landings.

Left: Unfolding a Swordfish's wings was a major, manual job.

Below left: Some Swordfish were float-equipped for capital ship spotter duty.

Far left, above: 'Stringbags' hung with bombs, mines, torpedoes and rockets were still more effective than some FAA monoplanes.

Far left, below: Pride of the FAA museum its preserved Swordfish.

flares, torpedoes and bombs, weaved its way through the protective umbrella of barrage balloons and pressed home its attack. The Italian fleet responded with a barrage of light and heavy anti-aircraft fire but with great skill the attack was pressed home. The second wave of nine followed soon after successfully deploying both bombs and torpedoes against the fleet. Reconnaissance sorties the following morning revealed the remarkable results; the new battleship *Littorio* had been sunk at its moorings, two other battleships, a cruiser and two destroyers were crippled and two auxiliary vessels had been sunk for the loss of two of the attacking Swordfish. This one raid had cut Italy's naval power in half and changed the balance of naval power in the Mediterranean.

For the next 18 months Swordfish squadrons continued to harry Axis shipping in the Mediterranean, sinking over 1,500,000 tons of enemy vessels in this period. By mid-1942 it was becoming obvious that it was no longer practical to deploy Swordfish on torpedo attacks. The aircraft's slow speed and long attack run made them easy targets and losses were prohibitively high. This was demonstrated at great cost in February 1942 when Lt Cdr Eugene Esmonde was detailed to intercept the German warships *Scharnhorst*, *Gneisenau* and *Prinz Eugen*, which were attempting to escape along the English Channel. Flying from Manston, Esmonde led a force of six Swordfish, which located the warships mid-Channel. Meeting a barrage of flak defences and enemy fire all six aircraft were downed before they could press home a successful attack, Esmonde subsequently received a posthumous VC for his bravery. Esmonde had previously led the vital attack on the battleship *Bismarck* that was causing havoc amongst Allied shipping in the North Atlantic. Nine Swordfish attacked with torpedoes crippling the steering mechanism thus allowing the British fleet to catch and sink the crippled vessel.

As torpedo raids were ending a new variant of the Swordfish was making its impact. The Mk III was equipped with an ASV (Air-to-Surface Vessel) Mk X radar and a strengthened wing to hold rocket projectiles and mines. This combination proved deadly against enemy shipping, submarines and coastal targets highlighted by the achievement of the Swordfish Mk IIIs aboard the escort carrier HMS *Vindex* which managed to sink four U-boats on a single voyage in September 1944 escorting a convoy to Russia.

By this time the Swordfish's intended replacement, the Albacore, had already been retired from frontline service and the venerable 'Stringbag' went on to serve throughout the war in Europe with the final frontline squadron retiring the aircraft on 21 May 1945.

Above: The canvas covering of the 1930s vintage Swordfish is seen to advantage on this pre-served example.

Left: An attempt to 'modernise' the Swordfish was to add a cockpit, but none saw action like this.

Below left: Radar-equipped Swordfish performed useful anti-shipping strikes.

Far left: Classic wartime view of the 'Stringbag'.

Above: Slow speed for torpedo drop was one Swordfish asset.

Left: With three men a Swordfish cockpit became very crowded.

Below: D-Day stripes on this preserved example: the Swordfish was about the slowest aircraft in the air on D-Day.

GLOSTER GLADIATOR

With the monoplane fighter still an unproven concept in the early 1930s, Gloster decided to develop its Gauntlet design, then in service with the RAF, as a private venture. With new single bay wings, improved aerodynamics, an enclosed cockpit and the new Bristol Mercury engine, it was envisaged that the design, named Gladiator, would have a maximum speed of over 250 mph.

In 1935 the Air Ministry placed an initial production order and, fitted with four machine guns, the first examples were delivered in spring 1937. By late 1938 the original Gladiator Mk Is had been replaced in RAF service by the Mk II with the more powerful Mercury VIIIA engine which was also the chosen powerplant for the Fleet Air Arm's 60 Sea Gladiators.

Most front line UK-based squadrons had re-equipped with Spitfires and Hurricanes by the outbreak of the Second World War. Nos 607 and 615 Squadrons were dispatched to France in November

1939, seeing little action before being totally outclassed by Luftwaffe Messerschmitt Bf 109s in the Battle of France. In April 1940 No 263 Squadron operated from a frozen lake in Norway against the advancing Luftwaffe. Despite 14 of the 18 aircraft being destroyed on the ground six confirmed and eight probable 'kills' were made in three days before the squadron was evacuated. In the Mediterranean Nos 6,

33, 80, 94, 112 and 127 were involved in action mainly against Italian opposition in North Africa and Greece until March 1941, proving a match for the Fiat CR.42.

Four Sea Gladiators were involved in the defence of Malta in June 1940, a local journalist named three of the aircraft *Faith*, *Hope* and *Charity* and the much-romanticised exploits of these aircraft have passed into aviation folklore.

Specification: Gladiator Mk II
Manufacturers: Gloster
Number built: 747 (inc export orders; 378 Mk I, 270 Mk II, 98 Sea Gladiators)
Entry into service: February 1937
Powerplant: One 830 hp Bristol Mercury VIIIA/IX
Length: 27 ft 5 in (8.36 m)
Height: 11 ft 7 in (3.53 m)
Wingspan: 32 ft 3 in (9.83 m)
Weight empty: 3,444 lb (1,562 kg)
Range fully loaded: 440 miles (708 km)
Max speed: 257 mph (414 km/h)
Service ceiling: 33,500 ft (1,0211 m)
Armament: 4 x 0.303-in (7.7-mm) forward-firing machine guns

Above: With Norwegian national insignia this preserved Gladiator is one of the few left.

Right: Many colouful markings were sported by pre-war RAF Gladiators.

Below: When camouflage came, the Gladiator had to go to war.

Below left: A Gladiator in pre-war 'silver' finish.

GLOSTER METEOR

Not only was the Gloster Meteor the first jet-powered RAF aircraft to enter operational service it was the only such-powered aircraft to see combat with the Allies during the Second World War. The legendary pioneering work on jet engines completed by Sir Frank Whittle laid the foundations for the development of more powerful turbojet engines, and in February 1941 an order for 12 prototypes of a twin-engined Gloster design were placed. Six different engines were tested on the 12 prototypes but it was the Rolls-Royce W.2B/23C Welland that was chosen to power the first production version, the Meteor Mk I.

On July 12, 1944 No 616 Squadron became the first unit to operate the type and on July 23 moved to Manston to begin V-1 flying bomb interception duties. The first 'kill' was claimed by Flying Officer Dean on 4 August, tipping the V-1 over with his wingtip after his guns had jammed. Later that day Flying Officer Roger gained a more conventional victory using the aircraft's four 20-mm cannon.

In December 1944 the unit received the improved Derwent-powered Meteor Mk III and in January 1945 deployed to Belgium as part of the 2nd Tactical Air Force. In March No 504 Squadron joined No 616 Squadron in Belgium becoming the second and only other Meteor unit to see combat in the Second World War.

Specification: Meteor Mk I
Manufacturers: Gloster
Number built: 20 (Mk I), 210 (Mk III)
Entry into service: July 1944
Powerplant: Two 1,700-lb Rolls-Royce W.2B/23C Wellands
Length: 41 ft 3 in (12.57 m)
Height: 13 ft 0 in (3.96 m)
Wingspan: 43 ft 0 in (13.11 m)
Wt empty: 8,140 lb (3,692 kg)
Max endurance: 1 hr 15 min
Max speed: 415 mph (668 km/h) at 10,000 ft (3,050 m)
Service ceiling: 40,000 ft (12,190 m)
Armament: 4 x 20-mm forward-firing cannon

Below: Mk I Meteors on an early postwar training flight.

Bottom: No 616 Squadron Meteor in 1945.

Above right: A long program tuned the Meteor into a postwar RAF stalwart.

Right: Wartime view of a No 616 Squadron Meteor.

Below right: Preserved Mk I Meteor.

HANDLEY PAGE HALIFAX

Although overshadowed by the more glamorous Avro Lancaster, the Handley Page Halifax played a vital role in the RAF night bombing campaign between 1942-45. Unlike the Lancaster, it also served in other roles including glider towing, maritime patrol and casualty evacuation.

The Halifax stemmed from the twin-engined HP.56 design study of 1936, which was developed to meet the RAF's need for a new medium bomber. Doubts expressed about the Rolls-Royce Vulture in 1937 prompted Handley Page to study alternative powerplants, a decision which was vindicated by the problems the Avro Manchester was to encounter with this engine. With no twin-engined layout able to produce sufficient power Handley Page proposed the installation of four Rolls-Royce Merlin engines taking the aircraft into the class of heavy bomber.

Faith in the aircraft was reflected in the fact that over 500 were on order over a year before the prototype first flew on October 25, 1939.

The aircraft showed good load-carrying ability and performance in trials at the A&AEE and the production specification was set to include nose and tail Boulton Paul turrets containing two and four machine guns respectively (four beam machine guns were added to later production Mk Is). The first production aircraft flew on 11 October 1940 and the first operational unit, No 35 Squadron, made the first Halifax Mk I raid during a daylight attack on Le Havre in March 1941.

By mid-June No 76 Squadron had joined No 35 as part of No 4 Group and day and night raids increased in frequency. In June 1941 five out of 15 attacking Halifaxes were lost during a daylight attack on the battleship *Scharnhorst* and shortly afterwards Bomber Command abandoned almost all daylight operations to concentrate on the night offensive. In October 1941, No 10 Squadron became the third operational unit equipped with the Halifax Mk II, which had improved defensive armament in the shape of a Boulton Paul dorsal turret replacing the beam guns. As the rate of production increased in the early part of 1942 Halifaxes began to replace the Whitleys and Hampdens in frontline squadrons and were to go on to be, with the Lancaster and to a lesser extent the Stirling, the main exponents of 'Bomber' Harris' controversial strategic bombing offensive against German cities.

In April 1942 No 76 Squadron became the first Halifax unit to deploy Bomber Command's new 8,000 lb bomb during a mission on Essen, the aircraft having modified bomb doors. By the time the first '1,000 bomber' raid took place in May 1942 six squadrons were equipped with a mixture of Halifax Mk Is and Mk IIs, and the aircraft's superiority over its twin-engined counterparts was demonstrated by the fact that only four of 118 Halifaxes were lost — a much lower percentage than for other types. Further massed raids against Essen and Bremen followed in June and the Halifax was at the forefront of these tactics which would be employed until the end of the war.

Specification: Halifax Mk I Series III

Manufacturers: Handley Page, English Electric, London Aircraft Production Group, Rootes Securities, Fairey

Number built: 6,179 (inc: 84 Mk I, 1977 Mk II, 904 Mk V, 467 Mk VI and 413 Mk VII)

Entry into service: November 1940

Powerplant: Four 1,280 hp Rolls-Royce Merlin X

Length: 70 ft 1 in (21.36 m)

Height: 20 ft 9 in (6.32 m)

Wingspan: 98 ft 8 in (30.12 m)

Weight empty: 34,020 lb (15,431kg)

Range: 1,260 miles (2,028 km) with maximum bomb load

Max speed: 262 mph (422 km/h) at 17,750 ft (5,410 m)

Service ceiling: 22,800 ft (6,949 m)

Armament: 2 x 0.303-in (7.7-mm) machine guns in nose turret, 4 x 0.303-in (7.7-mm) machine guns in tail turret, 4 x 0.303-in (7.7-mm) machine guns in beam positions, 2 x 0.303-in (7.7-mm) machine guns ventral position plus up to 13,000 lb (5,909 kg) of bombs

Specification: Halifax B.Mk III

Powerplant: Four 1,615hp Bristol Hercules XVI

Length: 71 ft 7 in (21.82 m)

Height: 20 ft 9 in (6.32 m)

Wingspan: 98ft 10 in (30.12 m)

Weight empty: 38,240 lb (17,345 kg)

Range: 1,985 miles (3,149 km) with maximum bomb load

Max speed: 282 mph (454 km/h) at 13,500 ft (4,115 m)

Service ceiling: 24,000 ft (7,315 m)

Armament: 1 x 0.303-in (7.7-mm) machine guns in nose, 4 x 0.303-in (7.7-mm) machine guns in tail turret, 4 x 0.303-in (7.7-mm) machine guns in dorsal turret plus up to 13,000 lb (5,897 kg) of bombs

In September 1942 No 35 Squadron was transferred to become one of the founding units of the Pathfinder Force, helping to determine the procedures that would become so valuable for the Main Bomber Force in the last two years of the war. The introduction of H2S radar in 1943 led to much improved bombing accuracy and as the war progressed more and more Halifaxes were equipped with the system. In October 1943 a major new variant was introduced in the shape of the Bristol Hercules-powered Mk III. With an increased wing span and a new streamlined nose the aircraft had a much higher service ceiling and went on to be built in greater numbers than any other variant. Earlier instability problems during asymmetric flight were also cured on this variant with the introduction of large rectangular tail fins. At its peak in the winter of 1944-45 no fewer than 34 squadrons operated the Halifax in the European theatre with more units based abroad and large

Below left and Below: Rembered for its bombing role, the Halifax undertook many RAF tasks. Modifications and improvements made the later marks far superior to those of 1940.

numbers remained in Bomber Command service in the spring of 1945, however after VE-Day most of the UK-based Halifaxes were rapidly withdrawn from front line service.

The Halifax has the distinction of being the only British four-engined bomber type to be deployed to the Middle East and North Africa. First deployed in July 1942 as No 249 Wing, the Halifaxes were heavily involved in the bombing of Tobruk in the summer of 1942. The Australian-manned No 462 Squadron remained in the theatre participating throughout the battles for North Africa and Italy, often in the Pathfinding role before finally returning to the UK in March 1944. A number of other squadrons also served in the Far East during the final year of the war

From November 1941 Halifaxes were operated in support of the Special Operations Executive (SOE). Duties included dropping agents behind enemy lines and marathon supply dropping sorties to eastern Poland. No 100 Group was another Halifax operator using the type on radio countermeasures and electric intelligence missions.

The Halifax's excellent range made it an obvious acquisition for RAF Coastal Command and maritime patrol versions of the Mk II, Mk III, Mk V and Mk VI were produced. Equipped with ASV Mk III search radar and additional fuel tanks in the bomb bay the Halifax GR.Mk II entered service at the end of 1942. With operational patrol endurance of over 13 hours the Halifax could range far out into the Atlantic and the two Coastal Command squadrons, Nos 158 and 405 sank at least seven U-boats during 1943 and damaged several others before re-equipping with Hercules-engined versions for the duration of the war.

In the latter part of the war Halifaxes were adapted for airborne assault as Halifax A.Mk IIIs, A.Mk Vs and A.Mk VIIs. Used for the deployment of paratroops or gliders they were actively involved in the Sicily,

Normandy, Arnhem and Rhine deployments of airborne forces.

During the European campaign Halifaxes flew 75,532 sorties and the 227,610 tons of bombs dropped was second only to the Lancaster for all RAF types in the conflict, and the aircraft was unique among four-engined bombers in the number of other roles it performed.

Above: A Halifax Mk III with a rarely-fitted ventral gun.

Right: A Mk II Halifax with Merlin engines.

Below: A dispersed Halifax on a wartime RAF airfield.

Above: Coastal Command used various Halifaxes primarily to hunt down U-boats.

Below: Uprated Hercules engines made the Halifax III a very effective bomber.

HANDLEY PAGE HAMPDEN

A specification for a new bomber, issued by the Air Ministry in 1933, would produce the RAF's two main medium day-bombers equipping RAF squadrons at the outbreak of the Second World War — the Handley Page Hampden and the Vickers Wellington. The design of these two aircraft was governed by the restrictions imposed by the Geneva Disarmament Conference which limited the total empty weight of all new bombers to 6,000 lb. The new aircraft was to have good performance and range characteristics and carry a bomb load of 1,500 lb and to meet this criteria the two manufacturers produced markedly different designs.

Vickers adopted a fuselage of large radius with good bombload capacity and incorporating power-operated turrets and beam guns. Handley Page opted for an extremely narrow but deep pod fuselage with three manually operated gun positions and tail empennage attached by a tapered boom. It was

the lack of space for power-operated turrets defensive armament that was later to be the Hampden's 'achilles heel' and the unusual arrangement led to the aircraft's sobriquet 'the Flying Panhandle'.

In June 1934 the Air Ministry withdrew the weight limitation and

Handley Page opted for the heavier but more powerful Bristol Pegasus as their chosen powerplant. Development continued and on June 21, 1936 the prototype made its first flight. Early tests were impressive with a top speed higher than the Wellington or Whitley, and the range

---

Specification: Hampden Mk I
Manufacturers: Handley Page, English Electric, Canadian Associated Aircraft, Short and Harland (Hereford)
Number built: 1,432 plus 152 Herefords
Entry into service: August 1938
Powerplant: Two 980 hp Bristol Pegasus XVIII
Length: 53 ft 7 in (16.33 m)
Height: 14 ft 11 in (4.55 m)
Wingspan: 69 ft 2 in (21.08 m)
Weight empty: 11,780 lb (5,343 kg)
Normal range: 1,885 miles (3,034 km) with 2,000 lb (907 kg) of bombs
Max speed: 254 mph (409 km/h) at 13,800 ft (4,206 m)
Service ceiling: 22,700 ft (6,919 m)
Armament: 2 x 0.303-in (7.7-mm) forward-firing machine guns, twin 0.303-in (7.7-mm) machine guns in dorsal and ventral positions plus up to 4,000 lb (1,814 kg) of bombs

with a full bomb load was also superior. In August of that year the first production contract was made and with tensions in Europe increasing a further contact was awarded shortly afterwards. Doubts that Bristol could meet the demand for Pegasus engines resulted in a new variant, later to be named Hereford, to be produced under licence in Northern Ireland with Napier Dagger engines. Although 150 Herefords were eventually produced the Dagger engines proved to be woefully unreliable and most were relegated to training units and never saw operational service.

The first deliveries of production Hampden Mk Is to the RAF occurred in August 1938 and by the outbreak of war there were 10 squadrons with No 5 Group, Bomber Command. The Hampden was committed to active operations from the first day of the war and early tasks mainly involved mine-laying operations in the North Sea and the English Channel. On September 29, 1939 the Hampden's lack of defensive armament and vulnerability to enemy fighters was tragically illustrated when five out of 11 aircraft from No 144 Squadron were lost to Luftwaffe fighters during an attack on destroyers in the

Above: An early wartime photo shoot for the Hampden.

Left: Bombing up activity around Hampdens early in WWII.

Far left: No 455 Squadron was one of the early Hampden bomber units.

Heligoland Bight. Further losses during the autumn prompted a gradual switch to night operations and by January 1940 No 5 Group Hampdens were conducting regular night bombing raids against enemy coastal targets and propaganda leaflet dropping raids over German cities, as well as continuing day mine-laying operations.

The invasion of the Low Countries in May 1940 saw a stepping up of night raids against mainland German targets. On July 1/2, 1940 a No 83 Squadron Hampden became the first aircraft to deploy the 2,000 lb semi armour-piercing bomb, however it missed its intended target, the battle cruiser *Scharnhorst*. At the height of the Battle of Britain Hampdens made one of their more successful raids with the attack on the Dortmund-Ems canal causing major damage with 1,000 lb bombs. For his efforts during this raid, No 49 Squadron pilot Flt Lt R. A. B. Learoyd became the first Bomber Command airman to receive the Victoria Cross.

Early losses had highlighted the need for improved armament and by the time of the first raid on Berlin, conducted by Hampdens and Whitleys on August 25 1940, the aircraft had been equipped with twin Vickers machine guns in the dorsal and ventral positions. As Hitler laid plans for the ill-fated Operation Sea Lion the Hampdens were called on for bombing raids on troops and barges in the Channel ports and intensified operations against military targets in occupied France. One such operation led to the award of the VC for Sgt John Hannah of No 83 Squadron for attempting to extinguish the flames consuming his burning aircraft.

At the end of 1940 No 5 Group Hampdens were involved in the RAF's first mass raid against a German city when Mannheim was attacked by 102 bombers and from this time onwards were assigned to night raids until the aircraft were withdrawn from active operations in September 1942. One of the few exceptions was the daylight raid on the battleships *Scharnhorst* and *Gneisenau* moored in Brest harbour in May 1941 with one Hampden from No 44 Squadron claiming a direct hit on the latter with a 2,000 lb bomb.

By spring 1941 further Hampdens were being delivered, many from licence-production in Canada, and it was aircrew from this country as well as Australia and New Zealand who were to form four new squadrons over the next 12 months. After participating in the first of the '1,000 bomber' raids in May 1942 the Hampdens were rapidly replaced by newer types and by mid-summer most had been relegated to secondary duties.

However, the Hampden was to continue in front line service until October 1943 with Coastal Command for which the Hampden TB.Mk I torpedo bomber had been specially developed. From 1942-43 these aircraft flew anti-shipping and convoy escort patrols before being replaced by the more capable Beaufighter. On retirement a number were allocated to the Soviet Air Force for operations in the northern seas.

The Hampden's lack of defensive armament and limited scope for additional weapons in the narrow fuselage ensured that it served for a shorter period and in fewer roles than the contemporary Wellington. The aircraft did, however, make a valuable contribution to the early war years by carrying the war to the enemy at a time when the Luftwaffe was in the ascendency and the threat of invasion was very real.

Top: Low power, light armament and modest range curtailed the Hampden's usefulness to the RAF.

Above: Hampdens did help 'hold the line' until larger and better bombers were ready.

Right: While they were mainly bombers Hampdens undertook other duties, including minelaying.

Left: On night operations, Hampdens were rarely effective due to their small bomb load.

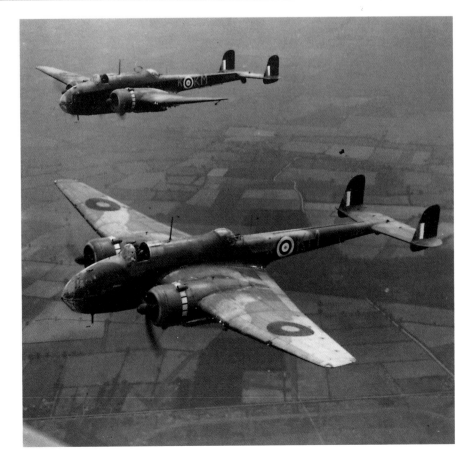

HAWKER HURRICANE

The Hurricane will be remembered for the contribution it made in the defeat of the Luftwaffe during the Battle of Britain. Indeed it was this aircraft, rather than the more glamorous Spitfire, that equipped the most operational units and gained more 'kills' than all other aircraft and ground defences combined.

In 1934 the Air Ministry expressed an interest in acquiring an eight-gun monoplane fighter and, anticipating the need for such an aircraft, Hawker's chief designer Sidney Camm had already begun work on such an aircraft. The advent of Rolls-Royce's Merlin engine (then known as the P.V.12) was crucial in providing sufficient power and this, married to Camm's brilliantly designed airframe, produced an aircraft that the Air Ministry felt obliged to write a new specification around.

The prototype first flew on November 6, 1935 and official trials in spring 1936 exceeded all performance predictions and represented a massive increase in capabilities over the RAF's current biplane fighter force. The trouble-free installation of eight 0.303-in machine guns in the wings of the prototype posed little difficulty and, highly impressed, the Air Ministry ordered 600 of the new aircraft in the summer of 1936. A production facility was established at Langley, Berkshire and, almost two years after the prototype the first production aircraft took to the air in October 1937.

First RAF squadron deliveries of Hurricane Mk Is commenced at the end of 1937 to No 111 Squadron based at RAF Northolt, and as production rates increased in the spring of 1938 Nos 3 and 56 Squadrons soon followed. The worsening political situation in Europe in the autumn of 1938 gave added urgency to the re-equipment programme and a further production facility was established by Gloster at Hucclecote which had produced over 1,000 examples by the end of the Battle of Britain.

When war broke out in September 1939 the Hurricane Mk I had become Fighter Command's most important asset with 19 squadrons fully equipped. Four squadrons (Nos 1, 73, 85 and 87) were immediately despatched to France, the former pair for service with the Advanced Air Striking Force and the latter pair with the British Expeditionary Force. On October 30, 1939 a Hurricane from No 1 Squadron became the first RAF aircraft to gain a victory over the Western Front by shooting down a Dornier Do 17, but action for the Hurricane pilots was sporadic during the Phoney War of the next seven months. This was all to change in May 1940 with the German invasion of France and the Low Countries. Five further Hurricane squadrons

Specification: Hurricane Mk I
Manufacturers: Hawker, Austin and Gloster plus licence production in Canada, Belgium and Yugoslavia
Number built: 12,975 in the UK (inc 3844 Mk I, 451 Mk IIA, 2929 Mk IIB, 471 Mk IIC, 296 Mk IID and 580 Mk IV)
Entry into service: December 1937
Powerplant: One 1,030 hp Rolls-Royce Merlin II
Length: 31 ft 4 in (9.55 m)
Height: 13 ft 1 in (3.99 m)
Wingspan: 40 ft 0 in (12.19 m)
Weight empty: 4,734 lb (2,151 kg)
Range: 525 miles (845 km)
Max speed: 318 mph (512 km/h)
Service ceiling: 33,400 ft (10,180 m)
Armament: 8 x 0.303-in (7.7-mm) machine guns mounted in outer wings

Specification: Hurricane Mk IIC
Powerplant: One 1,280 hp Rolls-Royce Merlin XX
Length: 32 ft 3 in (9.83 m)
Height: 13 ft 3 in (4.04 m)
Wingspan: 40 ft 0 in (12.19 m)
Weight empty: 5,658 lb (2,569 kg)
Range: 920 miles (1,480 km) with two drop tanks
Max speed: 329 mph (529 km/h)
Service ceiling: 35,600 ft (10,850 m)
Armament: 4 x 20-mm cannon in wings plus up to 1,000-lb of bombs beneath the wings

were committed to the battle in mid-May and ferocious fighting against the advancing Germans ensued. Despite claiming a substantial number of victories, losses within the Hurricane units both in the air and on the ground was high. The speed of the German advance necessitated a change of base every few days and unserviceability rates climbed alarmingly high. By the end of May the surviving Hurricanes were recalled to the UK to support the evacuation at Dunkirk. The cost had been high with over 260 Hurricanes lost in France and more by UK-based squadrons — a quarter of the RAF's front line fighter strength.

Production was by now in full swing and the losses had more than been made up by the outbreak of the Battle of Britain. By this time the RAF had 32 squadrons of

Below left: The first prototype Hurricane which flew in November 1935.

Below: Cannon-armed Hurricane Mk IIs of No 1 Squadron.

Hurricanes at its disposal which, together with 19 squadrons of Spitfires, would bear the brunt of the hectic fighting of the next three months. The new and then secret series of radar stations around Britain's coast would provide vital warnings of the armadas of Luftwaffe bombers approaching over the Channel, and often two or three times per day the squadrons launched to intercept. Faster and more manoeuvrable, the Spitfire squadrons were tasked where possible with engaging the fighter escorts, leaving the Hurricane squadrons as the main bomber destroyers. A stable gun platform, the Hurricane inflicted severe losses on the attacking formations and dedicated work by the ground crews ensured sufficient numbers were kept airworthy to finally defeat the Luftwaffe. The bravery shown by Fighter Command's Hurricane pilots was exemplified by the action of Flt Lt J. B. Nicholson who, on August 17, 1940, pressed home his attack on a Messerschmitt Bf 110 despite his aircraft being consumed in flames and having suffered severe injuries. For his efforts Nicholson was awarded the only Fighter Command VC of the war.

Following production of the Mk I, the Mk II introduced the Merlin Mk XX engine and was produced in four variants each with differing armament. Before these were introduced Mk Is had been deployed to other theatres of war. No 261 was heavily involved in the defence of Malta in the summer of 1940 and from the autumn Nos 73 and 274 Squadrons were active against the Italians in North Africa, gaining significant aerial victories. During the following 12 months Hurricanes were active in the Balkans campaign and the defence of Crete and by mid-1941 deliveries to the theatre of the new Mk IIs had commenced. Hurricanes subsequently plated a vital role in the North African campaign with duties switching from air combat to ground attack. The use of

four 20-mm cannon-armed Mk IICs against tanks and convoys was a major success and led in June 1943 to the introduction of the 'tank busting' Mk IID fitted with two 40-mm cannon. These aircraft could destroy any German armour and caused widespread destruction of Rommel's tank corps during the Allies final advance.

Fighter bomber Mk II Hurricanes were also employed extensively in the Burma region, being heavily involved in the second Arkan campaign and the Chindit expeditions at the end of 1943. In 1944 the Mk IV capable of carrying rockets, bombs or anti-tank guns on a 'universal' wing were introduced to

the theatre and served until the end of the war.

After the defeat of the Luftwaffe in the Battle of Britain, Hurricanes were employed by UK-based units on daylight Rhubarbs and night intruder sorties over occupied Europe. The final Hurricane Mk IVs in the UK were eventually replaced by the Typhoon in 1943-44.

The Royal Navy also operated the aircraft in the form of the Sea Hurricane from the catapult aircraft merchantmen, converted merchant ships with a small flight deck and later from escort carriers. The aircraft served in the North Atlantic and Mediterranean theatres with moderate success.

Above left: Hurricane scrambles during the Battle of Britain.

Below left: Hurricane squadrons took the lion's share of victories in the summer 1940 air battles.

Above: Cannon gave the Hurricane Mk IIC an effective night intruder punch.

Right: A Hurricane of the 'Battle of Britain Memorial Flight'.

Below: One of the few surviving flyable Hurricanes.

Above: All warbird Hurricanes are 'late build' examples although they are often painted to represent earlier models.

Right: Hawker named this Hurricane Mk IIC *The Last of the Many*.

Below: New engines have given some Hurricanes six exhaust stacks which they rarely had in wartime.

Above: A Hawker test pilot tests another new Hurricane 'off the line'.

Right: Warbird Hurricanes often fly in changed markings.

Below: A wartime Hurricane Mk IIC night intruder.

Above: In line astern a Hurricane leads a Spitfire.

Left: A Duxford air show which regularly has Hurricanes flying in mock combat.

Below: A Hurricane in No 56 Squadron markings.

HAWKER TEMPEST

Suffering from disappointing performance in its intended fighter role, design work began in 1941 to develop a new version of the Hawker Typhoon with a thin section laminar-flow wing and a revised radiator position. Originally referred to as the Typhoon Mk II, this new aircraft was ordered to prototype stage to test various power-plant installations comprising of the Napier Sabre, the Bristol Centaurus and the Rolls-Royce Griffon. Progress was most rapid on the Sabre Mk II-powered variant and, after the version with the repositioned radiator had been abandoned due to technical difficulties, the new aircraft was ordered into production as the Tempest Mk V.

Retaining the Typhoons twin-radiator and featuring a lengthened fuselage, a redesigned tail unit and the new elliptical wing, the Mk V entered service in April 1944 when the first Tempest Wing formed at RAF Newchurch. In June 1944 the Tempests were committed to countering the V-1 flying bomb threat and became the most successful type in these operations. By March 1945 the five Tempest squadrons assigned to the task had claimed 638 out of a total 1,771 V-1s destroyed with the top scorer being Squadron Leader J. Berry of No 501 Squadron with 61 kills.

From the summer of 1944 other Tempest squadrons moved to the Continent as part of the 2nd TAF. With the Luftwaffe threat diminishing the aircraft were employed on highly successful cab rank operations in support of the ground forces. The Tempests high speed was also used to good effect against the new jet-powered Messerschmitt Me 262 fighter claiming 20 kills before the end of the war.

Specification: Tempest Mk V
Manufacturers: Hawker
Number built (wartime): 806 (Mk V)
Entry into service: April 1944
Powerplant: One 2,180 hp Napier Sabre IIA
Length: 33 ft 8 in (10.26 m)
Height: 16 ft 1 in (4.90 m)
Wingspan: 41 ft 0 in (12.50 m)
Weight empty: 9,000 lb (4,082 kg)
Maximum Range fully loaded: 1,530 miles (2,462 km)
Max speed: 426 mph (686 km/h) at 18,500 ft (5,639 m)
Service ceiling: 36,500 ft (11,125 m)
Armament: 4 x 20-mm forward-firing cannon plus up to 2,000 lb (907 kg) of bombs or eight rocket projectiles

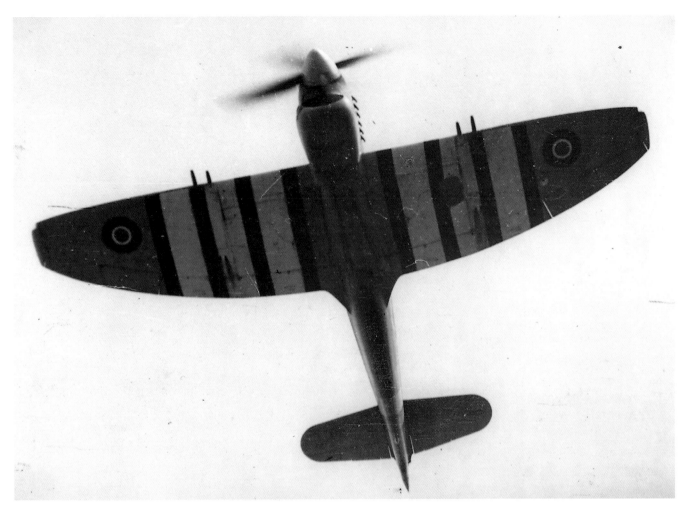

Above: Recognition stripes were added to Tempests to avoid confusion with the FW 190.

Right: The Tempest V was one of the RAF's best wartime fighters.

Left: Drop tank-equipped Tempest Vs of No 501 Squadron.

Below: The first Tempest V wing was formed in June 1944.

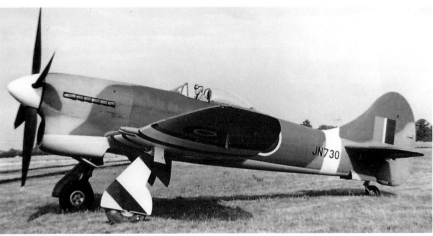

HAWKER TYPHOON

Designed as an interceptor, the Hawker Typhoon was plagued by numerous problems, which almost led to its cancellation. It was to emerge however, as the RAF's most important close support aircraft of the war. The Typhoon's origins date to a 1938 Air Ministry request for a heavily-armed single-seat fighter aircraft capable of 400 mph. Hawker's chief designer Sidney Camm had already seen the Hurricane enter production and in 1937 had started work on a new design anticipating the Air Ministry requirement.

The new fighter was to be armed with four 20-mm cannon and would be tested with two engines: the Napier Sabre and Rolls-Royce Vulture. The air-cooled Bristol Centaurus was overlooked due to official distrust of this type of powerplant, a decision that would later be regretted. Named Tornado the Vulture-powered version showed much promise but Rolls-Royce's decision to abandon the project to concentrate on Merlin production left the way clear for the Sabre-powered Typhoon.

With Hawker factories running to capacity production was initiated by Gloster factory at Hucclecote and the first production example flew

Specification: Typhoon Mk IB (late production)
Manufacturers: Hawker, Gloster
Number built: 3,270
Entry into service: August 1941
Powerplant: One 2,260 hp Napier Sabre IIC
Length: 31 ft 11 in (9.73 m)
Height: 15 ft 4 in (4.67 m)
Wingspan: 41 ft 7 in (12.67 m)
Weight empty: 8,840 lb (4,010 kg)
Range: 510 miles (821 km) with full weapons load
Max speed: 412 mph (663 km/h) at 19,000 ft (5,791 m)
Service ceiling: 35,200 ft (10,729 m)
Armament: 4 x 20-mm cannon in wings plus 8 x 60-lb (27-kg) rocket projectiles or up to 2,000 lb (907 kg) of bombs

from here on 27 May 1941. Trials carried out shortly afterwards were to prove to be extremely disappointing. The Napier engine was extremely unreliable, often failing in flight and requiring major overhaul every 25 hours. Performance and climb rate were also well below expectations especially at altitude where most of the dogfights were

likely to occur. Problems in production of the intended cannon armament resulted in many of the first production Typhoons being fitted with an eight-machine gun wing as the Mk IA before production finally centred on the cannon armed Mk IB. No 56 Squadron received its first Typhoons in September 1941 with No 266 Squadron following on

Right: RAF armorers sweat rocket projectiles onto the rail of a Typhoon in France shortly after D-Day.

Opposite, above: The Typhoon Mk Ib was one of the most effective Allied fighter-bombers.

Opposite, below: Typhoon cannon and rockets became the scourge of the Panzers in Normandy.

in February; however, by now an even more serious problem had been identified. Elevator flutter at low speeds was leading to structural failure of the tail assembly and many Typhoons were lost during the first half of 1942. The two operational squadrons were achieving little success in the interception role and there was a growing feeling within the Air Ministry that the Typhoon should be cancelled.

The turning point in the Typhoon's career came in the autumn of 1942 when feelings against the Typhoon were running at their highest. Squadron Leader Roland Beaumont requested to transfer his unit, No 609 Squadron, to Manston to support Hurricane and Spitfire Rhubarb ground-attack missions against targets in the Low Countries. In the next five months the squadron destroyed over 100 locomotives and numerous other ground targets as well as 14 Focke-Wulf FW 190s in low-level combat. No 609 Sqn's efforts combined with the much-needed cure for the structural problems secured the Typhoon's future in a new role.

The addition of bomb racks and rocket projectiles beneath the wing, trialled in the spring of 1943 turned the Typhoon into a formidable attack aircraft. As more bomb- and rocket-equipped versions reached an increasing number of RAF squadrons, the attacks on targets of opportunity such as trains and convoys, pioneered by No 609 Sqn, increased in frequency. Typhoons also made a valuable contribution to the Channel Stop operations, firing salvos of rockets against German shipping in the English Channel. Eventually, 26 squadrons flew the Typhoon and many of these were involved in attacking German radar stations and lines of communication throughout northern France in preparation for D-Day.

Following the D-Day invasion 2nd Tactical Air Force Typhoons played a vital role in the Allies breakout from the beachheads. With air superiority assured the Typhoons destroyed columns of troops, artillery, tanks and machinery at will, causing monumental damage to the German defences. The 'cab rank' system of standing patrols was established as the Allies advanced, allowing specific targets to be destroyed on request, at short notice by army units. Rocket-equipped Typhoons of the 2nd TAF continued to wreak havoc on ground targets throughout 1945. However, after VE-Day, having playing such a vital role in the Allies victory, the Typhoons were rapidly withdrawn from service and reduced to scrap.

SHORT STIRLING

Along with the Avro Lancaster and Handley Page Halifax, the Short Stirling comprised the trio of four-engined heavy bombers that carried out the RAF's night bombing campaign from 1942. The requirement for an aircraft in this class stemmed from the rapid expansion of the Luftwaffe in the mid-1930s. To keep pace the Air Ministry realised that bigger and faster bombers would be needed to counter the threat. In 1936 a specification for a high-speed long-range strategic bomber was issued and Short Bros and Supermarine were chosen to construct prototypes.

Shorts designed the aircraft around the Sunderland's wing; however, official insistence that the aircraft's span should not exceed 100 ft (allowing the aircraft to fit into existing hangars) resulted in a 12 ft reduction. This in turn reduced the aircraft's service ceiling which would be one of the major factors in the

type's premature withdrawal from front-line service. After a half-scale research aircraft was successfully flown the first full-scale prototype was built making its maiden flight in May 1939 although the aircraft was

written off the following day after its undercarriage collapsed.

The destruction of Supermarine's competitor in a bombing raid left the way clear for Stirling production and an initial requirement for 1,500

Specification: Stirling Mk I Series 3
Manufacturers: Short Bros, Short & Harland, Austin Motors
Number built: 2,374 (inc 758 Mk I, 875 Mk III, 579 Mk IV, 160 Mk V)
Entry into service: August 1940
Powerplant: Four 1,595 hp Bristol Hercules XI
Length: 87 ft 3 in (26.59 m)
Height: 22 ft 9 in (6.93 m)
Wingspan: 99 ft 1 in (30.20 m)
Weight empty: 42,300 lb (19,187 kg)
Range: 915 miles (1,473 km) with maximum bomb load
Max speed: 260 mph (418 km/h) at 10,500 ft (3,200 m)
Service ceiling: 18,000 ft (5,486 m)
Armament: 2 x 0.303-in (7.7-mm) machine guns in nose turret, 4 x 0.303-in (7.7-mm) machine guns in tail turret, 2 x 0.303-in (7.7-mm) machine guns in dorsal turret plus up to 14,000 lb (6,350 kg) of bombs

Specification: Stirling Mk III
Powerplant: Four 1,650 hp Bristol Hercules XVI
Length: 87 ft 3 in (26.59 m)
Height: 22 ft 9 in (6.93 m)
Wingspan: 99 ft 1 in (30.20 m)
Weight empty: 46,900 lb (21,200 kg)
Range: 2,010 miles (3,235 km) with 3,500 lb (1,588 kg) of bombs
Max speed: 270 mph (435 km/h) at 14,500 ft (4,420 m)
Service ceiling: 17,000 ft (5,182 m)
Armament: 2 x 0.303-in (7.7-mm) machine guns in nose turret, 4 x 0.303-in (7.7-mm) machine guns in tail turret, 2 x 0.303-in (7.7-mm) machine guns in dorsal turret plus up to 14,000 lb (6,350 kg) of bombs

examples was outlined. The plans to equip many RAF bomber squadrons with the Stirling by mid-1941 were severely held-up by the Battle of Britain, with the Air Ministry rightly insisting that production priorities leant towards Hurricane and Spitfire fighters. However, production eventually got into full swing and by the end of 1941 150 examples had reached squadron service.

The first operational unit to receive the Stirling Mk I was No 7 Squadron, based at RAF Leeming, thus becoming the first RAF squadron to fly a four-engined bomber since the Handley Page V/1500 in 1919. The Stirling's introduction to combat occurred on the night of 10 February 1941 when No 7 Sqn, then operating from Oakington, attacked oil-storage tanks in Rotterdam. In April No 7 Sqn was joined by No 15 Sqn and the first raid on Berlin followed on the 30th of that month. As more units re-equipped during the latter part of 1941 and early 1942 operations intensified with both unescorted daylight and night raids and mine-laying operations being flown. Unable to reach a service ceiling of 20,000 ft the aircraft could easily be intercepted by enemy fighters, however the Stirling's remarkable manoeuvrability for an aircraft of its size was a useful defence. This ability is reflected in the achievement of a Stirling Mk I from No 218 Squadron which, returning from a night raid in June 1942, beat off attacks from four Luftwaffe night-fighters destroying three of them, before returning safely to base.

A number of long-distance raids were also flown against targets in Italy. Encountering heavy defences losses were high but the operations were deemed a success with two pilots posthumously being awarded the VC. In early 1943 the Stirling Mk I began to be replaced by the more powerful Mk III and by May a total of 13 squadrons were operating Stirlings, however by the summer many Stirling Squadrons began to re-equip with the Halifax and Lancaster. The fact that the Stirling was unable to reach 20,000 ft or carry bombs larger than 2,000 lb had signalled the end of its Bomber

Below left: A No 7 Squadron Stirling awaits its next sortie.

Below: The bomb train delivering the night's load a No 7 Sqn Stirling.

Command service. A small number of Stirlings were retained for more specialised tasks; Nos 138, 161 and 199 Squadrons undertook long-range missions to drop supplies to the resistance groups in occupied France and No 138 later transferred to No 100 Group for electronic countermeasures work including the employment of 'window'.

From 1944, RAF Transport Command began to receive large numbers of Stirlings for both paradropping and glider-towing duties. With nose and dorsal turrets removed the Stirling Mk IV could tow two fully-laden Airspeed Horsas or one General Aircraft Hamilcar on airborne assault sorties and were

employed successfully during the Normandy invasion in June 1944 and the attack across the Rhine in March 1945. The Mk V was a dedicated unarmed transport which could carry 40 troops or 20 paratroops and could also be adapted for casualty evacuation.

As the first of the four-engined bombers for the RAF the Stirling made a valuable contribution carrying the war to the enemy before the more capable Lancasters and Halifaxes were available. Between 1941 and 1944, 27,821 tons of bombs and over 20,000 mines were laid for the loss of 769 aircraft. A remarkable achievement considering that the raids were unescorted.

Above: A poor ceiling and inability to carry the RAF's heaviest bombs cut short the Stirling's operational career.

Above right: OTU Stirlings on a formation flying training sortie.

Right: The height of the Stirling's landing gear was truly impressive.

Below: A Stirling Mk III of No 149 Squadron on its dispersal.

Above: A Stirling Mk III with its revised top turret.

Overleaf: Busy scene around a Stirling base.

SHORT SUNDERLAND

The Short Brothers company of Belfast was one of the leading manufacturers of seaplanes in the 1920s and 1930s, producing such revolutionary designs as the S.23 'Empire' flying-boat, and it was from this basic design that the most capable and best known British-built flying-boat of the war would emerge.

In 1933 the Air Ministry called for a new maritime reconnaissance flying boat to replace the Short Singapore Mk III which was currently in production. Short's chief designer, Arthur Gouge, was already well advanced with the design of the all-metal stressed-skin S.23 intended for civilian airline operations and began adapting the aircraft for the military role.

Approval for a prototype was received and this aircraft first flew in

Specification: Sunderland Mk III
Manufacturer: Short Bros & Harland and Blackburn
Number built: 749 (90 Mk I, 43 Mk II, 456 Mk III/IIIA, 10 Mk IV [Seaford] and 150 Mk V/VI)
Entry into service: June 1938
Powerplant: Four 1,066 hp Bristol Pegasus XVIII
Length: 85 ft 4 in (26.01 m)
Height: 32 ft 2 in (9.79 m) on beaching chassis
Wingspan: 112 ft 10 in (34.39 m)
Weight empty: 33,000 lb (14,969 kg)
Range: 3,000 miles (4,828 km) or an endurance of 20 hours
Max speed: 212 mph (341 km/h)
Service ceiling: 15,000 ft (4,570 m)
Armament: 1 x 0.303-in (7.7-mm) machine guns in nose turret, 4 x 0.303-in (7.7-mm) machine guns in tail turret, 2 x 0.303-in (7.7-mm) machine guns in dorsal turret, 4 x 0.303-in (7.7-mm) fixed forward-firing machine guns, 2 x 0.5-in (12.7-mm) machine guns in waist hatches plus up to 4,960 lb (2,250 kg) of various ordnance including bombs, depth charges or mines

October 1937. After initial flight trials a new wing with a tapered leading edge was adopted and the defensive armament of a hydraulic tail turret with four 0.303-in machine guns and a bow turret with a single VGO (Vickers gas-operated) machine gun was incorporated. Cleared for production the Sunderland Mk I carried a crew of seven and the main offensive load comprised up to 2,000 lb of bombs, mines, depth charges and other stores housed within the

Below left: A welcome sight to merchant seamen!

Above right: No 230 Squadron flew Sunderlands for most of the war.

Right: A Sunderland taking off was an impressive sight.

Below: Soldiering on into the postwar era Sunderlands operated during the Berlin Airlift.

central fuselage and cranked out under the wings prior to an attack.

The first RAF unit to receive the Sunderland was No 230 Squadron at Seletar, Singapore in June 1938 representing a great leap forward in terms of capability. The Mk I, despite having manually driven controls was pleasant to fly and surprisingly manoeuvrable and the two-step hull provided good lateral stability in moderately choppy water.

As war broke out in Europe, four squadrons in the UK (Nos 204, 210 and 228; plus No 10 RAAF) had re-equipped with the Sunderland Mk I and were immediately pushed into action. Mainly tasked with convoy escort and long-range patrol duties the first attack on was made on September 8, 1939 by a No 204 Squadron aircraft bombing two U-boats. Ten days later the squadron claimed a probable U-boat 'kill' as well as picking up the crew from the torpedoed merchant ship *Kensington Court* managing to transfer the

whole complement to hospital in Plymouth within an hour of their ship sinking.

Throughout 1940 Sunderlands continued to patrol and escort convoys in the Atlantic, North Sea and the Mediterranean. By this time defensive armament had increased with the addition of two VGO guns either side of the upper deck and a second gun in the nose turret. This extra armament proved invaluable for a No 204 Squadron Sunderland patrolling over the Norwegian coast on April 3, 1940. Attacked by six German Junkers Ju 88s, the Sunderland downed two and drove the others off before ditching itself. Later in the year another was attacked by eight Ju 88s over the Bay of Biscay and shot down three of the attackers. Despite only carrying rifle-calibre weapons the Sunderland gained a reputation for spirited defence and earned the nickname 'the Flying Porcupine' amongst Luftwaffe pilots.

With U-boat captains learning to hide from Sunderland patrols interceptions were becoming sparse by the end of 1940. This was remedied in 1941 with the introduction of the Sunderland Mk II fitted with ASV Mk II radar. In the Mediterranean Squadron Leader Garside made particular use of the new radar between October 1941 and February 1942 he attacked six U-boats destroying two and crippling two others. Sunderlands were also employed in the evacuation of Crete carrying up to 82 fully armed soldiers in addition to its crew which had by then risen to 10.

By the end of 1942, U-boats fitted with the Metox detection system could again avoid the Sunderlands attentions. However, the introduction of the Sunderland Mk IIIA with the new ASV Mk III radar, operating on a different frequency band, returned the advantage to the Sunderland crews and the frequency of attacks rapidly increased.

Sunderlands were also employed in the Far East, most notably with No 230 Squadron, which returned to this theatre with Sunderland Mk IIIs in the winter of 1943-44. Anti-submarine and convoy escort work was interspersed with casualty evacuation duties and, at the end or the war, repatriation of prisoners of war. The final variant to see wartime

Below left: ASV radar was a vital asset to Sunderlands engaged on anti U-boat operations.

Above right: An early production Sunderland I.

Right: Heavily armed and with crew stations for long patrols, the Sunderland was a Coastal Command mainstay.

Below: A flight of postwar Sunderlands with long-range wing fuel tanks.

Above: One of the few surving Sunderlands

Right: In typical weatherbeaten finish these Sunderlands are seen towards the end of the type's 21 years' RAF service

Above right: A new Sunderland fitted with ASV radar on the slipway.

276

service was the Mk V powered by Pratt & Whitney R-1830-90b Twin Wasp engines providing much improved climb and ceiling performance. By this time armament had been increased to 18 guns with the introduction of four fixed forward-firing machine guns, additional beam guns and a mid-upper turret first employed on the Mk III.

After VJ-Day many of the Sunderland units were disbanded, yet the aircraft was to continue in RAF service for another 14 years making a valuable contribution to the Berlin airlift and the Korean War. The Sunderland will best be remembered for the vital role it played in countering the U-boat threat during the Battle of the North Atlantic.

SUPERMARINE SEAFIRE

The lack of modern front line naval fighters led to the development of a new version of the exceptional Supermarine Spitfire Mk V able to operate from aircraft carriers. Despite its narrow-track and rather fragile undercarriage, which made operations from a moving carrier deck highly perilous, the Seafire, as it was named became a vital aircraft in the Fleet Air Arm inventory. A total of 1,699 Seafires was eventually produced.

The first version to be embarked for operations was the Mk IIC, which operated from HMS *Furious* with Nos 801 and 807 Squadrons in the latter half of 1942 for operations in the Mediterranean. In November the aircraft were heavily involved in the Allied Operation Torch landings in North Africa and by the end of 1942 another four squadrons were operational with the type.

In 1943 Seafires began operations from escort carriers and, in September of that year eight squadrons, operating from HMS *Formidable* and *Illustrious* and four escort carriers, were involved in fighter operations over the Gulf of Salerno during the Allied invasion of Sicily, claiming a number of enemy aircraft. During 1944 the squadrons began to re-equip with the improved Mk III featuring folding wings. Based on aircraft carriers in the Mediterranean and on the island of Malta the Mk III provided vital air cover for operations in Italy and, in August 1944 the invasion of France. In June 1944 Mk IIs from Nos 808, 885, 886 and 897 Squadrons took part in the invasion of northern

---

Specification: Seafire Mk III

Manufacturers: Supermarine, Cunliffe-Owen, Westland

Number built: (wartime versions) 167 Mk I (including 48 conversions from Spitfire Mk VBs), 372 Mk II, 1,250 Mk III

Entry into service: June 1942

Length: 30 ft 0 in (9.14 m)

Height: 11 ft 2 in (3.40 m)

Wingspan: 36 ft 8 in (11.18 m)

Weight empty: 5,400 lb (2,449 kg)

Range fully loaded: 725 miles (1,167 km) with drop tank

Max speed: 352 mph (566 km/h) at 12,250 ft (3,735 m)

Service ceiling: 33,800 ft (10,300 m)

Armament: 2 x 20-mm forward-firing cannon and 4 x 0.303-in (7.7-mm) forward-firing machine guns

France, operating from land bases as part of the 2nd TAF.

From late 1944 Seafires were also deployed in the Far East, and aircraft aboard HMS *Indefatigable* provided fighter cover during Allied attacks on oil installations on the island of Sumatra. As the Allies advanced towards Japan Seafire squadrons were increasingly used for ground-attack, carrying up to 500 lb of bombs. In March–April 1945 for example, Pacific Fleet Seafires were in action over the Sakishima Islands and in June at Truk. By the time Japan finally capitulated, 12 squadrons were operating the type in the theatre.

Below left: A carrier 'batsman' brings a Seafire in for a safe wire 'trap'.

Above right: Bouncing down the deck was a common sight on Seafire squadrons, the aircraft not being well suited to deck landings.

Right: A Griffon-engined Seafire pictured after the war.

Below: Seafires launching from a Royal Navy carrier.

SUPERMARINE SPITFIRE

Arguably the most famous British warplane of all time, the Spitfire was created as a private venture by a team led by Reginald J. Mitchell. Designed around Rolls-Royce's PV.12 power-plant, also a private venture, the Supermarine Type 300 impressed an RAF whose F.7/30 specification of 1930 had failed to produce a design any faster than the Gloster Gladiator. To Specification F.37/34, describing a short-range interceptor and written around Mitchell's machine, a prototype was constructed and made its first flight on 5 March 1936.

Using an all-metal monocoque structure, the Spitfire's airframe was strong yet light, making its handling and performance with a 1,030-hp (768-kW) Merlin engine (as the PV.12 was soon named), including a top speed of 355 mph at 19,000 ft, most impressive. The Air Ministry immediately ordered 310 examples, the first entering service in June 1938, with No 19 Squadron at RAF Duxford. Nine Fighter Command squadrons were fully equipped with the type by the outbreak of war, together with two Auxiliary Air Force squadrons that were partly equipped.

Armed with eight 0.303-in machine guns, the Spitfire Mk I made its combat dbut on October 16, 1939, when aircraft of Nos 602 and 603 Sqns shot down two German bombers over Scotland. Kept back from France for the defence of Great Britain, the Spitfire did not see its first real test until the summer of 1940, when 19 squadrons joined 29 Hurricane units in defending the British Isles against the Luftwaffe during the Battle of Britain. Spitfire Mk Is were joined by Mk IIs (with more powerful

Above: Echelon formation of Spitfire Mk Is early in WWII.

Left: By way of contrast this echelon is composed of Griffon-engined Spitfires with both 'bubble' and in-line cockpit canopies.

Right: Late Mk XVI Spitfires were markedly different from the Mk IX from which they were developed.

Specification: Spitfire Mk IA
Manufacturers: Supermarine, Westland, Cunliffe Owen, Castle Bromwich Aircraft Factory
Number built: 20,360 (inc 1,583 Mk IA, 750 Mk IIA, 170 Mk IIB, 94 Mk VA, 3,923 Mk VB, 2447 Mk VC, 100 Mk VI, 140 Mk VII, 1,658 Mk VIII, 5,665 Mk IX, 471 Mk XI, 957 Mk XIV, 1,054 Mk XVI, 300 Mk XVIII, 225 Mk 225, 454 F21/22/24)
Entry into service: August 1938
Powerplant: One 1,030 hp Rolls-Royce Merlin III
Length: 29 ft 11 in (9.12 m)
Height: 12 ft 8 in (3.86 m)
Wingspan: 36 ft 10 in (11.23 m)
Weight empty: 4,517 lb (2,049 kg)
Normal range: 415 miles (668 km)
Max speed: 362 mph (582 km/h) at 15,000 ft (4,572 m)
Service ceiling: 31,500 ft (9,601 m)
Armament: 8 x 0.303-in (7.7-mm) machine guns mounted in wings

Specification: Spitfire Mk IX
Powerplant: One 1565 hp Rolls-Royce Merlin 61 or 1710 hp Merlin 63/63A
Length: 31 ft 1 in (9.47 m)
Height: 12 ft 8 in (3.86 m)
Wingspan: 36 ft 10 in (11.23 m)
Weight empty: 5,634 lb (2,556 kg)
Range: 980 miles (1,577 km) with drop tank
Max speed: 408 mph (657 km/h) at 25,000 ft (7,620 m)
Service ceiling: 43,000 ft (13,106 m)
Armament: 2 x 20-mm cannon and 4 x 0.303-in (7.7-mm) machine guns or 4 x 20-mm cannon mounted in wings plus up to 1,000 lb (454 kg) of bombs

engines) from July 1940, a handful of the latter equipped with a pair of 20-mm cannon, as Mk IIBs.

After the battle, Mk IIs took part in the first offensive sweeps across the English Channel, but it was the Mk V, the next major Spitfire production variant, that was to form the backbone of Fighter Command from early 1941. Powered by a 1,440 hp Merlin 45, the Mk V's strengthened airframe was able to carry long-range fuel tanks (thereby addressing one of the aircraft's few weaknesses) and bombs. The first examples were converted from Mk Is and IIs and were delivered to Malta in March 1942 by the Royal Navy in an effort to bolster the beleaguered island's defences. Later that year further aircraft were issued to squadrons in North Africa, while others were shipped to Australia to assist in its defence from Japanese attack.

Before long the Luftwaffe's new Focke-Wulf FW 190 forced the Spitfire's designers to again improve the fighter's performance, especially at altitude. Though it was intended that the resulting Mk VIII would replace the Mk V on production lines, the urgency of the requirement resulted in the Mk IX entering service first and in much greater

numbers. Both types had a 1,710-hp Merlin 63 series engine, with a two-stage, two-speed supercharger, the latter mark utilising a Mk V airframe with minimal modification other than those associated with the new engine. The Mk IX had a top speed of 408 mph (compared to 337 mph for the Mk VC) and entered service in July 1942. Most served in north-western and southern Europe, with the 2nd TAF and the Balkan and Desert Air Forces, in both fighter and fighter-bomber roles.

Over 5,600 Mk IXs were built, equipping 90 squadrons and, with the Mk XVI, was the most numerous of all Spitfires. The Mk XVI was the last major Merlin-engined variant, entering service in late 1944. Essentially a Mk IX with a Packard-built Merlin engine, the Mk XVI became best known as a fighter-bomber with the 2nd TAF. Late-production examples of both Mks IX and XVI were notable for their clear-view 'bubble' cockpit canopies, extra internal fuel and revised armament, including 20-mm cannon and 0.5-in machine guns.

Other important Spitfire variants included those engaged in unarmed photo-reconnaissance. The most numerous early examples were the PR.Mk IVs, though these were superseded by the Mk XI in late 1942. Based on the Mk IX fighter, the Mk XI had a top speed of 422 mph and served in Europe, the Mediterranean and the Far East, 471 being built in all.

The never-ending search for better performance from a Spitfire airframe and Merlin engine nearing the end of their development 'lives' prompted the development of a variant powered by the considerably larger Rolls-Royce Griffon. The Spitfire Mk XII of April 1943 was the first Griffon-powered variant to enter service and was a stop-gap based on the Mk V. It proved highly effective against low-level raids by FW 190s and Bf 109Fs across the Channel and was soon followed by the Mk XIV, based on the Mk VIII, though better suited than the Mk XII to carrying the larger power-plant. As the aircraft was intended for service at altitude, its Griffon engine also boasted a two-stage supercharger, resulting in a longer airframe and a larger fin; later production aircraft had a 'bubble' canopy.

The Mk XIV entered service in January 1944 and was to be one of the first types engaged in the fight against V-1 flying-bombs, while others joined 2nd TAF and Southeast Asia Command in the fighter and fighter-reconnaissance roles. The Mk XVIII, which followed, was outwardly identical to a late-production Mk XIV, but carried more internal fuel in a strengthened airframe. Though entering service in March 1945, it saw little action before VE-Day. The definitive, redesigned Griffon-engined Spitfires, of Marks 21, 22 and 24 were all too late for wartime service.

In the same way that Merlin-engined fighters had served as the basis for photo-reconnaissance derivatives, the Mk XIV provided the starting point from which the PR.Mk XIX was developed, once again in response to the threat posed by the FW 190. From mid-1944, the Mk XIX began to replace Mk XIs with RAF PRUs, 225 being delivered in all. Serving as widely as the earlier type, most had pressurised cabins which allowed operations at higher altitudes out of the reach of enemy fighters.

Top: Low pass by a Mk V Spitfire at an air show.

Above: The same machine, painted in Battle of Britain colours.

Left: The distinctive elliptical wing shape of the Spitfire was retained until the last marks.

Far left: One of many flyable Spitfires to be seen in the UK today.

Overleaf:
Main photo: The Spitfire Mk IX was the RAF's successful answer to the deadly FW 190.

Inset left: Largest production mark of the Spitfire was the Mk V.

Inset right: A wartime shot of a Spitfire Mk Vb of No 222 Squadron.

Above and Below: This warbird Spitfire IX is in No 121 (Eagle) Squadron markings.

Left: A Spitfire Mk V landing.

Above right: Another Eagle Squadron representative is Spitfire Mk of No 71 Squadron.

Below right: Devoid of its wing cannon is this warbird Mk IX in No 133 Squadron markings.

SUPERMARINE WALRUS

Designed by R. J. Mitchell and built by Supermarine as a private venture, the Walrus was initially ordered by the Royal Australian Navy for shipborne reconnaissance and communications as the Seagull Mk V. In contrast with previous Seagull models the Mk V was completed with a metal hull and a pusher rather than a tractor engine. By the time the aircraft entered service in Australia, the British Air Ministry had also ordered the aircraft for the Fleet Air Arm, and in 1936 the first of 12 aircraft, by then named Walrus, were delivered. Intended for use with catapult flights aboard the Royal Navys battleships, battle-cruisers and cruisers the Pegasus-powered Walrus was tasked with reconnaissance and gunnery spotting for its parent ships guns and by the outbreak of war was well established in this role. Soon after war broke out No 710 Squadron was formed to operate from Sierra Leone escorting British convoys in the area, if necessary attacking enemy vessels with bombs or depth charges. Also used for ship-to shore communications the Walrus remained with the FAA in its primary duty with catapult flights until March 1944.

Specification: Supermarine Walrus Mk II
Manufacturers: Supermarine, Saunders-Roe
Number built: 761 (551 Mk I, 183 Mk II; plus 26 Seagull Vs for RAAF)
Entry into service: March 1936
Powerplant: one 775-hp Bristol Pegasus VI
Length: 37 ft 7 in (11.45 m)
Height: 15 ft 3 in (4.65 m)
Wingspan: 45 ft 10 in (13.97 m)
Weight empty: 4,900 lb (2,223 kg)
Range: 600 miles (965 km)
Max speed: 135 mph (217 km/h) at 4,750 ft (1,448 m)
Service ceiling: 18,500 ft (5,640 m)
Armament: 1 x 0.303-in (7.7-mm) machine gun in bow position and 2 x 0.303-in (7.7-mm) machine guns in midships position and up to 760 lb (345 kg) of bombs or depth charges

From 1941 the Walrus was operated by the RAF for air-sea rescue. Serving with four Middle East and seven UK-based units, the Walrus became the darling of downed aircrew swooping in low for the rescue often under enemy fire. No 277 Squadron alone rescued 598 aircrew from the sea.

Below left: Antiquated though it looked, it was a beautiful sight to airmen 'down in the drink'.

Bottom left: The first production Walrus Mk I seen in 1936.

Above right: A good view of the Walrus in flight.

Right: A Walrus crew practising a water rescue

Below: Using fore and aft hatches the crew could haul men aboard without difficulty.

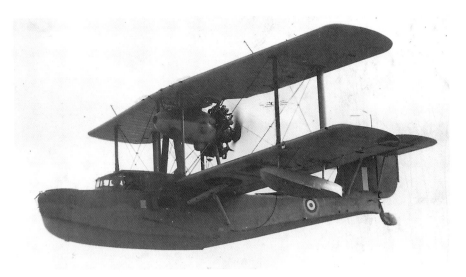

VICKERS WELLINGTON

Numerically the most significant British bomber of the Second World War the Vickers Wellington was the most important asset at Bomber Command's disposal for the first three years of the conflict.

Responding to the same Air Ministry specification which produced the Handley Page Hampden, the Wellington was one of the most ambitious aviation designs of the 1930s. The need to comply with the weight limits set at the Geneva Disarmament Conference of 1932 ensured that the Wellington would be of twin-engine layout of not more than 70 ft in length. To give the aircraft the desire strength while keeping within the weight limits, Vickers employed the geodetic fuselage structure previously used in the Vickers Wellesley, the only aircraft produced in the Second World War to use this technique. Without the need of supporting spars the fuselage had a large cross-section allowing adequate stowage space for ordnance and room for, what was at the time, heavy defensive armament.

Powered by Bristol Pegasus engines the prototype first flew in May 1936 and the relaxation of the weight restrictions allowed the Wellingtons range and load-carrying capabilities to be improved substantially. Displaying performance well beyond the specification a production order was granted in August 1936 and the aircraft was officially named Wellington.

Deliveries of the first production Wellington Mk Is began in October 1938, these aircraft differing from the prototype in having an extended nose, nose and tail turrets and a retractable tail wheel. By the outbreak of war six front line Bomber Command squadrons had been equipped with the Mk I and production was switched to the Mk IA fitted with a ventral turret. The

Above: Mk I Wellingtons on an early practise flight.

Left: Semi-circular line up of Wellingtons of No 30 Operational Training Unit.

Right: The best of the RAF's early-war bombers, the 'Wimpey' served through the war.

Specification: Wellington Mk IC
Manufacturer: Vickers-Armstrong
Number built: 11,462 (inc 181 Mk I, 187 Mk IA, 2,685 Mk Ic, 401 Mk II, 1,519 Mk III, 220 Mk IV, 394 Mk VIII, 3,803 Mk X, 180 Mk XI, 884 Mk XIII, 841 Mk XIV)
Entry into service: October 1938
Powerplant: Two 1,000 hp Bristol Pegasus XVIII
Length: 64 ft 7 in (19.69 m)
Height: 17 ft 6 in (5.35 m)
Wingspan: 86 ft 2 in (26.26 m)
Weight empty: 18,556 lb (8,417 kg)
Range: 1,805 miles (2,905 km) with 2,800 lb (4,506 kg) of bombs
Max speed: 234 mph (377 km/h) at 15,200 ft (4,633 m)
Service ceiling: 18,000 ft (5,486 m)
Armament: 2 x 0.303-in (7.7-mm) machine guns in nose turret, 2 x 0.303-in (7.7-mm) machine guns in tail turret, 2 x 0.303-in (7.7-mm) machine guns in beam positions plus up to 4,500 lb (2,041 kg) of bombs

Specification: Wellington Mk III
Powerplant: Two 1,425 hp Bristol Hercules III or XI
Length: 64 ft 7 in (19.69 m)
Wingspan: 86 ft 2 in (26.26 m)
Height: 17 ft 6 in (5.35 m)
Weight empty: 22,000 lb (9,980 kg)
Range: 1,470 miles (2,366 km) with maximum bomb load
Max speed: 255 mph (411 km/h) at 12,500 ft (3,810 m)
Service ceiling: 18,000 ft (5,486 m)
Armament: 2 x 0.303-in (7.7-mm) machine guns in nose turret, 4 x 0.303-in (7.7-mm) machine guns in tail turret, 2 x 0.303-in (7.7-mm) machine guns in beam positions plus up to 4,500 lb (2,041 kg) of bombs

Wellington made its combat debut on the second day of the war when 14 aircraft from Nos 9 and 149 Squadrons attacked German warships in a daylight raid at Brunsbuttel. Despite having what at the time was considered to be more than adequate defensive firepower, two Wellingtons were lost and the raid was entirely unsuccessful.

Doubts about the wisdom of employing the aircraft on unescorted raids mounted during the autumn as losses steadily rose, culminating in 16 out of 34 Wellingtons being lost in two raids on German warships at Heligoland and Wilhelmshaven. These experiences demonstrated the vulnerability of the Wellington during daylight raids and modifications led to the production of the Wellington Mk IC fitted with beam machine guns. As with the Hampden daylight raids were largely abandoned early in 1941 and the first modest phase of Bomber Command's night strategic offensive against Germany began. Proving to be more combat capable than either the Whitley or the Hampden, production of the Wellington in two new versions started: the Merlin-engined Mk II and the Hercules-engined Mk III, both variants having self-sealing fuel tanks.

With the threat of invasion diminishing, Bomber Command

stepped-up its night bombing offensive during the spring of 1941 and on April 1 a Wellington of No 149 Squadron dropped the first 4,000 lb 'blockbuster' bomb during a raid on Emden. In the autumn of 1940 Wellington Mk I-equipped No 75 Squadron was designated an RNZAF unit, becoming the first of many Commonwealth squadrons in Bomber Command, and in July 1941 Sgt J. Ward from this unit became the only member of a Wellington crew to receive a VC when he climbed out on to the aircraft's wing to extinguish a fire.

In March 1942 Air Chief Marshal Arthur 'Bomber' Harris took charge of Bomber Command and shortly afterwards his policy of massed night raids against German industrial sites and cities began. By this time the Wellington comprised over half of all Bomber Command aircraft and equipped some 20 operational squadrons. Of the 1,043 aircraft which participated in the first '1,000 bomber' raid on Cologne in May 1941, 599 were Wellingtons and Nos 1, 3, 4 and 6 Group's Wellington Mk Is and Mk IIIs continued to fly

the lion's share of night bombing raids until sufficient numbers of the four-engined Lancasters, Halifaxes and Stirlings appeared in 1943. The spring and summer of 1943 saw the Wellington largely replaced in main bomber force squadron service and the last raid by Bomber Command Wellingtons was flown in October. The Wellington did, however, continue to serve with No 100 Group, Bomber Command well into 1944, tasked with electronic intelligence and radio countermeasures.

The Wellington's wartime role was by no means confined to Bomber Command. With the spread of hostilities in the Mediterranean, North Africa and the Middle East during 1940 Nos 37 and 70 Squadrons moved to the theatre to assist with the Allies defence of the region. No 70 Sqn was soon in action in September 1940 attacking ships and harbour installations at Benghazi. No 37 Sqn was involved the following spring in supporting Allied operations in Greece and Iraq. By mid-1943 seven other Wellington squadrons, mostly equipped with the new Mk X, had been deployed to

the theatre and played a vital role in attacking German installations and convoys during the North African campaign. At least four Squadrons continued operations in the region during the invasion of Italy before finally being replaced by Liberators in March 1944.

In the Far East Nos 99 and 214 Squadrons began operations with Wellington Mk ICs in the spring of 1942. Successively re-equipped with Mk IIIs and Mk Xs these squadrons mounted numerous raids against land and maritime targets until the autumn of 1944.

Not only was the Wellington the backbone of Bomber Command in the early war years, but was also a vital tool of Coastal Command. Three variants fitted with increasingly more capable ASV radar were developed for the Command and from 1942 played a vital role in the Battle of the Atlantic. Using the Leigh searchlight the Wellingtons were particularly effective in 'killing' U-boats at night, the first such success being by a Wellington GR.Mk VIII against U-Boat U-502 in July 1942. Coastal Command

Wellingtons continued in service throughout the remainder of the war and were joined in 1945 by the Vickers Warwick GR. Mk V which, due to engine problems, had been unable to fill its intended role as a complementary bomber to the Wellington.

In addition to these roles, the Wellington also served as a transport aircraft and trainer as well as modified versions being used for new experimental engines, highlighting the fact that the Wellington was one of the RAF's most versatile and important aircraft of the conflict.

Below left: With Rolls-Royce Merlin engines the Wellington became the Mk II.

Above right: The Mk III was the last to serve with Bomber Command.

Right and Below: Although the Wimpey was better than some bombers, poor gun defense made the RAF switch it to night bombing

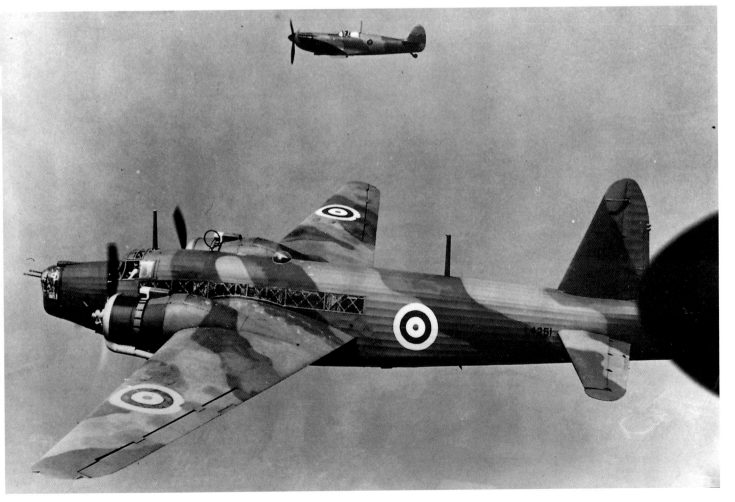

WESTLAND LYSANDER

Responding to an Air Ministry request in 1934 for a new army co-operation aircraft the Westland company designed the high-wing monoplane Lysander. Entering service in 1938 the aircraft had excellent short take-off and landing capability and was fitted with one or two trainable machine guns in the rear cockpit and one or two forward-firing machine guns, as well as bomb racks on stubs attached to the wheel spats.

With the attack on the Low Countries in the spring of 1940, four squadrons of Lysanders were attached to the Air Component of the British Expeditionary Force for the support of the ground troops. With the Luftwaffe having gained air superiority losses were high with over 100 Lysanders being lost in six weeks although one Lysander from No II Squadron did manage the unlikely feat of shooting down a Henschel Hs 126 and a Junkers Ju 87 on the same day with a combination of its rear and forward-firing machine guns.

In the Middle East Nos 6 and 208 Squadrons flew the Lysander in the reconnaissance and light ground-attack roles operating in Egypt Palestine and the Greek campaign between 1939 and 1942. A number of other squadrons used the aircraft in for similar purposes in the Burma campaign with No 20 Squadron still

Specification: Westland Lysander Mk III
Manufacturers: Westland, National Steel Car Corporation (Canada)
Number built: 1,652 (169 Mk I, 442 Mk II, 367 Mk III, 347 Mk IIIA, 100 TT Mk IIIA and in Canada 75 Mk II, 150 TT Mk IIIA)
Entry into service: May 1938
Powerplant: One 870-hp Bristol Mercury XX or XXX
Length: 30 ft 6 in (9.30 m)
Height: 14 ft 6 in (4.42 m)
Wingspan: 50 ft 0 in (15.24 m)
Weight empty: 4,365 lb (1,980 kg)
Range fully loaded: 600 miles (966 km)
Max speed: 212 mph (341 km/h) at 5,000 ft (1,524 m)
Service ceiling: 21,500 ft (6,553 m)
Armament: 2 x 0.303-in (7.7-mm) fixed, forward-firing, machine guns and 2 x 0.303-in (7.7-mm) machine guns in rear cockpit and up to 500 lb (227 kg) of bombs

Above right: A Lysander used for long range liaison work by South East Asia Command, RAF.

Right: An early war Lysander with Lewis gun defence and wheel spat bomb racks.

operating the Lysander in the region until November 1943.

At the time highly secret, the Lysanders most famous wartime exploits were in the hands of the SOE. Using the aircraft's exceptional STOL performance, black-painted Lysander Mk IIIs and Mk IIIAs, operating under the cover of darkness, landed agents and supplies in small fields in German-occupied territory at great risk. Other late-war uses of the Lysander included target towing and air-sea rescue with RAF Coastal Command.

Above right: Many training duties were undertaken by the 'Lizzie'.

Right: No 225 Squadron aircraft with wheel spat small bomb carriers in place.

Below: A fine view of a preserved Lysander.

Above: With its high wing the 'Lizzie' could be flown at remarkably low speeds.

Right: Among its wartime duties the Lysander flew agents into occupied territory.

Below: To pick up agents a Lysander with good 'rough strip' capability, usually did the job.

ITALY

CANT Z.506

Cantieri Riunity dell'Adriatico (CANT) followed a similar route to Savoia Marchetti to produce the Z.506, by adopting a three-engine layout. This aircraft was derived from the Z.505 prototype that was planned as a mail plane to connect Italy with its East Africa colonies, virtually all of which lacked major airfields. Flight testing revealed outstanding performance and the aircraft was subsequently placed in production as a 15-passenger civil transport (20 aircraft). Production then switched to the Z.506B Airone (Heron) military derivative that entered service in 1938. Production of the Z.506B, which also involved Piaggio up to January 1943, totalled some

Below: A Cant Z.506 about to lift off.

Specification: Z.506B

Type: Five-seat maritime reconnaissance and bomber floatplane

Powerplant: Three 750 hp (559kW) Alfa Romeo 126 R.C.34 nine-cylinder single-row radial engines

Length: 63 ft 1.7 in (19.24 m)

Height: 24 ft 5.5 in (7.45 m)

Wingspan: 86 ft 11.33 in (26.50 m)

Weight empty: 18,298 lb (8,300 kg); maximum take-off 28,008 lb (12,705 kg)

Range: 1,705 miles (2,745 km)

Max speed: 217 mph (350 km/h)

Climb to: 13,125 ft (4,000 m) in 20 minutes

Service ceiling: 26,245 ft (8,000 m)

Armament: 1 x 1 mm trainable machine gun in dorsal turret, 1 x 7 mm trainable rearward-firing machine gun in rear of the ventral gon dola, and 1 x 7.7 mm trainable lateral-firing machine gun in each of two lateral positions, plus an internal bomb load of 2,646 lb (1,200 kg)

324 aircraft of which 95 were in service at the time of Italy's entry into the Second World War.

The type was initially operated in the bomber role, but then revised with stronger defensive armament and reassigned to the maritime reconnaissance, convoy escort and anti-submarine roles. A number of aircraft were also converted to the Z.506S standard for the air/sea rescue task, and a number of the aircraft were retained in service by the air-sea rescue service up to 1959.

CANT Z.1007

Together with the SM.79 and BR.20, the Z.1007 typified the bombers of the Regia Aeronautica. Designed by Filippo Zappata, and first flown in prototype form during March 1937, the Z.1007 Alcione (Kingfisher) entered service late in 1938 and became one of Italy's most important medium bombers. Production of the Z.1007 totalled only about 35 aircraft with 840 hp (626 kW) Piaggio Asso XI radial engines and a defensive armament of four 7.7 mm machine guns.

Below: One of Italy's trimotor bombers, the Cant Z.1007 was deployed in large numbers.

Specification: Z.1007bis
Type: Five-seat medium bomber
Powerplant: Three 1,000 hp (746 kW) Piaggio P.XI R2C.40 14-cylinder two-row radial engines
Length: 60 ft 2.5 in (18.35 m)
Height: 17 ft 5 in (5.22 m)
Wingspan: 81 ft 4.33 in (24.80 m)
Weight empty: 20,715 lb (9,396 kg); maximum take-off 30,029 lb (13,621 kg)
Range: 1,087 miles (1,750 km) with a 2,646 lb (1,200 kg) bomb load
Max speed: 290 mph (466 km/h)
Climb to: 13,125 ft (4,000 m) in 10 minutes 30 seconds
Service ceiling: 26,900 ft (8,200 m)
Armament: 1 x 12.7 mm trainable machine gun in dorsal turret, 1 x 12.7 mm trainable rearward-firing machine gun in ventral step position, and 1 x 7.7mm trainable lateral-firing machine gun in each of two beam positions, plus an internal bomb load of 2,646 lb (1,200 kg)

This initial variant, which suffered problems with inadequate power provided by the Asso XI engines, was followed by 526 examples of the Z.1007bis and 50 Z.1007ter. The former introduced a larger airframe, an uprated powerplant with engines in revised nacelles, and different armament as well as two types of tail unit (single vertical surface in first three batches and twin surfaces in the last six batches). The latter had the uprated powerplant of three 1,175 hp (876 kW) Piaggio P.XIX radial engines but a reduced 2,205lb (1,000 kg) bomb load. The operational debut of the Kingfisher was not brilliant as it coincided with the ill-fated participation of the Corpo Aereo Italiano over the Channel in September 1940. The aircraft was used in large numbers over Greece and was extensively used in operations in the Mediterranean theatre. From 1943 the Z.1007ter version became available.

300

Right and Below: The Cant Z.1007 Alcione (Kingfisher) entered service late in 1938 and became one of Italy's most important medium bombers.

FIAT BR.20

The third major Italian bomber was the Fiat BR.20 Cicogna (Stork), which was designed in 1936 by Celestino Rosatelli. It was the first 'modern' medium bomber produced in Italy during the period leading up to the Second World War, and first flew in prototype form during February 1936 for service from the autumn of the same year. Although it was modern and advanced at the time of its appearance (it first saw action in Spain in 1937), this twin-engine low-wing monoplane betrayed its obsolescence from the beginning of its operational career in the Second World War.

Specification: BR.20M
Type: Five-seat medium bomber
Powerplant: Two 1,030 hp (768 kW) Fiat A.80 R.C.41 14-cylinder two-row radial engines
Length: 53 ft 0.5 in (16.17 m)
Height: 14 ft 1.25 in (4.30 m)
Wingspan: 70 ft 8.8 in (21.56 m)
Weight empty: 14,859 lb (6,740 kg); maximum take-off 22,795 lb (10,340 kg)
Range: 770.5 miles (1,240km) with a 2,205 lb (1,000 kg) bomb load
Max speed: 267 mph (430 km/h)
Climb to: 16,405 ft (5,000 m) in 17 minutes 56 seconds
Service ceiling: 23,620 ft (7,200 m)
Armament: 1 x 7.7 mm trainable forward-firing machine gun in the nose turret, 2 x 7.7 mm or 1 x 12.7 mm trainable rearward-firing machine guns in the dorsal turret, and 1 x 7.7mm trainable rearward-firing machine gun in the ventral hatch position, plus an internal bomb load of 3 527 lb (1,600 kg)

Delivery of 320 aircraft, incuding 85 for Japan and one for Venezuela, was followed by production of 264 improved BR.20M bombers. This model featured improved nose contours, revised armament and increased armour protection. The final variant was the BR.20bis (15 aircraft) with two 1,250 hp (932 kW) Fiat A.82 R.C.42S radial engines, a redesigned nose, two 7.7 mm machine guns in waist positions, and a power-operated dorsal turret. More than 160 Cicogna bombers were available when Italy entered the Second World War, and all but a handful of the 500+ aircraft that were constructed were lost in extensive operations before Italy's September 1943 armistice with the Allies.

Above left: Late BR.20s had a single-gun nose turret.

Left: A revised nose gave the BR.20 bombardier more visibility.

FIAT CR.42

This aircraft was the last in a series of excellent biplanes designed at Fiat by Celestino Rosatelli. Drawing on experience gained from the CR.1, CR.20, CR.30 and then the superb CR.32, the CR.42 was developed under the mistaken belief that there was still a role for a highly maneouvrable biplane fighter in the late 1930s. This belief had been strenghtened by the achievements of biplane fighters in Spain. The prototype took to the air for the first time in May 1938, when all other countries were developing monoplanes. Power was provided by a Fiat A.74 R1C 38 radial engine in a long chord cowling. Flight testing was concluded successfully and the Ministro dell'Aeronautico lost no time in ordering 200 of the machines, the first of them delivered during February 1939. Total production amounted to some 1,781 aircraft in seven variants, incuding 150 built for the Luftwaffe. The basic aircraft was exported to Belgium, Hungary and

Specification: CR.42
Type: Single-seat fighter biplane
Powerplant: One 840 hp (626 kW) Fiat A.74 R1C.38 14-cylinder two-row radial engine
Length: 27 ft 1.5 in (8.27 m)
Height: 11 ft 9.25 in (3.59 m)
Wingspan: 31 ft 10 in (9.70 m)
Weight empty: 3,929 lb (1,782 kg); max take-off 5,060 lb (2,295 kg)
Max speed: 267mph (430 km/h)
Climb to: 16,405 ft (6,000 m) in 8 minutes 40 seconds Service ceiling: 33,465 ft (10,200 m) range 482 miles (775 km)
Armament: 2 x 12.7 mm Breda-SAFAT fixed forward-firing machine guns in the upper part of the forward fuselage, plus an external bomb load of 440 lb (200 kg)

Sweden during the war, and first saw service in the former country in May 1940. When Italy declared war in June 1940 the Regia Aeronautica had 242 CR.42s with the fighter squadriglie, and these were active during the Italian campaign in southern France and were also used sporadically in the Battle of Britain. The CR.42 was then used exclusively for operations over the

Mediterranenean and in Northern and East Africa, and in the desert they proved effective against ground targets. In July 1941 the first CR.42 AS (Africa Settentrionale) with tropical dust filters and racks for two 200 lb bombs were delivered, but losses mounted from September 1942 and the remainder were withdrawn to Mediterrenean operations. The CR.42 CN was a night-fighter

variant wih exhaust flame-dampers, radio and underwing searchlights; the CR.42 DB a one-off prototype with a 1,160 hp Daimler-Benz DB 601E engine; the ICR.42 was a float-equipped CR.42 built by Fiat-subsidiary CMASA; the CR.42 LW was the night harassment and anti-partisan version built for the Luftwaffe after September 1943; and the CR.42 two-seater were Swedish single-seat aircraft converted after the war as liaison aircraft with a second open cockpit immediately behind that of the pilot.

Top: Many Fiat fighters were used by the Luftwaffe for second line duties.

Above: An early CR.42 with characteristic staggered wing layout.

Left: An airman checks a CR.42's engine cowling.

Far left: A nicely finished Fiat CR.42 as a museum exhibit.

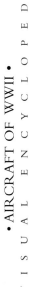

304

Above: The snug cockpit of the CR.42.

Right: Elaborate camouflage was a Regia Aeronautica speciality.

Below: In its heyday the CR.42 proved an excellent design.

Above: Dusty take off for a trio of CR.42s.

Left: The Italians' one big raid on Britain had poor results.

Below: Coloured cowlings helped identify Regia Aeronautica units.

Opposite, above and below: The Italians favoured biplanes for their outstanding manoevrability, but their aircraft were quickly outclassed by modern monoplanes.

FIAT G.50 FRECCIA

The G.50 was one of the six entries to the fighter competition launched in 1935, to find a low-wing monoplane for the Regia Aeronautica. Although the Macchi MC.200 eventually emerged dominant, the initial winner was Guiseppe Gabrielli's G.50 design. Flight trials began in February 1937 and went smoothly, and an order was placed in September for 45 aircraft. Deliveries began in early 1938 and the first of these were sent to Spain to reinforce the Aviacon Legionare. In combat pilots appreciated their good qualities of speed and manoeuvrability but disliked the enclosed cockpit, which was troublesome to open and restricted visibility. The next batch of 200 aircraft was therefore produced with a semi-enclosed cockpit. One of the most obvious failings, and one that was not rectified after Spain, was the poor armament that consisted of only two

12.7 mm machine guns. Production from the CMASA plant at Marina di Pisa got under way in 1939 and totalled some 778 aircraft.

When Italy entered the war some 97 aircraft were in service and these fought in Finland, in southern France in June 1940 and through the winter of 1940-41 against Britain. The G.50 was handicapped by a very limited range, leading to the introduction of the G.50bis, the main production variant. This had increased fuel tankage, redesigned vertical tail surfaces, a reprofiled fuselage to give better visibility, armour and self-sealing tanks. Other versions incuded the tandem-seat G.50B trainer, the G.50ter (single example with more powerful 1,000 hp Fiat A.76 engine), and the G.50 A/N two-seat fighter prototype with four 12.7 mm machine guns and racks for two bombs, that was intended for use on the ill-fated

Specification: G.50
Type: Single-seat fighter
Powerplant: One 840 hp (626 kW) Fiat A.74 R1C.38 14-cylinder two-row radial engine
Length: 25 ft 6.75 in (7.79 m)
Height: 9 ft 8.5 in (2.96 m)
Wingspan: 35 ft 11.5 in (10.96 m)
Weight empty: 4,354 lb (1,975 kg)
Range: 416miles) 670km
Max speed: 293 mph (472 km/h)
Service ceiling: 32,265 ft (9,835 m)
Armament: 2 x 12.7 mm Breda-SAFAT fixed forward-firing machine guns in the upper part of the forward fuselage

Italian aircraft carriers *Aquila* and *Sparviero*. From this last aircraft was developed the G.55.

The G.50bis served extensively in the Mediterranean and North African theatres. For operations in the desert most aircraft were fitted with dust filters and some were equipped with racks for bombs, incuding anti-personnel bombs. It was retired from front line service in September 1943, but soldiered on in Finnish service in the war against Russia until 1945.

Above right: There was little protection for the Fiat G.50 pilot in the event of attack.

Below left: A Fiat G.50 escorting a Luftwaffe Bf 110.

Right: Highly manoeuvrable, the G.50 quickly needed updating.

Below: The answer was the superb G.55 one of Italy's best wartime fighters.

MACCHI MC.200 SAETTA

The Saetta (Lightning) was one of the first generation of Italian low-wing monoplane fighters with advanced features such as retractable main landing gear units, but like many of its contemporaries was limited in capability by a low-powered engine and wholly inadequate system of armament.

Feasibility studies were began at Macchi in 1935 under engineer Mario Castoldi, the 'father' of the most successful Italian racing seaplanes incuding the M.39 (winner of the 1926 Schneider Trophy) and the MC.72 (World Speed Record holder in its class). The project was a private venture, but in 1936 the Italian Government issued an official requirement for a defence fighter. Castoldi's design was tendered as the MC.200 and this was first flown in prototype form on Christmas Eve 1937. Despite winning the ministerial fighter contest, held in 1938, that pitted the MC.200 against the Fiat CR.42, Fiat G.50 and Reggiane Re.2000, a ridiculous situation arose where all of these aircraft were produced simultaneously. Had a more practicable solution been followed, and development concentrated on either the MC.200 or G.50, a really outstanding aircraft might well have materialised.

Large numbers of the MC.200 were ordered by the air ministry and at the outbreak of war 144 machines had been delivered to the fighter squadrons, before entering service in

October 1939. The original type of enclosed cockpit was initially altered to an open and finally a semi-enclosed type ostensibly because Italian pilots preferred this layout! Production from June 1939 to July 1942 totalled 1,150 aircraft, later aircraft having the outer wings of the MC.202 with two 7.7 mm machine guns. With the advent of the more capable MC.202, the MC.200 was

generally relegated to the escort fighter and fighter-bomber roles (MC.200CB). The MC.20AS (Africa Settentrionale) was a tropicalised type for North African service, where the aircraft saw most service. Against the Hawker Hurricane Mk II and Curtiss P-40 the aircraft was generally inferior, and at the time of the Allied invasion of Italy only 43 aircraft remained in the front-line.

Specification: MC.200CB
Type: Single-seat fighter and fighter-bomber
Powerplant: One 870 hp (649 kW) Fiat A.74 R.C.38 14-cylinder two-row radial engine
Length: 26 ft 10.4 in (8.19 m)
Height: 11ft 5.75 in (3.51 m)
Wingspan: 34 ft 8.5 in (10.58 m)
Weight empty: 4,451 lb (2,019 kg); normal take-off 5,597 lb (2,339 kg)
Range: 541 miles (870 km)
Max speed: 312 mph (503 km/h)
Climb to: 16,405 ft (6,000 m) in 5 minutes 51 seconds
Service ceiling: 29,200 ft (8,900 m)
Armament: 2 x 12.7 mm fixed forward-firing machine guns in the upper part of the forward fuselage, plus an external bomb load of 705 lb (320 kg)

Right: The MC 200's cowling had distinctive cylinder head fairings.

MACCHI MC.205V VELTRO

Type: Single-seat fighter and fighter-bomber
Powerplant: One 1,475 hp (1,100 kW) Fiat RA.1050 RC.58 Tifone
  12-cylinder inverted-Vee engine (licence-built Daimler-Benz DB 605)
Length: 29 ft 0.5 in (8.85 m) **Height:** 9 ft 11.5 in (3.04 m)
Wingspan: 34 ft 8.5 in (10.58 m)
Weight empty: 5,691 lb (2,581kg); normal take-off 7,108 lb
  (3,224 kg); maximum take-off 7,514 lb (3,408 kg)
Range: 646 miles (1,040 km) **Max speed:** 399 mph (642 km/h)
Climb to: 16,405 ft (5,000 m) in 4 minutes 47 seconds
Service ceiling: 36,090 ft (11,000 m)
Armament: 2 x 12.7 mm fixed forward-firing machine guns in the
  upper part of the forward fuselage, and 2 x 20mm fixed forward-
  firing cannon in the leading edges of the wing, plus an external bomb
  load of 705 lb (320 kg)

The failure to produce a high-powered engine suitable for military use and light armament were two key factors that hampered Italian fighter design in the Second World War. With the MC.205V Veltro, Macchi addressed at least the first of these two limitations to produce what was undoubtedly the finest Italian fighter of the war. Progress was made from August 1940 when Mario Castoldi unveiled the excellent MC.202 Folgore (Thunderbolt), a development of the MC.200 with a licence-built (by Alfa-Romeo) version of the Daimler-Benz DB 601A engine producing some 1,075hp. Many of the best features of the MC.200 were incorporated into the design, easing the process of manufacture.

The Folgore's performance roughly compared to the Spitfire Mk V, although the armament of four machine-guns was still inadequate. During the Axis advance to El Alamein the Folgore fought its most successful campaign against the Hurricanes and Tomahawks of the Desert Air Force. However, by summer 1943 it had been outclassed by the Spitfire Mk IX, P-40 Warhawk and P-38 Lightning.

By this time Macchi had created the MC.205 as a still further improved version of the same basic concept with a licence-built version of the DB 605 engine. The MC.205 prototype was an MC.202 conversion that first flew in April 1942 with the new engine as well as larger outer wing panels. The new fighter entered production and was built to

the extent of 262 MC.205V *Veltro* (Greyhound) aircraft that were committed to combat from July 1943. Later machines had 20 mm cannon rather than 7.7 mm machine guns in the wings, and most of the aircraft served with Aeronautica Nazionale Republicana (the air force of the revised Fascist state) after the Italy's September 1943 armistice with the

Allies. Had the superior German engine been made available earlier, the MC.205V could thus have entered service earlier in the war and would have certainly had a greater impact on the war in the desert. A high-altitude version completed only in prototype form was the MC.205N-1 Orione, with four 12.7 mm and one 20 mm MG 151 guns.

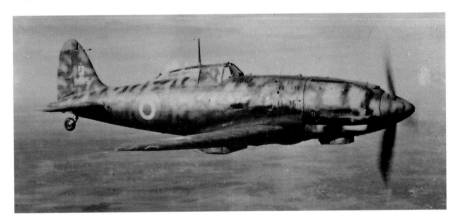

**Above right and right:
The MC.202 was a fine fighter but poorly armed and, until fitted with the DB 601 underpowered.**

SAVOIA-MARCHETTI SM.79 SPARVIERO

Whereas the SM.81 was a military version of an airliner, the SM.79 was a completely new design that shared only the three-engine, low-wing monoplane configuration of its predecessor. The SM.79P civil transport prototype (with eight-passenger seating) from which it was developed was designed to take part in the international London–Melbourne race and first flew in October 1934. This proved to be an excellent aircraft in all respects, winning a number of speed/distance/payload records in 1935. These achievements attracted the attention of the military, who asked that the second prototype be built in a bomber version. This did not differ structurally from the civil version, the only variations

being the addition of a ventral gondola and a distinctive raised central cockpit, which earned it the nickname 'Hunchback'. Production started in October 1936 and proceeded uninterrupted until June 1943, with deliveries totalling 1,230 aircraft.

The type entered service as the SM.79-I in late 1936 with the powerplant of three Alfa Romeo 126 radial engines. Its operational debut came in Spain in February 1937

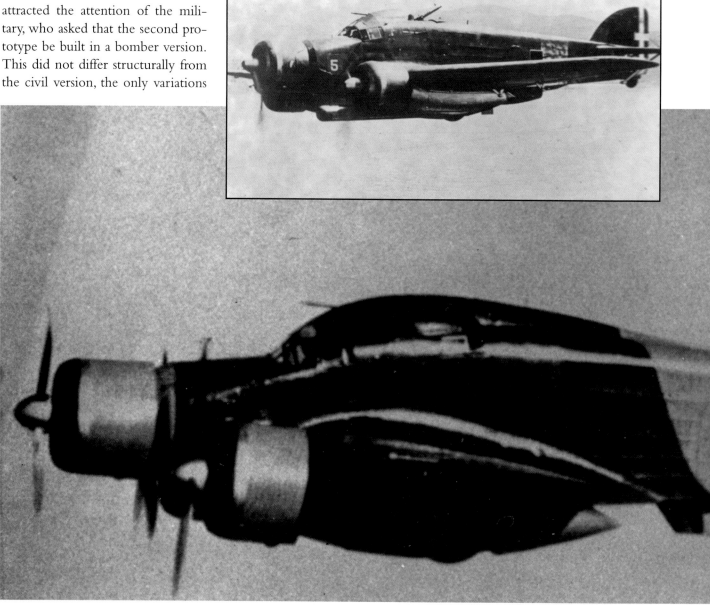

with the Aviacon Legionaria, in the role of medium reconnaissance bomber and in this theatre the aircraft performed with some distinction. Shortly after the outbreak of war the aircraft was adapted to a wider range of roles, incuding torpedo bombing. The SM.79-II, which entered service in October 1939, was optimised for the anti-ship role with two 450 mm torpedoes and a powerplant of three 1,000 hp

Specification: SM.79-I
Type: Four/five-seat medium reconnaissance bomber
Powerplant: Three 780 hp (582 kW) Alfa Romeo 126 RC.34 9-cylinder single-row radial engines
Length: 51 ft 3.1 in (15.62 m)
Height: 14 ft 5.25 in (4.40 m)
Wingspan: 69 ft 2.7 in (21.20 m)
Weight empty: 14,991 lb (6,800 kg); max take-off 23,104 lb (10,480 kg)
Range: 1,181 miles (1,900 km) with a 2,756 lb (1,250 kg) bomb load
Max speed: 267mph (430km/h)
Climb to: 16,405 ft (5,000 m) in 19 minutes 45 seconds
Service ceiling: 21,325 ft (6,500 m)
Armament: 1 x 12.7 mm fixed forward-firing machine gun above cockpit, 1 x 12.7mm trainable rearward-firing machine gun in dorsal position, one 12.7 mm trainable rearward-firing machine gun in ven tral position, and one 7.7 mm trainable lateral-firing machine gun in two beam positions, plus a bomb load of 2,756 lb (1,250 kg)

Specification: SM.79JR
Type: Four/five-seat medium reconnaissance bomber
Powerplant: Two 1,120 hp (835 kW) Junkers Jumo 211Da 12-cylinder inverted-Vee engines
Length: 52 ft 9.9 in (16.10 m)
Height: 14 ft 5.25 in (4.40 m)
Wingspan: 69 ft 2.7 in (21.20 m)
Weight empty: 15,840 lb (7,185 kg); maximum take-off 23,754 lb (10,775kg)
Range: 1,243 miles (2,000 km)
Max speed: 276 mph (445 km/h)
Climb to: 9,845 ft (3,000 m) in 8 minutes 36 seconds
Service ceiling: 24,280 ft (7,400 m)
Armament: 1 x 13 mm fixed forward-firing machine gun above the cockpit, 1 x 13 mm trainable rearward-firing machine gun in the dorsal position, 1 x 13 mm trainable rearward-firing machine gun in the ventral position, and 1 x 7.92 mm trainable lateral-firing machine gun in either of the two beam positions, plus an internal bomb load of 2,756 lb (1,250 kg)

(746 kW) Piaggio P.XI RC.40 or 1,030 hp (768 kW) Fiat A.80 RC.41 radial engines. In this capacity the aircraft excelled and many historians regard it as the finest torpedo-bomber of the war. After serving on all fronts the aircraft continued in service after September 1943 as a torpedo-bomber.

The final Italian model was the SM.79-III, and improved SM.79-II with heavier defensive armament but no ventral gondola. The aircraft continued in service after the Second World War as a transport with the Aeronautica Militare Italiana.

The SM.79 was also exported in a number of twin-engined forms. The SM.79B was the SM.79-I version for Brazil (three machines) with 930 hp (694 kW) Alfa Romeo 128 RC.18 engines, Iraq (four machines) with 1,030 hp (768 kW) Fiat A.80 RC.41 engines and Rumania (24 machines) with 1,000 hp (746 kW) Gnome-Rhône 14K Mistral-Major engines, while the SM.79JR was another model for Rumania (40 machines), similar to the SM.79B, with 1,120 hp (835 kW) Junkers Jumo 211Da engines. Sixteen of the latter were built under licence. The last export model was the SM.79K version of the SM.79-I for Yugoslavia (45 machines). Italian variants were the SM.79C VIP transport conversions of 16 SM.79-Is with 1,000 hp (746 kW) Piaggio P.XI RC.40 engines and no dorsal or ventral gun positions, and the SM.79T long-range version of the SM.79C with 780 hp (582 kW) Alfa Romeo 126 RC.34 engines and significantly increased fuel capacity.

Above left: Best of Italy's wartime bombers, the SM.79 excelled in the anti-shipping role.

Left: The fuselage hump on the SM.79 enclosed a defensive gun position.

SAVOIA-MARCHETTI SM.81

During the mid-1930s Savoia-Marchetti produced a series of aircraft for the Regia Aeronautica that were a considerable advance on the previous generation of Italian bombers, and that served Italy well throughout the course of the war. The first of these was the SM.81, a tri-engine low-wing monoplane that was developed from 1934 in parallel with the SM.73 airliner, with which it shared a basically common airframe. The Pipistrello (Bat), as it was dubbed, was a dual-role bomber and transport that first flew in prototype form in 1934 and entered service in 1935. Fast, well armed and with a good range, this aircraft saw extensive service in the Italian conquest of Abyssinia in the mid-1930s and in the early part of the Spanish Civil War. It performed well in these theatres, under conditions that were in no way representative of the coming war, but none the less was ordered in large numbers. Some 535 aircraft were built in three subvariants that differed only in their powerplants, which could comprise any of three types of radial engine (two Italian and one French, the last from

captured stocks). When tested in more hostile conditions, the aircraft's limitations were exposed.

From the time of Italy's June 1940 entry into the Second World War was used increasingly in the dedicated transport role, although it did undertake night bombing raids in North Africa. The type survived the war in modest numbers and remained in Italian service to 1950.

Specification: SM.81

Type: Five/six-seat bomber and transport

Powerplant: Three 670 hp (499.5 kW) Piaggio P.X RC.35 nine-cylinder single-row radial engines, or 650 hp (485 kW) Alfa Romeo 125 RC.35 or 126 RC.34 nine-cylinder single-row radial engines, or 650hp (485 kW) Gnome-Rhône 14-K 14-cylinder two-row radial engines

Length: 58 ft 4.75 in (17.80 m)

Height: 19 ft 8.25 in (6.00 m)

Wingspan: 78 ft 9 in (24.00 m)

Weight empty: 13,889 lb (6,300 kg); max take-off 22,167 lb (10,055 kg)

Range: 1,243 miles (2,000 km)

Max speed: 211 mph (340 km/h)

Climb to: 9,845 ft (3,000 m) in 12 minutes

Service ceiling: 22,965 ft (7,000m)

Armament: 2 x 7.7 mm or 1 x 12.7 mm trainable machine guns in dorsal turret, 2 x 7.7 mm trainable machine guns in power-operated ventral turret, and 1 x 7.7 mm trainable lateral-firing machine gun in beam positions, plus an internal bomb load of 4,409 lb (2,000 kg)

Below: Allied fighter pilots came to recognise the SM.81 by its fixed landing gear.

AICHI D3A ('VAL')

A formidable dive bomber that sank more Allied warships than any other Japanese type in the Second World War, the Aichi D3A was present at the beginning of the conflict in the Pacific, being one of three types of navy aircraft that struck Pearl Harbor. While it proved to be a worthy adversary, especially at Midway the Val, as it was obliged to operate primarily from land bases, it was gradually outclassed.

The D3A1 the last Japanese carrier-borne type to have a fixed landing gear, originated in a summer 1936 specification for a monoplane dive bomber, both Aichi and Nakajima receiving contracts. Aichi's entry was judged the winner because it was a more economical prospect than a design with retractable landing gear. After the maiden flight in January 1938 the production D3A1 was fitted with the 840 hp Mitsubishi Kinsei 3 radial engine, enlarged tail surfaces and stronger dive brakes. Most significantly, the wing was extended by more than a foot.

Specification: D3A1
Type: Two-seat dive bomber
Manufacturer: Aichi Kokuki K.K and Showa Hikoki Kogyo K. K.
Number built: 1,495
Entry into service: 1940
Length: 33 ft 5 in (10.195 m)
Height: 12 ft 7 in (3.847 m)
Wingspan: 47 ft 1 in (14.365 m)
Weight empty: 5,309 lb (2 408 kg)
Range: 915 miles (km)
Max speed: 240 mph (km/h)
Service ceiling: 30,050 ft (9 300m)
Armaments: (D3A1/ D3A2) 2 x 7.7-mm Type 97 cowl machine guns and 1 x 7.7-mm Type 92 machine gun for rear defense; 1 x 551 lb (250 kg) bomb on fuselage rack and 2 x 132 lb (60 kg) bombs under wings

These improvements enhanced the flight characteristics enough for production of the D3A1 to begin, a further increase in engine power to 1,000 hp (in the Kinsei 43) or 1,070 hp (Kinsei 44) and a new dorsal fin eliminating the directional instability that had bedevilled the prototype.

The D3A1 saw some service in China, prior to carrier qualification trials aboard the *Kaga* and *Akagi* in 1940 proving successful. For the Pearl Harbor operation, 126 examples of the D3A1 were embarked and although the Japanese dive bombers helped wreak havoc on the

Pacific fleet on December 7, 1941, reaction to the raid saw 15 of them shot down. Dive bombers were subsequently used in the Indian Ocean where D3A1s heavily damaged units of the British fleet.

Previous page: The film *Tora, Tora, Tora* brought mock Aichi D3As onto the US air show circuit.

Above: Convincing replicas were made from BT-13 trainers for the film reconstruction of the Pearl Harbor attack.

Left and Far left: Close to, the mock 'Vals' give away their US origins.

But the IJN's string of victories was to be brief. Losses of carriers at Coral Sea and Midway decimated the elite crews trained to fly the 'Val' with alarming speed. The Midway action saw a 100% loss when 72 out of 72 D3A1s embarked went down with their four carriers or were shot down by USN fighters. The situation did not improve with the subsequent attrition suffered in the Solomons. Thereafter, the JNAF had little choice but to land-base the D3A1.

An improved model, the externally similar D3A2, with increased fuel tankage for greater range, began entering service in the autumn of 1942. As well as flying from land bases the D3A2 served aboard the smaller remaining IJN carriers which could not handle its faster replacement, the Yokosuka D4Y4 Suisei. After suffering heavy losses off the Philippines in 1944, the 'Val' was largely relegated to training duties although it made a brief reappearance as a Kamikaze before the war's end.

Inset below: Retouched wartime photo of a D3A.

Main photo: Echelon formation of *Tora* film 'Kates' with a 'Val' in the low slot.

Inset top: A film 'Val' in Imperial Japanese Navy colours.

KAWANISHI H8K2 ('EMILY')

Widely regarded as the best all-round flying boat of the war, the H8K2 made its operational debut on March 4/5, 1942 when it made a night attack on Oahu Island. Bearing in mind the vastness of the Pacific Ocean it was an astute move by the Imperial Navy to integrate its long-range flying boat operations with submarines which handled replenishment and refuelling at predetermined rendezvous points.

Making its maiden flight in January 1941 the H8K prototype was, powered by four 1,530 hp Mitsubishi MK4A Kasei radials. Flight trials indicated a need for a deeper hull and improved keel contours and with this and other modifications completed the navy authorised production, as the H8K1. Well armoured, with fuel tank protection, and defended by cannon

and machine guns, the big 'boat was a worthy successor to its forerunner, the H6K 'Mavis'. Offensive load comprised two torpedoes, depth charges or bombs.

After building 16 H8K1s, Kawanishi turned to the improved H8K2 with 1,850 hp engines and increased armament. Codenamed 'Emily' by the Allies, the H8K2 was

Specification: H8K2
Type: Four engined long-range flying boat
Manufacturer: Kawanishi Kokuki K K
Number built: 167
Entry into service: February 1942
Length: 92 ft 2 in (28.13 m)
Height: 30 ft (9.15 m)
Wingspan: 124 ft 8 in (38 m)
Weight empty: 34,176 lb (15,502 kg)
Range: 3,000 miles (4,800 km)
Max speed: 269 mph (433 km/h)
Service ceiling: 25,035 ft (7,630 m)
Armaments: 5 x 20-mm Type 99 cannon in each of bow, dorsal and tail turrets and beam hatches, plus 4 x 7.7-mm Type 92 machine guns in ventral, port and starboard fuselage and cockpit hatches

the fastest flying boat operated by any of the combatants and it often proved a worthy opponent in combat. Able to operate over ranges exceeding 3,800 nautical miles, it made numerous maritime patrol sorties, late production aircraft being fitted with ASV radar. The Emily's capacious hull made it particularly useful as a staff and troop transport configured to carry up to 29 passengers or 64 troops; 36 examples of this variant, the H8K2-l, were built.

In order to obtain even better performance, an original design for

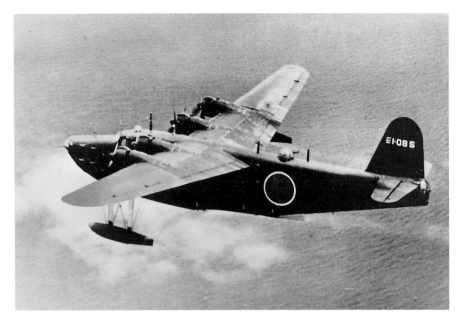

retractable wing stabilising floats was revived; two resulting H8K3 prototypes showed much promise although neither this model or a transport derivative could be built in quantity owing to Kawanishi's preoccupation with the Shiden Kai fighter.

Left: Shown beached on its land handling gear, the H8K2 was the best combat flying boat of WWII.

Top: Well armed, the 'Emily' was capable of very long range patrolling.

Above: Captured by the US at war's end an 'Emily' survived to be fully restored.

KAWANISHI N1K1-J SHIDEN ('GEORGE')

Unique in being the world's only operational fighter derived from a floatplane, the Kawanishi N1K1's metamorphosis reflected Japan's enforced change of strategy when her dream of Asian conquest was shattered. Sound enough in principal, the deployment of floatplane fighters needed a far safer environment than actually existed if they were to be of value in combat. Enemy fighters, invariably superior to any aircraft hampered by the drag of a float, made such deployment extremely risky.

But a perchant for combat floatplanes enabled the Japanese to bring six types into front line service, the Kawanishi N1K1 *Kyofu* (Mighty Wind) being the most advanced. Even while the Kyofu design was being finalised it became clear that the potentially high performance lent itself to a land-based derivative. The conversion from floats to wheeled landing gear seemed to be an economical way to create a new fighter, but there were difficulties.

The floatplane lineage of the N1K1 was reflected in a mid-wing layout, which meant that the four-blade airscrew for the landplane's engine required long main undercarriage legs for adequate ground clearance. As they retracted the main oleo legs had to contract for correct stowage, due to space restrictions also stemming from the floatplane origins. The conversion took only seven months and the fighter prototype flew on December 27, 1942.

Powered by a 1,820 hp Homare 11 radial engine, the N1K1 was armed with two fuselage-mounted machine guns and two cannon in underwing gondolas. Flight trials were plagued by engine and landing gear problems, the steep ground angle also being criticised by pilots. Although the aircraft was

pleasant to fly its top speed fell below that anticipated.

Having been accepted by the IJN for production as the N1K1-J, the aircraft received a 1,990 Homare engine to boost performance and a pair of cannon was installed in the wings outboard of the gondola-mounted guns. By the end of 1943, 70 examples had been built and the first units deployed to the Philippines in 1944. During the US invasion of the islands, the Shiden-Kai ('George' to the Allies) was found to be a tough opponent but Japanese ground crews had a heavy

workload keeping the 'Violet Lightning' operational.

Development continued — the N1K1-Ja, with four wing cannon and no fuselage weapons; the N1K1-Jb, with four cannon and two wing bomb racks and the similar N1K1-Jc Kai interceptor, with four wing racks. Production of the Shiden Kai was modest and only four first line units were able to deploy it operationally.

Below: Many Shidens were found abandoned when airfields were captured.

Specification: N1K1-J
Type: single seat interceptor fighter
Manufacturer: Kawanishi
Number built: 1,007
Entry into service: April 1944
Length: 29 ft 1 in (8.885m)
Height: 13 ft 3 in (4.06 m)
Wingspan: 39 ft 4 in (12m)
Weight empty: 6,387 lb (2,897 kg)
Range: 989 miles (1430 km)
Max speed: 363 mph (583 km/h)
Service ceiling: 41, 010 ft (12,500m)
Armaments: 2 x fuselage mounted 7.7-mm Type 97 machine guns plus 2 x wing mounted 20-mm Type 99 cannon and 2 x 20 -mm Type 99 cannon in underwing gondolas.

KAWANISHI N1K2 ('GEORGE')

As the N1K1 had showed such promise in combat it made sense in view of Japan's increasingly critical need for modern interceptors, to initiate a redesign to eliminate its major problem areas, particularly the complex landing gear. Consequently, the Shiden's wing was lowered to make way for a more conventional landing gear.

The first N1K2-J Model 21 flew on December 31, 1943 and the Navy, much impressed with the results obtained during a 15-week trials period, ordered the aircraft into production.

As the *Shiden Kai* (Violet Lightning Modified) the N1K2 began to equip operational units during 1944 and encouraging reports of its excellent combat capability gave impetus to a second variant, the N1K2-Ja Model 21a. Able to deliver four 551 lb (250 kg) bombs from underwing racks, this variant quickly became the standard Navy land-based fighter bomber.

Production of the Shiden-Kai was disrupted by B-29 raids and led to numerous shortages of parts and engines so that only a small proportion of planned output actually

materialised as fully combat ready aircraft. A desperate need for trainee pilots to build up their flying hours was partially met by a few N1K2-K Shiden Kai Rensen trainers with a second seat installed aft of the pilot.

To overcome the problem of the Shiden Kai's centre of gravity having always been a little too far aft, Kawanishi developed the N1K3-J Model 31. The Homare engine was moved forward 6 in which provided space for the installation of two machine guns in the forward

fuselage. Only two prototypes were built. Other variants completed only as prototypes at the time of the surrender incuded the N1K3A, a carrier-borne derivative of the Model 31 and initial examples of the proposed N1K4 and N1K5 series.

Below: A 'George' found on a Japanese airfield.

Specification: N1K2
Type: Single-seat interceptor fighter
Manufacturer: Kawanishi Kokuki K K
Number built: 401
Entry into service: Summer 1944
Length: 30 ft 7 (9.345 m)
Height: 12 ft 1 in (3.96 m)
Wingspan: 39 ft 4 in (12 m)
Weight empty: 5,858 lb (2,657 kg)
Range: 989 miles (1,430 km)
Max speed: 362 mph (583 km/h)
Service ceiling: 35,300 ft (10,760 m)
Armaments: 4 x wing mounted 20-mm Type 99 cannon; 2 or 4 x 551 lb (250 kg) bombs on wing racks

KAWASAKI KI-45 ('NICK')

An attempt by the Japanese Army to deploy a twin-engined fighter modern enough to hold its own against single-engined types, the Ki-45 proved how challenging this concept could be. Issuing a requirement allowing for broad interpretation in March 1937, the Army agreed to Kawasaki continuing development of its Ki-38 design study pending a detailed official specification. This was forthcoming and the company was able to proceed that December.

The new fighter, now known as the Ki-45, was to have a maximum speed of 217 mph (540 km/h), an operating altitude of 6,560 ft to 16,405 ft (2,000 to 5,000 m) and be powered by the Nakajima Ha-20b engine, a licence-built version of the British Bristol Mercury.

Flight trials, beginning about January 1939, revealed low engine power and excessive drag. A number of modifications failed to raise the top speed past the 300 mph mark which the JAAF required and the project was shelved until April 1940. Nakajima was then instructed to fit two of its own 1,000 hp Ha-25 radials in production aircraft. In the meantime a major redesign was initiated, primarily to simplify manufacture but also to improve the

Specification: Ki-45 KAIa
Type: Twin-engined ground attack and interceptor fighter
Manufacturer: Kawasaki Kokuki Kogyo K.K.
Number built: 1,370
Entry into service: October 1941
Length: 36 ft 1 in (11 m)
Height: 12 ft 1 in (3.7 m)
Wingspan: 49 ft 3 in (15.02 m)
Weight empty: 8,818 lb (4,000 kg)
Range: 1,243 miles (2,000 km)
Max speed: 335 mph (540 km/h)
Service ceiling: 32,810 ft (10,000 m)
Armaments: (Ki-45 KAIc) 1 x 37-mm Ho-203 cannon in ventral position plus 2 x 20-mm Ho-5 cannon firing obliquely and 1 x 7.92-mm Type 98 machine gun for rear defence.

fighter's performance and handling characteristics.

As the Ki-45 KAI, a prototype flew in May 1941 and the aircraft was accepted for service. Designated Ki-45 KAIa, the *Toryu* (Dragon Killer) entered front line service with the 21st Sentai in Burma and the 16th Sentai in China by the fall of 1942.

Among the most heavily armed of all Japanese fighters, the Toryu in Ki-45 KAIb form mounted a 37-mm cannon in an offset ventral tunnel, plus a 20-mm cannon in the nose. Japanese crews had considerable confidence in their ability to survive if their Toryus,

which also had protection for the fuel tanks, were hit during ground or anti-shipping sorties.

Equally effective against US patrol boats and heavy bombers, the Toryu was increasingly used as a night interceptor, for which some examples carried twin upward-firing 12.7-mm machine guns behind the cockpit. This 'field modified' weapons configuration led to the purpose-built Ki-45 KAIc night fighter, which retained the 37 mm cannon but had two cannon in the oblique position. This version was also scheduled to have airborne radar but this was never fitted to combat models, Toryus nevertheless being quite successful against B-29 night raids. Other armament combinations were tested but only the Ki-45 KAId was actually built. This anti-shipping version had an additional machine gun for rear defence but dispensed with the oblique cannon, similar weapons being positioned in the extreme nose. In total, 12 combat units flew the Ki-45, which was known to the Allies as 'Nick'.

Left: Ki-45 'Nick'.

KAWASAKI KI-61/KI-100 ('TONY')

Japan's alliance with the European Axis led to tenuous links in the field of military aviation and a number of co-operative ventures were explored. A not inconsiderable factor in this partnership failing to bear much fruit was the sheer distance between Europe and Asia. Allied intelligence nevertheless became aware that the Messerschmitt Bf 109 had been tested in Japan and unfounded rumours persisted that the type was being built under license. This was not the case but partnership with Germany was given substance when the Kawasaki Ki-61 emerged, powered by a license-built Daimler-Benz inline engine. A rare instance of the Japanese opting for a liquid rather than air-cooled powerplant for a fighter, the Ki-61 flew for the first time in December 1941.

Similar in configuration to the abandoned DB 601A powered Kawasaki He 60, the lighter Ki-61 had more pleasing lines with a better proportioned fuselage. The powerplant was a Kawasaki Ha-40, a

Below: Daimler Benz engine powered, the Ki-61 was unique among JAAF fighters.

Specification: Ki-61-Ib
Type: Single-seat fighter
Manufacturer: Kawasaki Kokuki Kokuki K K
Number built: 3,078
Entry into service: February 1943
Length: 28 ft 8.5 in (8.75 m)
Height: 12 ft 1 in (3.7 m)
Wingspan: 39 ft 4 in (12 m)
Weight empty: 4,872 lb (2,210 kg)
Range: 373 miles (600 km)
Max speed: 368 mph (592 km/h)
Service ceiling: 37,730 ft (11,600 m)
Armaments: 2 x fuselage mounted 12.7-mm Ho-103 machine guns and 2 x 20-mm Mauser MG 151/20 wing cannon; 2 x 551 lb (250 kg) bombs on wing hardpoints or 2 x 44-Imp gal (200 l) drop tanks

Specification: Ki-100-I
Manufacturer: Kawasaki Kokuki Kogyo K K
Number built: 377 (inc conversions)
Entry into service: Spring 1945
Length: 28 ft 11.25 in (8.82 m)
Height: 12 ft 3 in (3.75 m)
Wingspan: 39 ft 4 in (12 m)
Weight empty: 5,567 lb (2,525 kg)
Range: 870 miles (1,400 km)
Max speed: 360 mph (580 km/h)
Service ceiling: 36,090 ft (11,000 m)
Armaments: 2 x fuselage mounted Ho-5 20-mm cannon and 2 x Ho-103 12.7-mm wing machine guns; 2 x 551 lb (250 kg) bombs on wing racks

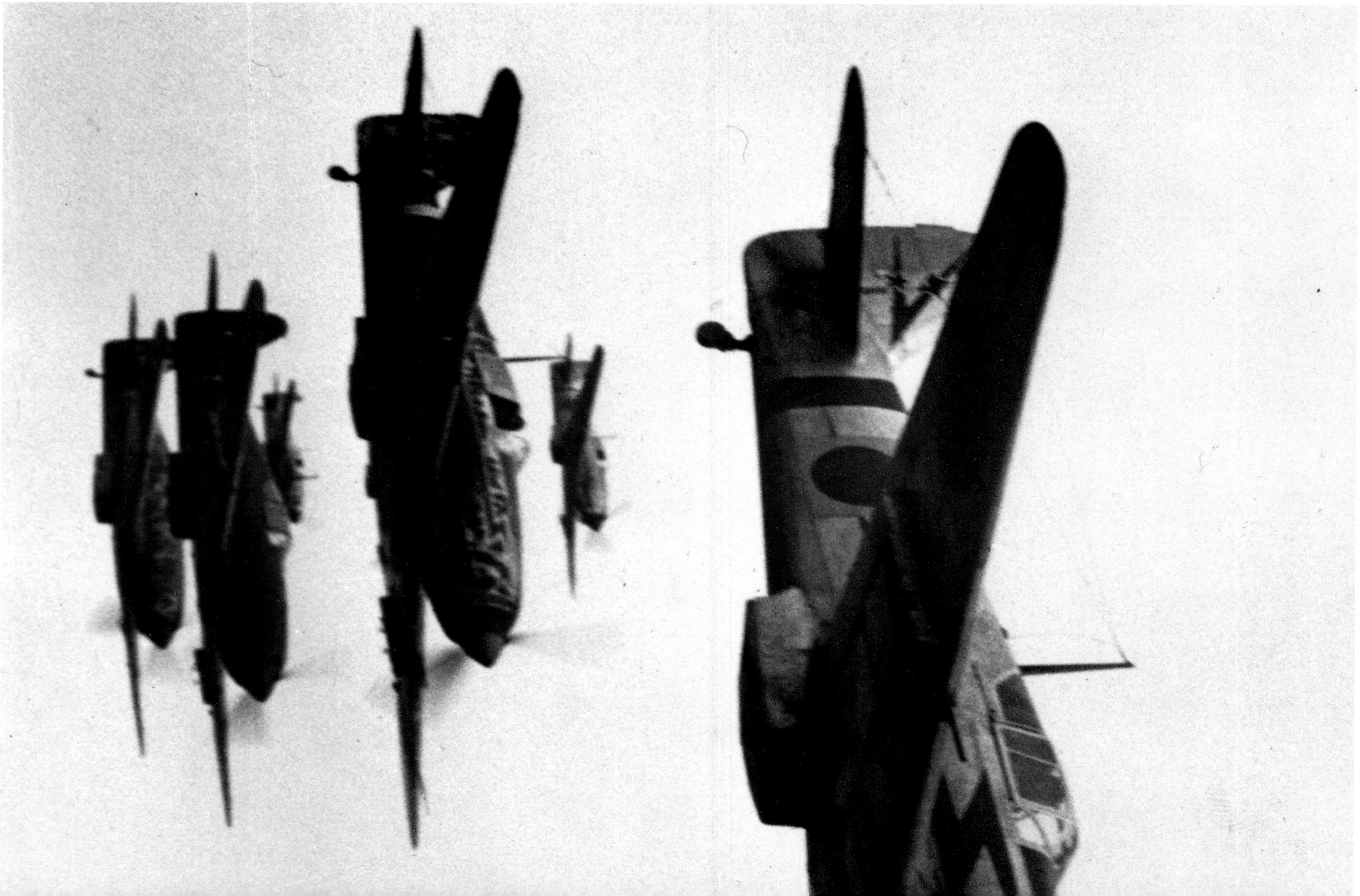

DB 601 copy, 12 prototypes being built before the first production airframe was completed in August 1942. Pre-service trials impressed Army pilots, who saw merit in the armament, armour protection and high performance. First deliveries took place in February 1943 and the Ki-61 entred combat in April with the 68th and 78th Sentais.

As the Allies still believed that the Ki-61 had foreign origins, Italy being a strong contender, 'Tony' seemed an appropriate code name. Initially armed with four machine guns, the Ki-61-Ia and Ib had the wing guns replaced by 20-mm Mauser cannon which had to be mounted on its side due to limited space in the wing.

Front line operations in New Guinea highlighted some maintenance problems and these were

Left: Left: Impressive training formation of Ki-61s, some in natural metal finish.

Below: A Ki-61 fighter trainer found abandoned by the US Marines.

attended to in the new model, the Ki-61-I KAIc (built from January 1944). By then the indigenous Ho-5 cannon was available to replace the fuselage machine guns, the model also having a stronger wing which enabled stores pylons to be incorporated. As production picked up, some examples were built as the Ki-61-KAId which had Ho-105 wing cannon.

In developing a more powerful engine for subsequent Hein variants Kawasaki produced the 1,500 Ha 140. Designed for installation in an improved Ki-61 this powerplant exhibited numerous teething troubles, few of which were completely overcome. The recipient fighter was the Ki-61-II which had greater wing area and a redesigned cockpit canopy. Its handling qualities turned out to be disappointing and this, coupled with the engine problems, resulted in only 11 examples of this model Hein being built.

A solution was sought by lengthening the Ki-61's fuselage and retrofitting standard wings to produce the Ki-61-II KAI. The modifications proved sound and when the Ha 140 ran smoothly, the Ki-61-II KAI was revealed as an excellent interceptor with a speed of 379 mph (610 km/h) and a ceiling of over 36,000 ft. Confident that the engine problems — which centered on a weak crankshaft — could be cured, Kawasaki tooled up to produce the latest Hein, starting in September 1944.

Two models of the Ki-61-II were built, the 2A and 2B, these differing only in armament fit. The engine problem was unexpectedly solved in a B-29 raid on 19 January 1945 when the Akashi engine plant was destroyed. This meant that of the 374 Ki-61-II completed, about 275 airframes were lacking engines, leaving Kawasaki with little alternative but to substitute another engine.

Ki-100

Having chosen the Mitsubishi Ha-112-II radial as the powerplant for the Ki-61, the Japanese Army was still in desperate need of an interceptor able to effectively counter B-29 raids. Much had been pinned on the Ki-61-II but engine reliablity had blunted this fighter's potential even without the disasterous loss of the Akashi plant. The problem was that engine plants were stretched to their limit and supplies for one more aircraft type were next to impossible. Kawasaki also needed an engine with a diameter not exceeding about 2 ft 9 in (0.84 m) if a time-consuming redesign of the Ki-61 airframe was to be avoided. Although the 1,500 hp Mitsubishi engine was 4 ft (1.22 m) in diameter, an answer was found by studying what had been achieved in Germany with the mating of the BMW 801 with the FW 190. The Japanese had carried out a smilar exercise when the Mitsubishi engine had been fitted into the Aichi D4Y3.

Work to convert the Ki-61 airframes culminated in the first flight of the redesignated Ki-100 on February 1, 1945. A lighter aircraft than its liquid-cooled forerunner, the Ki-100 showed much-improved handling qualities, causing considerable enthusiasm in JAAF circles. Most importantly, the new engine was reliable. This enabled rapid delivery of Ki-100s to first line units, 271 Ki-61 airframes having been re-engined by June. Their appearance came as a nasty shock to American pilots, whether flying fighters or bombers, as the Ki-100-Ia was easily

their equal, capable of high speeds at altitudes over 36,000 ft (11,000 m).

In the event it availed the Japanese little to have a handful of excellent interceptors, for their situation was dire by the time the Ki-100 got into service. Kawasaki nevertheless began bulding new airframes and two new Ki-100 versions, the -Ib with an all-round vision canopy and the -II. Only 12 examples of the Ki-100-Ib had been delivered to combat units — which incuded the 5th and 11th Sentais — out of 106 built before the surrender. The Ki-100-II was a version fitted with a turbocharger and water methenol injection for its 1,500 hp Ha-112 Ru engine. Only three had flown when the war ended.

Above: Front line Ki-100s.

Below left: A shortage of German derived engines led to installation of a Mitsubishi radial creating the Ki-100.

Below: Among surviving Japanese fighters is this Ki-100 with a Ki-61 colour scheme!

MITSUBISHI A6M2/A6M8 ('ZEKE')

By the time Japan decided that war with the Western Allies was inevitable the Imperial Navy had a formidable air component built around an efficient carrier force. To support dive and torpedo bombers the JNAF also had a superb fighter, the Mitsubishi A6M2. The country's location meant that the admirals required aircraft with the necessary range to strike over long distances. In this respect, the 1,000 mile range of the Mitsubishi Type 0 Reisen (Zero Fighter) succeeded all expectations.

Despite the official Allied codename 'Zeke' the Mitsubishi fighter's Type 0 — 'Zero' — designation entered popular mythology and has endured over the years. In late 1941 and early 1942 the 'Zero' came as a nasty shock to nations which had tended to disregard the ability of Eastern countries to match the technological achievements of the West.

Mitsubishi surmounted considerable difficulties in designing the A6M2 in the timescale required. Following the test flight of the prototype on April 1, 1939, a series of disasterous crashes — for which there was no immediately obvious cause or solution — theatened the entire project. These difficulties were

Specification: A6M2
Type: Single-seat fighter
Manufacturer: Mitsubishi Jukogyo K K and Nakajima Hikoki K K
Number built: 3,432
Entry into service: July 1940
Length: 29 ft 8.75 in (9.06 m)
Height: 10 ft 1 in (3.05 m)
Wingspan: 39 ft 4.5 in (12.00 m)
Weight empty: 3,704 lb (1 680 kg)
Range: 1,940 miles (3,110 km)
Max speed: 316 mph (509 km/h)
Service ceiling: 33,790 ft (10,300 m)
Armaments: 2 x 20-mm Type 99 Mk 1 wing cannon plus 2 x fuselage-mounted 7.7-mm Type 97 machine guns; bomb load: up to 264 lb (120 kg) on fuselage and wing racks

Specification: A6M5
Type: Single-seat interceptor fighter
Manufacturer: Mitsubishi Jikogyo KK and Nakajima Hikoki K K
Number built: 5,704★
Entry into service: September 1943
Length: 29 ft 11 in (9.121 m)
Height: 11 ft 6 in (3.509 m)
Wingspan: 36 ft 1 in (11 m)
Weight empty: 4,136 lb (1,876 kg)
Range: 1,200 miles (1,920 km)
Max speed: 356 mph (570 km/h)
Service ceiling: 38,520 ft (11,740 m)
Armaments: 2 x 20-mm Type 99 wing cannon and 2 x fuselage-mounted 13.2-mm Type 3 machine guns; bomb load up to 1,102 lb (500 kg); 8 x 22 lb (10 kg) rockets or 2 x 132 lb (60 kg) rockets.
★ This figure incudes some A6M7s

overcome with application and skill and the A6M2 entered service in July 1940, 328 being in IJN inventory by the time of Pearl Harbor. Following early victories, Japan's come-uppance at Midway in June 1942 resulted in the loss of 247 aircraft incuding 94 A6M2s when the four carriers went down, all but ending Imperial ambitions in Asia.

With the heart of its carrier force neutralised, the IJN land-based many of its fighters and deployed a cadre of highly qualified pilots to contain Allied airpower, be it Australian, British, American or Dutch, throughout the entire East Indies for some months. Pilots such as 86-victory ace Nishizawa, Ota (34) and Sakai (60 plus) of the Tainan Air Group, took a steady toll of opposing aircraft fighting to maintain a foothold in New Guinea.

Ever stronger Allied airpower steadily whittled down the numbers

Below left: The superlative A6M Zeke, more popularly known as the 'Zero'.

Above right: One of the few genuine A6Ms exiting today.

Right: Adapted as a floatplane the A6M also served the Imperial Navy well.

Below: A fine example of the refurbished A6M in full flying trim.

of skilled prewar trained pilots, but throughout the Pacific war the A6M2 was developed and improved to keep it in inventory. Much of the Zero's early success was thanks to the Japanese perchant for ignoring such niceties as self-sealing fuel tanks or armour protection for the pilot, engine and fuel tanks. The result was that, when pitted against better protected Allied aircraft, the light and highly manoeuvrable Zero showed an alarming propensity to burn, causing many pilots who might otherwise have survived a reversal in combat to become fatal casualties. These lessons were addressed and each A6M2 model was improved. The 780 hp Zuisei engine in the original A6M2 Model 21 gave way to the A6M3 Model 32 with a 1,100 hp engine, an improved exhaust system being fitted to the A6M5 Model 52 and the final model, the A6M8 Model 64, had an MK8P Kinsei radial offering 1,560 hp for take-off and bestowing a max speed of 356 mph.

Despite growing air superiority, few Allied pilots cared to prejudge the outcome of combat with a Zero. In the early part of the war numerous individuals paid the price for ignoring the edict 'Never dogfight with a Zero'. But as the war dragged on, the number of Japanese pilots able to get the best out of the Zero grew fewer. The worsening war situation culminated in Jiro Hirokoshi's superlative fighter being expended in difficult interception sorties against B-29 raids and Kamikaze attacks.

Far fewer A6Ms than Navy pilots survived the war but the handful that have been refurbished are now prized museum exhibits, tangible reminders that have enabled many Japanese veterans, long reticent about their part in the war, to admit with justifiable pride to having flown the formidable Zero in action.

Inset: A *Tora, Tora, Tora* A6M adapated from a T-6 Texan.

Main picture: Wartime view of the A6M; note drop tank.

Opposite, above and below:
Finished in Pearl Harbor attack
unit colours, the A6M2 is a
popular air show star.

Above: A late production A6M
was test flown in the US.

Left: An A6M in Chinese
Nationalist colours.

Below: Given away by its short
gear legs, a movie Zero still
looks good.

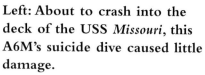

Left: About to crash into the deck of the USS *Missouri*, this A6M's suicide dive caused little damage.

Below left: About to impact a carrier, this kamikaze Zero is seconds from destruction.

Below: Rolling in to land the A6M2 shows its wing flaps to advantage

Right: A Mitsubishi Zero, half a decade on.

Below right: A field full of A6M5s being readied for another sortie.

MITSUBISHI G3M ('NELL')

Another prewar design that stood up well enough to the severe test of the Japanese Army's wartime combat operations, the G3M won early notoriety among the Western Allies when 60 aircraft participated in the sinking of the battlecruisers Prince of Wales and Repulse on December 10, 1941. It should have come as no surprise to the Allies that Japanese bombers could operate at hitherto unheard of ranges, as Imperial Navy crews flying G3M2s had on August 14, 1937 made a 1,250-mile flight from Taipei to China. This raid on Chinese targets represented the first transoceanic bombing raid in history.

Flying for the first time in prototype form as the Ka-15 in July 1935, the aircraft had an exceptional range and altitude capability, its 82-ft wingspan being nearly the longest of any Japanese Second

World War-era landplane. This attribute was shared with the Mitsubishi G4M, which had a slightly greater span and although the two Navy bombers were

comparable, their designs were significantly different. The slim fuselage and twin fins of the G3M contrasted sharply with the portly fuselage and single fin of the G4M.

Specification: G3M1
Type: Twin-engined heavy bomber
Manufacturer: Mitsubishi
Number built: 1,048
Entry into service: Autumn 1936
Length: 53 ft 11.5 in (16.45 m)
Height: 12 ft 1 in (3.685 m)
Wingspan: 82 ft 0.25 in (25.00 m)
Weight empty: 11,551 lb (5,243 kg)
Range: 3,871 miles (6,228 km)
Max speed: 216 miles (348 km)
Service ceiling: 33,730 ft (10,280 m)
Armament: 3 x 7.7-mm Type 92 machine guns in two retractable ventral turrets and one retractable dorsal turret; up to 1,764 lb (800 kg) of bombs or 1 x 1,764 lb (800 kg) torpedo carried externally

There were 21 Ka-15s, these testing various military equipments and engines; after bomber production began in June 1936, these machines were subsequently used for service trials. Production initially covered the solid nose G3M1a powered by 750 hp Hiro Type 91 radials and with a ventral bomb aimer's panel, and the G3M1b. This latter had 910 hp Kinsei 3 radials but was otherwise similar, while the G3M1c had a fully equipped bomb aimer's station in a glazed nose.

Installation of higher performance Kinsei 41/42 engines led to the G3M2, examples of this aircraft making many extreme-range raids into China. But the attribute of range highlighted a deficiency in defensive armament and Chinese fighters shot down a number of the bombers. Three machine guns in each G3M was no compensation for operating beyond the range of escort fighters.

Although the G3M was on the verge of obsolescence when the Pacific war began, Mitsubishi had re-engined the aircraft with 1,075 hp Kinsei 45 engines which had been fitted to a number of transport conversions designated G3M1-L. About 24 of these undertook prewar long-range 'showing the flag' flights and during the war they maintained a transport service between the various war zones.

In the meantime more bomber versions had appeared, incuding the GM32 Model 22 with a large 'turtle-back' dorsal gun turret housing a single 20-mm Type 99 cannon. In addition, blisters were added on the sides of the fuselage, each with a single 7.7-mm machine gun. The forward retractable dorsal turret was retained and a fourth machine gun

which could be fired from either side of the cockpit, was introduced on late production Model 22s.

By 1942 the G3M, identified as the 'Nell' by Allied intelligence, was approaching phase out, the Navy by then having established the G4M at its principal long-range bomber. A final version of the Nell, the G3M3 powered by two 1,300 hp Kinsei 51 engines, had been produced in 1941, this being not only the fastest of the series but the model capable of the greatest range. The main G3M transport derivatives, the L3Y1 based on the G3M1 and the L3Y2 derived from the G3M2, were identified by the Allies as 'Tina'.

Left: The slim, twin-tailed 'Nell' flew many early war missions over China.

Right: Enjoying very long range, the G3M had a massive wingspan.

MITSUBISHI G4M ('BETTY')

Dubbed the 'Flying Lighter' by Allied pilots who met it in combat, the Mitsubishi G4M Betty was a true workhorse of the Imperial Navy. Suffering more from doctrinal rather than technical deficiencies that often made it vulnerable in combat, the G4M again emphasised Japan's philosophy of sacrificing crew safety and airframe protection for speed and, in this case, enormous range. This asset was demonstrated by 20 aircraft that joined G3Ms in sinking the British capital ships off Malaya in December 1941. In terms of wingspan the G4M was also the largest bomber the Japanese deployed; it was an able torpedo bomber, often a transport, and finally a manned missile 'mother ship' for the MX7 Baka bomb.

The G4M1 prototype first flew on October 23, 1939, powered by two 1,530 hp Kasei radials and was delivered for Navy evaluation in January 1940. A second aircraft was handed over for trials in February and among other data, it recorded a top speed of 279 mph. Production

did not immediately follow however as the Navy was preoccupied with escort fighters, even proposing that the G4M be modified as a heavily armed escort for standard G3M formations. This, the G6M1, was built but excessive weight meant that it could hardly keep up with stan-

Specification: G4M2
Type: Twin-engined heavy bomber
Manufacturer: Mitsubishi Jukogyo K K
Number built: 2,446
Entry into service: June 1941
Length: 65 ft 7.5 in (19.63 m)
Height: 19 ft 8 in (6 m)
Wingspan: 82 ft 0.75 in (25 m)
Weight empty: 17,990 lb (8,160 kg)
Range: 2,982 miles (4,800 km)
Max speed: 271 mph (437 km/h)
Armaments: 2 x 7.7-mm Type 92 machine guns in fuselage side hatches plus 1 x 20-mm Type 99 cannon in dorsal turret and 1 x 20mm Type 99 cannon in tail cone; bomb load 2,205 lb (1,000 kg) or 1 x 1,762 lb (800 kg) torpedo externally; (G4M2e) 1 x 4,718 lb (2,140 kg) Ohka Model 11 missile semi-recessed into fuselage bomb bay area

Below: Notoriously prone to taking fire, the 'Betty' was an IJN mainstay during WWII.

Below right: Awaiting restoration, this G3M is stored at Silver Hill, Maryland.

dard bombers, which relegated it to training and transport duties.

The first G4M was completed in April 1941 and the type entered service in June. Long-range sorties into China showed the potential of the G4M, a fact proved in the opening rounds of the Pacific war. Attacking Allied ships and installations including Darwin, Australia in February 1942, the IJN bombers appeared all but unstoppable. It was when enemy fighters were met that its deficiencies were highlighted, many aircraft being lost over New Guinea when they failed to survive even light-weight bullet strikes in the unprotected fuel tanks or crew positions.

In an effort to redress the G4M's drawbacks, the Navy instigated a beefing-up of the armament along with more powerful Kasei 15 engines. More protection and a 20-mm tail cannon increased weight and reduced speed to offset any advantage, the G4M continuing to suffer casualties. Bettys carrying Admiral Isokoru Yamamoto for an inspection tour were on the receiving end of the interception by P-38 Lightnings on April 18, 1942. The admiral, brilliant architect of the Pearl Harbor attack, died in the wreckage of a shot down G4M1.

Development of the G4M2 extended to a number of models, incuding the G4M2a with 1,850 hp Kasei 25 engines, bulged bomb bay doors and ASV radar on late production examples. There were further variations within the Model 21, 22, and 24 series. The G4M2e was adapted to carry a single piloted Baka with the bomb bay doors removed and shackles fitted. Slowed down by the weight of the one-man rocket plane, the G4M became even easier meat than usual for the deadly American Navy fighters, destruction of the Japanese crew with their air-

craft and its 0payload often being achieved with little difficulty. On March 21, 1945, 16 Bettys were shot down on the first operational Ohka sortie before they could even launch.

The Betty gained some 11th-hour fame when it bore the Japanese surrender delegation to the island of Ie Shima, en route to the Philippines on August 19, 1945. By then a total of 24 Kokutais had been equipped with various G4M1 and 2 models.

Below: Thrown in to attack Allied ships, 'Bettys' suffered terrible losses.

MITSUBISHI J2M ('JACK')

'Jack' to Allied airmen and Raiden (Thunderbolt) to the Japanese, the Mitsubishi J2M represented new thinking on the part of the Imperial Navy planners who had previously stressed the attributes of manoeuvrability and range as paramount for carrier-based fighters. Remarkably, the J2M specification, initially explored in October 1938, reflected a prophetic future need for land-based interceptors. This meant that high speed and climb rate were most important and A6M designer Jiro Horikoshi strove to meet an official specification which was finally confirmed in September 1939 after numerous delays.

Armament was to be similar to that of the A6M but among the requirements was (for the first time), armour plate protection for the pilot. A 1,430 hp Kasei radial engine was installed, an extension shaft and frontal cooling fan allowing the smallest possible cowling area. Making its maiden flight on March 20, 1942 the J2M1 proved to be a basically sound design, but early early teething troubles were compounded by complaints from Navy pilots, who roundly criticised it, particularly for poor cockpit visibility. Mitsubishi initiated modifications and production finally started in October 1942

as the J2M2, now powered by a Kasei Model 23a engine, the first in Japan to feature water-methanol injection. This powerplant developed faults that required further modification, delays being compounded by two inexplicable crashes in mid-1943. Development continued, the J2M3 introducing four cannon armament and becoming, as the Model 21, the major production model.

When they finally took the J2M3 into action in 1944, primarily against US heavy bomber formations, IJN pilots came to appreciate its good performance, heavy armament and

armour protection. At that stage of the war, volume production was understandably hampered by shortages but as well as the primary Raiden model, Mitsubishi completed 21 examples of the J2M3a which had two of the four cannon mounted in underwing gondolas. Some Raidens were also field modified with upwards firing cannon similar to the guns that had been tested on the two J2M4 prototypes, no production of which was undertaken.

Operationally, Raidens were deployed primarily on home defence duties and many were used as interceptors during B-29 raids. Some success was achieved although a lower standard of pilot training and the toughness of the Superfortress, mitigated heavily against the Navy pilots.

Specification: J2M3
Type: Single-seat fighter
Manufacturer: Mitsubishi Jukogyo K K
Number built: 476 (all models inc prototypes)
Entry into service: December 1943
Length: 32 ft 7.5 in (9.94 m)
Height: 12ft 11.5in (3.94 m)
Wingspan: 35 ft 5 in (10.8 m)
Weight empty: 5,423 lb (2,460 kg)
Range: 655 miles (1,055 km)
Max speed: 380 mph (612 km/h)
Service ceiling: 38,385 ft (11,700m)
Armaments: 2 x 20-mm Type 99 Model 2 cannon and two 20-mm Type 99 Model 1 cannon in wings; (J2M4) as for J2M3 plus two oblique-firing 20-mm Type 99 Model 1 cannon; two 132 lb (60kg) bombs underwing

---

Left: The 'Jack' was one of the best Navy fighters of the war.

MITSUBISHI KI-21 ('SALLY')

A twin-engined aircraft classed as a heavy bomber by the Japanese, the Ki-21 was very important in that it helped put the Army on a par with its world contemporaries. Despite its shortcomings it was favoured by its crews and continued to fly combat missions throughout the war, long beyond its replacement date. It was not alone in that fact nor was it unique in being regarded as superior to its intended successor, the Ki-49 'Helen'.

The Ki-21 stemmed from a Mitsubishi response to a specification issued on February 15, 1936 for a twin-engined bomber to replace two older designs. With a crew of four, the new aircraft was to carry a standard bomb load of 1,653 lb (750 kg) plus three machine guns for defence.

Two prototypes were completed at Nagoya in December 1936, the second of which introduced the characteristic dorsal 'greenhouse' that was to hallmark the Ki-21. The prototype made its maiden flight on December 18. A production order for 143 examples of the Ki-21-Ia was confirmed in November 1937 and while Mitsubishi was meeting this, Nakajima was also awarded a contract for 351 Ki-21-Ia, -Ib and -Ic models, the latter two of which had improved armament and protected fuel tanks. Flight tests showed that the Ki-21 could also benefit from more powerful engines and following the testing of the third prototype fitted with the 850hp Nakajima Ha-5, the Ki-21-II appeared. Substitution of the Ha-101 engine created the Ki-21-11a.

Specification: Ki-21
Type: Twin-engined heavy bomber
Manufacturer: Mitsubishi Jukogyo K.K. & Nakajima Hikoki K.K.
Number built: 2,064
Entry into service: August 1938
Length: 52 ft 5 in (16 m)
Height: 14 ft 3 in (4.35 m)
Wingspan: 73 ft 9in (22.5 m)
Weight empty: 19,342 lb (4,691 kg)
Range: 932 miles (1,500 km)
Max speed: 268 mph (432 km/h)
Service ceiling: 28,215 ft (8,600 m)
Armaments: Single flexible 7.7 mm Type 89 machine guns in nose, ventral, tail and beam positions plus one x 12.7-mm Type 1 machine gun in dorsal turret (Ki-21-IIb); normal bomb 1,653 lb (759 kg)

Combat operations showed that the Ki-21's defensive armament, comprising three hand-held machine guns, was clearly too weak and a dorsal turret mounting a single 12.7 mm weapon was installed in the Ki-21-IIb, 688 of which were built.

Initially known as 'Jane' to the Allies, the Ki-21's codename was changed to 'Sally' and the bomber became one of the best known of the war. The Allies were initially fooled into thinking that the dorsal turret model was a new type and allocated the codename 'Gwen' to it. Although the mistake was realised, this name still turned up in encounter reports rather than the specified 'Sally 1 to 3' to cover all versions.

Transport duties were undertaken by numerous Ki-21s as they approached obsolescence, the bomber versions having fought well in China against ever-increasing odds during the early part of the war. The Ki-21 was gradually phased out and by the end of the war, the 58th Sentai was the sole remaining first line unit equipped with it. Special missions such as the flight to Yontan airfield on Okinawa in 1945 to deliver commandoes to destroy US aircraft and fuel dumps, were also undertaken by the Ki-21.

Right: Japan's war with China saw many sorties flown by the Ki-21.

MITSUBISHI KI-46 ('DINAH')

All combatant nations of the Second World War produced aircraft that were widely acknowledged to be the best in their class. This was not a total prerogative of the Allies for despite their ultimate defeat the Axis countries produced some of the world's most advanced designs. Among Mitsubishi combat aircraft, the Ki-46 Dinah was considered to be outstanding in the fast reconnaissance role. So clean was the airframe design that the Ki-46 was seriously considered for manufacture in Germany, powered by BMW engines. That did not come about but nevertheless remains a testimonial to a high international regard for the achievement of Mitsubishi engineers by a nation that led the world in aeronautical innovation.

The protype Ki-46 flew for the first time September 1939. Examples of the Ki-46-I followed and despite a number of technical faults incuding a weak landing gear, crews flying it in action over China were highly enthusiastic about its handling qualities. No enemy interceptor could reach the altitudes adopted by the Japanese reconnaissance crews.

More power was obtainable from the 1,055 hp Ha 102 engine, and fitted in the Ki-46-II it enabled the top speed to be increased to 375 mph.

Deployed over the Pacific battle zones early in the Second World War the aircraft given the code name 'Dinah', also excelled at virtually uninterrupted reconnaissance flights as far afield as Australia, but it was over Darwin that the Ki-46 began to be intercepted by P-38s and Spitfires. Mitsubishi attempted to counter this threat by installing the 1,500 hp Ha-112-II engine in the Ki-46-III which also had some significant airframe modifications. These incuded replacing the stepped

Specification: Ki-46-I	

Specification: Ki-46-I
Type: Twin-engined reconnaissance aircraft
Manufacturer: Mitsubishi Jukogyo K K
Number built: 1,742
Entry into service: July 1941
Length: 36 ft 1in (11.0m)
Height: 12 ft 8.75 in (3.88 m)
Wingspan: 48 ft 2.75 in (14.7 m)
Weight empty: 7,450 lb (3,379 kg)
Range: 1,305 miles (2,100 km)
Max speed: 336 mph (540 km/h)
Service ceiling: 34,500 ft (10.500m)
Armaments: 1 x 7.7-mm Type 89 machine gun in rear cockpit

cockpit of the first two production models with a beautifully streamlined canopy which faired smoothly into the dorsal line of the fuselage.

Dinahs continued to obtain intelligence data on Allied activities although the game grew increasingly tougher. Once fuel injection problems with its engines had been cured, the Ki-46-III could however, operate at heights exceeding 32,000 ft which gave its crews a degree of immunity from enemy interception.

As a matter of expediency in Japan's worsening war situation, the Army attempted to deploy the Ki-46 as an armed interceptor, a programme that was not a great success. Having first flown in armed configuration as the Ki-46-III KAI in October 1944, the aircraft possessed a poor climb rate. Saddled with the weight of two forward-firing Ho-5 cannon, ammunition tanks and so forth, its performance suffered accordingly. A third cannon, a 37-mm Ho-203, was obliquely mounted in the fuselage.

Examples of the Ki-46-III KAI, all of which were converted Ki-46-III airframes, were issued to home defence units, and the following Ki-46-IIIb was also built in small numbers. Finally, the Dinah reverted to the high-speed reconnaissance role as the prototype Ki-46-IVa with supercharged Ha-112-II Ru engines. One example flew at a sustained average speed of 435 mph in 1945, proving that the Dinah had not lost its reputation as one the best reconnaissance aircraft of the time. An armed version, the Ki-46-IVb, was also built in prototype form.

Opposite: A leaping tiger adorns the fin of this Ki-46.

Above: This Ki-46-II can today be seen in England.

Left: Built for high speed the Ki-46 rarely let down its crews.

Below: Widely rated as a top recon type, the Ki-46-II had very closely cowled engines.

Above: A major airshow attraction, this Ki-46 is probably the sole survivor of 1,742 built.

Right: Notable in this view is the wide chord propeller blades of the Ki-46.

Below: There was to be a German version of the Ki-46, so highly regarded was the design.

NAKAJIMA B5N1/B5N2 ('KATE')

Known to the Allies as 'Kate', the B5N was the third Imperial Navy type to be launched against the US fleet at Pearl Harbor. Kates carried the torpedoes to Hawaii that fateful Sunday, the combination of the Nakajima bomber and soon-to be-legendary Japanese torpedo proving deadly to the anchored warships. At that time the B5N was the most modern carrier-borne torpedo bomber in service anywhere in the world.

Development of the B5N began in 1932 following selection of the 'stopgap' B4Y1 biplane for production in 1936. It was intended that the Nakajima design would be a more modern and capable aircraft, built as it was in response to a later specification, issued in 1935. Among the requirements was provision for a 1,764 lb (800 kg) torpedo or equivalent bomb load, wing folding and a fuselage length not exceeding 40 ft to enable the aircraft to fit on a standard carrier deck elevator.

Specification: B5N2
Type: Three-seat torpedo bomber and ASW aircraft
Manufacturer: Nakajima Hikoki K K
Number built: 1,149
Entry into service: Spring 1940
Length: 33 ft 9.5 in (10.3 m)
Height: 12 ft 1 in (3.7 m)
Wingspan: 50 ft 10 in (15.518 m)
Weight empty: 4,643 lb (2,106 kg)
Range: 1,237 miles (1,990 km)
Max speed: 235 mph (378 km/h)
Service ceiling: 24,280 ft (7,400 m)
Armaments: 1 x 7.7-mm Type 92 machine gun for rear defence; 1,764 lb (800 kg) or bombs or 1 x 1,764 lb (800 kg) torpedo carried externally.

A sleek monoplane incorporating Fowler wing flaps and with the crew of three housed under an elongated 'greenhouse' canopy, the B5N1 flew for the first time in January 1937. Powerplant was a single Nakajima Hikari 2 radial.

Anticipating difficulties in maintaining the B5N1's systems, many of which were new, the Navy directed that the hydraulic wing folding be replaced by manual folding and that a simpler flap system be substituted for the Fowler design. Thus revised, the B5N1 was ordered into production in November 1937. Carrier service followed and the new torpedo bomber was also land-based for combat operations over China, where it served quite successfully in

the tactical bombing role, usually escorted to its target by Ki-27 fighters.

The derivative B5N2, first flown in December 1939, was externally similar to the B5N1 apart from a 1,000 hp Sakae 11 engine with a slighty smaller frontal area which gave an improved view forward. The Navy accepted this configuration for production and by the time of Pearl Harbor the B5N2 had entirely replaced its forerunner in fleet units.

As with other Japanese aircraft, the end of the nation's early war successes proved to be the swansong of the B5N2, at least in its primary torpedo bomber role. At Midway, 81 out of 93 embarked machines were lost. Kates subsequently operated mainly from land bases, seeing service in the Solomons and the Philippines, the latter area recording its last large scale operational area. Relegation to second line duties meant however a second lease of life for the Kate, as it became a useful maritime reconnaissance and ASW type. Some examples were fitted with ASV radar and Jikitanchiki magnetic airborne submarine detection (MAD) gear.

Above: A 'Kate' taxying to take off on December 7, 1941.

Below left: A bombed–up B5N 'Kate'.

Below: Multiple bomb racks can be seen below the fuselage.

Overleaf: B5N configured as a torpedo bomber

Insets: Imaginative camouflage applied to ex-*Tora! Tora! Tora!* B5N mock-ups.

All these photographs show the remarkably convincing US–derived B5Ns. With no real 'Kates' left, movie makers had to convert US trainers into convincing lookalikes. Note in particular, the torpedoes angled down for good airplane clearance on launch.

NAKAJIMA B6N ('JILL')

Built to meet a 1939 requirement for a three-seat carrier-borne torpedo bomber, the Nakajima B6N1 Tenzan (Heavenly Mountain) had to conform to some restrictions, among them the need for a wingspan similar to the B5N2 it was replacing and a fuselage under 40 ft long to fit carrier elevators. A 1,870 hp Nakajima Mamoru 11 radial engine gave the B6N 80% more power than its predecessor and data from flight trials in the spring of 1942 indicated an early carrier deployment. In the event technical difficulties postponed the B6N's service debut until 1943. Thrown into action in the battle for the Marianas, the B6N1s lost most of their fighter cover to USN combat air patrols and could achieve little. Forced to re-engine the aircraft with the 1,859 hp Mitsubishi MK4T Kasei radial, Nakajima produced the B6N2 and the B6N2a with minor changes. Of the total of 1,268 B6Ns built, a number were expended as Kamikazes, the crews of the last operational Tenzans selling themselves dearly in both suicide and conventional (the difference was often academic) air strikes on the US fleet operating off Okinawa.

Specification: B6N2
Type: Three-seat carrier-borne torpedo bomber
Manufacturer: Nakajima
Number built: 1,268
Entry into service: 1943
Length: 35 ft 7.75 in (10.865 m)
Height: 12 ft 5 in (3.8 m)
Wingspan: 48 ft 10 in (14.894 m)
Weight empty: 6,636 lb (3,010 kg)
Range: 1,084 miles (1,745 km)
Max speed: 299 mph (465 km/h)
Service ceiling: 29,660 ft (9,040 m)
Armaments: 1 x flexible 7.7-mm Type 97 machine gun for rear defence and 1 x 7.7-mm Type 97 machine gun firing through ventral tunnel; bomb load up to 1,764 lb (500 kg) or one torpedo.

Above right: The high and wide landing gear of the B6N helped carrier handling.

Right: Radar was fitted to the late model 'Jill', a potentially formidable attack type.

NAKAJIMA C6N ('MYRT')

Designed for the IJN to fulfill fast, long-range reconnaissance duties, the Nakajima C6N Saiun or Painted Cloud, did so outstandingly well. Otherwise known by its Allied codename 'Myrt', the type also found a niche in other areas. Early flight trials proved disappointing in terms of the reliabilty of its Homare engine but the C6N incorporated advanced features incuding a laminar flow wing with combination of split and Fowler flaps and leading edge slats, and forward angled vertical tail surfaces.

Completed in March 1943, the first C6N1 flew on May 15. Mainly for tests, 19 more aircraft were built up to April 1944, the Homare 21-powered C6N1 entering production shortly afterwards. Flight trials had recorded a C6N1 reaching 397 mph and in service the type was able to evade USN interceptors when it shadowed enemy naval units during the peripheral sea battle when the US invaded the Marianas.

A handful of C6N1s were converted as C6N1-S night fighters, a role in which they were much praised for their able defence of the home islands in 1945 as they proved to be among the fastest aircraft available for this demanding role. A total of 463 C6Ns were built and one luckless Myrt crew became the last confirmed US Navy kill of the war when their aircraft was shot down at 05.40 on August 15, 1945.

Specification: C6N1
Type: Three-seat reconnaissanc aircraft
Manufacturer: Nakajima Hikoki K K
Number built: 463
Entry into service: Summer 1944
Length: 36 ft 1 in (11 m)
Height: 12 ft 11 in (3.96 m)
Wingspan: 41 ft (12.5 m)
Weight empty: 6,543 lb (2,968 kg)
Range: 1,914 miles (3,080 km)
Max speed: 379 mph (609 km/h)
Service ceiling: 35,236 ft (10,470 m)
Armaments: 1 x flexible 7.92-mm Type 2 machine gun for rear defence; (C6N1-S) 2 x oblique-firing Type 99 20-mm cannon in fuselage; 1 x 160.6 Imp gal (730 litres) drop tank

Below: Nakajima C6N codenamed 'Myrt' by the Allies.

NAKAJIMA J1N1 ('IRVING')

Known to the JNAF as the Gekko (Moonlight) the J1N1 became Japan's most effective night fighter, having been derived from the J1N1-C reconnaissance aircraft. Originally ordered as a long-range fighter, the J1N1 first flew on May 2, 1941. Teething troubles with items such as the innovative twin remotely controlled gun barbettes, the hydraulic system and general heaviness resulted in an official view that a good turn of speed was the J1N's only saving grace. Revised to meet a reconnaissance role as the J1N1-C, low volume production was authorised.

By codenaming the J1N1 'Irving' as it appeared to be a fighter, Allied intelligence anticipated the aircraft's future role. The Navy meanwhile authorised an experimental fitting of a huge, drag-inducing rear turret with a 20-mm cannon which was not a success. Units based at Rabaul recommended fitting a reconnaissance Irving with dorsal and ventral oblique cannon for night fighting. The first kill by a Rabaul-based

Specification: J1N1-S
Type: Twin-engined night fighter
Manufacturer: Nakajima Hikoki K K
Number built: 486
Entry into service: July 1942
Length: 39 ft 11.5 in (12.18 m)
Height: 14 ft 11.5 in (4.562 m)
Wingspan: 55 ft 8.5 in (16.98 m)
Weight empty: 10, 697 lb (4,852 kg)
Range: 1,585 miles (2,550 km)
Max speed: 315 mph (507 km/h)
Service ceiling: 30,578 ft (9320 m)
Armaments: 1 x 20-mm Type 99 cannon and 2 x 7.7-mm Type 97 machine guns in nose; 2 x 20-mm Type 99 cannon, firing obliquely downwards and 2 x 20-mm Type 99 cannon firing obliquely upwards

J1N1 took place on May 20/21, 1943 when two B-17s were shot down, a success that led to official acceptance and production that August.

As the J1N1-S, the new variant had a redesigned upper fuselage decking without a step and four oblique cannon in dorsal and ventral locations, although combat experience showed that the lower pair were not very effective and they were deleted from late production aircraft. These latter were known as J1N1-Sa Model 11As. AI radar was fitted to most of the late-war Gekkos, some examples having a searchlight in the nose. If neither the radar or searchlight was fitted, a forward-firing cannon was usually installed. Despite being able to catch the B-29 and make a single pass, the Gekko could hardly blunt the bomber offensive and in a last desperate gesture of defiance this interesting night fighter was thrown into Kamikaze attacks.

Left: A relatively successfully design for a twin engined fighter, the J1N1 was a useful night fighter

NAKAJIMA KI-27 ('NATE')

The diminutive Ki-27 was the embodiment of Japanese prewar aeronautical design: light, agile and easy to fly, it quickly gained mastery over the motley collection of antiquated aircraft of the Chinese forces opposing Japan's invasion of that country in 1937. Perpetuating the fixed landing gear of a past era, the Ki-27 carried the Japanese Army Air Force fighter units through to the verge of the Second World War, many pilots believing that they could conduct wider war operations in the Pacific with such fighters.

Having selected the largest possible wing for the Ki-27 out of three possibilities, the Army achieved an extremely low wing loading of 19.9 lb/sq ft. Service pilots delighted in the manoeuvrability of their tiny fighter which achieved almost total ascendency over the aircraft of the Chinese and Soviet air forces in 1939. Japanese pilots flying the Ki-27 claimed hundreds of victories that year, an incredible achievement with such lightly armed machines.

There were two main models of the Ki-27. The prototype was powered by a 650 hp Nakajima Ha-1a engine which had been derived

Specification: Ki-27
Type: Single-seat fighter
Manufacturer: Mitsubishi
Number built: 3,399
Entry into service: Spring 1938
Length: 24 ft 8.5 in (7.35 m)
Height: 9 ft 2.25 in (2.8 m)
Wingspan: 37 ft 0.75 in (11.3 m)
Weight empty: 2,403 lb (1,090 kg)
Range: 389 miles (625 km)
Max speed: 286 mph (460 km/h)
Service ceiling: 34,400 ft (10,500 m)
Armaments: 2 x 7.7-mm Type 89 machine guns in fuselage; 4 x 55 lb (25 kg) bombs on wing racks

from the British Jupiter. This aircraft made its maiden flight on October 15, 1936, with Ki-27a production machines reaching first line units early in 1938. An Ha-1a uprated to 710 hp powered both the main production models, the Ki-27a and Ki-27b.

Production figures for this prewar fighter exceeded many first line combat aircraft of the war before Japan began fighting for her very life — it was no wonder that her Army pilots preferred flying the Nate to anything else, at least when the war seemed to be going so well.

Below: Very agile and a delight to fly, many Army pilots preferred the Ki-27 to the Zeke — at first

Right: An 'Oscar' photographed in protective pen as a US aircraft zooms over its airfield.

NAKAJIMA KI-43 ('OSCAR')

While the Japanese Navy's A6M tended to hog the headlines in combat reports of air combat in the Pacific, many of the Allies' adversaries were actually examples of the Army's Ki-43 Hayabusa (Peregrine Falcon). As the frequency of encounters increased the aircraft was recognised for what it was and the codename 'Oscar' was allocated.

Probably the most important Japanese Army fighter of the Pacific war, the Nakajima Ki-43 was also one of the most durable, the type being deploying in most combat zones throughout the conflict. Making its debut over Burma and Malaya in late 1941, the Ki-43 enjoyed outstanding manoeuvrability although its armament was soon seen to be too light.

Departing from traditional practice under which a contract was won by competing companies, the JAAF went direct to Nakajima in December 1937 to order a modern fighter to replace the Nakajima Ki-27 but retaining some of the pleasing aspects of the older fighter, particularly its manoeuvrability. It was a demanding task.

Flying for the first time in January 1939 powered by a 925 hp Ha-25 engine, the first Ki-43 had, like the Ki-27 and two more prototypes, only twin machine gun armament. Appearing at a crossroads for Japanese military aviation, the Ki-43 was viewed with some scepticism by Army pilots, many of whom believed that future air combat would involve dogfights and therefore any new fighter would need manoeuvrability above all else. They thought that the Ki-43 needed more agility.

Ten trials aircraft were completed by September 1940 and an experimental Ha-105 supercharged engine

was fitted into one of the prototypes. 'Butterfly' combat flaps were also introduced, these proving to be very effective, the airframe meanwhile undergoing radical changes. The early production Ki-43-IA had a two-bladed propeller for its 950 hp engine, the similar Ki-43-IB and -IC differing only in the type of armament fitted.

By February 1942 the Ki-43-II had appeared, this being powered by a 1,150 hp Ha-115 engine driving a three-bladed metal propeller. Early flight trials led to the production Ki-43-IIa of November 1942 and the Ki-43-III made its combat debut over Thailand in late October 1944 the 64th Sentai being the first to receive the last mass production model of the Hayabusa. Although the Ki-43's main use was in the early part of the war, prototypes of the advanced Ki-43-IIIb were being tested when Japan surrendered. The importance of the Hayabusa to the JAAF is shown by the fact that no less than 26 JAAF Sentais operated it during their existence as combat units.

Specification: Ki-43-IIb
Type: Single-seat fighter
Manufacturer: Nakajima Hikoki K K & Tachikawa Hikoki K K
Number built: 5,919
Entry into service: July 1942
Length: 29 ft 3 in (8.92 m)
Height: 10 ft 8.5 in (3.27 m)
Wingspan: 35 ft 5.75 in (10.84 m)
Weight empty: 4,211 lb (1,910 kg)
Range: 1,095 miles (1,760 km)
Max speed: 329 mph (530 km/h)
Service ceiling: 36,750 ft (11,200 m)
Armaments: 2 x 12.7-mm Ho-103 machine guns or 2 x 20-mm Ho-5 cannon in fuselage; 2 x 66 lb (30 kg) or 2 x 551 lb (250 kg) bombs under wings

NAKAJIMA KI-44 ('TOJO')

Less well known than its contemporaries the Ki-44 neverthless was a significant fighter in the inventory of the Japanese Army Air Force. Designed to a somewhat radical specification which departed from 'traditional' practice, the new fighter was to have a greater speed and climb rate at the expense of manoeuvrability. Top speed was to be 373 mph (600 km/h) and four machine guns was the specified armament.

Fortunately the 1,250 hp Nakajima Ha-41 radial was then just becoming available for installation in fighters and despite its large size, this engine was chosen to power what had become the Ki-44. The first prototype was flown in August 1940, observers noting the deep rear fuselage profile and very small wing, which spanned only 31 ft (9.45 m). This inevitably imposed a substantial wing loading and high landing speed but the Ki-44 passed its initial flight and handling tests without problems. These did however appear when the prototypes failed to meet a basic requirement of the specification — the ability to reach combat altitude

in under five minutes. Top speed too was lower than expected and either of these factors could have resulted in cancellation. But with Nakajima also then experiencing problems with the Ki-43, the Ki-44 was considered as something of an insurance.

The Ki-44 needed modification and after strengthening the engine mountings, altering the shape of the cowling and the supercharger intake

and changing the cowling flaps, the aircraft was still a little slow even without armament. Further modifications led to a speed of 389 mph (626 km/h) being attained and the company proceeded with seven pre-production aircraft, delivering the last of these in September 1941. On the 15th of that month they were passed to an experimental unit for combat trials, these early aircraft

---

Specification: Ki-44-II
Type: Single-seat interceptor fighter
Manufacturer: Nakajima Hikoki K K
Number built: 1,225
Entry into service: September 1942
Length: 28 ft 8.5 in (8.75 m)
Height: 10 ft 8 in (3.25 m)
Wingspan: 31 ft (9.45 m)
Weight empty: 4,286 lb (1,944 kg)
Range: 575 miles (926 km)
Max speed: 360 mph (580 km/h)
Service ceiling: 35,500 ft (10,820 km)
Armaments: (Ki-44-IIb) 2 x 12.7-mm Type 1 (Ho-103) machine guns in fuselage and 2 x 12.7-mm Ho-103 in wings; (Ki-44-IIc) 2 x 20-mm Ho-3 cannon in fuselage and 2 x 20-mm Ho-103 or 2 x 37-mm Ho-203 cannon in wings; 2 x 28.6 Imp-gal (130 litre) wing drop tanks.

being armed with a quartet of machine guns in the fuselage and wings, the former being of light, 7.7-mm calibre.

Following successful evaluation and action over China, the decision to begin meeting the first production order for the Shoki or 'Demon' earlier that year, was seen as timely. To the Allies the Ki-44 became the 'Tojo'.

Uprated machine guns were fitted to the Ki-44-IIb, all weapons now being the Type 1 Ho-103 of 12.7-mm (equivalent to 0.50-in) calibre. This model was also distinguished by having the oil cooler in an external fairing below the engine cowling. The similar Ki-44-IIc, 40 of which were built, could be distinguished by inboard mainwheel doors hinged at the fuselage wells rather on the oleo legs.

To make the Shoki a more effective interceptor, the armament was again boosted to incude two 37-mm or 40-mm Ho-301 wing cannon or 20-mm cannon in all four positions, in the Ki-44-IIc. The Ho-301 cannon was not as effective as it might seem, for it was light for its calibre and had a very slow rate of fire. Better was the 37-mm H-203 weapon, which had a range of 1,000 yd as against only 150 yd for the 40-mm gun.

In June 1943 the final Shoki model, the Ki-44-III, made its maiden flight, this model being powered by the 2,000 hp Ha-145 engine and having increased wing area and enlarged tail surfaces. Despite being phased out of production in late 1944, the Shoki finally achieved a degree of fame by defending the Empire against B-29 attacks. Young pilots appreciated its performance in this role even though it was restricted from performing certain flight manoeuvres which were considered to be dangerous.

Above and Below: Abandoned on an airfield, the Allies found this Ki-44 complete with twin drop tanks.

Below left: The Ki-44 was one of Japan's best fighters.

NAKAJIMA KI-84 ('FRANK')

Nakajima's Ki-84, code-named 'Frank', ousted the Ki-44 as the Army's principal fighter after Ki-43 production terminated and was widely regarded as the best JAAF fighter of the war. Although hampered by low quality materials in some components, a well-built Ki-84 with a good pilot at the controls could out-pace the P-47N and P-51D.

Designed as a replacement for the Ki-43 early in 1942, the Ki-84 was one of the 'second generation' of Japanese fighters which finally incorporated as standard armour protection for the pilot and self-sealing fuel tanks. The first example was completed in March 1943 and the first flight took place the following month. Capable of a top speed of 388 mph (624 km/h) and a ceiling of 40,680 ft (12,400m), pre-service test machines demonstrated that this was the best new fighter produced for the JAAF.

Specification: Ki-84-Ia
Type: Single-seat fighter
Manufacturer: Nakajima Hikoki K K
Number built: 3,382
Entry into service: April 1944
Length: 32 ft 6 in (9.92 m)
Height: 11 ft 1 in (3.385 m)
Wingspan: 36 ft 10 in (11.238 m)
Weight empty: 5,864 lb (2,660 kg)
Range: 1,053 miles (1,696 km)
Max speed: 392 mph (631 km/h)
Service ceiling: 34,450 ft (10,500 m)
Armaments: 2 x fuselage mounted 12.7-mm Ho-103 machine guns plus 2 x 20-mm wing mounted Ho-5 cannon; 2 x 551 lb (250 kg) bombs or 2 x 44 Imp gal (200l) drop tanks.

Cannon armament as well as the 'traditional' fuselage-mounted machine guns, also gave the Ki-84 ,which was named Hayate (Gale), a potential advantage in combat.

Powered by the 1,900 hp Nakajima Ha-45 radial, early Hayates were fitted with series 11 or 12 engines which provided 1,800 hp and 1,825 hp respectively for take off. Engine rating was raised to the full 1,900 hp in the series 21, the Ki-84s powerplant driving a four-bladed propeller.

In the Ki-84-Ib the cowl machine guns were replaced by twin Ho-5 20-mm cannon and the few Ki-84-Ic models completed were specialised bomber destroyers with the standard wing cannon replaced by 30-mm Ho-105 cannon. Encouraging tests with two pre-production batches led to a mass production go-ahead in late 1943, the Ki-84-I being first issued to the 22nd Sentai. Transferred to China, this unit cut its teeth against aircraft of the US 14th Air Force. Five weeks later it was in the Philippines.

Combat revealed some short-comings in the Hayate, incuding a weak landing gear and frequent failure of hydraulic and oil pressure lines. The disconcerting and sudden loss of fuel pressure was addressed but not entirely solved until the introduction of the Ha-45 series 21 engine fitted with a low-pressure fuel injection system.

The 10 Sentais equipped with the Ki-84 failed to hold US forces in the Philippines but the Army's appreciation of the aircraft's qualities culminated in the record output of 373 examples in December 1944. This was the highest figure for any JAAF aircraft, despite an increasingly critical shortage of raw materials and manpower. A second production line for the Ki-84 was established by Mansyu Hikoki in Manchuria, not so exposed to Allied bombing; this plant managed to produce 95 aircraft in 1945.

Bombing adversely affected the number of Ki-84s issued to front line units, however. To offset a shortage of aluminium, Nakajima incorporated a new fuselage, wingtips and ancilliary items made of wood into the Hayate design, this model becoming official-ly known as the Ki-84-II. In spite of this, Ki-84s continued to be logged as models Ib or Ic by combat units, depending on armament fit.

The Ki-84-III was a high-altitude version powered by an Ha-45 Ru engine with a turbocharger. Other projected variants remained on the drawing board although the raw materials shortage resulted in the Ki-106, an all-wood version of the Ki-84. Only three examples were built and test flown before the Japanese surrender. In all 25 Sentais were fully or partially equipped with the Ki-84 during the war.

Above: Allied fighters often had a hard time catching the Ki-84, which was rated the best JAAF fighter of the war.

Left: This 'Frank' was one of many Japanese aircraft taken to the US after the war.

YOKOSUKA MXY-7 (OHKA)

The very act of producing an aircraft that was little more than a bomb with a human being at the controls finally confirmed to many how much Japan's primitive philosophy clouded her conduct of the war. The notorious Ohka, which translated as 'Baka' or Fool, guided bomb was not produced or deployed in numbers high enough to force any major change in Allied policy but it remains one of the few true 'suicide' weapons to actually enter service.

Although self-immolation was a concept initially widely resisted by most Japanese airmen, the plight of the nation by mid-1944 led to a grim realisation that Kamikaze tactics were the only way to halt the inexorable slide into utter defeat that then seemed likely. Surrender was unthinkable and invasion of the home islands an terrible prospect — supreme sacrifice to save the nation could have no higher honour.

Specification: MXY-7
Type: Single-seat rocket-engined suicide plane
Manufacturer: Yokosuku
Number built: 852
Entry into service: October 1944
Length: 19 ft 10.75 in (6.7 m)
Height: 3ft 11.73 in (1.20 m)
Wingspan: 16 ft 4.75 in (5 m)
Weight empty: (no warhead) 970 lb (440 kg)
Range: 55 miles (88 km)
Max speed: 534 mph (860 km/h)
Service ceiling: (launch height) 27,000 ft (8,200 m)
Armament: One 2,645lb (1,200 kg) warhead containing tri-nitroaminol

To the Japanese militarists, expending young, fanatical pilots and obsolete aircraft on one-way missions was an expedient forced upon them — but a carefully planned refinement in the form of a piloted bomb took some time to grasp, even by extremist elements in the armed forces. Many airmen were

Right: The Baka was built strictly for one-way flights

Below right: The rocket engine of the early Bakas was to be replaced by a turbojet.

Below: An Ohka on museum display.

against the concept but doubts were swept aside and by mid-1944 the first of the Okha Special Attack weapons were ready for operational use. The 'Thunder gods' the corps which led the pilots, soon had ample volunteers.

Powered by a three-barrel Type 4 Model 20 rocket motor, which gave a thrust of 1,746 lb (800 kg) the MXY-7 Model 11 Ohka was capable of a speed of 534 mph (860 km/h) and a final diving speed of 621 mph (1,000 km/h). To achieve optimum performance it was ideally released from the mother ship at an altitude

of 27,000 ft (8,200 m), about 50 miles from its target. The pilot held the tiny aircraft in a glide until he ignited the rocket fuel by electrical charge and pushed over into a dive.

When they achieved a clean launch, the tiny Ohkas were almost impossible to stop but in general they were not a success, as their G4M mother ships were vulnerable to fighter attack. The problem was addressed and plans were executed to give the Ohka more thrust, using a turbojet engine. As the Model 22, the Ohka was fitted with a 441 lb (200 kg) thrust TSU-11 engine

which was deemed not as suitable as an Ne-20 turbojet, which would have powered the Ohka Model 33. In the event, neither of these versions reached operational status.

Above: Light and easy to transport, the Baka was often lost when its carrier aircraft was shot down.

Below: The nose area back to the ring held the MXY-7's warhead.

SOVIET UNION

ILYUSHIN IL-2

One of the few wartime aircraft designed principally to attack ground targets, the Ilyushin Il-2 emerged as one of the best in its class. Built in huge numbers and dubbed Sturmovik by its German adversaries, the Il-2 carried that nickname more or less throughout its lifetime. German fighter pilots, even the many Eastern Front Experten, were often hard-put to bring down the Il-2. It did have its vulnerable spots, particularly from behind and below where fire from a pursuing fighter could sever the control runs to the tail — but a more conventional attack often met with frustration. An all but impervious armoured 'bathtub' protected the crew and further armour plate shielding was provided for the engine and fuel tanks.

A prototype flew for the first time on December 30, 1939 and at first the designer envisaged a single-seater, primarily to bring performance within the parameters of the specification. The 'true' Il-2 prototype, still a single-seater and still under the designation CCB-55, flew on December 29, 1940. A wing with modest leading edge sweep was fitted, the landing gear retracting

Specification: (Il-2M)
Type: One- or two-seat close support aircraft
Manufacturer: Ilyushin
Number built: 36,163 (by November 1944)
Entry into service: Spring 1941
Length: 38 ft (11.6 m)
Height: 11 ft 1.75 in (3.4 m)
Wingspan: 47 ft 10 in (14.6 m)
Weight empty: 9,976 lb (4,525 kg)
Range: 384 miles (618 km)
Max speed: 246 mph (396 km/h)
Service ceiling: 27,890 ft (8,500 m)
Armaments: 2 x wing-mounted VYa-23 cannon and 1 x UBT for rear defence; up to 8 x RS-132 rockets under wings

backwards into prominent fairings bulged out at the leading edge to enclose the retraction gear. Broad chord vertical and horizontal tail surfaces and a seemingly 'cut short' cockpit canopy were instant recognition features of the Il-2. Official pre-service testing was completed in March 1941 and production began immediately, the Il-2 designation being confirmed that April.

Initial combat sorties with the single-seat Il-2 during the early stages of Operation Barbarossa highlighted some deficiences, including

an urgent need for a rear observer/gunner. This was instigated without delay and by the summer the Il-2M, with no less than 2,183 lb (990 kg) of armor incorporated in the airframe, became a potent weapon. Anti-tank armament was boosted, as was engine output, this enabling a maximum speed of 230 mph (370 km/h). Although the Il-2 was never very fast, its main task did not require high speed and despite frequent interception by enemy fighters, on many occasions Russian crews escaped unscathed. Output

was so high that combat losses were rapidly made good.

The succeeding Il-2AM (introduced in July 1942) and Il-2M3 looked similar to earlier examples, although the outer wing panels had greater sweepback. Heavier cannon were adopted to deal with the heaviest German tanks and in 1944 the composite wood-metal structure was replaced by an all-dural airframe. A ski landing gear was developed to help Il-2 crews cope with ice-covered runways, the Red Air Force being one of the best in the world at coping with conditions that would, and often did, keep their adversaries on the ground.

Enormous production facilities were provided for the Il-2, arguably

the most important aircraft in the Soviet inventory. It spearheaded most major offensives on the Eastern Front. By the war's end it had been built in greater numbers than any other military aircraft, Allied or Axis.

Far left: Chocks away for a front line Il-2.

Top: The Sturmovik was an Eastern Front war-winner.

Above: Early Il-2s were notable for their short canopy.

Left: A section of Il-2s with their wing cannon firing.

ILYUSHIN DB -3

The most important Soviet bomber of the war, the DB-3 began life under the designation CCB-30 which was in its turn an improved CCB-26 which first appeared in May 1936. A twin-engined bomber of pleasing proportions, the aircraft was unusual in having a separate raised cockpit on top of the fuselage. Selected for production late in 1936 as the DB-3, the aircraft had provision for internal and external wing bombs and up to four defensive guns; subsequently the DB-3T was able to carry a torpedo below the fuselage.

A DB-3 modernisation programme (the first models had no self-sealing fuel tanks) incuded extending the fuselage, the forward part of which was redesigned. The revision was more extensive than was obvious externally, improved engines also being substituted. Production was initiated in January 1940.

It was not unusual for the Russians to introduce redesignations that appeared to indicate completely new designs when these were actually modifications or when the individual designer's name or that of his bureau was allowed to be incor-

porated into the designation. Thus the DB-3 became the Ilyushin Il-4 in March 1942 and a number of new configurations emerged until production ceased in 1945. These incuded a power-operated dorsal gun turret, revised M-87B engine cowlings with cooling gills and a streamlined nose, which dispensed with the original nose turret with its single hand-held machine gun.

Among its many combat successes, the DB-4 bombed Berlin from August 1941, flew recce missions and towed gliders — a true 'maid of all work' invaluable to any air force.

Specification: Ilyushin Il-4
Type: Twin-engined long-range bomber
Manufacturer: Ilyushin
Number built: 6,784
Entry into service: May 1937
Length: 48 ft 6.5 in (14.8 m)
Height: 13 ft 9 in (4.2 m)
Wingspan: 70 ft 4.5 in (21.44 m)
Weight empty: 13,230 lb (6,000 kg)
Range: 1,616 miles (2,600 km)
Max speed: 255 mph (410 km/h)
Service ceiling: 32,808 ft (10,000 m)
Armaments: 3 x 12.7-mm BS machine guns in nose, dorsal and ventral positions; 10 x 220 lb (100 kg) inter nally; external racks for up to 3 x 1,102 lb (500 kg) bombs or 1 x 2,072 lb (940 kg) torpedo

Above left: The DB-3 served throughout the war.

Left: Aerial torpedoes being loaded into DB-3s.

LAGG-1/3

A very simple fighter built primarily of a birch plywood and bakelite composite, the LaGG-1 was the first type to be built by the Lavochkin, Gorbunov and Gudkov (LaGG) bureau. A well-proportioned, low-wing fighter with a characteristically deep rear fuselage profile, the LaGG-1 was powered by a M-105P liquid-cooled engine offering a top speed of 320 mph (515 km/h).

Between the maiden flight of the first prototype on March 30, 1940 and early 1941, 322 aircraft had been delivered. In the meantime the I-301 (designated after the GAZ-301 plant which built the first 100 aircraft) had flown as the forerunner of an improved model designated LaGG-3, the original having exhibited numerous faults. Four plants were selected for volume production and by the end of 1941 2,141 LaGG-3s had been completed. Early models were armed with one ShVAK cannon and ShKAS machine guns, plus RS-82 rockets under the wings.

Despite improvements — fitting a radio, new hydraulics and brakes and balancing the elevators — pilots continued to refer to the LaGG as a 'varnished, guaranteed coffin' there being numerous crashes both in

training and front line service. But thrown in to stem the German advance after June 22, 1941 the LaGG-3 was better than no fighters at all and it was developed further although poor build quality was an ongoing problem. A lightened Series 23 model was produced with one machine gun and one cannon armament but performance remained poor. In May 1943 the Series 66 appeared, this proving to be the fastest of the line with a top speed of 360 mph (580 km/h).

Throughout its lifetime the LaGG-3 suffered from low engine power as well as the inevitable result of employing unskilled labour in its construction. The real answer lay in a better engine and with the war situation stabilised, the decision was taken to fit an air-cooled radial into the airframe, and the LaGG-3 was transformed to became the superlative La-5.

Below: The LaGG-3 was nick-named the 'varnished, guaran-teed coffin'.

Specification: LaGG-3
Type: Single-seat fighter
Manufacturer: Lavochkin, Gurbunov & Gudkov design bureau
Number built: 6,528
Entry into service: January 1941
Length: 28 ft 11.75 in (8.82 m)
Height: 8 ft 10 in (3.22 m)
Wingspan: 32 ft 1.75 in (9.8 m)
Weight empty: 5,463 lb (2,478 kg)
Range: 345 miles (556 km)
Max speed: 320 mph (515 km/h)
Service ceiling: 31,500 ft (9,600 m)
Armaments: (typical) 1 x 20-mm ShVAK centerline cannon plus 2 x 12.7-mm BS machine guns in cowling plus wing racks for light bombs or up to six RS-82 rockets.

LAVOCHKIN LA-5/LA-7

In common with most Soviet fighters, the Lavochkin series of interceptors embodied necessary high performance with light weight and modest armament but sheer weight of numbers tended to nullify any drawback that this latter might have represented in combat. This is not to imply that the Soviet approach was in any way flawed as it followed a proven design philosphy that was highly successful.

Stemming from the disappointing LaGG-3 single-seater, which was transformed by the substitution of a radial engine for an inline, the La-5 became one of the most capable fighters of the war.

Work to install an M-82 radial in the LaGG-3 airframe was begun in late September 1941. Among the challenges were absorbing about 550 lb (250 kg) more weight while maintaining the centre of gravity and widening the forward fuselage of the LaGG-3 to accept an engine larger in cross section than the one it replaced. There were huge advantages to be gained from a successful conversion, however, and changes to the LaGG-3 airframe were kept to a minimum to save time.

The first flight of the re-engined machine was in March 1942. Test pilot reports initiated further minor changes but when Stalin received positive feedback from these tests, production was ordered immediately. The Soviet military position was then critical.

By July authorisation for full production of the La-5 had been given, which initially meant re-engining all existing LaGG-3 airframes. But production of new fighters was in time for a special trials regiment to introduce the La-5 to combat at Stalingrad in September. Pilots were highly enthusiastic, particularly when finding that they could execute a loop at only 186 mph (300 km/h) ASI.

Refinements incuded boosting internal fuel, installing the ASh-82F engine (in the La-5F) and reducing a blind spot to the rear of the cockpit

Specification: La-5FN
Type: Single-seat fighter
Manufacturer: Lovochkin
Number built: (est) 9,920
Entry into service: September 1942
Length: 28 ft 7in (8.71 m)
Height: 9 ft 3 in (2.84 m)
Wingspan: 32 ft 1.75 in (9.8 m)
Weight empty: 6,149 lb (2,789 kg)
Range: 475 miles (765 km)
Max speed: 403 mph (648 km/h)
Service ceiling: 36,090 ft (11,000 m)
Armaments: 2 x 20-mm ShVAK cannon in fuselage; up to 440 lb (200kg) bombs or 4 or 6 x RS-82 rockets under wings

Specification: Lavochkin La-7
Type: Single-seat fighter
Number built: 5,753
Entry into service: May 1944
Length: 28 ft 3 in (8.64 m)
Height: 8 ft 5 in (2.6 m)
Wingspan: 32 ft (9.80 m)
Weight empty: 5,842 lb (2,650 kg)
Range: 392 miles (630 km)
Max speed: 407 mph (655 km/h)
Service ceiling: 34,448 ft (10,500 m)
Armaments: 2 x ShVAK 20-mm fuselage-mounted cannon

with a new braced 'bubble' canopy. The definitive wartime version, the La-5FN, had fuel injection for its more powerful ASh-82FN engine and was distinguished by a full length supercharger air intake on top of the cowling. Twin cannon armament, remained virtually unchanged, the La-5FN also being able to carry bombs or rockets under the wings. Production of the 'Lavochka' continued until late 1944 after more than 9,000 had been built.

Lavochkin La-7

The La-7 entered Red Air Force service in May 1944. Essentially a 'cleaned up' La-5, it was in fact a new design which took advantage of alloy construction, the supply of this material having been put at some risk by the early Soviet war situation.

Changes made to the La-5 were minimised to ensure little disruption to output. The main external differences were the relocation of the supercharger air intake which was moved from the engine cowling to the left wing root, while the oil cooler was set back aft of the wing trailing edge. Pilot reports were even more positive than with the La-5FN, just over six months elapsing between the first flight of the prototype on 19 November 1943 and entry into service.

As with the La-5, the La-7 was also built as a two-seat trainer with reduced armament and a second cockpit aft of the original with dual controls. A number of experimental variants were test flown incuding the La-7R with an RD-1 liquid rocket engine installed in the rear fuselage below a taller vertical tail.

Above left: The final La-7s were the epitome of wartime Soviet fighter design.

Left: The final La-7s were the epitome of wartime Soviet fighter design.

MIG-1/3

Development of the MiG-1 began in late 1938, the desire for high performance at altitude overriding most other considerations. The first of three protypes was flown on April 5, 1940.

Although the Mikoyan design bureau had opted to fit the most poweful engine available, the liquid-cooled Mikulin AM-35A of 1,350 hp, the MiG-1's build quality was crude and it had a disappointing performance — sometimes bordering on the lethal. But it was a starting point for another design bureau to supply the fighters Russia would soon so desperately need and a basic modification was authorised under the designation MiG-3. This came about when the 101st production MiG-1 was reconfigured with extra fuel tankage (the range had previous-

Specification: MiG-3
Type: Single-seat fighter
Manufacturer: Mikoyan and Gurevich
Number built: 3,322
Entry into service: March 1941
Length: 27 ft 0.75 in (8.25 m)
Height: 12 ft 2.75 in (8.25 m)
Wingspan: 33 ft 5 in (10.20 m)
Weight empty: 5,721 lb (2,595 kg)
Range: 776 miles (1,250 km)
Max speed: 298 mph (480 km/h)
Service ceiling: 39,370 ft (12,000 m)
Armamants: 1 x 12.7-mm UB machine gun and 2 x 7.62-mm ShKAS machine guns in fuselage

ly been quite limited) and although few other faults were attended to, the type entered service in March 1941.

Pilots soon found that the MiG-3 required a very high standard of skill to keep it in the air. After the German invasion the air force had no choice but to use it in combat, Russian pilots finding themselves at a distinct disadvantage in trying to

take on their opponents at low level in a heavy, high-altitude interceptor. Losses were inevitable.

It was probably a blessing in disguise when AM-35A engine production was suddenly terminated and after the front stabilised in 1943 and far better fighters were in service, the MiG-3 was relegated to second line duties.

Below: Soviet pilots being briefed with their MiG-3s lined up behind them.

PETLYAKOV PE-2

S temming from a design study for a twin-engined fighter and dive bomber known as the PB-100, the Pe-2 became one of the best Soviet combat aircraft of the war and the Red Air Force's standard tactical bomber. The sleek PB-100 flew for the first time on December 22, 1939 with a similar configuration to the later Pe-2 although its intended role was briefly revised to concentrate on dive bombing and wing dive brakes were fitted. Pressure cabins had also been specified for the crew of two (pilot and radioman/gunner) but officialdom required a simpler, more conventional approach. There followed a frantic effort to redesign in the short timescale allowed and two prototypes were completed. Design authorisation was given on July 23, 1940 and less than six months elapsed before the first flight, the PB-100 meanwhile becoming the Pe-2.

By the time of the German invasion in June 1941, 459 Pe-2s, affectionately known as 'Peshka' or 'Little Pe', had been delivered and over

Specification: Pe-2
Type: Twin-engined close support aircraft
Manufacturer: Petlyakov
Number built: 11,427
Entry into service: July 1940
Length: 41 ft 4.25 in (12. 6 m)
Height: 11 ft 6 in (3.5 m)
Wingspan: 56 ft 3.5 in (17.2 m)
Weight empty: 12,900 lb (5,870 kg)
Range: 746 miles (1,200 km)
Max speed: 336 mph (540 km/h)
Service ceiling: 28,870 ft (8,800 m)
Armaments: 4 x 7.62-mm ShKAS machine guns, two in nose and one each in ventral and dorsal positions for rear defence; up 2,205 lb (1,000 kg) of bombs

1,000 had been built by the end of that year. The aircraft was initially deployed as an attack bomber with a crew of three, armament including a mid-fuselage periscopic sighting system for the single ventral gun and small bombs carried in the rear of each engine nacelle. The extreme nose was glazed for bomb aiming purposes but the gunner was isolated from the pilot behind a fuel tank .

Following the rapid German advance, the Pe-2 production facilities were moved north to Kazan, beyond the reach of the Luftwaffe. Three other factories quickly came on stream to boost deliveries to combat units. Numerous sub-variants of the Pe-2 were to appear during the war, among them the Pe-2 Series 105 with reduced nose glazing, the Pe-2FT which relocated the navigator in a dorsal turret with a single UBT machine gun to protect the aircraft from the rear, and the Series 205, which had an enlarged bomb bay. The Series 275 introduced a novel form of aft protection in the form of twin ejectors for five AG-2 grenades. A second pilot's cockpit was introduced on the Pe-2UT trainer and all armament in the Pe-2R was deleted in favour of cameras for the daylight reconnaissance role.

Above left: An early production Pe-2 without an visible armament.

Left: A dispersed Pe-2 with an elite Guards unit badge on its nose.

PETLYAKOV PE-8

Although it was the only four-engined bomber produced by the Soviet Union during the war, the Pe-8 ssw little front line service. Soviet air policy had not embraced a strategic heavy bomber force, as built up by the Western Allies. The philosophy remained tactical rather than strategic, the greatest possible effort being put into close support of ground armies.

Designed around a 1934 specification, the prototype Pe-8 first flew (as the ANT-40) on November 9, 1936 with four 1,100 hp M-105 inline engines and a separate fuselage engine to power the superchargers. Production machines (TB-7s) had AM-34s without the complexity of superchargers, these engines enabling the aircraft to reach an altitude of 30,200 ft (9,200 m). With a broad chord single fin, the armament of the TB-7 incuded nose and tail turrets and gun positions built into the rear of each inboard engine nacelle. With a span of 127 ft (39 m), the TB-7 was one of the largest bombers of the war, having crew accommodation for up to 11 men. The bomb load was carried both in a fuselage bay — the largest single weapon accommodated therein weighing 4,410 lb (2,000 kg) — and externally on inner wing racks.

Production was halted in 1939 and just as suddenly reinstated in 1940 with M-30/M-40 diesel engines specified. Availability of these engines was erratic, some machines having instead four AM-35As fitted, but 18 aircraft were supplied to 412 *Polk* (Regiment) in 1940 and this unit attacked Berlin on 9 August 1941. The Pe-8 created international interest when a single aircraft, with AM-35A engines, flew to Washington with a stop in England in May and June 1942, carrying foreign minister Molotov to meet Western leaders.

Therafter the diesel engines of the Pe-7 gave so many problems that further expansion of a heavy bomber force was postponed. Substitution of ASh-82 radial engines enabled production to proceed steadily through 1943 and 1944, the aircraft being redesignated as the Pe-8 in the course of 1943.

A final attempt to get the Pe-8's unreliable diesel engines to function smoothly met with little success and production was stopped, seven short of 100 examples. The Pe-8 nevertheless carried out many long-range flights within the Soviet Union, incuding some as an engine test bed, with a fifth powerplant installed in the nose.

Specification: Pe-8
Type: Four-engined heavy bomber/transport
Manufacturer: A. N. Tupolev
Number built: 93
Entry into service: June 1940
Length: 76 ft 9.25 in (23.4 m)
Height: 20ft (6.1 m)
Wingspan: 127 ft 11.75 in (39.01 m)
Weight empty: 39,429 lb (17 885 kg)
Range: 2,231 miles (3,590 km)
Max speed: 257 mph (305 km/h)
Service ceiling: 34,120 ft (10,400 m)
Armamants: 6 x ShVak machine guns in nose, engine nacelle, dorsal and tail positions; mixed bomb load up to max 8,818 lb (4,000 kg)

A groundcrew man 'flags off' a Pe-8, the only four-engined WWII Soviet bomber.

POLIKARPOV I-153

Biplane fighters were largely rendered obsolete by the new 1930s generation of monoplane combat aircraft but in a few notable instances they soldiered on and made their mark when nothing more modern was available. The I-153 was an outstanding example of this expediency foisted on the Russians after the German invasion of June 22, 1941 and it helped to hold the line against the enemy in the early days of the war in the East.

As the final biplane fighter designed by Polikarpov the I-153 was given construction approval on October 11, 1937. Apart from installation of an M-62 engine the gull-winged aircraft had a retractable landing gear and for the time, the heavy armament of four ShKAS machine guns. Underwing stores stations were also standard, in advance of many other designs. Production began soon after the first flight and pre-service testing during 1938. There was some urgency to get

modern aircraft to the Far East where the Japanese were having things much their own way in their war with China. The I-153 equipped the 70 IAP which saw its first action in July 1939.

The I-153BS had, as its designation implied, provision for four BS guns and the M-62 engine, while the I-153P had two ShVAK guns instead. The I-153 was also made capable of carrying underwing drop tanks and launching RS-82 rockets.

The M-63 engine powered both the single I-153V which featured a pressure cabin, and the I-153V used to test ramjets. Taking some initial blows from the German onslaught the I-153 was clearly outclassed by modern monoplane fighters. It did however give valuable service when Russia's choice of combat aircraft was limited and it continued in second line service in Russia and in Finland, which operated 14 captured examples.

Specification: I-153
Type: Single-seat biplane fighter
Manufacturer: Polikarpov
Number built: 3,437
Entry into service: Spring 1939
Length: 20 ft 3 in (6.17 m)
Height: 9 ft 2.25 in (2.80 m)
Wingspan: 32 ft 9.5 in (10.00m)
Weight empty: 3,291 lb (1,452 kg)
Range: 292 miles (470 km)
Max speed: 227 mph (366 km/h)
Service ceiling: 22,966 ft (7,000 m)
Armaments: 4 x 7.62-mm ShKAS machine guns in fuselage

Below: An I-153 makes for a rare museum exhibit.

POLIKARPOV I-16

A tiny monoplane whose achievements totally belied its size, the I-16 was the first fighter anywhere to mount an 20-mm cannon. Blooded in Spain where it was dubbed *Rata* (Rat) the I-16's nickname followed it into the Second World War and it became synonymous with Russian tenacity in the air, its pilots ramming the enemy if all other tactics failed.

Conceived during the 1930s 'biplane versus monoplane' years when nobody was quite sure which configuration would be most effective in actual combat in the future, the I-16 was a remarkable aircraft.

In 1933, Polikarpov decided to opt for a monoplane and he created the smallest possible airframe using mixed materials and it became the leading Soviet fighter for nearly a decade. That this was a little too long was shown after the Germans invaded in June 1941, the I-16 being declared obsolete the same month.

The first I-16 flew on December 31, 1933, the low power of the M-22 engine being duly noted. There was no alternative powerplant unfortunately although the second example

was flown in 1934 with an imported US Cyclone F3 engine.

Production went ahead in May 1934 despite the I-16's shortcomings which incuded a lack of trimmers, stability best described as marginal with a tendency to stall, and engine vibration. A two-seat unarmed trainer was built as the UTI-2, the fuselage of this model being used as a basis for the UTI-3 trainer. Other trainers conversions followed, based on later Rata models.

The main first production I-16 was the *tip* (type) -4 which had a slightly longer cowling, a Hamilton propeller and other changes. The armoured I-16Sh was a ground attack variant, with four ShKAS cannon and a 220 lb (100 kg) bomb load. In 1938 the I-16P appeared with long-barrelled wing cannon. This configuration, along with two fuselage guns, became the standard armament of the succeeding Type 17 and later models.

The I-16's model designations extended to the Type 24, 27, 29 and 30, production continuing throughout 1939 and into 1941. Most of these were powered by the

M-62 or M-63 engine and all late-production I-16s had a variety of armament options, incuding RS-82 rockets under the wings or a bomb load of 1,102 lb (500 kg).

Specification: I-16 Rata
Type: Single-seat fighter
Manufacturer: Polikarpov
Number built: 9,450
Entry into service: 1935
Length: 19 ft 7.75 in (5.99 m)
Height: 8 ft 4.75 in (2.56 m)
Wingspan: 29 ft 6 in (9.00 m)
Weight empty: 2,976 lb (1,350 kg)
Range: 497 miles (800 km)
Max speed: 242 mph (389 km/h)
Service ceiling: 27,130 ft (8,270m)
Armaments: 2 x 7.62-mm ShKAS machine guns in fuselage and 2 x 7.62-mm machine guns in wings

In service the Rata or Mosca (Fly) could be a formidable opponent, as some German airmen found to their cost — if they could not bring enemy bombers down by conventional means, some Russian pilots would attempt to ram their adversaries which invariably resulted in the loss of both aircraft involved. This air combat tactic, born out of desperation in the early days of Barbarossa, was known as a 'Taran' or ramming victory. The first occurred when an I-16 rammed an He 111 one hour after the German invasion began. In this case the Rata pilot was killed although physical contact with enemy aircraft did not always result in the demise of the Russian pilot. And of course it was not confined to pilots flying the I-16!

Right: Ratas patrol over the Russian steppes.

Below left: Few combat aircraft were as compact as the 'Rata'

Below: An early model I-16, probably in Spain where it was flown by the Republicans.

TUPOLEV SB-2

A very important Soviet bomber type, the SB-2 also boosted the offensive air arms of several other countries after a combat debut during the Spanish Civil War. It had its origins in the Ant-37 and Ant-40 designs and was submitted in response to an air force requirement for a *Skorostnoi Bombardirovshchik* — SB or 'fast bomber' issued in October 1933.

The first aircraft, flown on October 7, 1934, was rebuilt after a landing accident later that month. A mid-wing design then known simply as the SB, the new bomber was rebuilt with a longer fuselage and more tapered outer wing sections. Fitted with M series engines, the SB completed testing on July 31. A second aircraft, designated SB-2HS, was built primarily to test water-cooled engines with flat-fronted radiators. This configuration was an immediate success and mass production was planned without delay, deliveries taking place from early 1936. Seeing action with Republican forces in Spain from October 1936, the SB-2 proved faster than opposing fighters but it was noted that the bomber was ill protected and had a tendency to catch fire easily.

Development of the SB-2 incuded a licence to build it in Czechoslovakia as the B-71, some of this production subsequently going to the Luftwaffe, mainly for training. Russian developments incuded a dual-control trainer and a transport,

the SB-2M-103 designation denoting the M-103 engine which enabled an altitude of 41,650 ft (12,695 m) to be attained. This engine was chosen as the standard powerplant; along with numerous changes that led to the SB bis 3, the 14th series version.

The SB-2 became firmly established in Soviet air force service during the last years of peace but it was not, considering its origins, capable of much modernisation. The

last of 6,831 SB-2s was completed early in 1941, shortly before the German invasion.

SB-2s saw a considerable amount of action after the initial onslaught, which caught numerous Russian aircraft, incuding SB-2s, on the ground.

With crew losses rising steadily at the hands of the Luftwaffe '*Experten*' in the early months of Barbarossa, the SB-2-equipped units nevertheless survived this ordeal, regrouped and fought back.

Specification: SB-2
Type: Twin-engined medium bomber
Manufacturer: Tupolev
Number built: 6,831
Entry into service: Spring 1936
Length: 40 ft 3.25 in (12.29 m)
Height: 10 ft 8 in (3.28 m)
Wingspan: 66 ft 8.5 in (20.34 m)
Weight empty: 8,267 lb (3,750 kg)
Range: 746 miles (1,200 km)
Max speed: 255 mph (410 km/h)
Service ceiling: 31,000 ft (9,500 m)
Armaments: 4 x 7.62 ShKAS machine guns in nose, dorsal and ventral positions; 6 x 220 lb (100 kg) bombs of 1 x 1,100 lb (500 kg) bomb in fuselage bay

---

Right: A Soviet workhorse bomber, the SB-2 was substantially adapted for many roles.

YAKOVLEV YAK-1 AND 7

Carrying on the Soviet tradition of building lightweight fighter airframes from non-strategic materials wherever possible, the Yakovlev series of single-seaters became the most famous Russian fighter types of the war.

Yakovlev's enthusiasm to build a small single-seat fighter began in November 1938 when he planned a design around the Klimov M-106 engine. This had to be changed to the lower-powered M-105P but an attractive, low-wing aircraft with a stepped cockpit canopy and deep rear fuselage emerged early in 1940 as the I-26. Despite the loss of this aircraft in a crash, the decision to mass produce had already been taken.

Flying as the I-26-2 with a strengthened wing and other refinements on April 14, 1940 and as the I-26-3 on September 18, the Yak-1 forerunner soon received increased offensive capability. It was able to carry bomb containers as well as RS-82 rockets under the wings and had increased ammunition for its guns.

A lightened model with no apparent new designation flew in March 1942. More manoeuvrable than its predecessors, this was followed by the Yak-1B with a cut-down rear fuselage in order to improve all-round vision from the cockpit. Production terminated in July 1944, by which time 8,734 aircraft had been completed

With a constant need for replacement fighters to make good attrition from combat, an interim conversion of a Yak-1 airframe into a two-seat trainer led to the Yak-7UTI. This was proposed as a fighter in its own right following encouraging test data and service use during spring 1941.

Again outwardly similar to the Yak-1 series, the Yak-7 was a different aircraft under the skin and ultimately ran to 18 models. These incuded the Yak-7A, -7B and the -7MPVO. Structurally the Yak-7 retained its two-seat trainer configuration, the rear cockpit space being used for equipment in the front-line fighter versions. Reconnaissance was a primary role of the Yak-7B which carried a camera in the rear cockpit while the MPVO sub types were intended as dual day or night interceptors. Other examples were used to test equipment and a few served as prototypes of versions that were not built in quantity.

Specification: Yak-7
Type: Single-seat fighter
Manufacturer: Yakovlev
Entry into service: October 1940
Length: 27 ft 9.75 in (8.48 m)
Height: 8 ft 8 in (2.64 m)
Wingspan: 32 ft 9.75 in (10 m)
Weight empty: 5,137 lb (2,375 kg)
Range: 582 miles (850 km)
Max speed: 373 mph (600 km/h)
Service ceiling: 32,800 ft (10,000 m)
Armaments: 1 x 20-mm ShVAK cannon firing through propeller hub and 2 x 7.62-mm ShKAS machine guns in upper front fuselage; up to 220 lb (100 kg) of bombs on wing racks

Below: One of the earlier Soviet fighters, the Yak-7 undertook many important sorties when the fate of Russia hung in the balance.

YAKOLEV YAK-3

A culmination of all that had been learned from combat with the earlier Yakolev single seaters, the Yak-3 emerged as one of the most capable fighters of the war. In contrast to Western designs, it appeared under-armed but it reflected a long-standing Russian philosophy of obtaining fine aerodynamic capability through the use of lightweight materials, particularly wood, which was easy to manufacture in vast numbers under less than ideal conditions. All these criteria the Yak-3 met admirably. Produced out of numerical sequence so that it entered Red Air Force service after the Yak-9, the Yak-3 flew for the first time in spring 1943.

The aircraft was in service in time to participate in the 1943 Battle of Kursk, which helped break the German stranghold on the central sector of the Eastern Front. So dangerous had the Yak fighters become that a directive was sent to Luftwaffe units to 'avoid combat below 5,000 meters with Yakovlev fighters lacking an oil cooler under the nose'!

Soviet airmen welcomed the nimble and tough Yak-3 which had an even better performance than its forerunner. All wartime examples had the 1,225 hp VK 195PF engine which enabled the aircraft to attain a top speed of 404 mph . A hallmark of Russian fighters was seemingly light armament although it had been a German philosophy in the Bf 109F (similarly armed to the Yak-3) that this did not prevent good pilots scoring kills, with the advantage of a light, very manoeuvrable airplane. In the Yak-3 that was particularly true.

As well as being the mount of many Soviet aces, French airmen of the Normandie-Niemen Regiment flew the Yak-3 in action over the Russian Front. The unit ended the war with a score of 273 victories, 99 of them on the Yak-3.

Below: Preserved in France this Yak-3 represents the *Armée de l'Air*'s effort in the East.

Specification: Yak-3
Type: Single-seat fighter
Manufacturer: Yakovlev
Number built: 4,848
Entry into service: July 1943
Length: 27 ft 10.25 in (8.50 m)
Height: 7 ft 10 in (2.39 m)
Wingspan: 30 ft 2.25 in (9.20 m)
Weight empty: 4,960 lb (2,250 kg)
Range: 506 miles (815 km)
Max speed: 404 mph (650 km/h)
Service ceiling: 35,450 ft (10,800 m)
Armaments: 1 x ShVAK cannon on centreline plus 2 x 12.7-mm BS machine guns in cowling

YAKOVLEV YAK-9

Experience with the Yak-1 and Yak-7 led to the Yak-9 which gained a fame far beyond its Russian frontiers and for good reason, for it was among the best fighters in its class anywhere. Making greater use of light alloy, supplies of which were unexpectedly assured when the limit of the German advance could be quantified, Soviet plants geared up to build enormous numbers of Yak-9s, a goal they rapidly achieved.

The new fighter had its origins in a much modified Yak-7 that was in November 1942 reworked as the Yak-9/M-106. A new designation was thought appropriate to distinguish a Yak-7 derivative with metal wings and numerous other refinements.

An all-round-vision canopy was fitted and armament was restricted to fixed guns, without any provision for external ordnance. As was usual with fighter design the world over,

Specification: Yak-9U
Type: Single-seat fighter bomber
Manufacturer: Yakovlev
Number built: 16,796
Entry into service: January 1944
Length: 28 ft 6.5 in (8.70 m)
Height: 8 ft (2.44 m)
Wingspan: 32 ft 9.75 in (10 m)
Weight empty: 5,100 lb (2,313 kg)
Range: 550 miles (890 km)
Max speed: 435 mph (700 km/h)
Service ceiling: 34,500 ft (10,500 m)
Armaments: 1 x 20-mm ShVAK cannon on centerline plus 2 x 12.7-mm BS machine guns in forward fuselage

reliable engine power was the cornerstone of success. The Yak-9T became the first major variant, this being considered a tactical fighter with an anti-tank capability. Powered by the Klimov M-105PF engine, it had the cockpit moved back 15.75 in (400 mm) compared with the Yak-7 (as did all Yak-9s) and was powerfully armed with a centreline 37-mm cannon, plus a single fuselage-mounted UBS machine gun,

which was used primarily for sighting the cannon. The former weapon, designed to penetrate armour up to 48-mm thick, was devastating against most tanks, which a skilled Yak-9 pilot could destroy with a single well-placed round.

Having made its combat debut over Stalingrad in December 1942 the Yak-9 had, depending on model, a top speed of 331 mph (533 km/h) at sea level and 371 mph (597 km/h)

Below: With a crewman guiding the pilot, a Yak-9 taxies out for a sortie.

at altitude. This performance enabled it to combat the Bf 109 and Fw 190 on equal terms.

The similar Yak-9D (*Dalnosty* — range) had increased fuel capacity for greater range and the Yak-9P differed only in the type of machine gun fitted. Obtaining a better altitude performance (primarily to intercept high flying Luftwaffe reconnaissance aircraft) from what was essentially a low level, battlefield support fighter, was achieved in the Yak-9PD. A deeper radiator and larger oil cooler were fitted, the former being moved forward. Only a single ShVAK cannon was fitted and in this form the aircraft attained an altitude of 44,690 ft, about 10,000 ft greater than the standard service ceiling.

Dual combat and PR capability was provided in the Yak-9R and -9TK, the Yak-9K, which was based on the earlier Yak-9T (*Tankovyi* —tank hunting), being a second anti-tank variant with reduced fuel load, an optical gunsight and a muzzle brake for the centerline NS-45 cannon.

In the Yak-9B, an ingenious bomb container mounted aft of the cockpit held four tubes for FAB-100 bombs or containers holding 32 x PTAB bomblets which were usually dropped in level flight without special sights.

Various improvements resulted in further variants including the Yak-9DD, which was an escort fighter with extended range capabilty, the Yak-9M with a reinforced wing and the Yak-9M/PVO, which had multi-channel radio, IFF equipment and reduced fuel capacity.

A Yak-9V trainer was built in 1944 ,the Yak-9S following in 1945, a short-lived partial update which was better addressed in the Yak-9U. A prototype of this latter model first flew in November 1943 and was a major all round airframe upgrade with better armor protection, improved radiators, more efficient cockpit controls and, at long last in the view of the pilots who had to fly it, increased firepower. However, this latter remained at three guns,

invariably two fuselage mounted 12.7-mm UB MGs and either a ShVak 20-mm or MR-23VV cannon firing through the airscrew spinner. To better accommodate the many changes, the Yak-9U had the wing moved forward by 3.9 in (100 mm).

With such a superb fighter in their hands Russian pilots finally wiped out the memory of the 1941-42 defeats as they hounded the Luftwaffe to the gates of Berlin. Reaching 433 mph (575km/h) in level flight, the Yak-9U was on a par with the world's best fighters - but the major achievement by Russian engineers to turn a mediocre design into a war winner with hardly a pause in output was little short of amazing.

Below: Fast and agile the Yak-9 was one of the world's best wartime fighters.

UNITED STATES
OF AMERICA

BEECH 18 AND UC-45 EXPEDITOR

The USAAF first ordered the Beech 18S commercial light transport under the military designation of C-45 in 1940. This initial order, for just eleven examples, was followed by deliveries of more than 4,000 aircraft, a measure of the type's usefulness in military service.

Subsequently designated the C-45A, B, and F, the latter model being the 'standardised' type, the 'twin Beech' performed numerous useful roles, including those of VIP transport and crew trainer. As a navigational trainer the designation AT-7 was introduced, along with the name Navigator. Several examples

Specification: UC-45 Expeditor
Type: Light transport
Manufacturer: Beechcraft Aircraft Corporation
Entry into service: 1939
Length: 34 ft 3 in (10.4 m)
Height: 9 ft 9 in (2.8 m)
Wingspan: 47 ft 8 in (14.56 m)
Weight empty: 5,420 lb (2,460 kg)
Range: 1,200 miles (1,930 km)
Max speed: 225 mph (360 km/h)
Service ceiling: 26,000 ft (7,930 m)
Armaments: None

were fitted with twin Edo floats and skis could be fitted as an alternative.

Eventually the Beech production line turned out 549 AT-7 Navigators. Most were fitted with uprated P&W engines to cope with increased weight, the aircraft being a basic six seater, including accommodation for six students.

Previous page: A P-47D Thunderbolt in full 'Invasion' stripes.

Above: Trainer, liaison airplane and top brass runabout the Beech 18 was one of the world's most successful designs.

Left: This star-spangled Beech is one of many still flying in the US.

The 'Expeditor' is the generic name for an entire family of Beech twin engined commercial transports adopted by US military forces, the Expeditor was coined by the British who tended to name all US aircraft they ordered. The Beech 18 first flew in 1941 and about 350 were shipped to the UK for RAF use in the liaison and light transport role. Many found their way to the Far East, where twin engined reliability was desirable when flying over inhospitable jungle terrain.

As the UC-45 Expeditor (after January 1943) the aircraft was powered by two Pratt & Whitney Wasp Junior engines of 450 hp each, which enabled it to operate at a maximum speed of 225 mph (360 km/h) over a range of 1,200 miles (1,930 km).

Right: Fanciful schemes abound on Beech 18s in private hands.

Below right: Painted in early US Air Corps colours, the Beech is an air show regular.

Bottom right: Beech 18s were flown by many nations as this Canadian representative shows.

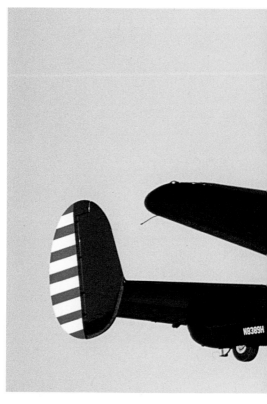

Below: Thousands of student aircrew remember the docile Beech.

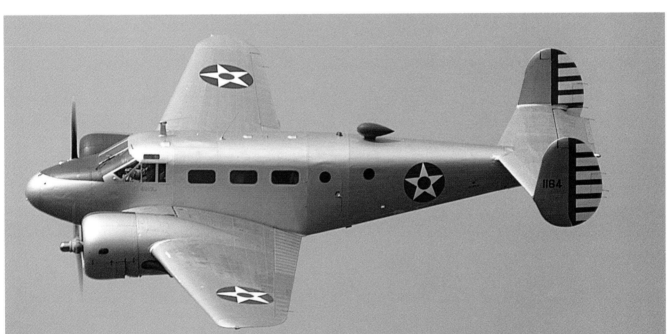

BEECH AT-11 KANSAN

Developed from the Beech AT-7, the AT-11 Kansan was a specialised bombing and gunnery trainer, ordered to enable the USAAF to supply an adequate number of combat crews to the war theaters as the American commitment increased. A bomb bay was cut in the floor and the extreme nose was modified to provide a realistic bombardier's station, complete with sights and bomb release gear.

Powered by P&W R-985-AN-1 engines, the AT-11 tipped the scales at a shade over 8,000 lb. Deliveries totalled 1,582, 36 examples being modified as AT-11s equipped for navsigation training. In addition, 24 AT-11s ordered by the Netherlands before the Axis powers curtailed such deliveries from abroad were impressed into US service.

Specification: Beech AT-11
Type: Bombing and gunnery trainer
Manufacturer: Beech Aircraft Corporation
Number built: 1,580
Entry into service:
Length: 34 ft 3 in (10.4 m)
Height: 9 ft 9 in (2.8 m)
Wingspan: 47 ft 8 in (14.5 m)
Weight empty: 8,160 lb (4,100 kg)
Range: 870 miles (1,390 km)
Max speed: 215 mph (344 km/h)
Service ceiling: 20,000 ft (6,100 m)

Above right: An AT-11 in the wartime colours of Nationalist China.

Top right: Olive drab early US based training twins.

Right: Smart 'natural metal finish' on an AT-11 navigation trainer.

BELL P-39 AIRACOBRA

Unlike some other WWII-era aircraft that departed significantly from accepted fighter design and were not put into mass production, the Bell P-39 turned in a reliable combat record. In common with numerous other types, it did so in a role for which it had not been primarily intended — that of ground attack. In the beginning, the Bell P-39 joined a fleet of international aircraft whose function was presumed to be that of bomber interception, this in the days before the war changed so many pre-conceived notions on combat aircraft.

When it first flew, as the XP-39, on 25 November 1939 the Airacobra was highly praised for its heavy 37-mm cannon armament, tricycle landing gear and engine, which was mounted behind instead of in front of the pilot. Looking conventional enough, the P-39 was different under the skin as the airscrew of the Allison V-1710-17 engine was driven via a five-foot extension shaft which allowed

ample room for the bulky cannon breech and its 30-round ammunition tank. The upper fuselage decking also had a pair of synchonised Browning machine guns enclosed within the very slim nose contours.

Unfortunately the P-39's overall performance turned out to be not as sparkling as the publicity men strove to make the pre-war world believe. Despite a number of changes made

> **Specification:** P-39Q
> **Type:** Single-seat fighter
> **Manufacturer:** Bell Aircraft Corp
> **Number built:** 9,588
> **Entry into service:** January 1941
> **Length:** 30 ft 2 in (9.2 m)
> **Height:** 11 ft 10 in (3.63 m)
> **Wingspan:** 34 ft (10.37 m)
> **Weight empty:** 5,600 lb (2,540 kg)
> **Range:** 675 miles (1,086 km)
> **Max speed:** 380 mph (612 km/h)
> **Service ceiling:** 35,000 ft (10,670 m)
> **Armaments:** (P-39D) 1 x 37-mm nose cannon
>   plus 2 x 0.50-in fuselage guns; up to 4 x 0.30-in wing guns
>   bomb on centerline rack

Right: P-39 trainers carried high visibilty 'buzz numbers'.

Below right: This US-based warbird represents the thousands of P-39s supplied to Russia.

Below: A revolutionary engine layout did not hamper the P-39 in combat.

to the XP-39, performance was still poor at altitude. Nevertheless an order for 80 aircraft had been placed in August 1939 comprising 20 P-39Cs and 60 fully militarised P-39Ds.

When the shooting war started and service chiefs knew the requirements for modern fighters, the last thing the USAAC or RAF wanted was to use the Airacobra as a front line interceptor against heavy opposition. The RAF turned down the P-39 after brief use by one squadron in England in June 1941.

But with little else to make up the numbers, the P-39 and its still-born RAF contract sister the P-400, were instead diverted to places such as Guadalcanal and the Marshall Islands, there to contain the Japanese until such times as something more effective was available. It was in April 1942 that the P-39D made its combat debut in the Pacific.

Contracts for the P-39 ran to more than 9,000, enabling Bell to

develop the line into the P-39F which was similar to the D apart from an Aeroproducts propeller replacing the Curtiss type. Then came the P-39K and L which were also similar and powered by a V-1710-63 engine. Installation of a V-1710-83 produced the P-39M, followed by the penultimate and most produced model, the P-39N. Finally there was the Q model, which had a 1,200hp Allison V-1710-85 engine.

Proving itself ideal in the ground attack role, USAAF P-39s gave a good account of themselves in the Middle East after Operation Torch, peak inventory of the Bell fighter being reached in early 1944 with 2,150 on strength. This figure was rapidly reduced as the US war inventory became adequately equipped with more modern fighters and the Aircacobra was released for sale or lease to Allied nations. Russia eagerly took up the American offer and eventual-

ly took delivery of 4,952. On the Eastern Front the P-39 was pressed into service in the traditional Red Air Force fighter role of ground support, a duty it performed remarkably well. Many of the top Soviet aces flew the Airacobra and it was probably more damaging to the enemy over the wastes of Russia than anywhere else. French and Italian airmen also flew the P-39 in action during the war.

During its production span the Airacobra's performance had remained more or less constant, the top speed rising from 368 mph to 385 mph; Bell had contained the inevitable weight spiral of military aircraft by keeping empty weigh down, the P-39Q being only about 200 lb heavier than the D model.

France and Russia were also the two nations that made most use of the derivative P-63 Kingcobra, which was not needed for service with the USAAF.

Below left: The Airacobra gave good early war service. This photograph shows well the high nose undercarriage.

Above: Many color schemes are applicable to preserved P-39s.

Below: A 'sand and spinach' Airacobra on a US flightline.

BELL P-63 KINGCOBRA

During WWII, the Bell Aircraft Company was if nothing else, innovative. Denied huge military contracts as a follow-on to the P-39, it nevertheless continued development of its radical single-seat fighter. The P-63 was the main result in terms of series production.

First flying as the XP-63 on December 7, 1942, the intended Airacobra successor was extensively tested, this programme extending into mid-1943. By that time an initial production order had been received and P-63 deliveries began at the end of the year.

The USAAF had in the meantime decided that it did not need the Kingcobra to equip its own units but the fighter could fill outstanding orders from abroad under Lend Lease arrangements. Bell completed 1,725 P-63s, the majority of them being shipped to the Soviet Union, where they performed well in the close support role, in much the same way as the P-39 had already done. France also received the P-63.

Various armament combinations were tested on the P-63, a single 37-mm nose cannon and two wing machine guns being standardised upon. Bombs could be also carried under the fuselage and the wings.

Production passed to the P-63C, 1,227 of which were built, the P-63D not being built. The war's end also curtailed the P-63E, all contracts being cancelled. USAAF use of the Kingcobra extended to the P-63As used as 'live' training targets under Operation Pinball. The idea was that the P-63s set themselves up to be shot at with frangible bullets, a strike triggering red wingtip lights, much like a pinball machine in an amusement arcade. Around 300 aircraft were modified for this unique role.

Specification: P-63A
Type: Single-seat fighter
Manufacturer: Bell Aircraft Corp
Number built: 1,725
Entry into service:
Length: 32 ft 8 in (10 m)
Height: 12 ft 7 in (3.84 m)
Wingspan: 38 ft 4in (11.7 m)
Weight empty: 6,694 lb (3,040 kg)
Range:
Max speed: 410 mph (655 km/h)
Service ceiling:
Armaments: : 1 x 37mm cannon, 2 x 50 cal machine gub in fuselage nose. Plus 2 x 50 cal guns in fairings undwer the wings.
   1 x 500lb bomb could be carried under the fuselage

Below left: This P-63 is now with the
Confederate Air Force.

Bottom left: Few original Bell P-63s
wore US camouflage, although the
Russian examples kept their paint

Above and Below: Bell developed the
P-63, adding a dorsal fin for late-war tests.

Right: France and Russia used the
P-63 in combat.

BOEING B-17 FORTRESS

Easily the most famous American bomber of the war, the 'Flying Fortress' won undying fame in the dangerous skies over Europe. The nickname was attributed to a Seattle Times newspaperman at the roll-out ceremony for the Y1B-17 prior to the first flight on 28 July 1935. The name stuck and the 'Fort' it became. A four-engined bomber was an enormous investment for both Boeing and the US Air Corps in those days and any positive publicity was more than welcome. Powered by the reliable 1,200 hp Wright R-1820 engine with exhaust-driven turbochargers for high altitude flight, the first production model, the Y1B-17 flew without a dorsal fin and had hand-held armament set to fire from streamlined blisters with limited fields of fire.

Specification: B-17F
Type: Long-range heavy bomber
Manufacturer: Boeing Airplane Co
Number built: 12,371
Entry into service: January 1937
Length: 74 ft 9 in (22.8 m)
Height: 19 ft 1 in (5.8 m)
Wingspan: 103 ft 9 in (31.47 m)
Weight empty: 32,720 lb (14,855 kg)
Range: 1,100 miles (1,760 km)
Max speed: 287mph (462 km/h)
Service ceiling: 35,000ft (10,670 m)
Armaments: (B-17E) 10 x 0.50-in machine guns in nose, turret, ball, waist and tail positions; up to 6,000lb (2,724 kg) of bombs internally; (B-17F) up to 13 x 0.50-in machine guns in nose, turret, radio room, ball, waist and tail positions; normal bomb load as other models, some carried externally for special missions; (B-17G) up to 13 x 0.50-in machine guns in chin, cheek, turret, radio room, ball, waist and tail positions; normal bomb load as other models but absolute maximum of 12,800 lb (5,800 kg)

War reports from Europe influenced US industry in many ways, Boeing accordingly updating the B-17 to undertake possible 'modern' war sorties with a much improved chance of success and crew survival. This modernisation had only partially been effected when the B-17C made an uncertain combat debut in the hands of the RAF in Europe and in the early Pacific fighting. The Japanese found the B-17 a tough nut to crack and even though the

Above left: When Boeing had completed 5,000 B-17s, a G model was signed by war workers and named *Five Grand*.

Left: B-17Gs of the 381st Bomb Group fly a training mission over England.

Bottom left: A B-17F on test flight from Boeing at Seattle.

Below: Early camouflaged B-17Fs head for Germany, turret gunners alert.

bomber's participation in that theater was disappointing, valuable lessons were learned. The USAAC recommended further refinements and Boeing incorporated many of these in the first of the 'big tail' B-17s, the E model. This was followed by the further improved B-17F which flew thousands of sorties during the build up the 8th Air Force in England from August 1942. Among its missions the European Theater of Operations were the two 1943 Schweinfurt strikes, on which more than 120 were lost but whatever the target the B-17F sailed majestically through fighters, flak and weather to help deliver a high explosive coup de grace to the Third Reich. A spiralling casualty rate did not stop the 8th Air Force, and its companion 15th based in Italy, from pounding the Third Reich's industrial capacity to a vitual standstill.

Although the standard bomb load of a B-17 was a modest 6,000 lb (2,724 kg) in comparison with other Allied heavies, its defensive guns helped to significantly reduce the enemy fighter force — but it did need fighter escorts all the way to prevent losses reaching prohibitively high numbers. Many believed that the Fort could fight its way through to the target but events proved that this could not be done without decimated formations and many lost or wounded crewmen. A failed attempt to rectify the situation was the YB-40, a 'war-weary' B-17 crammed with guns intended as a destroyer hidden in regular bomber formations. It proved too slow to keep up and a long-range fighter was the real answer.

Those Fortresses brought down by head-on fighter attack in the grim air battles of 1943 helped create the B-17G, the last wartime production model with a lower nose 'chin' turret and hand held 'cheek' guns to ward off deadly frontal fire.

The increasing technical sophistication of the air war saw B-17s carrying radar into action for daylight BTO (Bombing Thru Overcast) sorties when clear visibility was denied to bombardiers who usually relied on the Norden sight. While the standard internal load sufficed for the vast majority of missions, some Fortresses carried additional bombs externally on fuselage racks for special missions. These included Disney rocket bombs designed to destroy U-boat pens, and some of the first US radio-controlled glider bombs. Old B-17s themselves became bombs when

Above right: The genuine article. A B-17F of the 8th Air Force photographed in 1943

Right: All preserved B-17s are late production G models.

Below right: A 381st BG B-17 leads a 'natural metal' Fortress from the 'Fireball Outfit'.

Below: Preserved B-17G marked as an 8th Air Force 17F.

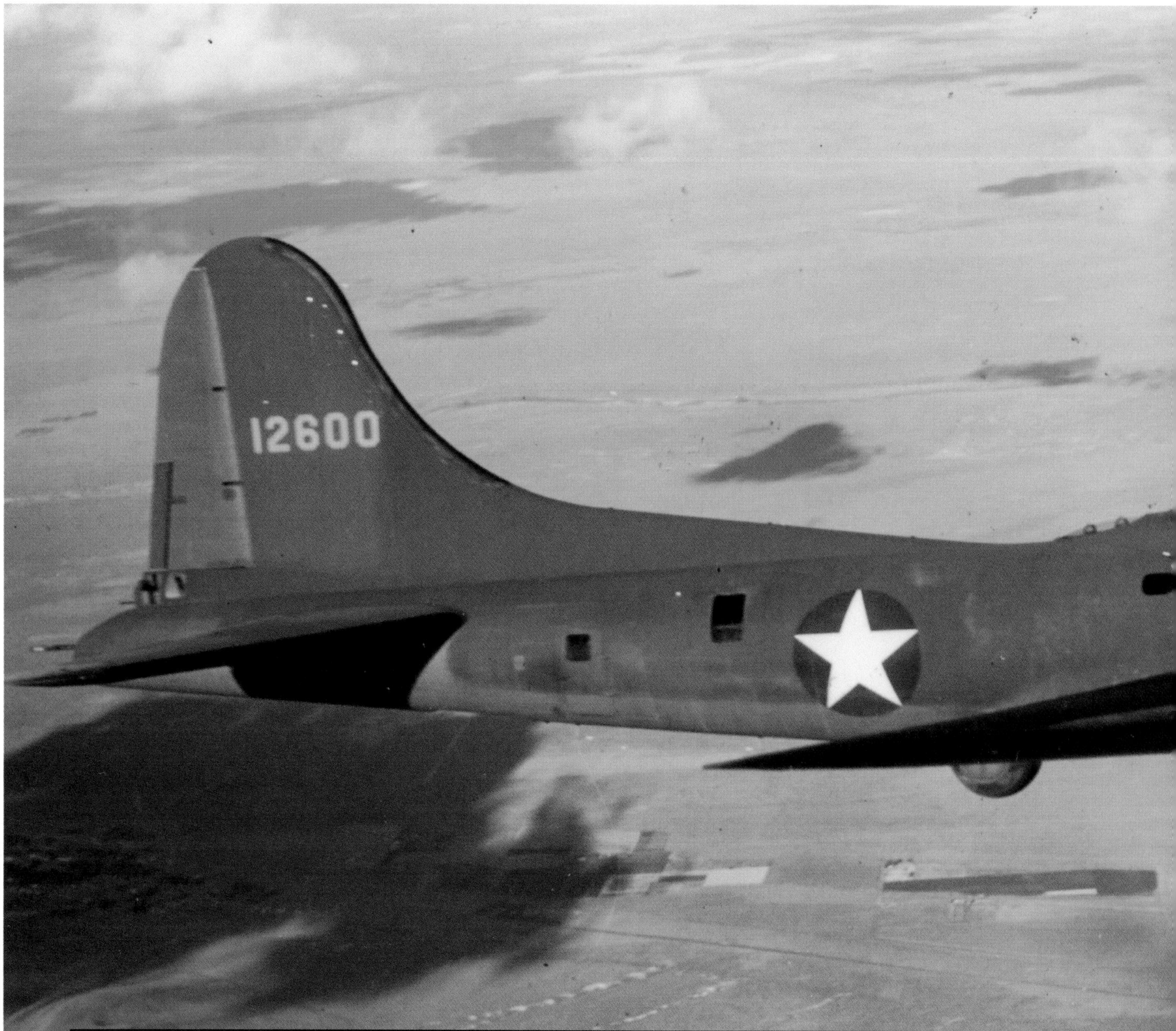
12600

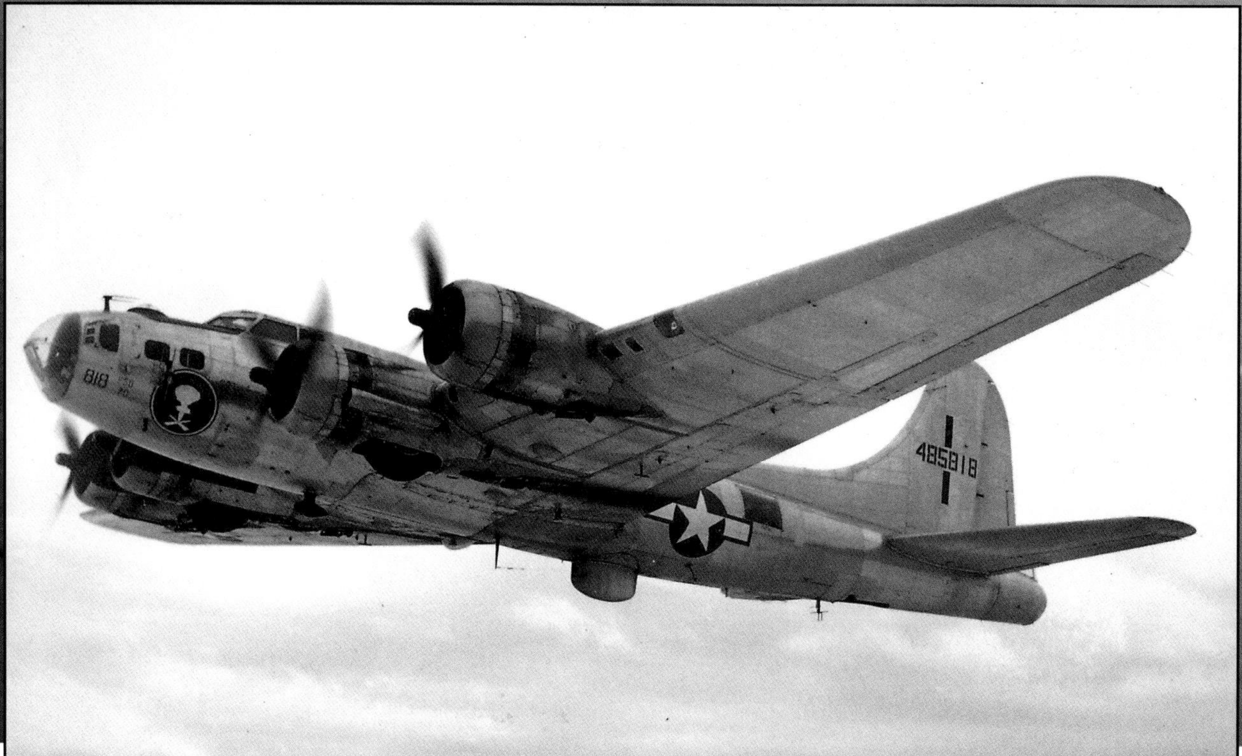
818
485818

Project Castor was launched to hurl pilotless Forts into German block-houses and other tough targets.

Used mainly in the European Theater, the B-17 got back into the Pacific war when rescue SB-17s dropped airborne lifeboats to downed aircrews and sailors.

By the time the European war ended the B-17 was nearly 11 years old but by anyone's reckoning it had been one of the USAAF's principal combat types.

Left: *Esmeralda* **was a B-17E pictured on test from Boeing**

Below left: A surplus B-17G with radar engaged on postwar weapons testing.

Below: A war-weary B-17F on a second-line training flight during the war.

Left: B-17Gs look a little like F models if the chin turret is left off.

Below left: One-wheel landings thrill air show crowds.

Bottom left: Famed as *Sally B* this UK based B-17 was painted for the movie *Memphis Belle*.

Right: Tender loving care is essential to keep warbirds flying.

Below: *Nine O Nine* of the 91st BG flew most 8th AF missions.

Bottom: Late war 8th AF markings on warbird B-17Gs.

Above: This B-17G is as fully equipped and armed as its wartime counterpart.

Right: A B-17G in the colours of the 34th Bomb Group of the 8th Air Force.

Below: B-17G *Nine O Nine* flies an airshow sortie.

BOEING B-29 SUPERFORTRESS

Destined to be remembered as the aircraft that finished WWII by dropping two atomic bombs on Japan, the Boeing B-29 was the culmination of conventional bomber design that had begun long before the conflict in which it won its spurs. Complex and expensive to build under an intensive 'war emergency' crash program, the B-29 entered combat later than had been hoped but it rapidly wiped out the ability of the Japanese to wage war as factory after factory in the home islands went up in smoke. Incendiaries and high explosives delivered almost exclusively by B-29s burned the heart out of the Japanese empire.

Initial high altitude, European type formation strikes on Japan by B-29s based in India met with only average success, due mainly to the relatively small numbers that could be deployed, and that ever present factor, weather.

But with bases in the Marianas secured, Gen Curtis LeMay Commanding General of XXIst Bomber Command, threw away the rule book and sent his Superforts in

at lower alititudes than was considered safe for heavy bombers. The results were spectacular. LeMay's very heavy bomb groups of the 20th Air Force began to systematically raze the Empire's cities to the ground.

Flying for the first time on 21 September 1942, the USAAF having ordered two 14 YB-29s and 500 production aircraft, Boeing

worked around the clock to meet demand. So great was the B-29 program that a network of plants, bringing in the facilities of Bell, North American, General Motors and Martin, had to be established. By a herculean effort these plants managed to complete more than 2,000 Superfortresses by VJ Day.

Defensively the B-29A was formidable. It was armed with 12

Specification: B-29
Type: Long-range heavy bomber
Manufacturer: Boeing Airplane Co
Number built: 2,181
Entry into service: June 1943
Length: 99 ft (30.2 m)
Height: 27 ft 9 in (8.46 m)
Wingspan: 141 ft 3 in (43.05 m)
Weight empty: 74,500 lb (33,795 kg)
Range: 3,250 miles (5,230 km)
Max speed: 357 mph (575 km/h)
Service ceiling: 36,000 ft (10,973 m)
Armaments: 1 x 20-mm cannon in tail turret and up to
   12 x 0.50-in machine guns in remotely controlled fuselage barbettes;
   up to 20,000 lb (9,072 kg) of bombs internally

.50-in guns, all but two of which were set in barbettes controlled by a remote sighting station which provided automatic tracking and ranging data. Rounding out the armament was a tail 'stinger' in the form of a 20-mm cannon and two machine guns. Combat brought about numerous changes to the B-29 in general and its armament was reduced to save weight when it was found that Japanese interceptors were far less coordinated or as numerous as their German counterparts and enemy AA fire was not the hazard it had been to bombers in Europe.

By the spring of 1945, 20 very heavy bomb groups had regularly had some 500 B-29s available for most missions from the huge Marianas bases. A 'halfway house' was established on Iwo Jima so that aircraft damaged in raids on Japan did not have to fly the entire distance

Below left: A B-29 hot off the Boeing line is flight-tested.

Above right: The Confederate Air Force maintains the B-29 Fifi in flying trim.

Below: Boeing at Renton built many wartime B-29s.

to their home base. This saved many crews from a risky ditching in the ocean not to mention a valuable aircraft.

The amount of destruction a single B-29 raid could inflict on Japanese cities was awesome. Toyko was devastated on an unprececented scale, greater than anything seen in Europe. The flimsy nature of Japanese buildings made them particularly vulnerable to incendiary bombs which the Superfortresses could haul across the Pacific on a regular basis in formations hundreds strong.

By mid-1945 the Manhattan Project had perfected the atomic bomb and on 6 August the first of these was dropped by a specially modified B-29 named *Enola Gay*.

This blast was followed by the devastation of Nagasaki on the 9th, bringing about the final surrender of the Japanese.

During the war Superfortresses were simply known as B-29s, without the familiar suffix letter to denote changes, for externally at least there were few major changes despite Boeing's multiple production blocks. Apart from a more streamlined profile when some of the gun turrets were removed, radar was the one item of equipment that altered the look of a B-29. When H2X was installed, the scanner necessitated a bulky ventral radome between the two bomb bays and some machines also had a small external ball radome at the extreme tail housing a gun-laying radar.

Top: A B-29 landing on a Marianas air base in late 1944.

Above: In Korea the B-29s were the mainstay of the UN bombing of the North.

Right: Sleek and well armed, the B-29 burned the heart out of Japan

Far right: An early production Superfort on its pre-delivery flight.

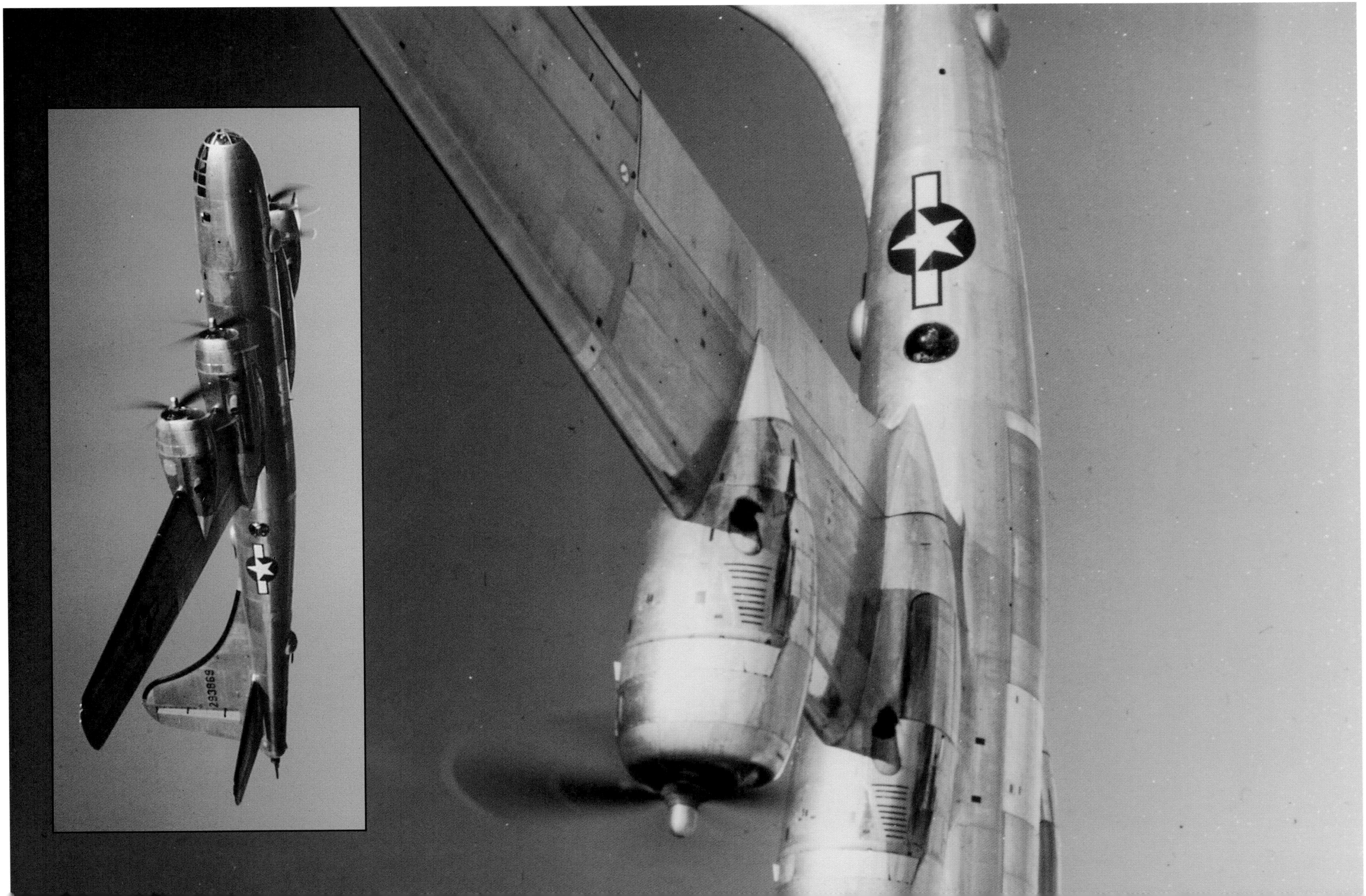

Above: Museum B-29s include this example named *Quaker City*.

Right: Korean veteran *It's Hawg Wild* is preserved at Duxford, UK.

Opposite, top: B-29 air show star *Fifi* makes a fine sight.

Opposite, centre: One of the earliest Confederate Air Force (CAF) acquisitions, the B-29 takes much dedication to keep it flying.

Opposite, below: Revving up its engines the CAF B-29 prepares for a show.

Overleaf: The CAF B-29 banks over Texas for the camera ship.

CHANCE VOUGHT F4U CORSAIR

One of the most outstanding fighters ever built, the F4U Corsair was highly regarded far outside naval aviation circles and was even contemplated as a practical escort for hard pressed USAAF bombers in Europe in 1943. First flown as the XF4U-1 on 29 May 1940, the Vought design was the first US warplane to exceed 400 mph in level flight. The early framed 'birdcage' cockpit canopy gave the pilot a restricted view and this was another reason why it was not immediately favoured as a carrier borne type. The original canopy, with minor changes, lasted through

Specification: F4U-1D
Type: Single-engined single-seat shipboard fighter
Manufacturer: Vought Aeronautics
Number built: 12,681 under various designations
Entry into service: July 1942
Length: 33 ft 8.25 in (10.27 m)
Height: 14 ft 9.25 in (4.49 m)
Wingspan: 40 ft 11.75 in (12.48 m)
Weight empty: 8,873 lb (4,025kg)
Range: 1,000 miles (1,609 km)
Max speed: 395 mph (635 km/h)
Armaments: 6 x 0.50-in wing machine guns and up to 2,000 lb (907 kg) of bombs on external racks; up to eight HVAR on wing racks

Above: Big and powerful, the F4U was one of the world's best carrier fighters.

Left: Wing folding was essential to stow F4Us in carrier hangars.

Far left: A preserved F4U Corsair leads a pair of FM-2 Wildcats.

Overleaf: Followed by another Corsair and an F8F Bearcat this F4U is one of many with the markings of Navy aces.

the F4U-1A but was changed to a 'bubble' canopy in the F4U-1D

Deliveries began in July 1942, the Corsair being powered by a 2,000 hp Pratt & Whitney R-2800-8 radial which was progressively uprated. The F4U-1A's R-2800 gave 2,250 hp with water-methanol injection, which gave it an outstanding performance compared with its main Japanese adversaries.

Carrier qualification trials were conducted by VF-17 beginning 25 September 1942. The results were not overly encouraging and the Navy rejected the Corsair as a primary carrier type. It was left to the Royal Navy, desperate for modern carrier fighters, to take the first aircraft into action. Launching from Fleet Air Arm carriers in 1943 the Corsair proved to be superior to any enemy aircraft it met, with a fine operating record. It was ironic that the US Navy held to its view that the Corsair's landing characteristics were too demanding for it to operate reliably from fleet carriers, despite eight months of Royal Navy experience.

It transpired that the British F4Us by having clipped wings (to allow them to stow aboard smaller RN carriers) and redesigned main oleos, had cured the alarming tendency of the aircraft to bounce on landing. It was left to the Marines to show that there were few problems in flying a full span F4U from a carrier deck, which the Corps proceeded to do.

The Navy re-examined the F4U and found that a potentially valuable aircraft was being denied a full carrier role. When modifications had been made to eliminate the bounce on landing, the Corsair passed fresh Navy scrutiny and was embarked in January 1944 for the type's first Navy war cruise — as a night fighter. The success of this cruise convinced the Navy and more squadrons were formed on the 'bent wing bird' well in time for the final assault on Japan's island bastions. Rugged enough to cope with crushed coral runways hastily laid down by the Seabees on Pacific islands, Marine F4Us fought ably in all the last Pacific campaigns, particularly Iwo Jima and Okinawa. Navy F4U squadrons embarked aboard Essex class carriers produced 24 aces on that type alone, while other pilots got part of their total on Grumman fighters as well as the Corsair.

Right: Authentic wartime markings are shown on this F4U — with that Bearcat closing in!

Below right: Navy ace Ira Kepford flew an F4U marked similarly to this warbird

Below: In French Suez operation markings this F4U-4 contrasts the Corsair warbirds in US colours.

CONSOLIDATED B-24 LIBERATOR

Built in greater numbers than any wartime bomber, the B-24 Liberator saw service around the world, flying missions everywhere that Allied forces operated. Like some of its smaller counterparts, the B-24 was the sole type in its category available for combat in some theatres and in areas such as China and Burma it remained the only US heavy bomber throughout the war. With huge production orders, Consolidated was able to adapt the basic design to undertake a variety of roles other than bombing, just some of which incuded transport, fuel tanker, radar-equipped 'snooper', maritime reconnaissance

Specification: B-24D-J
Type: Four-engined heavy bomber
Manufacturer: Consolidated Aircraft
Number built: 19,203
Entry into service: (USAAC) November 1941
Length: 67 ft 2 in (20.47 m)
Height: 18 ft (5.49 m)
Wingspan: 110 ft (33.5 m)
Weight empty: 37,000 lb (16,783 kg)
Range: 2,200 miles (3,540 km)
Max speed: 290 mph (467 km/h)
Service ceiling: 28,000 ft (8,534 m)
Armaments: (B-24D) 10 x 0.50-in machine guns in nose, turret, waist, tail and ventral positions; up to 8,000 lb (3,629 kg) of bombs internally

Above: A B-24J on a manufacturer's test flight.

Left: A B-24 pictured at Duxford before flying to the US for a museum.

Below left: A 'clean' B-24 testing its wings before USAAF delivery.

Far left: A mainly white colour scheme was used on UK-based PB4Y-1s

and patrol, electronic counter measures and formation 'lead ship' to assist regular bombers to form up.

British Liberators were instrumental in hunting U-boats far out into the North Atlantic and finally closing the Atlantic gap where the German boats had formerly been safe from air attack. Naval adapations under the designation PB4Y-1 flew from England to assist in this vital work. PB4Ys also patrolled the vast reaches of the Pacific, seeking out Japanese submarines and transports.

Navy Liberators later grew into the all-Navy single-tailed PB4Y Privateer which well lived up to its name in terms of sunken Japanese transports, wrecked port facilities and thousands of tons of supplies sent to the bottom. Flying countless miles on patrols often with the reward of little action on the fringes of the main thrust across the Pacific, the Navy Libs and Privateers did a vital if unsung job.

Among the Liberator's many claims to fame were the unescorted low level attack on the Rumanian oilfields at Ploesti on August 1, 1943, the first long-range strikes against Singapore and numerous gruelling flights over the Alps to tough German and Austrian targets as the backbone of the 15th Air Force based in Italy. It was an integral part of the dual B-17/B-24 double punch of the 8th Air Force in England.

Liberator transports, designated C-87s, flew dangerous sorties over the Hump, the Himalayan air bridge between India and Burma, to keep the forward combat units supplied with fuel and essentials. These tankers operated at great risk from enemy fighter attack and often appalling weather conditions that could destroy aircraft with terrifying ease.

The heart of the Liberator design was the Davis wing, which supplied substantial lift and enabled it to operate over ranges greater than any other Second World War bomber. It reflected a modern design approach in its tricycle landing gear — and also in its complexity, many of its operating systems being electrical.

First flight of the XB-24 took place on December 29, 1939 and initial production deliveries were as the LB-30A, a much needed transport model. Bomber versions were initially supplied to the RAF in June 1941 as Liberator Mk Is, the AAF

taking delivery of its first Liberators (B-24Ds) that November. Initial US combat operations were from North Africa and one unit, the 44th Bomb Group, shuttled back and forward between that theatre and Britain where it periodically joined the 8th Air Force daylight offensive.

Development programmes to keep the B-24 in the front line led to the upgunned B-24H and J models which had nose turrets.

Right: *Diamond Lil* **is the LB-30 transport Lib owned by the CAF.**

Below: With Mustangs of the 352nd FG keeping watch, 8th AF B-24s head for their target.

Above: Despite the 15th AF tail markings, this is the CAF's LB-30.

Left: Round engine cowlings denote a transport Liberator.

Below: The CAF Liberator has an early style greenhouse nose.

Above right and Right: A warbird B-24 with 15th AF markings on the right side and 8th AF on the left.

The B-24H was one of the final wartime Liberator variants.

CONSOLIDATED PBY CATALINA

Affectionately known as 'Dumbo' when they touched down to rescue Allied flyers obliged to ditch in the sea, the PBY Catalina enjoyed a combat record second to none, the vital task of air sea rescue being but one of its many roles. Catalina crews recall with pride the part the PBY played in giving the first airborne alert of the approaching enemy carrier force at Midway, the shadowing of the Bismarck into the north Atlantic and its part in defeating the U-boat in the Atlantic.

Flying for the first time on March 21, 1935 as the XP3Y-1, Consolidated won a contract to supply the first cantilever-wing flying boat to the US Navy against strong competition from Douglas. Powered by two 825 hp Twin Wasp radials, the early aircraft was fast for a flying boat, the 184 mph top speed causing great interest. The PBY-1 was first delivered to the service in October 1936. During 1939 with delivery of the Model 28-5 named Catalina to the Navy, three were bought by Russia with a view to license production as the GST and one by the RAF.

Specification: PBY-5A
Type: Twin-engined flying boat/amphibian
Manufacturer: Consolidated Aircraft
Number built: 3,276 (US/Can only)
Entry into service: Winter 1941
Length: 63 ft 11 in (19.5 m)
Height: 18 ft 10 in (5.65 m)
Wingspan: 104 ft (31.72 m)
Weight empty: 17,465 lb (7,974 kg)
Range: 3,100 miles (4,960 km)
Max speed: 196 mph (314 km/h)
Service ceiling: 18,200 ft (5,550 m)
Armaments: (PBY-5A) up to 5 x 0.50-in machine guns in bow, ventral and fuselage blister positions; underwing racks for up to 4,000 lb (1,814 kg) of bombs or depth charges or two torpedoes

Above: Cat on the prowl. A Navy patrol squadron PBY circa 1943.

Left: A taller tail identified the final Catalinas built.

Above right: A classic amphibian design the PBY was a winning wartime design.

Right: A refined hull and taller tail improved the last PBYs.

One of the first aircraft supplied to Britain under Lend-Lease to boost the patrol and anti-submarine capability of RAF Coastal Command, the Catalina was initially a flying boat per se. The high, pylon-mounted wing carrying the engines, the long sweep to the broad chord vertical tailplane and twin side blisters gave the Catalina a unique configuration. A nose turret, plus large fuselage blisters, carried the defensive guns although each position was ideally located for rescue work, often without the PBY crews having to get their feet wet!

The Catalina was given an important amphibian capability with the advent of the PBY-5A which first flew in this form on November 22, 1939. This more versatile model equipped many USN patrol squadrons as well as USAAF Emergency Rescue Squadrons around the world.

Under the Canadian name Canso the PBY also maintained a watch on Canada's vast coastline during the years of the U-boat menace. Consolidated produced its final Catalina model as the PBY-6A which had the standard hull but the larger area tail surfaces of the PBN-1 which was manufactured by the Government Aircraft Factory under yet another name, Nomad. These late war 'boats were significantly differ- ent to their forerunners, the basic Catalina design having undergone considerable modification. A new sharp bow section, a revised hull with new 'steps' and taller vertical tail surfaces with a wider span tailplane, were unmistakable. Production of the Nomad ran to 156 examples, 137 of them being supplied to the Russians to boost their own GST Catalina production (understood to have been about 150 aircraft) and the additional 48 PBY-6As furnished under Lend-Lease.

Right: Late-war PBY with radar in pod above the cockpit.

Inset: The original 'round tail' PBY flying in RAAF colours.

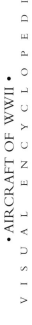

Above: Seen before a bad landing, this Cat was an air show favourite.

Left: Catalinas in Argentine Navy colours.

Below: A Catalina in the early war colours of the Netherlands.

Above right: Catalina makes an air show fly-by with its gear just retracting.

Below right: PBY in late-war US Navy colours.

Above: RAAF and US Catalinas on a rare flight together.

Left: The PBY could haul survivors in through the big fuselage blisters.

Below: The 'Dumbo' Cats saved many lives.

Above right: Devoid of nose turret and with a 'cropped' tail, this Cat is in late-war RAF colours.

Below: The RDAF was one of the last to use the PBY operationally.

CURTISS C-46 COMMANDO

With its portly fuselage able to accommodate cargo of around 12,000 lb (5,440 kg) the C-46 well complemented the more numerous C-47 on wartime operations. As the need for transports increased in proportion to Allied expansion around the world the C-46 came into its own in the Far East. Able to carry more and operate at higher altitudes than the C-47, the Curtiss transport was a natural choice for the Hump route over the Himalayas. In the South Pacific the Marine Corps version the R5C-1, equipped to carry 50 troops or freight, did sterling work on supply sorties to far flung bases. In Europe C-46s carried freight and towed gliders for the Rhine crossing in 1945.

The C-46 first flew as the CW-20 airliner on March 26, 1940, service deliveries of the A model starting in July 1941. With twin R-2800 radials, all C-46s were similar apart from 17 examples of the C-46E which had a stepped windscreen; all three other production models (C-46A, D, F) had smoothly faired cockpit windows.

Below: A smooth cockpit line was introduced after the first C-46s had been built with 'stepped' canopies.

Specification: C-46D
Type: Twin-engined transport
Manufacturer: Curtiss Wright Corp
Number built: 3,160
Entry into service: July 1941
Length: 76 ft 4 in (23.27 m)
Height: 21 ft 9 in (6.63 m)
Wingspan: 108 ft 1 in (32.92 m)
Weight empty: 29,483 lb (13,373 kg)
Range: 1,600 miles (2,575 km)
Max speed: 227 mph (366 km/h)
Service ceiling: 27,600 ft (8,410 m)
Armament: None

Top: A wartime Commando in USAAF olive drab and neutral gray camouflage.

Above: A C-46 is part of the CAF stable of flyable warbirds.

Overleaf: Big, fat and useful the C-46 backed up the C-47 to give the USAAF huge wartime air lift capability

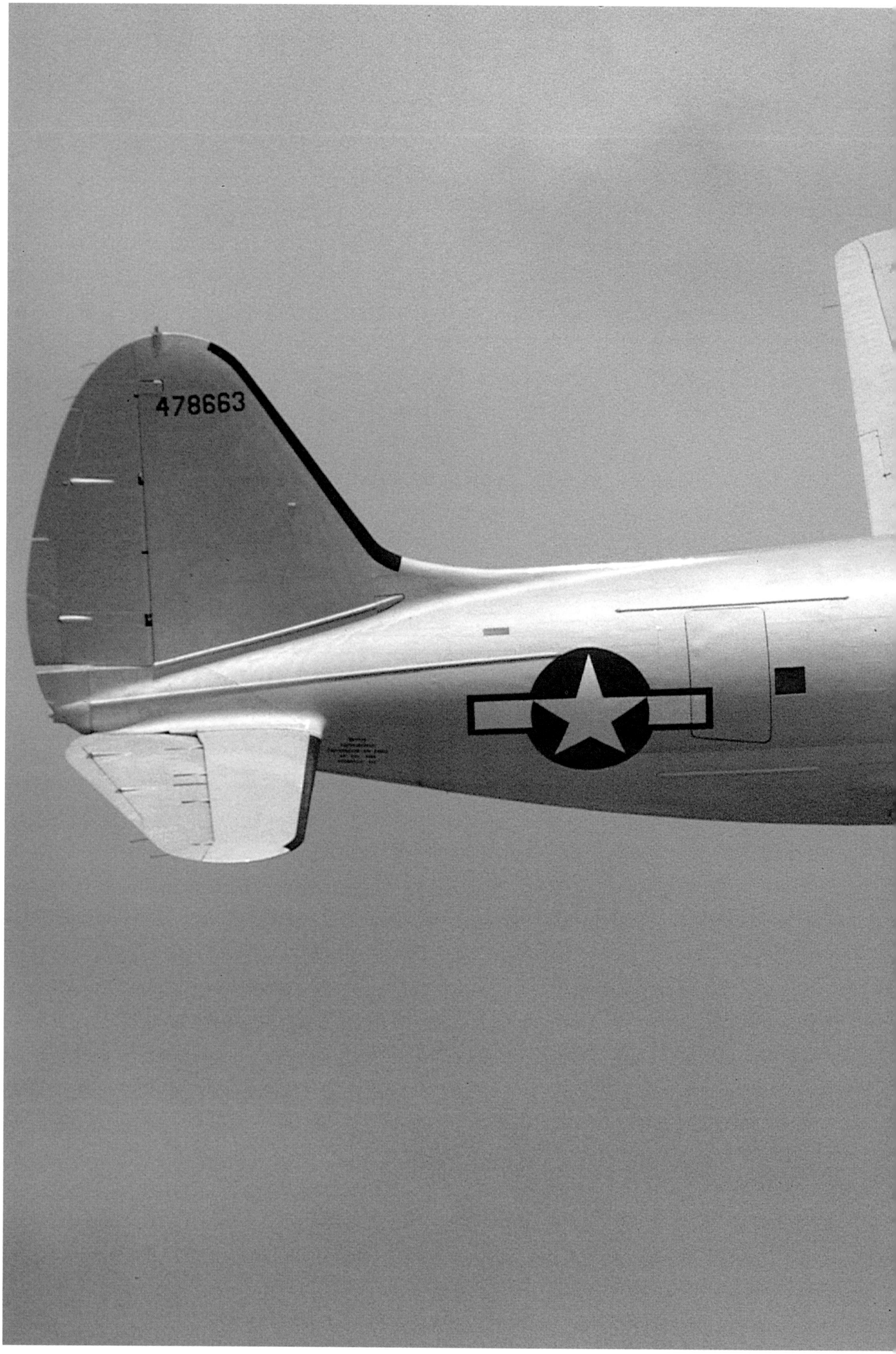
478663

CURTISS P-36

Destined not to see widespread service in American hands, the P-36 Hawk was nevertheless one of the few fighters able to give the Bf 109 a good run for its money during the early stages of the 1940 battle for France. Highly rated in French service for its heavy armament, the P-36 went on to serve briefly with the RAF in Burma and to see combat in the hands of the Finnish Air Force. In US service, the Hawk was too late to see much wartime service and was used mainly as a trainer.

First flown as the Model 75 in April 1935, the Curtiss design was powered by 900 hp Wright XR-1670 radial engine, this soon giving way to the XR-1820. Despite troubles with this new engine the Army ordered 210 P-36As on July 7, 1937. Before this order was completed the P-36C was introduced. This model had wing guns and more

Specification: P-36C
Type: Single-seat fighter
Manufacturer: Curtiss Wright Corp
Number built: 210
Entry into service: 1941
Length: 28 ft 6 in (8.69 m)
Height: 9 ft 6 in (2.90 m)
Wingspan: 37 ft 4 in (11.38m)
Weight empty: 4,620 lb (2,096 kg)
Range: 825 miles (1,328 km)
Max speed: 311 mph (500 km/h)
Service ceiling: 33,000 ft (10,000 m)
Armaments: 2 x cowl-mounted 0.50-in machine guns and
4 x wing-mounted 0.50-in machine guns

engine power but continual modification was required to rectify faults, the upshot being that the first pursuit squadrons, the 46th and 47th, did not receive the aircraft until 1941. Both units were in Hawaii on December 7 and the 46th scored two kills with the P-36. Overtaken by the pace of

aeronautical progress, the P-36 was considered obsolete by then and few saw combat in the Pacific.

Some 18 months before Japan brought America into the war, the Curtiss Hawk was considered to be anything but obsolete. In the Armée de l'Air the Hawk 75A-1, A-2 , A-3

**Above: In 'war games' camou-
flage, a P-36 beats the overcast.**

**Below left: A P-36 on test in
Britain during the war.**

**Below: French rudder stripes
show this to be an early Hawk.**

and A-4 saw much action when the
Germans invaded on May 10, 1940.
More French pilots reached ace
status flying the Hawk 75 than any
other type during the Battle of
France.

In November 1942 Vichy French
machines made a brief unsuccessful

attempt to challenge the Allies during Operation Torch in North
Africa. Service in Finland also belied
the Hawk's age although the RAF
aircraft inherited from France were
used mainly in the Far East, some
also being operated on second-line
duties in the UK.

CURTISS P-40 WARHAWK

Built in numbers high enough to ensure its deployment in many parts of the world when the Allied cause was taking a pounding from the Axis, the P-40 was available when little else was. Making an early stab at the enemy, P-40s took off from Bellows Field to hit the Japanese as they were attacking Pearl Harbor. Many enemy aircraft fell as a result of this courageous Air Corps action.

Subject of a continuous development programme, the P-40 eventually went into combat with two different types of engine, much improved armament, better cockpit visibility and a significant increase in capability; it remained in action in some parts of the world until the Axis finally surrendered.

Having produced a long line of Hawk fighters, Curtiss Wright substituted the radial engine of the 10th radial-engined P-36A for an Allison V-1710-19 air-cooled inline and redesignated it the XP-40. Having flown this prototype for the time on October 14, 1938, Curtiss was contracted by the USAAC to build 524 P-40s. Under a modified contract the company delivered 200

Specification: P-40B
Type: Single-seat fighter
Manufacturer: Curtiss-Wright Corp
Number built: 131
Entry into service: June 1941
Length: 31 ft 9 in (9.68 m)
Height: 12 ft 4 in (3.75 m)
Wingspan: 37 ft 4 in (11.36 m)
Weight empty: 5,590 lb (2,536 kg)
Range: 730 miles (1,175 km)
Max speed: 352 mph (566 km/h)
Service ceiling: 32,400 ft (9,875 m)
Armaments: 4 x 0.30-in machine guns in wings and
  2 x 0.50-in forward fuselage

Specification: P-40N
Type: Single-seat fighter
Number built: 5,200
Entry into service:
Length: 33 ft 4 in (10.6 m)
Height: 12 ft 4 in (3.75 m)
Wingspan: 37 ft 4 in (11.36 m)
Weight empty: 6,000 lb (2,722 kg)
Range: 750 miles (1,207 km)
Max speed: 343 mph (552 km/h)
Service ceiling: 38,000 ft (11,582 m)
Armaments: 6 x 0.50 in wing machine guns plus up to
  1,500 lb (680 kg) of bombs on belly and wing racks

early aircraft identified by the company designation Hawk 81-A2 rather than 'P-40A'. There followed the P-40B, which first flew on March 13, 1941. Similar to earlier machines the 131 P-40Bs retained the carburettor air intake above the nose, flanked by fairings over the barrels of twin 0.50-in machine guns firing through the airscrew disk. Armour plate was introduced and the wing guns were doubled to four.

In the P-40C, 193 of which were built, self-sealing of the fuel tanks was improved and two more wing guns were added. The 1,040 Allison V-1710-33 engine powered all the early model P-40s, which took the name Warhawk.

Apart from the destruction of 73 Curtiss fighters on the airfields adjacent to Pearl Harbor on December 7, 1941 and the concurrent action by US pilots to fend off the attack in P-40s, the Warhawk made its mark in China. There, the American Volunteer Group — the famed Flying Tigers — began

Below left: So many P-40s were flying in the US that wartime two-seaters became common.

Above right: Sharkmouths adorn most warbird P-40s.

Below: Well-painted P-40E shows the favourite Warhawk colours — the Flying Tigers.

operations against the Japanese from late December 1941.

An engine change, to the Allison V-1710-30, brought about the P-40D which had the fuselage guns removed and the wing weapons changed to 0.50-in Brownings. Drop tank racks and belly and wing pick-up points were also introduced on this model. Only 22 went to the USAAF, the bulk of production (560) going to the RAF as the Kittyhawk I.

The appearance of the similar P-40E saw production upped substantially to 2,320 examples and although the top speed was boosted

to 354 mph (570 km/h) compared to the 360 mph (579 km/h) of the D model, the aircraft was capable of a further increase in performance. This was achieved with the P-40F, which was powered by a Rolls-Royce Merlin 28 engine which enabled this model to achieve a top speed of 373 mph (600 km/h). From the P-40F-5 the fuselage was lengthed by 20 in, making the overall length 31 ft (9.44 m), 1,311 examples of the P-40F being built.

The long-fuselage P-40K reverted to the Allison V-1710-73 engine, some examples also having a small dorsal fin added to control a

Above: Even late-war P-40Ns have teeth today!

Right: The wartime Warhawk teeth craze was started by No 112 Sqn, RAF in the desert.

Below right: Flying Tigers' P-40B markings on a P-40N.

tendency to swing on take-off. The real answer to this problem was to lengthen the fuselage again and after 1,300 P-40Ks had been completed plus 600 similar P-40Ms with the Allison V-1710-81, Curtiss turned to improved models designed to keep the Warhawk in the front line.

Weight inevitably offset the improvements possible with a rapidly ageing design and the 700 P-40Ls had two wing guns removed, less armour and reduced fuel capacity, thus saving about 250 lb (113 kg). It was not really enough but the most-produced model, the P-40N, was more drastically lightened by 8,850 lb (4,014 kg) which enabled a top speed of 378 mph (608 km/h) to be attained by early aircraft with four guns. Six guns became standard and the majority of the 5,218 P-40Ns built were so armed.

Many P-40s went to Allied nations, Russia alone taking 2,397. From a peak US inventory of around 2,500 in April 1944, replacement by more modern types saw the number of P-40s rapidly dwindling until by July 1945 only one USAAF group was equipped with the type.

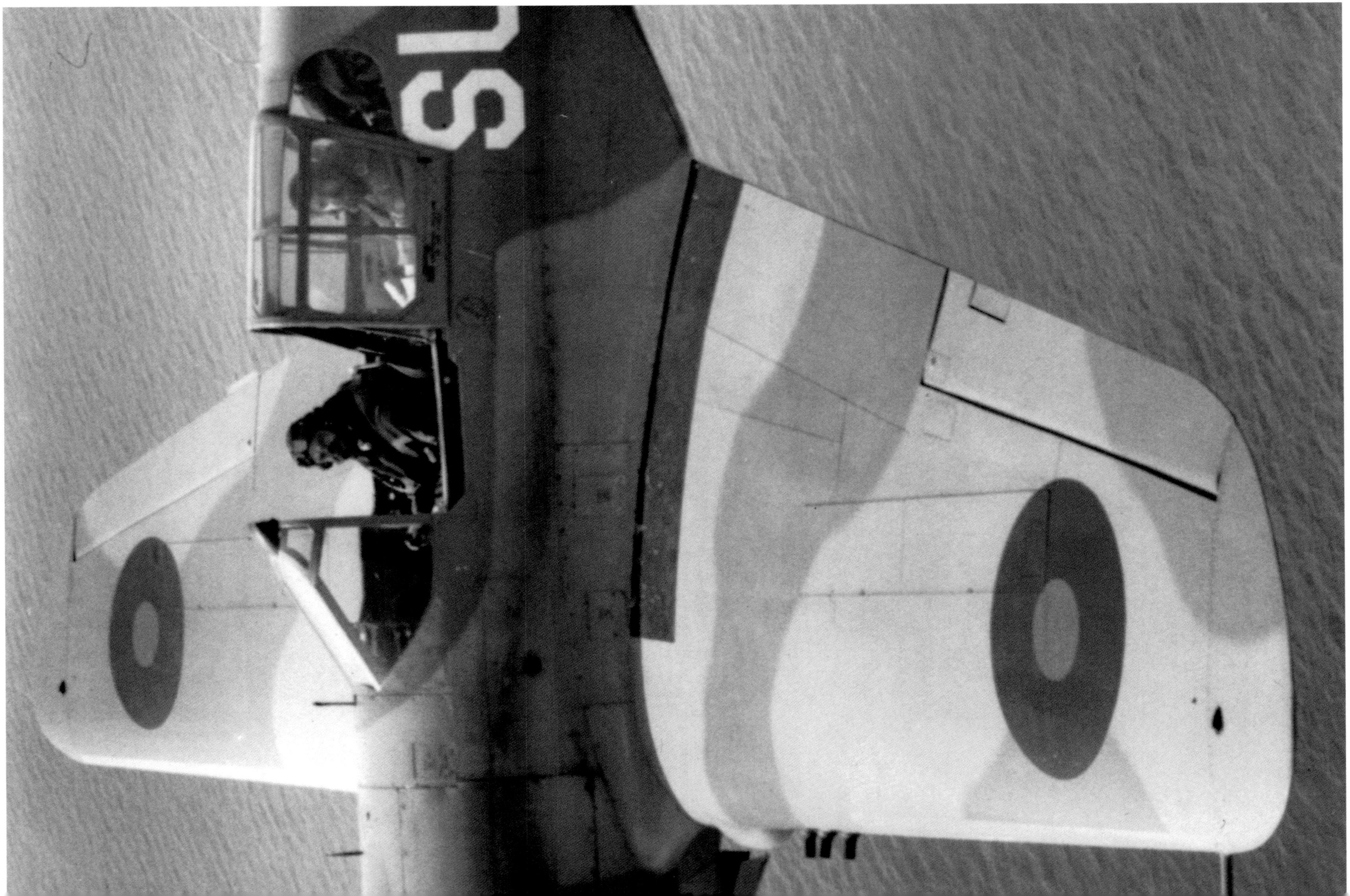
SU

CURTISS SB2C HELLDIVER

Winning a reputation as a naval attack aircraft in the face of many difficulties, the Helldiver managed to make a significant contribution to Naval victory in the Pacific. Unenviously having to succeed the Douglas SBD, victor at Midway and held in very high regard by its crews, the Helldiver would have to have been outstanding to be accepted right away. Outstanding it was not, at first. Despite being more modern, more powerful and better armed than its forerunner, it was also heavy and paradoxically, underpowered.

The XSB2C-1 flew on December 16, 1940, a time when the US air services were coming to terms with their needs for new aircraft; the Navy particularly explored the desirability of dive bombers versus torpedo bombers, it also being assumed by service chiefs that dive bombers would become an integral part of the Army's inventory. New naval aircraft therefore had ideally to undertake specific roles that would be adaptable fit all requirements. It was partially this that prevented the Helldiver from entering production until June 1942, plus the many changes required after early flight trials. The loss of the prototype within days of the maiden flight did not help matters.

With production underway by June 1942, the Navy was able to conduct carrier trials early in 1943, these showing that the SB2C needed dedicated work to bring it up to the required reliability for carrier operations. There were doubts that this could be achieved, but by then the die was cast; with the SBD phasing out, the Navy had little choice but to persevere with the 'Beast' (a nickname that derived from the growling noise its brakes made) to cure its

Specification: SB2C-4
Type: Two-seat dive and torpedo bomber
Manufacturer: Curtiss-Wright Corp
Number built: 1,194
Entry into service: December 1942
Length: 36 ft 8 in (11.2 m)
Height: 16 ft 11 in (5.1 m)
Wingspan: 49 ft 9 in (15.2 m)
Weight empty: 11,000 lb (4,990 kg)
Range: 1,110 miles (1,786 km)
Max speed: 281 mph (452 km/h)
Service ceiling: 24,700 ft (7,530 m)
Armaments: 2 x 20-mm wing cannon and 2 x 0.50-in machine guns for rear defence; up to 1,000 lb (454 kg) of bombs internally and on wing racks

drawbacks enough to pass it as carrier qualified. This finally occurred in time for the Helldiver's initial war sorties against Rabaul on November 11, 1943. A continuing programme to improve the SB2C led to the SB2C-3, SB2C-4 and SB2C-5, all of which differed in detail, an obvious external change being the introduction of a frameless cockpit canopy on the -5.

In the event the Helldiver was to prove very capable of doing the job it was designed for; USN carrier air

Below left: Preserved SB2C in wartime carrier markings

Bottom left: The Helldiver was an effective attack bomber.

Above right: Note 'bent' pitot head and tailhook on this warbird.

Below: An SB2C-4 with wings folded.

groups had with the Helldiver and Avenger the opportunity to tailor each of its attack aircraft to the roles they were best suited to. Therefore the Helldiver handled bombing missions, usually attacking its targets in a dive, while the TBF used torpedoes — on the relatively rare occasions that this weapon was still used — as well as bombs and rockets.

Among the Helldiver's claims to fame are the sinking of the IJN *Yamato*, the super-battleship that represented almost the last gasp of the Imperial Navy's surface fleet when it sortied against the US invasion forces in Leyte Gulf in 1944. A storm of bombs from wave after wave of Helldivers and TBFs quickly sank the ship.

DOUGLAS A-20

One of a long line of aircraft in the unique US 'attack' category, the Douglas A-20 Havoc joined a number of modern twin-engined bombers in the Allied inventory able to keep pace with the rapidly changing requirements of air combat. Along the way the A-20 proved capable of undertaking many roles which ensured its deployment through to the end of the war.

Flying in prototype form as the Douglas DB-7 on October 26, 1938 the forerunner of the A-20 was a slab-sided aircraft that belied its later potential. But innovative features such as a tricycle landing gear were to prove fortuitous in the war still

Specification: A-20G
Type: Three-seat light bomber
Manufacturer: Douglas Aircraft Co
Number built: 7,385
Entry into service: 1939
Length: 48 ft 10 in (14.88 m)
Height: 17 ft 7 in (5.36 m)
Wingspan: 61 ft 4 in (18. 69 m)
Weight empty: 12,950 lb (5,874 kg)
Range: 1,000 miles (1,610 km)
Max speed: 351 mph (565 km/h)
Service ceiling: 25,300 ft (7,720 m)
Armaments: 6 x 0.50 in machine guns in solid nose plus
2 x 0.50 in machine guns in dorsal turret for rear defence;
up to 4,000 lb (1,814 kg) of bombs in internal bay plus
up to 2,000 lb (907 kg) on wing hardpoints.

months away. The French Government, with indigenous new designs not yet in service, turned to America for modern aircraft and 100 DB-7s were ordered in February 1939. Such orders boosted the US industry at a time when revenue was sorely needed, putting many of them on a much firmer footing.

After the French armistice a number of DB-7s arrived in Britain, the forerunners of substantial orders for bombers, intruders and night fighters. British orders were placed without delay.

By December 1941 the US was at war; the US Army deployed the A-20C, the 15th BS flying the first missions by the 8th Air Force in England in July 1942. Early models were also sent to the Pacific where A-20s were first adapted to the role of 'strafer' to attack enemy shipping at mast height with guns and bombs.

Improvements to the A-20 resulted in the A-20G which modernised rear defence with a low drag Martin dorsal turret with two 0.50-in machine guns. The similar A-20J and A-20K had clear bombardier noses.

An aircraft that was the subject of smaller production contracts than its immediate successors, the A-20 was therefore spread a little thinly in some war theatres, there being three light bomb groups in England with the 9th Air Force and one in the Mediterranean. Three groups went to the 5th Air Force where they followed the advance across the Pacific often striking from rough forward airfields to harass enemy shipping.

Lacking any night fighters when the war broke out the USAAF adopted the P-70, a version of the A-20 that filled an important gap pending the service debut of the P-61. As well as operating in the front line in the Pacific, the P-70 undertook an important training role for crews of night fighter groups. Fitted with AI radar, the P-70 soldiered on against the Japanese until replaced by the P-61.

Many A-20s also boosted the striking power of the Red Air Force when the type was offered under Lend-Lease arrangments; 2,908 eventually went to Russia. RAF and SAAF squadrons deployed the A-20, under the name Boston, as a primary tactical bomber in North Africa when along with US aircraft of the 12th Air Force's 47th Bomb Group, it made a significant contribution to the defeat of Rommel's Afrika Korps and the Italian forces fighting on the southern front.

Far left: The CAF A-20 is a rare bird indeed.

Top left: The CAF A-20 represents the wartime combat group.

Above left: A-20s of the wartime 9th Air Force flying a typical tactical formation.

Left: A second line A-20 used on war transport duties.

DOUGLAS A-26 INVADER

Bringing the markedly differing requirements inherent in the US attack, light and medium bomber categories together in a single airframe was achieved remarkably well by Douglas in the A-26 Invader. Destined to replace both the B-26 Marauder and A-20 Havoc, the Invader was a relative latecomer to combat in Europe, late in 1944. Initial reaction by combat crews well used to the older types, was not always positive. But when crews converted they quickly enthused over the A-26's capability and quickly put it on the map. Examples reached the Pacific in time to action in the hands of three groups and it appeared in Italy to replace long serving A-20s in

Specification: A-26 Invader
Type: Three-seat light attack bomber
Manufacturer: Douglas Aircraft Co
Number built: 10,000
Entry into service: December 1943
Length: 50 ft (15.24 m)
Height: 18 ft 6in (5.64 m)
Wingspan: 70 ft (21.43 m)
Weight empty: 22,370 lb (10,145 kg)
Range: 1,400 miles (2,253 km)
Max speed: 355 mph (571 km/h)
Service ceiling: 22,100 ft (6,736 m)
Armaments: (A-26B) 10 x 0.50 machine guns in 'solid' nose and two remotely controlled fuselage barbettes; (A-26C) 2 x 0.50-in machine guns in 'clear' nose and four in fuselage barbettes plus up to eight machine guns in detachable underwing pods; up to 4,000 lb (1,824 kg) of bombs in fuselage bomb bay

the Mediterranean Theatre of Operations. One unit, the 39th Bomb Group, had begun the war in the MTO flying B-26s, had changed to B-25s and finally wound up in the Pacific as an A-26 outfit.

First flown as the XA-26A on July 10, 1942, the A-26's combat debut was delayed for various reasons, not the least of which was awaiting for the AAF to decide exactly what main role it wanted the aircraft to undertake. The wartime success of the single-seat fighter bomber had tended to reduce the need for medium bombers, although one twin could carry more ordnance than a fighter and a crew of three or four men had advantages, particularly in navigation and the operation of radar and blind bombing aids.

The A-26 was almost a victim of its own versatility as it could handle conventional bombing and ground strafing with a variety of weapons in a 'solid' nose, guns up to 75-mm calibre being tested. Powered by two 2,000 hp Pratt & Whitney R-2800-27 or -79 engines the Invader had a top speed of 355 mph making it the fastest US aircraft in the 'light to medium' category. As a strafer, the A-26B carried six 0.50-in guns in the solid nose, plus four more in remotely sighted dorsal and ventral turret and up to four twin gun packages could be carried below the wings. An internal bomb bay was able to accommodate up to 4,000 lb of mixed ordnance, normal load comprising eight standard 500 lb HE bombs.

It was November 9, 1944 before the A-26 entered front line service with the 9th AAF in the European Theater, where it initially began to replace the A-20 Havoc and at a slower rate, the B-26 Marauder. Both A-26Bs with a strafer nose and A-26Cs with a bombardier nose were issued to combat groups and these were operated on an 'as required' basis. Making its combat debut in the appalling winter of 1944/45, the A-26 crews were often confronted with cloud-covered targets that were bombed 'blind' on the signal of a lead navigator.

In the event the USAAF did not adopt the heavier gun noses flown experimentally on the early A-26s, a brace of standard 'fifty calibres' doing the job well enough — as one of the most heavily armed aircraft of the war, the Invader carried an ample number of these on every mission.

When the B-26 Marauder was phased out, the Invader became the B-26 when the 'attack' category was largely dropped from the inventory by the new United States Air Force. Ever since, the Invader and the Marauder have tended to be confused with each other, which is not surprising.

Far left: Windows were added to some surplus A-26s bought for executive use.

Left: Wartime A-26s were built with solid and clear bombardier noses.

Below: On final approach is the CAF B-26B painted in Korean war colours.

Above: The sleek lines of the A-26 are enhanced by removal of turrets.

Right: A Pacific war scheme was chosen for *Daisy Mae*, an A-26B.

Below: This A-26B also lacks turrets but owners do try to add them when they can be found or fabricated.

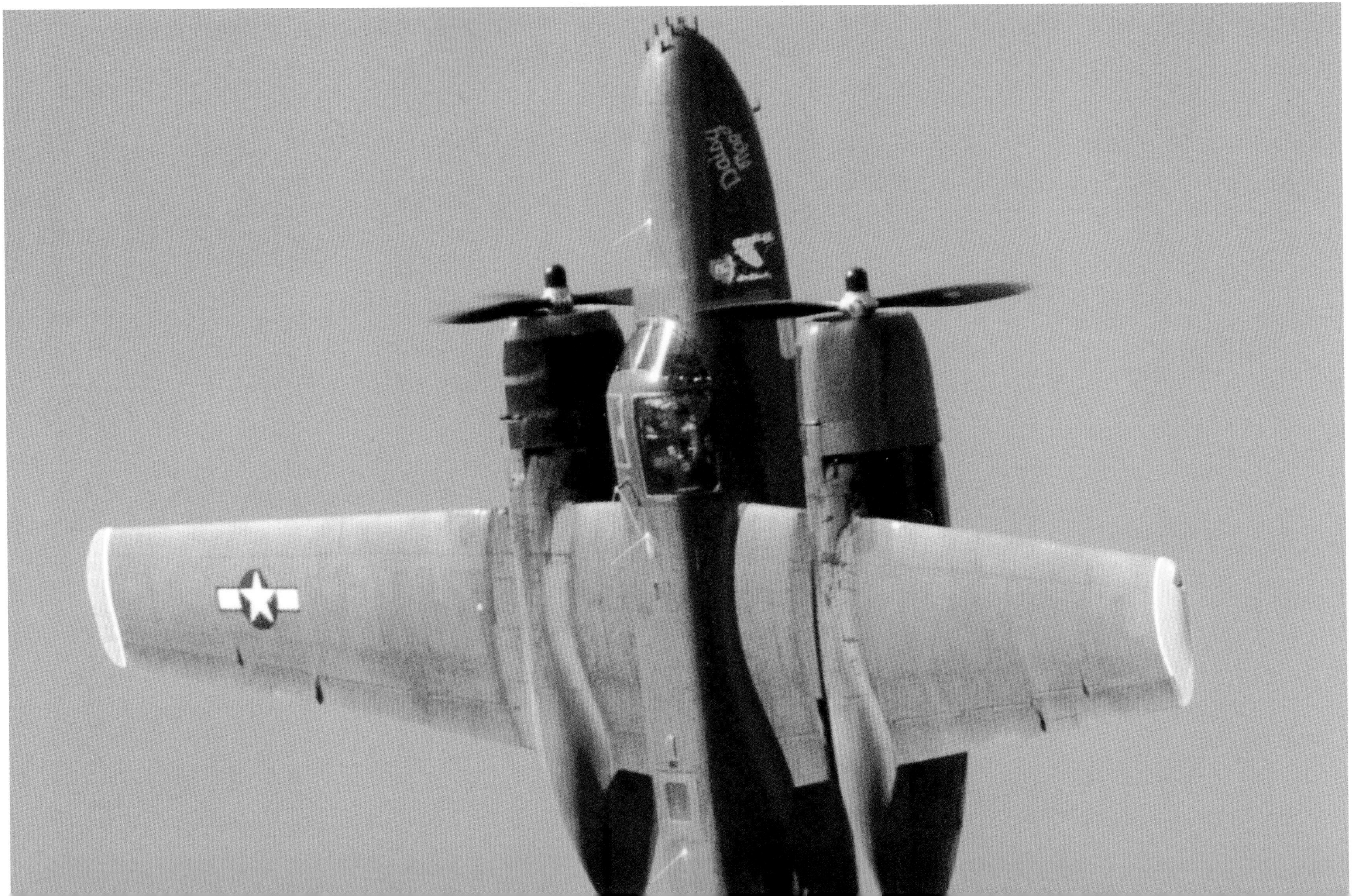
Daisy Mae

DOUGLAS C-47 SKYTRAIN

Few aircraft in history made such a contribution to winning a war without firing a shot in anger as did the Douglas C-47 Skytrain. Its huge catalogue of epic wartime operations incuded Overlord, Market Garden and the Rhine — all would have been very difficult if not impossible, without a fleet of military 'Douglas Commercial Threes'.

An aircraft that set new standards in the airline business it was built for, the DC-3 first flew on December 17, 1935. Military interest in its capabilities as a transport had already been shown by a purchase of the DC-2. After necessary modifications to the DC-3 which mainly centered on adding greater strength to the cabin floor, fitting fuselage loading doors and more powerful engines, the first Army orders for the C-47 were placed in 1940.

The engines of the C-47 were 1,200 hp Pratt & Whitney R-1830-92 radials, the aircraft having an operating weight of

Specification: C-47A
Type: Twin-engined transport
Manufacturer: Douglas Aircraft Co
Number built: 10,048
Entry into service: October 1938
Length: 64 ft 5.5 in (19.64 m)
Height: 16 ft 11 in (5.16 m)
Wingspan: 95 ft (28.96 m)
Weight empty: 16,970 lb (7,700 kg)
Range: 2,125 miles (3,240 km)
Max speed: 230 mph (370 km/h)
Service ceiling: 23,000 ft (7,000 m)
Armaments: None in US service but offensive loads carried by some aircraft in Russian and Finnish service.

29,300 lb (13,290 kg) although later models were cleared to fly at 35,000 lb (15,875 kg). Orders for the USAAF rapidly ran into thousands and the C-47 gave way to the C-47A which had a 24-volt as against a 12-volt electrical system. The following C-47B had R-1830-90 engines with high-altitude blowers and extra fuel especially for

operations in the China-Burma-India (CBI) theatre. The C-47 rapidly filled out other important roles such as that of navigational trainer.

When Air Transport Command was formed on July 1, 1942 the C-47 was its primary type; the USAAF's Troop Carrier Command was also formed that year and again the Skytrain represented the backbone

of the service it provided to military forces around the world. As a paratroop transport the C-47 was superior than any other aircraft type and it was also adapted to tow gliders to boost the number of troops that could be placed in a drop zone. This capability proved particularly useful on D-Day when the bulk of the Allied airborne forces were ferried to France by C-47s. One day before D-Day in Europe, Burma was invaded, the C-47 spearheading the assault by towing in Waco CG-4 troop-carrying gliders.

The C-53 Skytrooper was intended to carry personnel and only one entry door was provided; 20 of the 221 built were passed to the US Navy as R4Ds. The C-117 was

Far left: A C-47 in Argentine Navy colours shows how wide its customer appeal was.

Above left: C-47s make popular warbirds, too.

Left: D-Day stripes and 9th AF markings recall the most important C-47 war theatre.

Below: The RAF was a major C-47 user.

designed to carry staff officers in airline comfort and these as well as other variants with different designations, served long after the war.

Few British Army paratroopers will ever forget that the C-47 or Dakota was almost literally the only aircraft there was to carry them into battle; converted bombers were a very poor alternative and fortunately few of these had to be used. American transports aided the RAF when there was simply nothing else.

Some combat operations demanded appropriate equipment and radar training was brought into the front line by some C-47As fitted with H2S sets located in the fuselage aft of the wing. Radar was used for pathfinding purposes when overcast conditions obscured drop zones.

C-47s carried a variety of special loads, from field guns to mules and ice cream to ammunition. Slightly hampered by its side-loading configuration which would not allow passage for some very bulky loads, the Skytrain did have extra carrying capacity under the fuselage, a provision for freight panniers being an early USAAF requirement.

So versatile was the C-47 that the one drawback was that more of them had not been built; Eisenhower called the C-47 one of the four war-winning weapons the US had developed. Most Allied nations operated C-47s and the Russians built it as the Lisunov Li-2 with some fundamental airframe changes. There were a number of variants, some of which were armed.

Imitation by the enemy may not be readily appreciated in time of war but the Japanese built C-47s under a prewar license. Showa and Nakajima produced it for the IJN as the L2D2, 3 and 4 codenamed 'Tabby' by the Allies and inevitably some were destroyed in combat by US aircraft.

Right: Early US Army markings on a warbird C-47.

Below right: The classic C-47 'tail dragger' lines are seen well here.

Bottom right: Many C-47s have become movie stars.

Below: A C-47 and C-46 show their different noses.

458

A C-47 complete with 'Rebecca' homing aerials sits on a flightline with a C-46 and other Skytrains.

DOUGLAS SBD DAUNTLESS

By turning part of its designation into 'Slow But Deadly' US Naval aviators flying the Douglas Dauntless developed a fierce pride in their ability to dive-bomb their targets. That they could do this with accuracy was proven to the world during the battle of Midway when Dauntlesses sank four Japanese carriers and tore the heart out of the Imperial Navy's fleet. Indelibly stamping the SBD's place in history the Midway operation saw 128 dive bombers available for combat as the two sides prepared for action in June 1942. It was the Dauntless crews, diving into the melee caused by the enemy concentrating on warding off

Specification: SBD-3

Type: Two-seat dive bomber

Manufacturer: Douglas Aircraft Co

Number built: 5,936

Entry into service: Summer 1939

Length: 33 ft (10.06 m)

Height: 12 ft 11 in (3.94 m)

Wingspan: 41 ft 6 in (12.65m)

Weight empty: 6,535 lb (2,970 kg)

Range: 456 miles (730 km)

Max speed: 252 mph (406 km/h)

Service ceiling: 24,300 ft (7,400 m)

Armaments: 2 x 0.50-in wing machine guns and 2 x 0.50-in machine guns for rear defence; up to 1,000 lb (450 kg) bomb on external belly rack and 2 x 100 lb (45 kg) bombs on wing racks

low level, far less effective, American attacks, that did so much fatal damage to the IJN carriers.

Flying as the XBT-1 in July 1935 the development period to bring a new dive bomber into US Navy service was to take some time. Numerous tests and fly offs with rival designs were necessary before even the Dauntless forerunner was cleared for carrier operations.

The actual prototype Dauntless, the XBT-2, did not make its maiden flight until July 23, 1938, with the SBD-1 entering Navy service in June 1940. All SBDs, incuding the -2,-4, -4 -5 and -6 were externally similar but with detail improvements

Below left: SBDs rev up on a carrier deck shortly before they fought at Midway and changed the course of the war.

Above: This Dauntless was one of the first warbirds acquired by the CAF.

Below: Marked as a US Army A-24, this Dauntless represents the less successful part of the SBD's career.

such as self-sealing fuel tanks, additional armour, fuel capacity and in the SBD-6, a 1,350 hp R–1820-66 engine.

The Dauntless's relatively brief carrier career was all but over, in first line terms, by 1943 when its intended successor the SB2C Helldiver, began to join the fleet. The Dauntless was one of those designs that managed to bridge the gap between pre-war hypothesis and combat reality where other types such as the Devastator could not. But further modification of the SBD airframe would have been impracticable. The short time that this transition took surprised many people but it meant that modern, much improved aircraft were needed very quickly indeed.

Apart from the Navy, the Marine Corps which had been the first recipient of the type, continued to use the SBD to good effect on ground support operations, particularly during the Philippines campaign of 1944-45, where some units were still flying the type when the war ended.

The admirable early naval career of the SBD was not repeated by its Army A-24 equivalent. Ordered when dive bombing appeared to be an important capability for the Air Corps to possess, olive drab Dauntlesses were desperately deployed against the all-powerful Japanese. In small, ineffective numbers, the A-24 made no difference to the early war situation.

Left: The Navy and Marines were the main SBD users.

Below: Midway era markings on an SBD.

Bottom: Taxying an SBD.

Right: Note the 'Cheese grater' dive flaps and open wheel bays.

Below right: Warbird Dauntless on flightline.

GRUMMAN F4F WILDCAT

First of the Grumman 'Cats' to see combat in the Second World War, the F4F is remembered as another of an august band of aircraft types that so ably 'held the line' when Allied fortunes were at their lowest. Its early fame stemmed from the fighting in the Pacific but Wildcats did their bit to reduce the German U-boat menace by being one of the earliest types supplied to Britain under Lend-Lease. Put to work on escort carriers, the Wildcat was instrumental in sowing the seeds of Kriegsmarine defeat in the battle of the Atlantic. The XF4F-2 first flew on September 2, 1937.

The Pacific theatre had an urgent need for modern fighters to stem the Japanese at sea and on land and there were 88 machines attached to the air groups that emerged victorious at Midway. The price was 26 Wildcats lost. Marine F4Fs would later fight a gruelling rearguard action at Guadalcanal until the enemy finally abandoned the Solomons in 1943.

Wildcats were also the first US Navy fighters to see combat in Europe during Operation Torch when F4Fs took on rogue French air units that challenged the Allied

invasion of North Africa in November 1942.

Development of the F4F extended to the FM-2 which was fitted with a taller fin and rudder, to become the most capable of the Wildcat line. Flying for the first time in March 1943, it was built entirely by General Motors under contract to Grumman which was fully occupied with Hellcat production by that time. Able to carry HVARs or bombs as well as its fixed guns, the

'wilder Wildcat' was given an important new lease of life which freed up the fleet units flying F6Fs and F4Us on the fast carriers for the final operations against Japan. For its part the FM-2 was formed into smaller air groups which deployed aboard escort or 'Jeep' carriers. These groups, equipped mainly with Wildcats and Avengers, provided excellent back up to the fleet so that the issue of control of the Pacific was never really in doubt.

Specification: F4F/FM-2
Type: Single-seat fighter
Manufacturer: Grumman Aircraft
Number built: 7,251
Entry into service: November 1940
Length: 28 ft 9 in (8.5 m)
Height: 11 ft 11 in (3.6 m)
Wingspan: 38 ft (11.6 m)
Weight empty: 4,649 lb (2,767 kg)
Range: 900 miles (1,448 km)
Max speed: 318 mph (509 km/h)
Service ceiling: 35,000 ft (10,670 m)
Armaments: (F4F-4) four 0.50-in wing machine guns plus
   2 x 250 lb (113 kg) bombs on underwing racks or
   (FM-2) eight 2.75 HVAR on zero length wing launchers.

Above: A taller tail gives away this FM-2, marked as an F4F.

Right: Even earlier Navy F4F markings are applied to this FM-2.

Below left: The FM-2, the 'wilder' Wildcat.

Below: These markings were applied to FM-2s operating from 'Jeep' carriers

Brothers in arms, the FM-2 and F4U.

GRUMMAN F6F HELLCAT

Arguably the most successful shipboard fighter of all time, the F6F Hellcat was a brilliant example of combining sound engineering skills with the results of combat experience. Younger sibling of the F4F Wildcat, the Hellcat probably did more than any other US naval aircraft to defeat the Japanese.

Taking pilot experience with the F4F when finalising the design of its successor, Grumman had the F6F at least in mind as early as February 1938 when it envisaged a new fighter built around the Pratt & Whitney R-2600. The company went for a more conventional design than the F4F with its fuselage-mounted

Specification: F6F-3
Type: Single-seat shipboard fighter
Manufacturer: Grumman
Number built: 12,275
Entry into service: January 1943
Length: 33 ft 7 in (10.24 m)
Height: 13 ft 1 in (3.99 m)
Wingspan: 42 ft 10in (13.06 m)
Weight empty: 9,101 lb (4,128 kg)
Range: 1,090 miles (1,755 km)
Max speed: 375 mph (603 km/h)
Service ceiling: 38,400 ft (11,705 m)
Armaments: 6 x 0.50-in wing machine guns; up to 2,000 lb (907 kg) of bombs or eight HVAR on underwing racks

Above: An F6F-3 with three drop tanks flown by a carrier air group CO.

Left: A modern air show sometimes includes an F6F, although few remain.

Above right: Deadly looking F6F night fighters protected carriers from enemy attack.

landing gear which had to be labori- ously cranked up by hand and inevitably gave it a narrow track not ideal for carrier operations. With a big engine the F6F would be heavier and it emerged with a landing gear that retracted backwards into the wing the wheels turning through 90 degrees to lie flat in their bays. Design work lapsed for some two years while Grumman fulfilled con- tracts for the F4F but the F6F project was revived in September 1940.

By the time the Grumman mock-up was inspected by the Navy in January 1941 the XF4U-1 had become a significant factor in future planning for carrier operations; the Grumman F6F was envisaged as a Corsair alternative, a very wise move as it transpired.

Grumman flew the prototype Hellcat, as the XF6F-1, on June 26,

1942. The engine chosen to power production machines was the P&W R-2800 and the initial contract was placed about five months before the maiden flight of the prototype. The initial model was the F6F-3, first flown on October 3, 1942.

The F6F-3 was progressively improved during the course of pro- duction, which ran to 4,402 aircraft; among these was the radar-equipped F6F-3E night intruder, the F6F-3N night interceptor and the camera- equipped F6F-3P. The majority of Hellcats were, however, first line fighters pure and simple. Drop tanks, shackles and bomb rack were intro- duced during production, late war aircraft also being fitted with rocket launching capability.

The F6F-5 was the only other major wartime model of the Hellcat, this flying for the first time on

April 5, 1944. Powered by the P&W R-2800-10W engine with water injection it incorporated numerous detail changes and refinements as a result of combat, incuding a revised 'frameless' windshield. The two rear windows aft of the cockpit canopy that served to externally identify the F6F-3, were deleted. An additional bomb could now be carried on the inner wing racks, as could up to six HVARs on 'zero length' wing launchers.

At least 306 pilots achieved ace status while flying F6Fs with US Navy squadrons during the war, a larger figure than for any other air- craft type. And the Hellcat obtained a better kill-to-loss ratio of 19:1 — a figure unrivalled by any other type — for its Navy and Marine pilots were credited with 5,156 victories for the loss of just 270 F6Fs.

Left: F6Fs were the best Navy fighters in the Pacific.

Below left: An F6F with its intended successor, the F8F Bearcat.

Above: The F6F, a true war winner.

Right: A single belly tank took F6Fs into Japan's back yard.

Below: One of the many Hellcat aces is remembered by F6Fs such as this.

GRUMMAN F8F BEARCAT

One of the smallest fighters ever ordered by the US Navy, the Grumman F8F was to be the successor to the F6F Hellcat, the intervening number being taken up by the F7F Tigercat. The latter was, at the other end of the spectrum, a twin-engined fighter, the largest the Navy had ever ordered.

Delieveries of the F8F commenced before the war ended and carrier qualification trials looked set to be completed before the war with Japan ended., In the event the atomic bomb strikes curtailed operational deployment of the Bearcat in WWII.

Orders were maintained however despite contractural cutbacks and the F8F became a useful interim link between the piston engine and the turbojet in carrier aircraft. The post-war Navy deployed it from carriers and adopted for an initial type for its aerobatic team the Blue Angels.

Specification: F6F-3
Type: Single-seat shipboard fighter
Manufacturer: Grumman
Number built: 12,275
Entry into service: January 1943
Length: 33 ft 7 in (10.24 m)
Height: 13 ft 1 in (3.99 m)
Wingspan: 42 ft 10in (13.06 m)
Weight empty: 9,101 lb (4,128 kg)
Range: 1,090 miles (1,755 km)
Max speed: 375 mph (603 km/h)
Service ceiling: 38,400 ft (11,705 m)
Armaments: 6 x 0.50-in wing machine guns; up to 2,000 lb (907 kg) of bombs or eight HVAR on underwing racks

Right: Highly manoeuvrable, the F8F would have decimated the Japanese but the war ended before it got into combat.

Below right: Tiny compared with other USN fighters, the Bearcat was only used in combat by France.

Below: An early F8F warms up on a windswept carrier deck.

Grumman exported the Bearcat to the French, hard pressed in their war in Indo China in the early 1950s and these were the only F8Fs to see action. Operating from land bases, the Armee de l'Air hauled many tons of bombs and napalm to Viet Minh positions, to no avail. But pilots appreciated the versatility and manoevrability of the long-legged F8F and its ability to use forward landing strips without difficulty.

GRUMMAN TBF AVENGER

Named to reflect the nation's outrage over Pearl Harbor the Grumman TBF Avenger was thrown into action for the first time during the pivotal battle for Midway Island in April 1942. The new aircraft did not do well and five out of six were destroyed. Quickly putting that episode — which revealed few inherent problems with the Grumman design — behind them, TBF crews quickly mastered an aircraft that was surprisingly large for a carrier-based type but proved highly effective in combat. By the time the US Navy began operations on the long road back to Japan, the TBF was an integral part of the carrier air groups. Along with the F6F Hellcat

Specification: TBF-1C
Type: Three-seat torpedo bomber
Manufacturer: Grumman Aircraft
Number built: 9,836
Entry into service: January 1942
Length: 40 ft (12.19 m)
Height: 16 ft 5in (5.00 m)
Wingspan: 54 ft 2 in (16.51 m)
Weight empty: 10,080 lb (4,572 kg)
Range: 1,215 miles (1,9,55 km)
Max speed: 271 mph (436 km/h)
Service ceiling: 22,400 ft (6,830 m)
Armaments: 1 x cowl-mounted 0.50-in machine gun; 2 x 0.50-in wing-mounted machine guns plus 2 x 0.50-in machine guns for rear defence; one 22-in torpedo or up to 2,000 lb (907 kg) of bombs in fuselage bay

and SB2C Helldiver, these groups made an unbeatable team.

Avengers lived up to their name on numerous occasions, among them the reduction of the island garrisons of Saipan and Guam and the sinking of the mighty Japanese battleship Yamato. Having broken the enemy radio codes the Americans could set ambushes to prevent elements of the Imperial Fleet causing much disruption to their own operations.

Left: Able to deliver bombs and torpedoes with equal accuracy the TBF was a USN mainstay. This one wears Royal Navy colours.

Above: Early USN TBFs made their debut at Midway.

Below: An early CAF TBF at Harlingen, Texas.

Over the islands still held by the enemy Avengers 'softened up' enemy pillboxes, airfields and buildings and helped the ground forces winkle diehard troops out of well hidden foxholes. Using guns, bombs, rockets and napalm, Navy Avengers plastered a long list of targets.

Flying for the first time on August 7, 1941 the XBF-1 showed need for some improvements although a production contract had already been awarded for 286 aircraft. One of the most important early modifications was the addition of a dorsal fin to restore stability, a feature retained on all future aircraft. The TBF went operational on June 4, 1942, the Midway battle resulting in the disappointing early loss of five aircraft. Nothing daunted, the US Navy worked with Grumman to establish the type firmly in fleet inventory, the TBF-1 later being

joined by the TBM-1. This revised designation indicated an important second production centre at General Motors, which eventually built 2,882 TBM-1s and 4,4664 TBM-3s. Grumman bowed out after building 2,290 TBF-1s in order to make factory space primarily for the F6F.

The improved TBM-3 was similar to the TBM-1 and all wartime Avengers differed little externally, aside from equipment such as radar pods and ordnance. As it was built to attack targets with bombs or a torpedo the TBF handled the latter duty on the relatively few occasions when 'tin fish' were used, leaving dive bombing to its stablemate the SB2C Helldiver. Rockets also entered the Avenger's armoury, the aircraft being equally at home with British-type rail launchers and US 'zero length' launchers under the wings.

Authentic wartime markings adorn these two warbird TBFs.

Left: Postwar Avenger.

Below left: USS *Bunker Hill*'s arrowhead identification sits well on a warbird TBF.

Above: Tailhook extended, all this TBF lacks is a ventral gun.

Right: A long fuselage bomb bay enabled the TBF to deliver a variety of ordnance.

Below: This view shows the bomb bay doors opening.

LOCKHEED P-38 LIGHTNING

Designers of some of the outstanding combat aircraft of WWII were blissfully unaware how significantly natural hazards could adversely effect the performance of their brainchild. The P-38 was a fighter that excelled in the warmer conditions of the Pacific yet suffered a significant degree of technical malfunction in the damp, cold skies of Europe. In many minds this has tended to sully its reputation — and nothing could be less deserved.

In the Pacific the P-38 gave excellent service. It proved well able to take on the more nimble Japanese fighters once sound tactics had been developed and it became the favoured mount of numerous aces. A mission of extreme importance undertaken by the P-38Hs from Henderson Field, Guadalcanal, was to intercept the party of Admiral Yamamoto. To complete the mission

required a long-range flight of some 550 miles (885 km) but the Lightnings were there on time to shoot down the Japanese admiral's G4M 'Betty' bomber, a feat that may well have shortened the war. Among

the many highly skilled Army pilots that made the P-38 famous was America's top ace, Maj Dick Bong.

The XP-38 first flew on February 11, 1939. It appeared sleek and futuristic for its day and by the

Specification: P-38J
Type: Twin-engined single-seat fighter
Manufacturer: Lockheed Aircraft Co
Number built: 9,923
Entry into service: June 1941
Length: 37 ft 10 in (11.53 m)
Height: 12 ft 10 in (3.91 m)
Wingspan: 52 ft (15.85 m)
Weight empty: 14,000 lb (6,401 kg)
Range: 1,880 miles (3,025 km)
Max speed: 360 mph (579 km/h)
Service ceiling: 44,000 ft (13,410 m)
Armaments: 1 x 20-mm cannon and 4 x 0.50-in machine guns in fuselage nose and up to 2,200 lb (998 kg) of bombs on underwing hardpoints

time war came it was reckoned to be an exceptional fighter with heavy firepower, good range and the safety factor of two engines. Lockheed chose Allison V-1710-27/29 engines of 1,150 hp to power the first YP-38 pre-production models, as well as the first 30 P-38s from a contract for 673 aircraft. The balance were P-38Ds, followed by the P-38E and the similar P-38F. The latter had uprated engines and inner wing racks for bombs or drop tanks, later production aircraft incorporating what was known as a 'manoeuvring flap' which significantly enhanced the efficiency of the wing and gave a positive boost to performance.

Such attributes came together in the Pacific; the distances over which the 5th Air Force's P-38s were often required to operate were gradually extended with drop tanks. Although P-38s had been stationed in Iceland on the US entry into the war, the P-38F became the first widely-used combat model in Europe, from mid 1942. Hard put to outfly experienced German flyers the P-38 groups weathered a tough period of bomber escort missions from England and North Africa before the Axis was worn down and new aircraft better suited to the conditions were available.

With the advent of the P-38H with improved engines and greater ordnance carrying capability, Lockheed revised the engine radiator layout to create the much-improved P-38J. With Allison V-1710-98/91 engines and more fuel tankage the Lightning's endurance was boosted to about 12 hours enabling pilots to fly all the way to Berlin and to strike at axtreme distances in the Pacific.

The wartime P-38 series was rounded out by the further improved P-38L, more of which (3,810) were built than any other model. Mostly used as a fighter, the P-38 was adapted to perform bomber operations by having a bombardier nose fitted. These aircraft led other P-38s to their targets by handling the lead navigator/bombardier duties.

Numerous P-38s were also converted to the photo-reconnaissance role under the designation F-4 and F-5, depending on the original airframe upon which the conversion was based.

Left: P-38F on factory test.

Above: This ill-fated P-38J crashed in the UK, killing the pilot.

Right: Few P-38s still exist and they are highly sought after.

Overleaf, inset top and main photo: Many nose set-ups were fitted to surplus P-38s; main photo shows a modern variation for survey work.

Inset bottom: P-38 warbird in Pacific theatre markings.

UNITED STATES OF AMERICA •

485

LOCKHEED PV-1/2 HARPOON

The result of a design exercise that began with a passenger aircraft, the PV series of patrol bombers served widely and well in a number of far-flung war theatres. Stemming from the commercial Model 18 airliner, the PV series in turn owed much to the first military conversion which, as the Hudson, did much valuable work on coastal patrols when Britain needed all the help she could get. Developed into a medium bomber as the Ventura the RAF found that the Lockheed design had been overtaken by the speed of military aircraft development under the impetus of war. By 1943 the Ventura was unable to be effective in this role, at least if

Specification: PV-2
Type: Twin-engined patrol bomber
Manufacturer: Lockheed Aircraft Corp
Number built: 535
Entry into service: December 1942
Length: 51 ft 5 in (15.77 m)
Height: 13ft 2 in (3.9 m)
Wingspan: 75 ft (22.86 m)
Weight empty: 24,000 lb (10,886 kg)
Range: 900 miles (1,448 km)
Max speed: 282 mph (454 km/h)
Service ceiling: 44,000 ft (13,410 m)
Armament: 8 x 0.50-in machine guns in nose plus 2 x 0.50-in machine guns in dorsal turret and 2 x 0.50-in machine guns in ventral position; up to 4,000 lb (1,814 kg) of bombs in internal bay and wing hardpoints plus 2 x 1,000 lb (454 kg) bombs under the wings

Left: An Australian-operated PV-1 in the Pacific.

Below: Changes to the PV-1 created the potent PV-2 Harpoon.

Above right: Another rare warbird, existing PV-2s have often been drastically de-militarised.

Right: The CAF operates this PV-2 which still needs a dorsal turret.

deployed against targets well defended by German flak and fighters.

It was left to the US Navy, the Marines (which used some in the night fighting role) and the Royal New Zealand Air Force to put the PV-1 on the map, the type first being delivered to the Navy in December 1942. This move came about when the Navy confirmed a need for land-based aircraft — as against flying boats — for patrol duties, the PV being one of three types delivered.

Powered by 2,000 hp Pratt & Whitney R-2800 radials, the PV-1 was similar to the USAAF's B-34 Lexington, the first US Navy aircraft being in fact a batch of aircraft diverted from Army contracts. Other were diverted from British Lend-Lease orders and were used for crew training.

Lockheed's design department rounded out the PV line with the PV-2 which had a superficially similar configuration. It flew in

prototype form on December 3, 1943 and was far more than a cosmetic update. A totally new wing of greater span, larger fins and rudders, a reprofiled fuselage and heavier armament made the PV-2, named Harpoon, a much more effective warplane. Deliveries began in March 1944 and in the hands of US Navy patrol squadrons PV-2s carried out

many tedious overwater sorties often in the hostile climate of the Aleutians and Kurile islands, searching for Japanese subs and ships.

The 535 PV-2Ds built had eight nose guns compared to five in the original model, plus a dorsal turret with two more. The bomb load was 2,000 lb, wing hardpoints accommodating rockets and drop tanks.

Right: A four-gun belly tray was fitted to wartime PV-2s.

Far right: Heavily armed for patrol work, later PV-2s also carried rockets.

Below: Just touching down, a PV-2 warbird shows its salient features.

MARTIN B-26 MARAUDER

• AIRCRAFT OF WWII • A VISUAL ENCYCLOPEDIA

No other aircraft in the twin-engined medium bomber category turned in a better war record than the B-26 by flying the mission for which it was designed. That this was a comparative rarity in a combat arena that had so quickly changed from that envisaged before hostilities began only served to highlight the soundness of the design. Any aircraft that could turn in an exemplary record as a 'straight and level' bomber in the European Theatre of Operations had to be good, for this was considered to be the toughest war front of them all.

In 1940 Martin's Peyton Magruder achieved a streamlining that put the B-26 streets ahead of

any military aircraft extant anywhere else at the time. Flying for the first time on November 25, 1940, the first 210 examples built were plain B-26 models without any suffix. Capable of 310 mph (500 km/h), they were light and consequently the fastest of the line. These 'hot ships' were deployed quickly to the Pacific where a small force of B-26s did well to keep the Japanese from overrunning New Guinea and thereby help break the back of their offensive operations.

Output of early Marauder models was modest and subsequent operations in the Pacific, plus the fact that the B-25 proved a little easier to fly by pilots with limited experience,

resulted in the B-26 being allocated to Europe and the 8th Air Force, and to North Africa and the 12th Air Force .

Wrongly deployed by the 8th Air Force in Pacific-type low level attack against murderous European flak and fighter defence, the Marauder's fate hung in the balance after some heavy early losses, which tended to also be the case in the Mediterranean. But the B-26 was retained and as a primary medium bomber and in the ETO it became an outstanding success. Fighter escort was invariably provided and the loss rate to enemy fighter interception proved to be remarkably low, a fact primarily due to improved tactics, good formation

Specification: B-26B/G
Type: Seven-seat twin-engined medium bomber
Manufacturer: Martin Aircraft
Number built: 5,157
Entry into service: 1940
Length: 56 ft 1 in (17.09 m)
Height: 20 ft 4 in (6.20 m)
Wingspan: 71 ft (21.64 m)
Weight empty: 23,000 lb (10,432 kg)
Range: 1,100 miles (1,770 km)
Max speed: 310 mph (500km/h)
Service ceiling: 19,800 ft (6,035 m)
Armaments: (B-26B) Up to 12 x 0.50-in machine guns in nose, package, turret, waist and tail positions; up to 5,200 lb (2.359kg) of bombs in double fuselage bay

flying and crew loyalty. Soon the 9th Air Force's eight groups became an indispensible tactical medium bomber spearhead to support the invasion of Europe both before and after the troops went ashore. In the MTO the B-26 groups also came of age and groups, often operating from very rough forward airfields, pounded Axis airfields, supply lines and dumps until the ground war in Africa culminated in complete Allied victory.

Externally the B-26 changed from the 'short wing, short tail' B-26B with a stepped twin-gun tail position to the much more capable B-26B-10 with more firepower and a more efficient Bell tail turret. All subsequent models were based on this shorter fuselage sub-type, with many changes in equipment not obvious externally.

A more fundamental difference was to angle the wing up by some 4.5 degrees to improve landing characteristics and general handling. This feature introduced on the B-26F, was followed by the final production version, the B-26G, which also had the 'tilted wing' and numerous detail improvements, the culmination of considerable combat experience.

Specification (B-26G):
Type: medium bomber
Manufacturer: Martin Aircraft
Number built: 893
Entry into service: May 1944
Length: 56 ft 6 in (17.23 m)
Height: 21 ft 6 in (6.55m)
Wingspan: 71 ft 6 in (17.23 m)
Weight empty: 25,300 lb (11,490 kg)
Range: 1,150 miles (1,850 km)
Max speed: 280 mph (451km/h)
Service ceiling: 19,800 ft (6,040 m)
Armaments: up to 11 x 0.50-in machine guns in nose, package, turret, waist and tail positions; up to 4,000 lb (1,814 kg) of bombs in forward fuselage bay

Left: A box of 9th Air Force B-26Bs forming up over England in 1944.

Below: B-26 *Carefree Carolyn* **was once the pride of the CAF but sadly she crashed.**

Above: The sleek lines of one of the best medium bombers of the war, well shown by the Confederate Air Force's B-26.

Left: Marauders saw service in the Pacific as well as Europe where they often outran Japanese fighters.

Below: A recent US warbird is this early model B-26 with pointed tail, prop spinners and other changes compared to the major wartime Marauders.

NORTH AMERICAN T-6 TEXAN

Allied victory in the Second World War was the result of many factors, not the least of which was a well-planned training programme. This in turn required safe and reliable aircraft on which to train thousands of combat pilots and the T-6/SNJ filled that requirement admirably. Students usually obtained initial air experience on a primary type before graduating on to the T-6 for basic or advanced training. It could of course be flown as a single-seater if necessary and used for a whole range of aerial tuition including gunnery, blind flying, navigation and aerobatics, depending on what a given course required.

Stemming from a long line of North American single-engined trainers and fighters, the NA-16, forerunner of the NA-26 (AT-6), flew as a prototype in April 1935. As a two-seat trainer the AT-6A (which

took that designation in 1940) had docile flying qualities and was powered by a 550 hp Pratt & Whitney R-1430-AN1 radial engine driving a two-blade propeller.

As a gunnery trainer the aircraft was known as the AT-6B, and the AT-6C had a mix of steel and plywood in its construction but the AT-6D reverted to aluminium as

---

Specification: AT-6F
Type: Two-seat advanced trainer
Manufacturer: North American Aviation
Number built: 15,109
Entry into service: 1937
Length: 29 ft 6 in (8.99 m)
Height: 11 ft 8.5 in (3.56 m)
Wingspan: 42 ft (12.8 m)
Weight empty: 4,271 lb (1,938 kg)
Range: 870 miles (1,400 km)
Max speed: 212 mph (341 km/h)
Service ceiling: 24,750 ft (7,338 m)
Armaments: 1 x 0.30-in or 0.50-in machine gun in either wing root or 1 x 0.50-in machine gun in rear cockpit, all for training purposes; light practice bombs on underwing racks.

used before. The AT-6F was the final wartime model.

Known as the Harvard to the RAF and less often as the Texan to the Americans, the AT-6 soon became the most widely used US trainer of all time. Wartime expansion demanded thousands of crews who needed good training to be effective in combat and NAA eventually completed 15,109 examples of the T-6 to help. The Navy had its equivalent SNJ and the RAF and all Allied nations used it widely, Canada's Noorduyn company also building a similar version. There were also German and Japanese models, the latter country building 176 with the Allied code name 'Oak'. That was fame!

Left: If trainee pilots had to fly formation, a T-6 was a good aircraft to do it in.

Bottom left: A North American publicity shot of a wartime T-6.

Below: Many T-6s still exist, in variety of colour schemes like this Navy SNJ representative.

Left: T-6 in USAF colours.

Below left: Korean war buzz numbers appear on this T-6.

Above: T-6 masquaerading as a Hellcat.

Right: The USMC trained pilots on its SNJs.

Below: A T-6 on the ramp ready for an airshow.

NORTH AMERICAN B-25 MITCHELL

A medium bomber that undertook more varied roles than most of its Allied or Axis contemporaries, the B-25 not only excelled at them but managed to exploit an entirely new one to deadly effect on the enemy.

Having assured itself a place in aviation history for the daring carrier-borne raid on Tokyo on April 18, 1942, the Mitchell was named after that tenacious advocate of airpower, Gen William Mitchell. After the Tokyo raid the B-25C — built at Inglewood with the similar B-25Ds being built at Dallas — was among the first AAF bombers to combat the Japanese in the Pacific and it was there that the first experiments were made to attack ships with Mitchell strafers. With bombardier noses painted over and packed with machine guns, the low level B-25C/D model attackers devastated Japanese vessels which were also hit with bombs skipped into their sides from the wavetop flying B-25s. Para-frag bombs liberally sown from B-25 bomb bays over enemy airfields also wrecked numerous aircraft on the ground.

When the B-25G became available the number of targets needing the attention of a shells from a 75-mm nose cannon were not that many. But the G model saw combat, mainly in the Far East and Pacific and bridges, buildings and sometime ships, were rarely able to stand up to this kind of punch. While NAA went about a major redesign in the form of the B-25H — the second 75-mm cannon model — the combat groups were doing just fine with conventional B-25s configured as medium bombers and as strafers. Many targets did not require attack by from special weapons and many of the cannon-armed Mitchells fought their war as trainers.

No AAF B-25 groups flew from England, their theater being the Mediterranean. It was the RAF that deployed Mitchells from Britain, 2 Group squadrons developing admirably close formation flying to ward off enemy fighters. They followed the Allied advance into Germany and were still in the front line in 1945.

The ultimate Mitchell model was the B-25J. Like the B-25H it had a deeper fuselage with a turret just

Specification: B-25J
Type: Four/five-seat
   medium bomber
Manufacturer: North
   American Aviation
Entry into service: 1940
Length: 52 ft 11 in (16.13 m)
Height: 16 ft 4 in (4.98 m)
Wingspan: 67 ft 7in (20.55 m)
Weight empty: 19,400 lb
   (8,800 kg)
Range: 1,350 miles (2,172 km)
Max speed: 272 mph
   (438 km/h)
Service ceiling: 24,200 ft
   (7,376 m)
Armaments: (B-25B) 5 or 6
   x 0.50-in machine guns in
   nose, turret waist and tail
   positions; up to 2,000 lb
   (907 kg) of bombs internally; (B-25C/D) up to 9 x
   0.50-in machine guns in
   nose, turret, waist and tail
   positions plus up to 3,000 lb
   (1,316 kg) of bombs
   internally and on wing
   racks. (B-25G) One x 75-mm
   cannon and 4 x 0.50-in
   machine guns in nose;
   6 x 0.50-in machine guns
   in turret, waist and tail
   positions; bomb load as
   B-25C/D

behind the cockpit, 'bay window' waist gun positions and a custom made, twin gun tail turret. Issued to groups on an as required basis to replace worn out B-25C/D models, the J could be operated as a bomber or a strafer, interchangable nose sections providing for either role. As a strafer the B-25J could carry an absolute maximum of 18 x 0.50-in machine guns — which was usually enough to deal with any target!

The US Marines expanded the B-25's role furher with its PBJ series. Carrying radar, these aircraft became day and night Pacific 'hecklers' hunting the enemy on the seas or whittling down island garrisons bypassed by the Navy's thrust back across the Pacific.

Ably supporting the ground forces' advance through the Philippines, PBJ squadrons wound up on the islands of Guam and Iwo Jima, where just before the end, they introduced the mighty Tiny Tim rocket to combat. Stripped of all but one tail gun, and carrying two of the 11.75 in rockets under their bellies, the PBJ-1Js went hunting for an enemy who had already been utterly defeated.

Specification: B-25H
Type: Three-seat
   strafer/medium bomber
Manufacturer: North
   American Aviation
Number built: 1,000
Length: 52 ft 11 in (16.13 m)
Height: 16 ft 4 in (4.98 m)
Wingspan: 67 ft 7 in (20.55 m)
Weight empty: 19,480 lb
   (8,836 kg)
Range: 1,350 miles
   (2,172 km)
Max speed: 275 mph
   (442 km/h)
Service ceiling: 23,800 ft
   (7,254 m)
Armaments: 1 x 75-mm
   nose cannon and 10 or 14 x
   0.50-in machine guns
   respectively in nose, pack
   age, turret, waist and tail
   positions; (B-25J) up to
   18x 0.50-in machine guns in
   'solid' nose, package, turret,
   waist and tail positions; up
   to 3,000 lb (1,316 kg) of
   bombs internally (PBJ-1J)
   1 x 0.50-in machine gun in
   extreme tail plus 2 x 11.75-
   in Tiny Tim rockets below
   fuselage

Below left: A factory fresh B-25H, one of 1,000 built.

Left: A warbird with a difference, this B-25J was converted back to duplicate Doolittle's B model.

Below: Today's Mitchell warbirds include this 'Air Apaches' J model.

Left: The B-25J had a deeper rear fuselage than early versions.

Below left: B-25J marked as a 5th Air Force 81st TRG ship makes a simulated bombing run.

Right: B-25s come in all colours and with solid and clear noses.

Below: A warbird B-25J waving the flag for the combat groups in the Mediterranean.

Bottom: An unlikely wartime escort for a B-25C, a warbird P-63 flies over England.

NORTH AMERICAN P-51 MUSTANG

One of the most brilliant military aircraft of all time, the P-51 Mustang is principally remembered for its role as a long range escort fighter in Europe. That was a far cry from the full story, for the P-51 undertook a variety of roles and began life as a response to a requirement from Britain for a new aircraft for the demanding tactical reconnaissance role. North American Aviation assured the British Purchasing Commission that a new fighter would be ready for inspection in about three months, which was no mean feat. The first flight of the new fighter then known simply by the company designation of NA-73, took place on 25 October 1940. Powered by an Allison V-1710-F3R engine of 1,100 hp, it was almost immediately the subject of an initial British contract.

When it first arrived in England in 1942 the Allison-engined P-51 or Mustang Mk I re-equipped tactical reconnaissance units and the aircraft (subsequently joined by later models) flew many outstanding missions into Europe, bringing back vital target data and photographs until the end of the war. Meanwhile, the USAAF became interested in a single seat fighter that could used in the attack role, which it estimated that the P-51 (no suffix) could meet.

Armed with four 20-mm cannon, the redesignated Mustang became the A-36A, one of the few dive bombers in the Allied inventory. It flew thousands of sorties to support the ground forces in the Mediterranan Theatre of Operations and in the Far East. Such missions only stopped when the combat groups literally had no more aircraft beyond the 500 examples produced to fight with.

Rolls-Royce, North American and AAF technicians meanwhile experimented with installing a Merlin engine in the Mustang airframe, which was successfully done to result in the P-51B. With its very low fuel consumption, the new four gun Mustang possessed an impressive range and was able to escort US heavy bombers right into Germany. By the time of the invasion of Europe in June 1944, the Army Air Forces could confidentially put huge bomber formations over German targets better protected by Mustangs than ever before.

With combat reports to hand, NAA set about improving the Merlin Mustang which had had its share of technical faults, not the least of which was gun reliability stemming from an angled breech and feed installation in the thin wing,

Specification: A-36A
Type: Single-seat dive bomber
Manufacturer: North American Aviation
Number built: 500
Entry into service: (RAF) 1942, (USAAF) 1943
Length: 32 ft 3 in (9.83 m)
Height: 12 ft 2 in (3.71 m)
Wingspan: 37ft (11.28 m)
Weight empty: 6,610 lb (2,882 kg)
Range: 550 miles (885 km)
Max speed: 310 mph (499 km/h)
Service ceiling: 25,100 ft (7,650 m)
Armaments: 4 x 20-mm wing cannon plus up to 2,000 lb (907 kg) of bombs on underwing racks

Specification: P-51D
Type: Single-seat escort fighter
Manufacturer: North American Aviation
Number built: 7,956
Entry into service: Summer 1944
Length: 32 ft 3 in (9.83 m)
Height: 13 ft 8 in (4.16 m)
Wingspan: 37 ft (11.28 m)
Weight empty: 7,635 lb (3,463 kg)
Range: 950 miles (1,529 km)
Max speed: 437 mph (703 km/h)
Service ceiling: 41,900 ft (12,771 m)
Armaments: 6 x 0.50-in wing machine guns; up to 2,000 lb (907 kg) of bombs or 8 x HVAR on zero length launchers; (P-51B) 4 x 0.50-in wing machine guns; up to 2,000 lb (907 kg) of bombs or M10 triple-tube rocket launchers on wing racks

engine problems and visibility through the 'greenhouse' cockpit hood. In spring 1944 the P-51D emerged. With an all round vision bubble canopy and six machine guns in a reprofiled wing, the new variant became one of the most capable single-seaters of the war.

A propeller change brought about the P-51K, the final wartime sub-variant. This, along with the otherwise similar P-51D and its respective photo-recon variants the F-6D and K, continued to take the war right into the enemy's own backyard. As a fighter with an outstanding range the P-51 amazed some Germans, including Luftwaffe chief Hermann Göring who once said he knew the war was lost the moment he saw Mustangs over Berlin.

Over Japan the long range P-51D protected the B-29 formations and helped destroy the enemy aircraft on his airfields in the home islands. Being able to strike Japan from Iwo Jima meant that Mustangs could rove almost at will, bombing and strafing numerous enemy aircraft on the ground. By so doing they decimating a carefully marshalled air fleet that would have been used as kamikazes, had an invasion of Japan proved necessary.

Above left: With a Rolls-Royce Merlin engine, North American created the outstanding P-51B.

Left: Warbird Mustangs are numerous, 8th AF markings naturally being popular.

Right: Once based in England P-51D *Candyman* has since gone home.

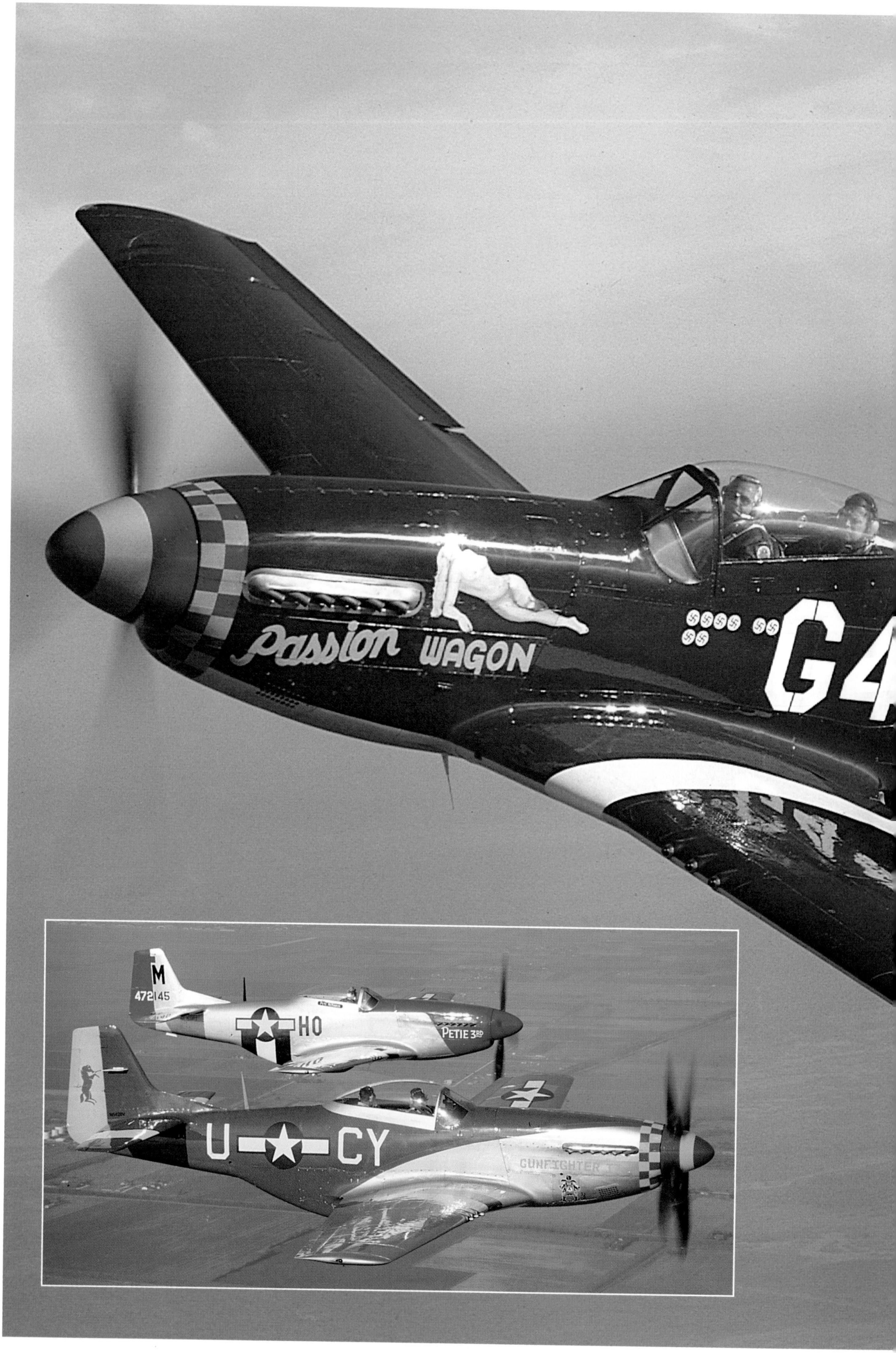
Passion WAGON
G4
M
472145
HO
PETIE 3RD
U CY
GUNFIGHTER

Above: The 55th Fighter Group's P-51Ds wore colours similar to these in England in 1944-45.

Left: P-51Ds are often fitted with a second seat.

Inset left: Wartime 8th Air Force colours on P-51Ds.

Below: Uprated props are among modern changes made to P-51 airframes like this 'Debden Eagles' representative.

NORTHROP P-61 BLACK WIDOW

The only US aircraft developed as a night fighter from the outset, the P-61 arrived in service after types such as the P-70, P-38, Beaufighter and Mosquito had provided the AAF with a night fighter capability. Like other nations, the US had not considered the need for a specialised nocturnal interceptor before the war but when the requirement was realised a substantial effort was made to develop one. Northrop took up the not inconsiderable challenge and flew a prototype XP-61 for the first time on May 26, 1942. The layout was of twin-boom type with the crew of three being housed in a central pod fuselage.

Specification: P-61B
Type: Three-seat night figther
Manufacturer: Northrop
Number built: 941
Entry to service: May 1944
Length: 49 ft 7 in (15.11 m)
Height: 14 ft 8 in (4.47 m)
Wingspan: 66 ft (20.14 m)
Weight empty: 23,450 lb (10,637 kg)
Range: 550 miles (566 km)
Max speed: 330 mph (531 km/h)
Service ceiling: 33,100 ft (10,089 m)
Armaments: 4 x 20-mm cannon in ventral position plus 4 x 0.50-in machine guns in dorsal turret; up to 1,600 lb (726 kg) of bombs on each of two or four wing racks

Early aircraft suffered numerous teething troubles, particularly in getting the SCR-720 AI radar, based on a British-developed airborne interception set, to work reliably, which delayed the programme considerably. A teardrop-shaped top turret with four 0.50-in machine guns was deleted from most of the initial 200 production P-61As as this was found to cause severe buffeting. The turret could afford to be dropped, for with four 20-mm cannon in the ventral position, the Black Widow was still very heavily armed. A P-61A recorded the Black Widow's first combat kill in the Pacific on July 7, 1944.

By that time the P-61B, able to carry drop tanks or bombs for the night intruder mission, had entered production. Problems with the four-gun turret had been solved and this was restored later in the P-61B production run. Some P-61Bs became P-61G weather reconnaissance aircraft with no armament. The P-61C, powered by 2,800 hp R-2800-73 engines, was the final production model, only 41 being completed. A similar twin-boom configuration was adopted for a P-61 derivative, the Northrop F-15 Reporter, an unarmed recce type which saw little service because of war's end and the changeover to turbojets for the 'high and fast' PR role.

Left: A P-61A hot off the Northrop line. A huge aircraft, the Black Widow was well named.

Above: A navigator demonstrates how to exit the P-61's fuselage pod.

Right: A four-gun top turret was not fitted to all P-61s due to buffeting problems.

REPUBLIC P-47 THUNDERBOLT

Occupying the top slot as the best all round fighter bomber of the war, the mighty P-47 was not unusual in taking on a role that its designers had not envisaged. The result of a quite tortuous series of compromises and specification changes, the original 'lightweight' P-47 interceptor proved to be one of the heaviest fighters of the war — single or twin-engined. It weighed as much as two Bf 109s in later form but in combat, size did not count against it.

Flying for the first time in 1940 the XP-47 evolved into the P-47C via the A and B models, both of which were useful trainers. The 'razorback' P-47C was the first considered suitable for combat operations, examples of this and subsequent production blocks being shipped to England where the 8th Air Force was desperate for an escort fighter. The P-47 was the only single-engined type available in numbers and from its operational debut in March 1943 its range was increased to take the bombers a few miles into Germany and hit the Luftwaffe hard. Battling the odds, the weather and its own short range the P-47 held on throughout 1943

and made way for the P-51 early in 1944. Thunderbolts went increasingly over to the ground attack role where its big, tough engine could take substantial damage and still get pilots out of trouble. And eight heavy caliber machine guns made it a deadly weapon even without any ordnance.

When the tactical 9th Air Force was formed in England for invasion support duties, most units flew P-47Ds while in the 8th the fighter

---

Specification: P-47D-30
Type: Single-seat fighter and fighter bomber
Manufacturer: Republic Aircraft
Number built: 15,660 (all models)
Entry into service: 1941
Length: 36 ft 1 in (10.99 m)
Height: 14 ft 7 in (4.44 m)
Wingspan: 40 ft 9 in (12.42 m)
Weight empty: 10,600 lb (4,812 kg)
Range: 850 miles (1,367 km)
Max speed: 398 mph (640km/h)
Service ceiling: 30,000 ft (9,144 m)
Armaments: (P-47D) 8 x 0.50-in wing machine guns and up to 2,000 lb (907 kg) of bombs on belly and wing racks; two three-tube M10 wing rocket launchers. (P-47N) eight 0.50-in wing machine guns; up to 2,500 lb (1134 kg) of bombs; four or eight HVAR on underwing launchers

---

Below left: P-47 pilot and instructor group in the Middle East with a P-47 from the same unit as above.

Above right: Warbird P-47s are not numerous but several fly in the US including this one in 9th Air Force colours.

Right: Duxford's P-47 carried the markings of the 78th Fighter Group, based there in World War II.

Overleaf:
Inset left: A warbird P-47 belonging to the Wolfpack, the wartime 56th Fighter Group.

Inset right: A very thirsty aircraft, the P-47 needed 100 gal of fuel an hour.

Main photo: The Duxford Thunderbolt screams for altitude, flying much lighter than its 1944 counterparts.

groups gradually gave up their P-47Ds for Mustangs but the 56th remained with the Thunderbolt and in 1944 got one model all to itself, the P-47M. Potentially excellent, the M unfortunately suffered lengthy engine problems that kept it from combat until the issue was no longer in doubt. Back on combat duties late in 1944, the P-47M showed how engine power with the aid of water injection and paddle bladed propellers, had been increased. The P-47M had a top speed of 470 mph (756 km/h).

The early 'razorback' P-47D models gave way to the D-25 with a 'bubble' canopy; subsequent production blocks introduced a dorsal fin to offset a marginal loss of stability but outwardly most bubbletop D models were similar.

Early on, the P-47 was not demanded so much in the Pacific theater where the P-38 had adequate range and two engines for insurance,

but razorback P-47Ds nevertheless did their bit with the 5th Air Force from 1943.

Republic developed the line into the P-47N under a major redesign program with a new wing and increased internal fuel tankage. The P-47N's enormous 2,350-mile (3.782 km) range made it a natural

for the Pacific. Flying many fighter and ground attack sorties by night and day before the end, the mighty N model was among the most capable of the entire series. Most heavily armed of the P-47 series, the N was able to carry up to 2,500 lb (1,134 kg) of bombs and rockets.

511

PHOTO CREDITS

The publisher wishes to thank the photographers and photographic libraries who supplied the illustrations on the following pages:

Front cover (all), pages 1, 2, 6-7, 8-9, 11 (bottom), 12 (top), 13, 14 (both), 15 (top), 16, 17, 22, 23, 24 (both), 25, 26, 31 (both), 32, 36 (top), 37, 39, 40-41 (main), 40 (inset, bottom), 43 (both), 44 (both), 46 ,47, 48, 49 (top), 50 (both), 51, 55 (top), 56, 57, 59 (top), 62, 63 (both), 64, 65 (all), 67 (top), 68 (both), 69, 70, 71, 72 (all), 74, 75 (both), 76 (bottom), 84-85, 88, 95 (top, middle, bottom), 97(inset), 107 (bottom), 119 (top), 123 (top, middle, bottom), 134 (middle), 135 (top), 136-137, 138 (bottom), 139 (all), 154, 156 (all), 157, 159 (top), 160 (top), 161 (top), 163 (bottom), 180, 181, 223 (bottom), 221 (all), 243 (top), 258 (bottom), 260 (middle), 261, 307 (bottom), 317 (bottom), 328, 329 (bottom), 331 (top), 332 (inset), 335 (bottom), 341 (bottom), 346 (inset, top), 352, 364, 377, 382, 395 (top), 405, 412 (bottom), 413 (bottom), 417 (bottom), 420, 423 (middle), 434 (middle, bottom), 436 (middle), 437, 445 (top), 449 (bottom), 456 (top, bottom), 457 (top, bottom), 458, 459 (middle, bottom), 470 (bottom), 495 (bottom), 496 (both), 497, 501 (bottom), 503, 505 (inset, bottom), 508 (bottom) and back cover (bottom) courtesy of Jeremy Flack/Aviation Photographs International;

Pages 10, 11 (top), 12 (bottom), 15 (middle, bottom), 19, 20, 21, 27, 29, 30, 33 (bottom), 34, 35, 40 (top), 42, 49 (bottom), 53 (top), 54, 55 (bottom), 59 (bottom), 61, 66, 67 (middle, bottom), 76 (top), 77, 99 (middle top, middle bottom), 101 (top, upper middle, lower middle), 107 (middle), 108 (middle), 112 (middle, bottom), 113 (all three), 114 (all), 115 (both), 117, 118 (middle), 124, 126, 127, 131, 132 (top, middle), 134 (top), 140, 141 (top, middle), 142 (bottom), 147, 148 (bottom), 149 (top), 151 (middle), 152, 153, 162 (top, middle), 164, 167 (bottom), 169, 175 (top, middle, bottom), 177, 179, 182 (top), 183 (middle, bottom), 186 (middle), 298, 300 (all), 301 (both), 303 (all), 304 (inset, top and inset, bottom), 306 (bottom), 309 (top, middle), 312 (inset), 317 (top), 322, 323, 324, 325, 335 (top, middle), 336 (top, middle), 338, 341 (top), 343, 349 (top), 360, 361 (top, bottom), 363 (top), 370 (top), 376, 378, 380, 383, 384 and 470 (top) courtesy of Alfred Price Collection/Aviation Photographs International;

Pages 33 (top), 52, 53 (bottom), 410 (inset, top), 423 (bottom), 444 and 451 (middle, bottom) courtesy of Roger Freeman/Aviation Photographs International;

Pages 45, 94, 142 (top, middle), 149 (bottom), 170-171 (main), 307 (top), 308, 321 (inset, middle), 356, 368, 369 (bottom), 371, 379 (top) and 490 courtesy of Bison Picture Library;

Pages 79, 80 (both), 81, 83, 85 (inset), 86 (all), 89 (both), 90 (both), 91 and 92 (both) courtesy of Coll. Musée de l'Air et de l'Espace/Le Bourget;

Pages 82, 87, 314, 324, 358, 359, 374, 442, 443 (both), 466, 474 (bottom), 475 (both), 494, 495 (top), 506 and 507 (both) courtesy of Aviation Picture Library;

Pages 93, 99 (top and bottom), 102-103 (main), 103 (top, middle), 104, 105 (all), 108-109 (main), 110, 111, 112 (top), 116, 118 (top, bottom), 119 (bottom), 120-121, 122 (top), 125 (top, bottom), 128-129, 132 (bottom), 133 (top), 133 (bottom), 135 (bottom), 138 (top, middle), 143 (top), 144 (top), 144-145, 150-151 (main), 155 (top), 158 (top, middle), 159 (bottom), 160-161 (main), 162 (bottom), 163 (top), 165 (top, bottom), 166, 167 (top, middle), 168, 170 (top), 171 (top), 172 (bottom), 173 (top, bottom), 174, 176 (all), 178-179 (main), 182 (middle, bottom), 183 (top), 187, 188, 189 (top), 192, 193 (top, bottom), 196 (bottom), 197 (bottom), 198, 199 (both), 200, 201 (top, bottom), 204-205 (main), 205 (top), 206, 207, 210 (top), 210-211 (main), 212, 214 (both), 215 (top, bottom), 216 (both), 217 (all), 218, 222-223 (all), 224, 225 (all), 226 (both), 227 (both), 228, 229 (middle, bottom), 231 (top, bottom), 232, 233 (top), 234, 235 (all), 237 (top, bottom), 238, 239 (all), 240-241 (main), 241 (top, bottom), 242, 243 (middle, bottom), 245 (top, bottom), 246, 247, 248 (top), 249 (top, middle), 250, 251 (top), 252, 253 (all), 257 (middle, bottom), 258 (top), 258-259 (main), 260 (top), 262, 263 (top, bottom), 264, 265 (both), 268 (top), 269 (top, bottom), 273 (top), 274, 275 (all), 276 (top), 276-277 (main), 277 (top), 278, 279 (top, middle), 282, 283 (all), 284 (top), 286 (all), 287 (both), 289 (all), 293 (middle, bottom), 295 (middle, bottom), 296 (middle, bottom), 297, 302, 304-305 (main), 306 (top), 309 (bottom), 311 (both), 315, 316, 317 (top), 318 (inset), 318-319 (main), 319 (inset), 320-321 (main), 321 (inset, top), 326-327 (main), 329 (top), 330, 331 (middle, bottom), 332-333 (main), 334 (both), 337 (top), 340, 344, 345 (all), 346-347 (main), 348, 350 (inset), 350-351 (main), 351 (inset), 353 (both), 366 (top), 385, 386-387 (main), 387 (top), 388-389 (all), 390-391 (main), 391 (top, middle), 392, 393 (top), 394 (left), 394-395 (main), 396 (middle, bottom), 397 (all), 399 (top, middle, bottom), 400, 401 (top, middle, bottom), 402 (inset), 402-403 (main), 403 (inset), 404 (all), 406-407 (all), 408, 409 (both), 410-411 (main), 412 (top), 413 (middle), 414-415, 416, 417 (top), 418-419, 421 (both), 422, 423 (top), 424-425 (main), 425 (top), 426 (all), 427 (both), 428-429, 430 (top), 431 (both), 432-433 (main), 434 (top), 435 (both), 436 (top, bottom), 438-439 (main), 439 (top, middle), 440-441 (main), 445 (bottom), 446-447 (all), 448 (both), 449 (top), 450, 451 (top), 452, 453 (top, bottom), 454-455 (all), 457 (middle), 460-461, 463 (bottom), 464 (all), 465 (both), 467 (all), 468-469, 471, 472 (both), 473 (all), 476, 477 (top), 478-479, 480 (both), 481 (all), 483 (bottom), 484-485 (all), 487 (top), 488-489 (all), 492-493 (main), 493 (inset, top and bottom), 499, 500 (both), 501 (top and middle), 502 (bottom), 504 (inset, bottom), 504-505 (main), 505 (inset top), 509 (both), 510-511 (all) and back cover (top) courtesy of Peter R March and Peter R March Collection;

Pages 96-97 (main), 100, 101 (bottom), 108 (bottom), 151 (top), 172 (top), 178 (top), 184-185 (main), 186 (bottom), 296 (top), 327 (inset), 342, 349 (bottom), 354-355 (main), 355 (top), 362-363 (main), 365 (top), 398, 411 (inset), 430 (bottom), 433 (inset), 462, 463 (top), 477 (bottom), 482, 486 (both), 498 (both) and 502 (top) via Jerry Scutts Collection

Pages 98, 106, 107 (top), 109 (bottom), 122 (bottom), 129 (top), 134 (bottom), 141 (bottom), 143 (bottom), 145 (top), 146, 148 (top, middle), 155 (middle), 170 (middle), 173 (middle), 184 (top), 185 (top), 186 (top), 189 (middle, bottom), 190, 191 (top, bottom), 193 (middle), 195 (all), 196-197 (main), 196 (top), 197 (top), 201 (middle), 202, 203, 204 (left), 207 (bottom), 208, 209 (both), 211 (bottom), 213 (all), 215 (middle), 219, 220 (both), 229 (top), 230, 231 (middle), 236 (both), 237 (middle), 244 (both), 245 (middle), 248 (bottom), 249 (bottom), 251 (bottom), 254, 255, 256 (both), 257 (top), 260 (bottom), 263 (middle), 266, 267, 268 (bottom), 269 (middle), 270-271, 272, 273 (middle, bottom), 279 (bottom), 280 (both), 281, 285 (top), 288 (both), 290 (both), 291, 292, 293 (top), 294 (both), 295 (top), 336 (bottom) and 337 (bottom) courtesy of Brian Strickland Collection;
Pages 130, 393 (bottom), 410 (middle), 459 (top), 487 (bottom) and 491 courtesy of Andrew P March;

Pages 155 (bottom), 284-285 (main) and 483 (top) courtesy of Daniel March;
Pages 299, 307 (middle), 310, 312-313 (main), 339, 346 (inset, bottom), 357, 365 (bottom), 366 (bottom), 367, 369 (top), 370 (bottom), 372 (inset, top), 372-373 (main), 375 (bottom), 379 (bottom) and 381 via Chris Ellis Collection;

Pages 369 (middle), 375 (top), 412 (bottom), 413 (top) and 435 (middle) courtesy of Aviation Photographs International.